MINORITY RULE

MINORITY RULE

THE RIGHT-WING ATTACK ON THE WILL OF THE PEOPLE—AND THE FIGHT TO RESIST IT

ARI BERMAN

FARRAR, STRAUS AND GIROUX

NEW YORK

Farrar, Straus and Giroux
120 Broadway, New York 10271

Portions of this work previously appeared, in different form, in *Mother Jones*, *The Nation*, *Rolling Stone*, and *The New York Times Magazine*. Citations are included in the notes.

Library of Congress Cataloging-in-Publication Data
Names: Berman, Ari, author.
Title: Minority rule : the right-wing attack on the will of the people—and
    the fight to resist it / Ari Berman.
Description: First edition. | New York : Farrar, Straus and Giroux, 2024. |
    Includes bibliographical references and index.
Identifiers: LCCN 2023045468 | ISBN 9780374600211 (hardcover)
Subjects: LCSH: United States—Politics and government—1989– |
    Conservatism—United States—History. | Democracy—United States—
    History—21st century. | White people—Race identity—United States. |
    Right and left (Political science)—United States—History—21st century.
Classification: LCC E893 .B476 2024 | DDC 305.809/073—dc23 /eng/20240109
LC record available at https://lccn.loc.gov/2023045468

Our books may be purchased in bulk for promotional, educational, or business use. Please contact your local bookseller or the Macmillan Corporate and Premium Sales Department at 1-800-221-7945, extension 5442, or by email at MacmillanSpecialMarkets@macmillan.com.

www.fsgbooks.com
Follow us on social media at @fsgbooks

10 9 8 7 6 5 4 3 2 1

In Memory of Harriet Berman

The supreme issue, involving all the others, is the encroachment of the powerful few upon the rights of the many.

—Robert "Fighting Bob" La Follette, 1913

CONTENTS

MINORITY RULE

PROLOGUE: FEAR OF A WHITE MINORITY

In May 1995, Republican presidential candidate Pat Buchanan appeared at the National Press Club in Washington, DC, to announce a new immigration policy as the centerpiece of his campaign. It was the start of immigration awareness week in the United States, but Buchanan was not in a welcoming mood. "If present trends hold," he said, "white Americans will be a minority by 2050."

Instead of reaching out to Latinos and other minority groups and embracing the country's changing demographics, Buchanan warned, "we have an illegal invasion of this country." He called for building a "Buchanan Fence" patrolled by the US military along the US-Mexico border to keep out undocumented immigrants, hiring five thousand new border agents, instituting a five-year moratorium on legal immigration, and changing the Fourteenth Amendment to deny citizenship to children born in the United States to undocumented parents. Buchanan wanted to "Make America First Again," borrowing a phrase from his former boss Ronald Reagan's campaign slogan "Let's Make America Great Again."

He was surrounded on the podium by the leaders of six groups devoted to restricting immigration, such as the California Coalition for Immigration Reform and Floridians for Immigration Control. He held a copy of a new book called *Alien Nation: Common Sense About America's Immigration Disaster* by the conservative journalist Peter Brimelow, which proposed harsh limits on non-European immigration.

A lengthy excerpt of Brimelow's book, titled "Time to Rethink

Immigration?," had run as a sixteen-page cover story in the conservative magazine *National Review*, accompanied by an image of Lady Liberty with her hand raised as a stop sign. "America will become a freak among the world's nations because of the unprecedented demographic mutation it is inflicting on itself," Brimelow wrote. He called for cutting legal immigration by two-thirds and repealing the 1965 Immigration and Nationality Act, which had overturned a 1924 law passed by Congress that instituted strict quotas on immigration from everywhere but northwest Europe. It was adopted in a nativist fervor after migration from southern and eastern Europe had skyrocketed in the late 1880s and early 1900s, making the country more urban than rural for the first time and diluting the power of Anglo-Saxon whites.

The 1990 census—which coincided with Buchanan's first presidential bid in 1992—was the first to predict that whites would one day become a minority in the country. "New projections show that the number of minorities, bolstered by heavy immigration and high birth rates, is growing much more rapidly than the number of white Americans," the Scripps Howard news service reported. Buchanan realized before any other major politician that white anxiety about their impending minority status could be a powerful issue, especially for Republicans, and he styled himself as a leader of a "new restrictionism" movement that advocated for the toughest limits on immigration since the 1920s.

"The question we Americans need to address, before it is answered for all of us, is: Does this First World nation wish to become a Third World country?" he wrote in 1991.

Buchanan himself came from a family of immigrants. His mother's family was German Catholic and his father's Irish Catholic, the type of people who once faced discrimination from Anglo-Saxon Protestants. But race, not country of origin, was the dividing line in the Georgetown neighborhood of Washington, DC, where Buchanan grew up as one of nine children. The Washington of his childhood in the 1950s was "a sleepy and segregated Southern city," he wrote. "The Negroes of

Washington had their public schools, restaurants, bars, movie houses, playgrounds, and churches; and we had ours."

His parents were fierce anticommunists and Buchanan's boyhood idols were Senator Joe McCarthy and Spanish dictator General Francisco Franco. The family took a dim view of the left-leaning civil rights movement. After graduating from Columbia Journalism School, Buchanan become an editorial writer for the conservative *St. Louis Globe Democrat* in 1962, writing columns denouncing the local NAACP as communist-infiltrated.

In St. Louis he met Richard Nixon, who would capitalize on domestic unrest and a white backlash against the civil rights movement. Buchanan became a speechwriter for Nixon and attended the 1968 Democratic Convention in Chicago. He stayed in a nineteenth-floor suite at the Hilton, overlooking Grant Park. One day, while hobnobbing with the likes of Norman Mailer, he watched as the police beat thousands of unarmed antiwar demonstrators. Much of the country recoiled from the violence, but Buchanan saw an opportunity. He wrote to Nixon and urged him to visit Chicago and "stand with the great silent majority against the demonstrators." The term "silent majority" became a memorable shorthand to describe aggrieved white Americans.

In the 1960s, a new commitment to equality had replaced the old age of explicit white supremacy, marked by a dramatic and sudden expansion of democratic rights. In a remarkable fifteen-month span from July 1964 to October 1965, President Lyndon Johnson signed the Civil Rights Act, the Voting Rights Act, and the Immigration and Nationality Act, a sweeping trio of antidiscrimination laws that would transform the politics and demographics of the country.

The Civil Rights Act of 1964 desegregated nearly every aspect of American life—from schools to public accommodations to workplaces—and expanded the promise of the Fourteenth Amendment by ending discrimination based on race, sex, and gender. The Voting Rights Act of 1965 struck down the literacy tests and poll taxes and other suppressive devices that had rigidly maintained Jim Crow in the South for nearly a century. It enforced the long-ignored provisions of the Fifteenth Amendment and enfranchised millions of voters of color. The Immigration and Nationality Act, also passed in 1965, opened the doors of the country to the developing world in the first significant way and embraced the language of the civil rights movement, specifying that no person would "be discriminated against in the issuance of an immigrant visa because of his race, sex, nationality, place of birth, or place of residence."

It was, in many ways, a Second Reconstruction, extending long-delayed rights of citizenship not just to African Americans but many other previously disenfranchised and marginalized communities. This put America on the path to becoming an enduring multiracial democracy for the first time in the country's history.

But Buchanan knew that the Second Reconstruction of the 1960s would spark a backlash like the first one had in the 1860s, and he understood better than most how to mobilize white voters who viewed the extension of new rights to African Americans and other minorities as threatening their power. Buchanan helped steer Nixon, who had supported the Civil Rights Act and the Voting Rights Act, away from the civil rights movement. He urged Nixon not to visit Martin Luther King's widow, Coretta, on the first anniversary of his assassination. "Initially, the visit would get excellent press," Buchanan wrote in a 1969 memo, but "it would outrage many, many people who believe Dr. King was a fraud and a demagogue, and perhaps worse."

Buchanan counseled Nixon to ignore "liberal issues" like housing, education, and unemployment. "The second era of Reconstruction is over," he wrote to the president in 1970. "The ship of integration is going down."

» » » » » »

Twenty years later, when Buchanan launched his first presidential campaign, he took this white backlash strategy directly to the South.

While campaigning in Georgia, he visited Stone Mountain outside of Atlanta to admire the giant carvings of the Confederate generals Robert E. Lee, Stonewall Jackson, and Jefferson Davis in the hillside, which he called "a beautiful monument." He denounced the civil rights laws of the 1960s, labeling the Voting Rights Act "an act of regional discrimination against the South" and endorsing its repeal.

When he traveled to Mississippi a week later, he laid flowers on the grave of a slaveholding Confederate ancestor who was captured by General William Tecumseh Sherman during the Civil War. Another relative, he said proudly, had died in action as a Confederate soldier. "They both tried to overthrow the government of the United States," he said. "They didn't. This time we're going to settle accounts for our ancestors in dealing with the Yankees in Washington, D.C."

Just as Nixon fended off Alabama's Dixiecrat governor George Wallace, Buchanan was now wooing supporters of David Duke, the KKK leader-turned-Louisiana state representative who had launched his own long-shot presidential bid on a platform of white supremacy. "The way to deal with Mr. Duke is the way the GOP dealt with the far more formidable challenge of George Wallace," Buchanan said. "Take a hard look at Duke's portfolio of winning issues; and expropriate those not in conflict with GOP principles." Duke, for his part, said, "I think Pat Buchanan sounds more like me every day."

Buchanan was the first major presidential candidate to mix antipathy toward the civil rights era with hostility to nonwhite immigration, making opposition to demographic change the centerpiece of his 1992 and 1996 presidential campaigns. With the white majority he'd built for Nixon well on its way to becoming a minority, this was the next major front in the nation's political and cultural wars. "Who speaks for the Euro-Americans?" he asked. "Is it not time to take America back?"

Buchanan mounted a strong challenge to incumbent president George H. W. Bush in the 1992 New Hampshire primary, winning more than a third of the vote against a sitting president and framing the race as "the Buchanan Brigade" versus "King George's army." Buchanan didn't win a single state that year, but he captured nearly three million votes, enough to receive a coveted keynote speech at the GOP convention in Houston. He electrified Republican delegates by speaking apocalyptically about "a cultural war . . . for the soul of America," denouncing "unrestricted abortion on demand," the "homosexual rights movement," and "radical feminism." The liberal columnist Molly Ivins famously remarked that Buchanan's speech "probably sounded better in the original German."

Republicans adopted some of Buchanan's positions on immigration as the official party platform, pledging to "equip the Border Patrol with the tools, technologies and structures necessary to secure the border." Buchanan's sister and campaign manager, Bay Buchanan, said "structures" meant walls. "They don't build lighthouses on the border," she quipped.

Four years later, Buchanan won the New Hampshire primary during his second presidential run. He called his followers "the true sons and daughters of the Founding Fathers." He portrayed his crusade to preserve Judeo-Christian values and maintain white power in the face of a massive demographic shift not as an aberration in US history, but as part of its oldest struggle. He ridiculed the media's "intoxication with 'democracy,'" and stated that "equal justice for the emerging white minority" was more important than extending new rights to formerly marginalized communities.

"The Founding Fathers did not believe in democracy," he wrote. "They did not believe in diversity. They did not believe in equality."

» » » » » »

Buchanan was dismissed by many as a fringe figure in the 1990s, and he never came close to winning his party's nomination, but his dire warnings about the disappearance of the country's white majority have become a central organizing principle for the conservative movement today. His nativism, racism, and skepticism toward democracy foreshadowed the ideology that now defines the Republican Party.

The country is roughly twenty years away from the majority-

minority future of Buchanan's nightmares, and new multiracial coalitions are gaining influence in formerly white strongholds like
Georgia. To entrench and hold on to power, a shrinking conservative
white minority is relentlessly exploiting the undemocratic features of
America's political institutions while doubling down on a wide variety
of antidemocratic tactics, such as voter suppression, election subversion, dark money, legislative power grabs, immigration restrictions,
census manipulation, and the whitewashing of history. This reactionary movement, which is drastically overrepresented in the Electoral
College, the Congress, and gerrymandered legislative districts because
of a political system that diminishes the voices of urban areas, young
Americans, and voters of color, has retreated behind a fortress to stop
what it views as the coming siege.

Conservatives like Buchanan have long pointed to the notion that
the United States was never intended to be a true democracy to justify
a deep hostility to broad-based political participation.

"We're not a democracy," the Utah Republican senator Mike Lee
tweeted on October 7, 2020, defining it as "rule by majority, the view
that it is the prerogative of government to reflexively carry out the will
of the majority of its citizens."

Three months later, a mob that explicitly presented themselves as
heirs to the American Revolution stormed the US Capitol on January
6, 2021, to overthrow the will of a majority of voters. But this crisis
didn't begin—or end—with Donald Trump's attempt to overturn the
2020 election.

America's democratic experiment has long been defined by a central tension over whether the government should benefit the many or
the few. The United States has historically been a laboratory for both
oligarchy and genuine democracy; that dualism is part of its DNA. At
the heart of this debate are contested ideas about legitimacy, freedom,
and who counts as an American.

To grasp the stakes of the present-day fight over democracy, one
has to understand the clash between competing notions of majority
rule and minority rights that date back to the country's birth.

It's certainly true that the founders, despite the lofty ideals in the Declaration of Independence, designed the US Constitution in part to check popular majorities and protect the interests of a propertied white upper class. The Senate was created to represent the country's elite and restrain the more democratic House of Representatives, while the Electoral College prevented the direct election of the president and enhanced the power of slave states through the three-fifths clause. Voting rights were restricted in most states to white male property owners, so that only 6 percent of Americans were eligible to vote in the first presidential election.

But as the United States has democratized in the centuries since, extending the franchise and many other rights to formerly disenfranchised communities, the antidemocratic features that were built into the Constitution have metastasized to a degree the Founding Fathers could have never anticipated, threatening the survival of representative government in America.

If the founders once feared what James Madison called "the superior force of an interested and overbearing majority," today the central threat facing American democracy is the tyranny of the minority.

For the first time in US history, five of six conservative justices on the Supreme Court have been appointed by Republican presidents who initially lost the popular vote and confirmed by senators representing a minority of Americans. The signature project of those justices has been to nullify the civil rights–era laws that Buchanan railed against.

The extreme direction of the court is emblematic of how the countermajoritarian distortions in American politics have intensified in recent years.

Before the 2000 election between George W. Bush and Al Gore, only three times in US history had the loser of the popular vote won the Electoral College. But that's happened twice in sixteen years since then. It almost occurred a third time in 2020, when Joe Biden won the popular vote by seven million but Trump lost the three closest states in the Electoral College by just 45,000 total votes. Trump never could have attempted to overturn the results—and there would have been no insurrection—if the United States had a system in which every vote mattered equally in presidential elections.

Similarly, the level of inequality in the Senate right now—by far the worst among any advanced democracy—would have shocked the likes of Madison. When the founders reluctantly decided to give each state the same number of senators regardless of population, the 1790 census showed that the country's most populous state, Virginia, had twelve times as many people as its least populous, Delaware. Today, California has sixty-eight times the population of Wyoming. Fifteen small states with 38 million people combined routinely elect thirty GOP senators; California, with forty million residents, is represented by two Democrats. This imbalance is getting worse: by 2040, roughly 70 percent of Americans will live in fifteen states with thirty senators, while the other 30 percent, who are whiter, older, and more rural than the country as a whole, will elect seventy senators. The structure of the Senate only magnifies the body's unrepresentativeness: due to the filibuster, which is not in the Constitution, forty-one Republican senators representing just 21 percent of the population have been able to block bills supported by huge majorities of Americans on issues like gun control, abortion, and voting rights.

This is not just a problem at the federal level. For much of the past decade, more than fifty million Americans have lived in states like Wisconsin, where Republicans controlled the state legislature despite receiving fewer votes and pioneered new ways to curb political participation. A record number of candidates in key state and local races in the 2022 midterm election sought to override one of the most fundamental principles of a democracy: accepting the outcome of a free and fair election.

The reactionary conservatives behind the drive for minority rule claim to be the only legitimate heirs of representative government, but they're seeking to delegitimize and warp the institutions created by the founders.

They claim to be appealing to freedom, but they're trying to limit freedom for historically marginalized groups that were written out of the country's original governing institutions.

They claim to be the only true Americans, but they're trying to sharply narrow the definition of citizenship and who is entitled to exercise those rights.

The struggle throughout US history between constricting and expanding democracy has reached a fever pitch today. A minority of Americans are hell-bent on nullifying the will of the people, but there is also a vibrant and growing resistance to these regressive efforts. The question of whether the United States will live up to Abraham Lincoln's ideal of a "government of the people, by the people, for the people" is the defining fight of our time.

1

LABORATORY FOR OLIGARCHY

In the late spring and early summer of 2011, soon after tens of thousands of progressive activists had demonstrated at the Wisconsin state capitol in Madison to protest Governor Scott Walker's bill stripping public-sector unions of collective bargaining rights, Republican members of the legislature walked across the street to the shiny glass office of Michael Best and Friedrich, the party's go-to law firm. The GOP was in control of the state's redistricting process for the first time since the 1950s, and Republicans were shown to the "map room," where their aides were drawing new political districts in secret following the 2010 census.

The legislators signed confidentiality agreements, pledging not to discuss the work with anyone, even though the redistricting process was financed with taxpayer funds and maps had traditionally been drawn at the capitol, not at a private law firm. "Public comments on this map may be different than what you hear in this room," read the talking points distributed to GOP legislators. "Ignore the public comments."

The new maps had titles like "Aggressive" to describe how they favored Republicans. "The maps we pass will determine who's here 10 years from now," a legislative aide told the Republican caucus. "We have an opportunity . . . to draw these maps that Republicans haven't had in decades."

On July 11, 2011, the maps were introduced in the legislature; no Democrat had seen them before they were released. There was one public hearing, two days later, and the reshaped districts were approved the next week on a party-line vote.

Publicly, Republicans downplayed the significance of the maps. "This looks fair to me," said the GOP state senator Van Wanggaard. "I don't have anything jumping out at me."

But state politics had been transformed virtually overnight. Nowhere was this more evident than in Wanggaard's hometown of Racine, one hundred miles east of Madison.

Wanggaard, a former cop with blond hair resembling Dennis the Menace, lived on a quiet, tree-lined street in a neighborhood known as the Danish Village for its Scandinavian ancestry and numerous bakeries. His two-story white house had a large American flag hanging from the porch and a pro-police "We Back the Badge" sign in the yard. Two houses to the south, his state senate district—the 21st—abruptly cut off to exclude the rest of the largely Democratic neighborhood near Lake Michigan.

It used to be one of the state's most competitive senate districts, encompassing all of rectangular-shaped Racine County, a fifty-fifty mix of urban and rural communities in southeast Wisconsin. But the new redistricting maps converted the swing district into one that favored a Republican by sixteen points.

It was now shaped like a horseshoe, pulling in the Republican countryside of Racine and Kenosha counties while excluding heavily Democratic urban areas, except for the block where Wanggaard lived. "It's a prime example of how a party in power chose a district for their guy," said John Lehman, a Democrat who represented the 21st before Wanggaard.

Lehman, a longtime public school teacher whose grandfather came to Racine in 1929 to work in a foundry, represented the district from 1996 to 2010. He lived five blocks from Wanggaard and used to teach at the same high school where Wanggaard was sometimes stationed as an off-duty cop. Wanggaard defeated him in 2010 by three thousand votes, but Lehman beat Wanggaard in a recall election in 2012 after Wanggaard voted for Walker's highly contentious antiunion legislation.

"I voted for every conservative item that the governor brought forward," Wanggaard told Wisconsin Public Radio. Wanggaard had once been the rep for his police union and his vote to strip public-sector unions of collective bargaining rights infuriated his constituents. Racine's police union endorsed Lehman, who won by 819 votes.

By then the new district lines had been drawn by Republicans, but they didn't take effect until *after* the recall, which put Lehman in the awkward position of winning an election in his competitive old district but serving in the new, deeply Republican one. He used to represent all of Racine, a city of seventy-five thousand with a large Black population, but his district now stretched to the resort town of Twin Lakes on the Illinois border. In between were old farms, new McMansions, and small towns with yard signs that said "Keeping Christ in Christmas."

Lehman was six feet five with a bushy gray mustache. Everyone knew him in Racine. But when he spoke at a Memorial Day parade in Twin Lakes, throwing candy to kids, "nobody knew who I was," he said. When he scheduled listening sessions in the district's rural areas, nobody showed up. "I tried to serve the district, but it was like a foreign land," he said.

The new boundaries effectively nullified the recall election Wanggaard had lost and all the unpopular votes he'd cast in favor of Walker's arch-conservative agenda. "It was unwinnable for a Democrat," Lehman said. Wanggaard ran again in 2014 and won by twenty-three points.

Most of the state legislature's Republican majority was just as secure. In 2012, Obama carried Wisconsin by seven points and Democratic legislative candidates received 51.4 percent of the statewide vote, but Republicans retained 60 percent of seats in the assembly. Under the Republican map, the number of safe GOP seats in the 132-member legislature had increased from 55 to 69 while the number of swing districts decreased from 24 to 13. It was a practically foolproof system: no matter the public mood or how extreme their agenda was, Republicans would maintain control of state politics. "Even when

Republicans are an electoral minority, their legislative power remains secure," one federal court noted.

Entrenching GOP dominance by manipulating core democratic institutions represented a huge shift not just in Wisconsin's politics, but in its culture as well.

The state had often swung between red and blue but had long been known for the idea that government should represent the common good regardless of who was elected. "The basic principle of this government is the will of the people," said Robert "Fighting Bob" La Follette, the state's influential governor and US senator from 1901 to 1925. La Follette pushed for progressive reforms such as women's suffrage, the direct election of presidential nominees and US senators, and a ban on corporate donations to political candidates to expand democratic participation and counter the influence of the robber barons.

Teddy Roosevelt called Wisconsin "a laboratory for wise experimental legislation aiming to secure the social and political betterment of the people as a whole." The state paved the way for landmark policies like Social Security, unemployment insurance, and collective bargaining rights for unions.

But Walker and the Republicans elected in 2010 launched a counterrevolution against what had come to be known as the Wisconsin Idea. The gerrymandering in Wisconsin, which was replicated by Republicans across the country in 2011, was just one part of a larger strategy to systematically tilt the state's democratic institutions in the GOP's favor. Rather than government working for the many, Walker wanted to concentrate power in the hands of an elite and wealthy conservative white minority. If he succeeded, he wrote, Republicans could "do it anywhere in the country."

» » » » » »

Todd Allbaugh became a Republican in 1980, when he was in the fifth grade, after meeting his local GOP chairman and putting a Reagan poster in his bedroom. Allbaugh worked for Wisconsin Representative Steve Gunderson, the first openly gay Republican in Congress, and then became chief of staff for the state senator Dale Schultz, whom the Madison *Capital Times* called "the last remaining moderate Republican in the state legislature."

"In the 1980s and '90s, when I went to Republican conventions, I heard about the need to create a bigger tent, to bring new people into the party," Allbaugh said. Republicans controlled the state government during much of that time but never passed laws limiting the ability to vote. Indeed, Wisconsin was one of the first states to adopt Election Day registration in the 1970s, which significantly boosted voter turnout, and trailed only Minnesota in voter participation in 2008.

Allbaugh received a rude awakening when he attended a closed-door meeting of the State Senate's Republican caucus in the late spring of 2011. They were considering a new bill requiring government-issued photo ID to vote, a top priority for Wisconsin Republicans since the 2000 and 2004 presidential elections, when George W. Bush lost the state by less than one point. The party blamed the losses on voter fraud by Democrats in Milwaukee, a majority-minority city long scapegoated by white conservatives, along with high turnout among Black and young voters.

These complaints resurfaced after Wanggaard lost his recall election by eight hundred votes in 2012. His lawyer said that election officials in Racine had "used procedures that would make Fidel Castro blush." Republicans claimed that voter registration forms were found in a dumpster, poll books were unsigned, and union members were bused in from Michigan to vote illegally. "Anyone who argues . . . that we do not need voter ID either wants to conceal these potential fraudulent activities or hasn't been paying attention," Wanggaard said.

Yet no evidence of fraud turned up when the county sheriff and district attorney, both Republicans, launched a month-long investigation. Behind closed doors, Republicans offered a different rationale for the law. Since gerrymandering only applied to US House and state legislative races, GOP senators argued the voter ID law would boost the party's prospects in all races by depressing the votes of core Democratic constituencies.

"We've got to think about what this could mean for the neighborhoods around Milwaukee and the college campuses around the state," the state senator Mary Lazich reportedly said, rising from her chair and smacking the table for emphasis.

Schultz asked his colleagues to consider not whether the bill would help the GOP, but how it would impact the voting rights of Wisconsinites. According to Allbaugh, the state senator Glenn Grothman cut him off. "What I'm concerned about is winning," he said. "We better get this done while we have the opportunity." Two other GOP senators were "giddy" and "politically frothing at the mouth" over the bill, Allbaugh recalled, while three others sat "ashen-faced" during the debate.

"It made me physically ill," Allbaugh said. "It was like a gut punch. I never thought, after all the years of dedicating my life to helping advance the Republican Party, that I would sit in a meeting of Republican officials and hear them openly plotting to impede another citizen's voting rights."

Schultz voted for the voter ID bill reluctantly, but his concern grew when Republicans passed another law eliminating early voting at night and on weekends, which was used more often by Democrats in large urban areas like Madison and Milwaukee.

Grothman, the author of the bill, said he wanted to "nip" early voting "in the bud" before it spread from Madison and Milwaukee to other areas. The county clerk of Waukesha County, a Milwaukee suburb that was 95 percent white and staunchly conservative, argued that early voting gave "too much access" to voters in the two Democratic strongholds.

Schultz asked Allbaugh to find three documented cases of voter fraud in the state. But Allbaugh could only find two instances of double voting, both, ironically, committed by Republicans. Neither case would have been stopped by a voter ID law or was related to early voting.

Schultz sharply criticized his party's voting restrictions before retiring from the legislature in 2014. "We should be pitching as political parties our ideas for improving things in the future rather than mucking around in the mechanics and making it more confrontational at our voting sites and trying to suppress the vote," he said.

The voter ID law was one of thirty-three election changes passed in Wisconsin after Walker took office, which included cutting early voting, curtailing voter registration drives, and adding new residency requirements to cast a ballot. "The Wisconsin experience," one federal judge later wrote, "demonstrates that a preoccupation with mostly phantom election fraud leads to real incidents of disenfranchisement, which undermine rather than enhance confidence in elections, particularly in minority communities."

That had been the point all along.

» » » » » »

On November 8, 2010, just days after his gubernatorial election, Walker had dinner with the board and senior staff of the Bradley Foundation at a sleek steakhouse in downtown Milwaukee near the lakefront.

The invite came from Bradley's president, Michael Grebe, the former general counsel to the RNC and state chair of Reagan's re-election campaign in 1984, who had also been the chairman of Walker's campaign. He presided over the most powerful conservative foundation in the state—and perhaps the country—even though it had never become a household name.

It was started by two brothers, Lynde and Harry Bradley, who manufactured electronic parts in Milwaukee. Along with Fred Koch, the patriarch of Koch Industries, Harry had been a founding member, in the 1950s, of the John Birch Society, the ultraconservative group that warned of an "international communist conspiracy" to take over the United States that included President Dwight Eisenhower, Supreme Court Chief Justice Earl Warren, and the civil rights movement.

These views remained on the fringes until 1985, when the Allen-Bradley corporation was bought by Rockwell International, one of the country's largest defense contractors. The Bradley family's wealth skyrocketed, and their private foundation's assets increased from $14 million to $290 million. The foundation hired Michael Joyce, the former executive director of the conservative Olin Foundation, to win "the war of ideas" and give tens of millions of dollars to foster a new conservative ecosystem that included groups like the Heritage Foundation and the Federalist Society.

Grebe took over in the early 2000s and began funding, with the help of key national donors like the Koch brothers, a sprawling network of think tanks, legal centers, media organizations, and political groups in Wisconsin that propped up Walker and the Republican majority. Wisconsin became the foundation's test case for creating a conservative counterrevolution in a place known for its progressive history.

Walker told the foundation's inner circle he wanted to "go big and go bold."

Bradley was ready to help. Two think tanks funded by the foundation, the Wisconsin Policy Research Institute and the MacIver Institute, drew up a list of policies for the incoming Walker administration. "We supplied the ideas," said James Klauser, chairman of the Wisconsin Policy Research Institute.

Their top priority was going after public-sector unions, which would make it far easier for corporate interests to influence the state's economic and political system by defunding and demobilizing one of the top allies of the Democratic Party and progressive causes.

Walker responded by introducing Act 10, which stripped public-sector unions—like teachers and municipal workers—of collective bargaining rights, ended automatic union dues, and required annual recertification, while exempting the few labor constituencies that tended to support Republicans, such as police officers, firefighters, and state troopers.

"If Act 10 is enacted in a dozen more states, the modern Democratic Party will cease to be a competitive power in American politics," wrote the influential conservative strategist Grover Norquist, president of Americans for Tax Reform. "It's that big a deal."

The bill was introduced in the state assembly on February 14, 2011—Valentine's Day. That day, teaching assistants at the University of Wisconsin–Madison wrote Valentine's Day cards to Walker saying, "We ♥ UW: Don't Break My ♥."

The next day, tens of thousands of pro-union activists showed up to demonstrate at the capitol and would remain there for months, going so far as to peacefully occupy the building's rotunda. Wisconsin was the first state to give collective bargaining rights to public employees in 1959, and polls showed that a majority of Wisconsinites supported the unions and viewed Walker's bill as an attack on the state's well-regarded democratic institutions.

Walker was in trouble. He was quickly surrounded by the largest resistance movement in state history. Just a year after assuming the governor's office, his opponents would gather more than a million signatures to trigger a recall election to remove him from office. And early polls showed him trailing his 2010 opponent, Milwaukee mayor Tom Barrett, in a rematch.

So he once again turned to the Bradley-Koch network for help.

» » » » » »

In January 2010, a conservative majority on the Supreme Court radically rewrote America's campaign finance laws to allow megadonors and corporations to contribute unlimited sums, often in secret, to political action committees. *Citizens United v. FEC* reversed a century of campaign-finance restrictions that saw money as a corrupting influence on politics, with Justice Anthony Kennedy writing for the 5-4 majority that limiting "independent political spending" from corporations and other groups violated the First Amendment's right to free speech. In practice, the decision gave wealthy donors unprecedented influence to buy elections.

Thanks in part to his Bradley connections, Walker had long been close to GOP billionaires like Charles and David Koch, who gave $9 million to Walker and his allies between 2010 and 2014. "We've spent a lot of money in Wisconsin," David Koch said in February 2012. "We are going to spend a lot more."

The recall election took on outsized national significance because conservative groups wanted to export Walker's agenda across the country. "Today, every other governor in the country and every state legislator in the country is watching Wisconsin," said Tim Phillips, president of the Koch-funded group Americans for Prosperity, which spent nearly $4 million defending Walker during the recall, at a rally in Madison. "You are the model for the country!"

Walker asked his advisers in September 2011 how he could raise enough money to survive the recall, despite intense public opposition to his attack on unions. "Corporations. Go heavy after them to give," wrote his fundraiser Kate Doner. "Take Koch's money. Get on a plane to Vegas and sit down with Sheldon Adelson. Ask for $1m now."

Walker did just that, but instead of raising money for his campaign—which was subject to disclosure requirements and contribution limits—he steered wealthy donors to the probusiness Wisconsin Club for Growth, which could raise unlimited sums in secret and was insulated from public accountability. "The Governor is encouraging all to invest in the Wisconsin Club for Growth [which] can accept Corporate and Personal donations without limitations and no donors disclosure," wrote Doner.

The group, an offshoot of the national Club for Growth, which supported policies like privatizing Social Security and cutting taxes for the wealthy while backing primary challenges to moderate Republicans, was run by Republican operative Eric O'Keefe. Sometimes called the "third Koch brother," O'Keefe had been national field coordinator for the Libertarian Party in 1980 when David Koch was the party's vice presidential candidate. Their platform called for radical policies like ending public education, repealing all taxation, and abolishing

Medicare, Medicaid, and Social Security. The campaign received only 1 percent of the vote nationwide, and when their platform proved unpopular, O'Keefe and the Kochs turned their attention to overturning limits on campaign contributions to give wealthy interests a much freer hand in influencing the political process.

The Bradley Foundation increased O'Keefe's prominence by giving $3 million between 1998 and 2012 to groups directed or founded by him, which he used to train conservative activists and lobby for the repeal of campaign finance laws.

Walker's campaign was banned from coordinating directly with outside groups like O'Keefe's, but in a highly unusual arrangement, Walker's top strategist, R. J. Johnson, a former executive director of the Wisconsin Republican Party whom Walker called "my Karl Rove," was hired as a consultant for Wisconsin Club for Growth. Walker went on an unprecedented fundraising spree, traveling to a conference in Georgia to raise $250,000 from the hedge fund magnate Paul Singer, barnstorming the length of Fifth Avenue to solicit checks from tycoons like Trump and Steve Forbes, receiving $200,000 from the casino magnate Adelson and persuading Wisconsin's richest man, John Menard, to give $1 million directly from the coffers of his home improvement store, Menards Inc. All of it went to Wisconsin Club for Growth. As Doner wrote, Walker wanted campaign funds "run thru one group to ensure correct messaging." (The donations were only made public because of leaked documents published by *The Guardian*.)

That money, in turn, funded a barrage of TV ads attacking Barrett and persuading Wisconsinites that even if they disagreed with Walker's policies, "recall isn't the Wisconsin way." Walker's aggressive fundraising—and the unlimited, secret contributions—gave the governor and his allies a huge financial advantage over Barrett: $58.7 million to $21.9 million. Despite his controversial agenda, he easily won the recall by seven points. More than $21 million would be spent by Wisconsin Club for Growth, which helped save Walker and four of six GOP state senators also facing recalls.

Johnson told donors afterward that Wisconsin Club for Growth's "soup to nuts campaign" played a decisive role in "[moving] independent swing voters to the GOP candidate." He delivered his findings at a retreat organized by the Bradley Foundation, which as a nonprofit foundation was prohibited from engaging in electoral politics.

Eighty percent of voters opposed the *Citizens United* decision, but O'Keefe saw nothing wrong with wealthy interests spending unlimited amounts to covertly influence political campaigns. "That's inside baseball," he said. "There's no moral issue involved."

But progressive reformers like Robert La Follette had long viewed the concentration of wealth and power as the gravest threat to democracy. The "tremendous influence" of corporate power in the political realm, La Follette said in an 1897 speech, had led to "a growing conviction in state after state, that we are fast being dominated by forces that thwart the will of the people and menace representative government."

More than a century later, it was particularly notable that the push to flood the political system with dark money was driven by the same forces that were behind efforts like voter suppression and gerrymandering, which accomplished similar goals through other means. "We are facing a dual attack on our democracy," said NAACP president Ben Jealous. "Everyday voters are being disenfranchised, while corporations are being hyper-enfranchised."

Wisconsin offered an early preview of the post–*Citizens United* political landscape. As the cost of federal elections increased by nearly $2 billion from 2008 to 2012, spending by outside groups in Wisconsin quadrupled in 2010 and 2012 compared to the two elections before *Citizens United*. In 2006, only 2 percent of outside political spending came from groups that did not have to disclose their donors. By 2010, that number had increased to 40 percent. Conservative "social welfare" groups—like Wisconsin Club for Growth—would outspend their liberal counterparts by nearly five to one.

By 2012, more than a quarter of all political contributions came from just thirty thousand people who represented the 1 percent of the 1 percent, the country's most elite and unrepresentative minority. Not a single member of the House or Senate would be elected without their support. In that election, the top thirty-two super-PAC donors gave as much money—$313 million—as Obama and Mitt Romney raised from their 3.7 million small donors combined. While money didn't always determine outcomes, it usually did: 90 percent of US House candidates who spent the most won.

In *Citizens United*, Justice Kennedy wrote that "independent expenditures, including those made by corporations, do not give rise to corruption or the appearance of corruption." But it was difficult to make that claim in Wisconsin with a straight face.

Walker's donors received a generous return on their investment. Between April 2011 and January 2012, Dallas billionaire Harold Simmons, whose company manufactured lead paint, a known danger for developing children, gave three checks totaling $750,000 to Wisconsin Club for Growth. Walker's adviser warned him about Simmons's background in a "red flag" email.

"We should discuss this so you are aware of what you might need to defend in terms of contributions from donors when these are disclosed," wrote Walker aide Keith Gilkes. "Harold Simmons has consistently been a target of environmentalists. One of the most immediate issues was that NL Industries (purchased by Simmons in 1986) was the leading maker of lead pigment paint." A few years later, lead would contaminate the water supply in neighboring Flint, Michigan, causing a massive public health crisis.

After Walker's recall election, in June 2013, Republicans in the Wisconsin Legislature inserted a late-night provision into a budget bill that blocked Wisconsin residents from suing manufacturers like Simmons for lead poisoning. The legislature also changed the definition of "lead-bearing paint" to allow greater amounts of lead, and reduced state lead-paint inspections. "Not since the days of the Robber Barons in the 19th century has one party in Wisconsin done so much damage to the common good while serving special private interests," said the Wisconsin Democracy Campaign, a progressive watchdog group.

Large campaign contributions didn't just buy special favors for the wealthy or prop up unpopular policies like Act 10; they frequently prevented widely supported policies from ever becoming law. There was often a striking disconnect between what the wealthy and the rest of the country believed, particularly on core economic issues. According to one in-depth survey, 68 percent of the public believed "the government in Washington ought to see to it that everyone who wants to work can find a job," but only 19 percent of the top 1 percent of Americans agreed. Fifty-four percent of the public favored raising taxes on the rich to combat income inequality, but only 17 percent of the wealthy concurred.

Even though the general public commanded a majority on these and other issues, state and federal policymaking was tilted in favor of a minority of wealthy conservatives. Research by political scientists Martin Gilens and Benjamin Page found that "economic elites and organized groups representing business interests have substantial independent impacts on U.S. government policy, while average citizens and mass-based interest groups have little or no independent influence." In the United States, they concluded, "the majority does *not* rule—at least in the causal sense of actually determining policy outcomes."

» » » » » »

Despite his recall victory, Walker still had a big problem: It was illegal under state law for his campaign to directly coordinate with outside groups like Wisconsin Club for Growth. An experienced special prosecutor who had served in the US Attorney's office in Wisconsin for thirty years opened an investigation alleging a "criminal scheme" between Walker and his outside allies. Conducted in secret, it was known as a "John Doe" inquiry. In June 2014, the state released documents showing how Walker's campaign had covertly worked with conservative groups to skirt Wisconsin's campaign finance laws. As the probe intensified, Walker and his allies turned to the four-member conservative majority on the Wisconsin Supreme Court, which had received $8 million in outside support from the very groups under investigation, for a get-out-of-jail-free card.

The Wisconsin Supreme Court, whose judges are elected, had long been regarded as a moderate body with a sterling reputation. Its longtime chief justice, Shirley Abrahamson, had once been shortlisted for the US Supreme Court seat that went to Ruth Bader Ginsburg. But a few years before Walker's victory, conservative business interests launched a campaign to transform the court into a firmly conservative institution, anticipating that it would become the final authority on major political disputes in a closely divided state.

In the spring of 2008, Wisconsin voters saw a chilling TV ad showing Louis Butler, the first Black member of the state supreme court, side by side with a Black man convicted of child rape, a man Butler had allegedly freed from jail.

"Louis Butler worked to put criminals on the street, like Reuben Lee Mitchell, who raped an eleven-year-old girl with learning disabilities," said the ad's ominous-sounding narrator. "Butler found a loophole, Mitchell went on to molest another child. Can Wisconsin families feel safe with Louis Butler on the Supreme Court?"

The ad was run by Michael Gableman, a little-known conservative state judge from rural Wisconsin who'd been recruited to challenge Butler. Judicial races tended to be restrained affairs, befitting the stature of a judge, but Gableman, a former prosecutor who called himself a "law and order judge," ran a notoriously ugly campaign.

The ad led to an outcry. Butler had been a public defender assigned to represent Mitchell and lost the case on appeal. Mitchell was sentenced for the crime and only committed another one after serving his original prison term, facts not mentioned in the ad. The watchdog group One Wisconsin Now called it "the most racist ad in the history of Wisconsin politics" while the Wisconsin Judicial Commission filed an ethics complaint against Gableman for his "reckless disregard for the truth."

In the past, such a negative ad—in a judicial race, no less—might have backfired in Wisconsin. Gableman, however, was supported by nearly $3 million in outside spending from Wisconsin Club for Growth and the state's largest business group, Wisconsin Manufacturers and Commerce, who dubbed Butler "Loophole Louie" and reinforced Gableman's hits on Butler in a barrage of attack ads.

These groups spent five times as much as Gableman's own campaign, outspending Butler's side by two to one on TV ads in the final days of the campaign. An incumbent judge hadn't been defeated in forty years, but Butler lost by twenty thousand votes, which he blamed on outside groups like Wisconsin Club for Growth. "This system is broken," he said in a concession speech. "Third-party issue groups who don't have to be accountable, don't have to follow campaign laws and don't have to disclose their donors siphoned huge amounts of money into this race."

Conservatives had finally won a majority on the state Supreme Court, but three years later it was in jeopardy when Justice David Prosser faced a tough re-election in April 2011 as protests against Act 10 swelled in Madison. The state court would soon consider the constitutionality of Walker's agenda and, in an unusually partisan message, Prosser's campaign manager said the judge's re-election would protect "the conservative judicial majority and act as a common sense complement to both the new administration and Legislature."

The fates of Prosser and Walker were widely assumed to be intertwined. "If Justice Prosser loses," Walker's chief counsel Brian Hagedorn, a former clerk to Gableman, wrote in an email to supporters on the eve of the election, "Governor Walker's agenda could be stopped in its tracks by this new activist majority."

The outside groups that backed Gableman sprang into action, with R. J. Johnson writing that Wisconsin Club for Growth was "leading the coalition to maintain the court." Wisconsin Club for Growth and Wisconsin Manufacturers and Commerce reprised the same message they used against Butler, attacking Prosser's opponent, assistant attorney general JoAnne Kloppenburg, for being "weak on criminals." They spent $3.5 million, five times as much as Prosser's campaign, on TV ads supporting his candidacy.

Once again, the liberal candidate and her supporters were outspent two to one. Prosser was re-elected in a nail biter by seven thousand votes. He told a donor that the outside spending on his behalf was "absolutely indispensable." Walker wrote to Karl Rove that "Club for Growth–Wisconsin was the key to retaining Justice Prosser."

The court's conservative majority went on to uphold Act 10, in a decision written by Gableman, along with nearly all of Walker's agenda, including the redistricting maps and voter ID law. But it was soon embroiled in controversy. Prosser was accused of calling Abrahamson a "total bitch" and putting his hands around the neck of another liberal justice, Ann Walsh Bradley, during a dispute over when the Act 10 decision would be released.

In 2015, as the Wisconsin Supreme Court was set to hear the John Doe case, ruling on whether Walker's coordination with outside groups violated the state's campaign finance laws, prosecutors asked Gableman and Prosser to recuse themselves, citing the massive spending on their behalf from the groups under investigation. But the conservative justices had already adopted an ethics rule in 2009—using language proposed by Wisconsin Manufacturers and Commerce—that said they didn't have to recuse in cases involving groups that had supported their campaigns. The conservative majority then canceled oral arguments in the case, denying the public the chance to hear the evidence compiled by prosecutors against Walker and his allies, which Abrahamson said was "highly unusual" and "alarming."

Conservative groups funded by the Bradley Foundation relentlessly attacked the investigation in the media. In July 2015, the court's conservative majority released a breathtaking decision, again written by Gableman, shutting down the probe against Walker and his allies. It called the defendants—who included Walker, his top aides, and outside allies like O'Keefe—"brave individuals" who had "played a crucial role in presenting this court with an opportunity to re-endorse its commitment to upholding the fundamental right of each and every citizen to engage in lawful political activity and to do so free from the fear of the tyrannical retribution of arbitrary or capricious governmental prosecution."

When special prosecutor Francis Schmitz, a longtime Republican who had voted for Walker, appealed the decision, the Wisconsin Supreme Court ruled that his appointment was invalid and removed him from the case, making it difficult for him to appeal to the US Supreme Court. "My career in the military and as a federal prosecutor fighting violent criminals and terrorists did not fully prepare me for the tactics employed by these special interest groups," Schmitz said.

The court's conservative majority went much further than just clearing Walker and his allies. It ruled that coordination between campaigns and dark money groups like Wisconsin Club for Growth was permissible so long as the outside groups didn't expressly tell voters who to vote for. This directly contradicted the *Citizens United* decision, which said that outside groups could accept unlimited donations with no disclosure precisely because they were independent of political candidates. "They went way, way beyond what *Citizens United* said," said Matthew Rothschild of the Wisconsin Democracy Campaign. O'Keefe's dream of a political system with no campaign finance regulation—where billionaire interests had unfettered access to secretly influence elections—was closer than ever to becoming a reality.

But Walker and his allies didn't stop there. The Bradley Foundation and its directors had given $18 million to groups and individuals connected to the John Doe investigation. After the probe was shut down, O'Keefe and the Bradley network persuaded the Republican legislature to launch a sweeping attack on the state's campaign finance system, once known as among the strongest in the country, to insulate them from future investigations and cement their political influence. The legislature allowed donors to contribute unlimited sums to political parties and let corporations give directly to them for the first time in a century; doubled the amount donors could give to political candidates; authorized outside groups to coordinate with political candidates on "issue advocacy" (the very thing Walker was under investigation for); exempted donors from disclosing where they worked; prevented future John Doe investigations from focusing on political crimes like bribery and misconduct in office; and dismantled the state's highly regarded watchdog agency comprised of retired judges. Wanggaard cosponsored the bill curtailing John Doe investigations, which he said were "like 1939 Germany."

The bills passed in the middle of the night on November 7, 2015. "It was just a systematic destruction of the good-government democracy that Wisconsin had enjoyed up to the election of Scott Walker and the Republicans," said Jay Heck, executive director of Common Cause Wisconsin.

A state that had prided itself on good governance for the people had fallen into minority rule and become the blueprint for radical conservatives to replicate nationwide. A onetime laboratory for democracy, said Rothschild, had turned into "a laboratory for plutocracy and a Petri dish for the Koch brothers and the right-wing revolution that Walker ushered in." The success of that strategy "signaled to right-wing forces across the country that the sky's the limit."

Wisconsin exemplified the clash throughout US history over whether America would be an experiment in democracy or oligarchy. That fundamental tension dates back to the debate over the country's most consequential political document and its founding institutions in 1787.

2

THE FURY OF DEMOCRACY

On May 29, 1787, Edmund Randolph, the thirty-four-year-old governor of Virginia and a former aide-de-camp to George Washington during the Revolutionary War, rose to "open the main business" of the Constitutional Convention. Tall and handsome, he came from one of Virginia's most distinguished families and represented the largest and most powerful state in the union.

In the late spring of 1787, fifty-five of the most illustrious men in America gathered in Philadelphia to draft a new constitution for the United States. Meeting in the Assembly Room of the Pennsylvania legislature, they included war heroes like Washington, elder statesmen like Benjamin Franklin, and young upstarts like Alexander Hamilton. In the words of James Madison, they "would decide forever the fate of Republican Govt."

Washington sat on a thronelike chair at the front of the sparsely decorated forty-by-forty-foot room, which included fourteen wooden tables covered in heavy green cloth and two marble fireplaces. The windows were shut and covered with heavy drapes to prevent eavesdropping on the secret proceedings.

Standing at the back of the room, across from the Pennsylvania delegation, Randolph took aim at the governments of the thirteen states, which in the minds of the delegates had led the country to the brink of collapse by being too solicitous of the common man. "Our chief danger arises from the democratic parts of our constitutions," Randolph said. "It is a maxim which I hold incontrovertible, that the powers of government exercised by the people swallows up the other branches. None of the constitutions have provided sufficient checks against the democracy."

The stated purpose of the convention was for the Articles of Confederation—the country's original constitution adopted in 1781—to be "corrected and enlarged." But in order "to restrain, if possible, the fury of democracy," Randolph laid out a blueprint, known as the Virginia Plan, for an entirely new national government to replace the Continental Congress and counter the power of the states.

The House of Representatives would be elected by the people, like the state legislatures, but would be matched by an upper house, known as the Senate, whose members would be nominated by the state legislatures and chosen by the lower house. The new national legislature would choose the country's president and appoint its judiciary. That meant the public would directly elect only one house of one branch of the federal government.

It was a stunning start to the convention. The new constitution proposed by Randolph limited the public's role in the selection of the country's leaders, separated the government into different branches and divided power between the federal and state governments to filter popular opinion and temper populist passions. That structure was designed to restrain popular majorities and curb the excesses of democracy in the states to protect the interests of a wealthy, propertied, white male minority. It marked a radical turnaround from the Declaration of Independence that had been signed in that very room eleven years earlier.

» » » » » »

When America declared independence from Great Britain in 1776—rebelling against a monarchy that harshly governed its colony from four thousand miles across the Atlantic—the revolutionary leaders created a government that strove to be one with its people.

Not only did the Declaration of Independence state that "all men are created equal" and endowed with "certain unalienable rights" that included "Life, Liberty and the pursuit of Happiness," America's founding document held that governments derived "their just powers from the consent of the governed." This was "the mother principle" of the revolution, said Thomas Jefferson, that governments are "republican only in proportion as they embody the will of their people and execute it."

This belief that majority rule and popular consent defined a democratic society dated back centuries. "For if liberty and equality, as some persons suppose, are chiefly to be found in a democracy, it must be so by every department of government being alike open to all; but as the people are in the majority, and what they vote is law, it follows that such a state must be a democracy," Aristotle wrote in *Politics* in fourth century BC. To Jefferson, a democratic republic was "a government by its citizens in mass, acting directly, according to rules established by the majority."

The new democratic republic created by Jefferson and the fifty-five other men who signed the Declaration of Independence was the first of its kind. Instead of a direct democracy, like in ancient Greece, in this representative democracy politicians elected by the people would faithfully reflect the views of their constituents.

The state constitutions drafted in 1776 placed the bulk of political power in popularly elected state legislatures that were expected to reflect and encourage democratic participation. Legislators were elected annually, with the slogan "where annual elections end, tyranny begins," so that they would be as accountable as possible to the public. Constituents could instruct their legislators on how to vote, and there were frequent town meetings and public gatherings. Most states had term limits to discourage career politicians. Property requirements were reduced for voting and office holding to create a broader-based electorate and political class. Ordinary citizens clung fervently to the notion of "VOX POPULI VOX DEI": "the voice of the people is the voice of God."

Of course, many people were still excluded from the political process. Only white men continued to hold office after the revolution.

Property requirements made roughly a quarter of white men ineligible to vote, women could vote only briefly in New Jersey, and free Black men were allowed to cast ballots in just five states. The 700,000 enslaved people had no legal rights and Native Americans were not even considered US citizens. Still, by the standards of the time, the postwar legislatures were far more reflective of everyday society than the colonial ones, which had been dominated by wealthy merchants and lawyers. In states like New Jersey and New York more than half of the legislators were farmers from modest backgrounds. "Government is, or ought to be, instituted for the common benefit, protection, and security of the people," said Pennsylvania's constitution, "and not for the particular emolument or advantage of any single man, family, or set of men who are only part of the community."

This new democratic egalitarianism might have defined America's political system for decades if an economic crisis hadn't hit in the 1780s. To pay off their staggering war debts—and a $3 million requisition in 1785 from the Continental Congress, which could not generate its own revenue—states enacted tax increases that fell most heavily on the farmers, who made up 90 percent of the country's population.

This devastated the economy, leading to the worst depression until the 1930s. Tens of thousands of people had their farms repossessed. In some Pennsylvania counties, 60 to 70 percent of taxpaying farmers lost their land. Jails were soon filled with debtors. In eight states, riots broke out among impoverished citizens who could not pay their taxes or debts. Ordinary citizens petitioned their legislatures for tax and debt relief, and politicians responded by forgoing tax collection and allowing debtors to repay their obligations with paper money instead of gold and silver coins, which were in short supply.

A flood of newly issued paper money soon led to massive inflation and became worthless for raising government revenue or satisfying public and private debts. To the country's economic and political elite, it appeared that the state governments were favoring the poor over the rich and debtors over creditors in order to win over the sentiments of the common man. "The general disease which infects all our constitutions [is] an excess of popularity," Alexander Hamilton told the Pennsylvania banker Robert Morris.

Things were most dire in Massachusetts. After the government cracked down on tax enforcement, struggling farmers took up arms in 1786, led by Daniel Shays, a thirty-nine-year-old former captain in the Revolutionary War who lived thirty miles west of Boston. They called themselves the Regulators and placed pine needles in their hats to signify a metaphorical liberty tree, inspired by the Declaration of Independence's command that "whenever any form of government becomes destructive . . . it is the right of the people to alter or to abolish it, and to institute [a] new government."

The Shaysites shut down courthouses in five counties so that taxes could not be collected and farms would not be foreclosed upon. They then marched to the federal arsenal in Springfield in search of more weapons and ammunition. It was one of the largest agrarian uprisings in American history. The state was on the verge of civil war.

The country's elder statesmen reacted with horror. Virginia congressional delegate Henry Lee told Washington that "the malcontents" in Massachusetts comprised a "majority of the people" (in fact, they numbered several thousand in a state with 375,000 people) and sought to abolish all debts and confiscate private property. Washington responded that "mankind left to themselves are unfit for their own government," and he feared the revolt would spread to other states. Leading figures became openly contemptuous of democracy and yearned for the days of monarchy.

"I was once as strong a republican as any man in America," the author Noah Webster wrote in November 1786. "Now, a republican is among the last kinds of governments I should choose. I should infinitely prefer a limited monarchy, for I would sooner be subject to the caprice of one man, than to the ignorance and passions of a multitude."

The rebellion was easily put down by Massachusetts's government, and the Shaysites were banned from voting or holding office. But what happened next was even more alarming to the political elite. The Shaysites took to the political process, "endeavoring to give the elections such a turn as may promote their views under the auspices of Constitutional forms," wrote Madison. Voter turnout increased three-fold in the 1787 election, and the state's hardline governor and legislature were replaced by a new government that pardoned the rebels and aided the farmers. The results, said Madison, were "not a little tainted by a dishonorable obsequiousness to popular follies." If the Shaysites could accomplish through the political process what they could not by taking up arms, thought Madison, then maybe the structure of the government was to blame.

Writing from Paris, where he was minister to France, Jefferson urged his old friend not to panic. "A little rebellion now and then is a good thing," he wrote to Madison on January 30, 1787, "and as necessary in the political world as storms in the physical." He urged Madison to "educate and inform the whole mass of the people, enable them to see that it is their interest to preserve peace and order, and they will preserve it, and it requires no very high degree of education to convince them of this. They are the only sure reliance for the preservation of our liberty. After all, it is my principle that the will of the majority should prevail."

But the will of the majority was exactly what Madison feared. When he arrived in Philadelphia that May, Madison said the "evils" of popular democracy in the states "had more perhaps than anything else, produced this convention."

» » » » » »

The thirty-seven-year-old Madison sat in the front row, short and sickly and dressed in black, as Randolph opened the convention. Although the Virginia Plan had been introduced by Randolph, it was Madison's blueprint.

When he gave his first major speech at the convention, on June 6, Madison expanded on Randolph's critique of the populist legislation passed by the states. "What has been the source of those unjust laws complained of among ourselves?" he asked. "Has it not been the real or supposed interest of the major number? Debtors have defrauded their creditors. The landed interest has borne hard on the mercantile interest. The holders of one species of property have thrown a disproportion of taxes on the holders of another species."

The upheaval in the states brought "into question the fundamental principle of republican government, that the majority who rule in such governments are the safest guardians both of the public good and private rights," Madison wrote in an extensive memorandum that he circulated a month before the convention to the likes of Jefferson and Washington.

In 1776, America's leaders had designed a government to protect the many from the few. Now, said Madison, it was time to protect the few from the many. "It is much more to be dreaded that the few will be unnecessarily sacrificed to the many," he wrote to Jefferson in October 1788.

Madison was a firm adherent to revolutionary principles. To maintain popular support, he believed that the government had to derive "all its powers directly or indirectly from the great body of the people . . . not from an inconsiderable proportion, or a favored class of it." But he didn't want 51 percent of Americans to be able to simply impose their will on the other 49 percent. He argued that democratic institutions could only achieve true legitimacy by balancing majority rule with the protection of minority rights. How to ensure both of these fundamental rights, which were often at odds, was the great dilemma he wrestled with at the convention. "To secure the public good, and private rights, against the danger of [a majority faction], and at the same time to preserve the spirit and the form of popular government, is then the great object to which our inquiries are directed," he wrote in the Federalist Papers.

Madison hadn't been afraid to take unpopular stands in support of minority positions. As a member of the Virginia legislature in 1785, he'd mounted a passionate attack on a bill introduced by Patrick Henry to provide government funding for Christian religious institutions, arguing that it violated religious freedom and could lead to discrimination against less dominant Christian sects or nonbelievers. "Who does not see that the same authority which can establish Christianity, in exclusion of all other religions, may establish with the same ease any particular sect of Christians in exclusion of all other sects?" he wrote.

Individual liberty, to Madison, was inextricable from the greater public good. He believed that majority rule was inevitable and, indeed, preferable in a democratic society; one of his main critiques of the Articles of Confederation was the requirement that all thirteen states agree on any amendment, which allowed "the most trifling minority" to block "the will of the majority." But he also worried that rash and impulsive majorities—of the kind that had fueled the populist uprising in the states—could trample minority rights and threaten the viability of self-government. "No other rule exists . . . but the will of the majority," he wrote during the debate over religious freedom in 1785, "but it is also true that the majority may trespass on the rights of the minority."

Madison had been refining these ideas for more than a decade. After growing up the son of the wealthiest man in Orange County, Virginia, who owned three thousand acres and one hundred slaves, and then graduating from Princeton, Madison became the youngest member of the Continental Congress at twenty-eight. He was so youthful-looking that an older delegate mistook him for a college freshman. He was an avowed opponent of populism, once losing an election for the Virginia House of Delegates because he refused to provide the customary free whiskey to the voters. Instead, he was a bookworm who devoured a cargo of works on history and politics that Jefferson had sent him from Paris before the convention. From his study of history and experience in the Continental Congress and Virginia legislature, Madison was skeptical of the fleeting nature of public opinion and even more distrustful of the politicians he believed exploited impetuous popular passions. "Had every Athenian citizen been a Socrates, every Athenian assembly would still have been a mob," he wrote in Federalist No. 55.

Madison regarded the protection of property to be of paramount importance in an enlightened republic. "Wherever the real power in a government lies," he told Jefferson, "there is the danger of oppression. In our governments the real power lies in the majority of the community, and the invasion of private rights is chiefly to be apprehended, not from acts of government contrary to the sense of its constituents, but from acts in which the government is the mere instrument of the major number of the constituents."

Other prominent founders, including most of those gathered in Philadelphia, shared his concerns. While the vast majority of American citizens were farmers or tradesmen of modest means, virtually all the delegates owned large amounts of land, many were extremely wealthy, and nearly half were slaveholders. Their views unapologetically reflected this class bias. The drafters of the Constitution had no conception that white people would one day become the minority, but they were keenly aware that they themselves were a distinct minority who needed to be shielded from the masses. "If a majority were to control all branches of the government," John Adams wrote in his famous 1786 treatise *Defense of the Constitutions of Government of the United States of America*, "debts would be abolished first; taxes laid heavy on the rich, and not at all on the others; and at last a downright equal vision of everything be demanded and voted."

Despite his general concern for minority rights and defense of religious minorities in Virginia, Madison ultimately wanted to protect a very specific minority group: not the economically downtrodden, nor those excluded from voting or political participation such as women or African Americans, but rather wealthy and powerful white male property owners like himself. He foresaw a day when "the great majority of people will not only be without land, but without any other sort of property," he said at the convention. "An increase of the population will of necessity increase the proportion of those who will labor under all the hardships of life, and secretly sigh for a more equal distribution of blessings."

One of his main aims in drafting a new Constitution was to protect the propertied minority from the propertyless majority. Madison's "remedy," he said on June 6, was "to enlarge the sphere [of government] and thereby divide the community into so great a number of interests and parties, that in the first place a majority will not be likely at the same moment to have a common interest separate from that of the whole or of the minority; and in the second place, that in case they should have such an interest, they may not be apt to unite in the pursuit of it." The purpose of the convention was "to frame a republican system on such a scale and in such a form as will controul all the evils which have been experienced."

In 1776, the people were meant to be as close to the government as possible. Now, in order to rescue the new American experiment, Madison strove to create a political system that resulted in "the total exclusion of the people in their collective capacity, from any share" in governing the country by vesting that power in the country's representatives through a powerful republic and complicated system of checks and balances. That was "the only defense against the inconveniences of democracy consistent with the democratic form of government." He wanted, in essence, to save the people from themselves.

» » » » » »

A day after Madison's speech against the excesses of majority rule, the convention considered his plan for a new upper house, known as the Senate, which Madison called the "great anchor of the Government" and the leading defender of "the rights of property."

In every state except Maryland the upper house was elected by the people, but the Virginia Plan proposed that members of the Senate be nominated by state legislatures and selected by the lower house, with no involvement from the public. There was broad agreement that it should be "the aristocratic part of our government," said Pierce Butler of South Carolina. "The Senate ought to come from, and represent, the wealth of the nation," Madison said, protecting "the minority of the opulent against the majority." John Dickinson, the state president of

Delaware, said senators should be "distinguished for their rank in life and their weight of property, and bearing as strong a likeness to the British House of Lords as possible."

Madison proposed that senators serve nine-year terms, so that they could be as insulated as possible from swings in the public mood. Hamilton believed that senators should be appointed for life, arguing that "nothing but a permanent body can check the imprudence of democracy."

A lone dissent came from Pennsylvania's James Wilson. He was one of the original signers of the Declaration of Independence and one of the most famous lawyers in America. Washington considered him one of the ablest men at the convention. An immigrant from Scotland with a thick brogue, Wilson wore his glasses low on his nose and was known as "James the Caledonian" for his stern demeanor. He was hardly a populist—an angry mob once attacked his house in Philadelphia and killed his aide, sending Wilson into hiding—but he had more faith in the public's democratic character than most of his counterparts did.

"If we are to establish a national Government, that Government ought to flow from the people at large," Wilson said on June 26. "If one branch of it should be chosen by the Legislatures, and the other by the people, the two branches will rest on different foundations, and dissentions will naturally arise between them."

But no one seconded Wilson's speech. His proposal for senators to be directly elected by the people failed 10–1. Only Pennsylvania, which had no upper house, backed him. Elbridge Gerry, the future governor of Massachusetts, summarized the feelings of the delegates when he said "the commercial and monied interest would be more secure in the hands of the state legislatures, than of the people at large. The former have more sense of character, and will be restrained by that from injustice."

Madison's proposal was modified only slightly; state legislatures, not the lower house, would select senators, and they would serve staggered six-year terms, longer than in any state.

But when this brief debate ended, another, a far more contentious one, began.

» » » » » »

In his opening speech at the convention, Randolph proposed that both houses of the legislature be apportioned according to the number of people in each state. Reflecting the tension among the founders between democracy and oligarchy, Randolph's plan both insulated the new Congress from popular majorities while striving to maintain the government's legitimacy by ensuring that it represented the greatest number of people. Though states had the same number of delegates in the Continental Congress, some of the most steadfast supporters of the new Constitution argued that representation in the states should be based on population instead. "As all authority was derived from the people, equal numbers of people ought to have an equal no. of representatives," Wilson said.

But the country was narrowly divided between large states and small ones. The smallest states in the union quickly objected, arguing that each state should have an equal number of senators. "N. Jersey will never confederate on the plan before the Committee," said William Paterson, the state's first attorney general. "She would be swallowed up." Paterson said he would "rather submit to a monarch, to a despot, than to such a fate." He vowed to "not only oppose the plan here but on his return home do everything in his power to defeat it there."

A heated debate broke out among supporters of equal representation versus backers of proportional representation.

"The number of Representatives should bear some proportion to the number of the Represented," Wilson responded to Paterson, reading a letter from his friend Benjamin Franklin. "The decisions should be by the majority of members, not by the majority of States."

He warned that it was "equally in the power of the lesser states to swallow up the greater," in which case "the minority overpowers the majority, contrary to the common practice of assemblies in all countries and ages." In a series of passionate speeches, Wilson said that "the present claims of the smaller states lead directly to the establishment of an aristocracy, which is the government of the few over the many."

Though he lost his fight to have senators directly elected by the people, Wilson won the first round over whether senators should be chosen proportionally, with the states voting 6–5 to apportion both houses based on population.

But the small states would not let the matter drop and grew increasingly aggressive. On the morning of Saturday, June 30, Gunning Bedford Jr., the attorney general of Delaware, who was a classmate of Madison's at Princeton and graduated at the top of his class, confronted the delegates from Massachusetts, Pennsylvania, and Virginia, the three largest states in the union. "I do not, gentlemen, trust you," he said, staring down the likes of Madison and Wilson. "If you possess the power the abuse of it could not be checked; and what then would prevent you from exercising it to our destruction?" He issued a startling ultimatum: "The large states dare not dissolve the Confederation. If they do, the small ones will find some foreign ally of more honor and good faith, who will take them by the hand and do them justice."

Rufus King of Massachusetts, a member of the Confederation Congress, jumped to his feet and scolded Bedford for his "vehemence unprecedented." Threatening to leave the union and side with a foreign power—the very thing America had rebelled against—represented a dramatic escalation of the convention debate.

A second vote was taken on July 2, and this time the states deadlocked five to five. The five states opposing equal representation represented 56 percent of the country—and twice as many people as the states favoring it—but the majority was now powerless to stop the minority. "A government founded in a vicious principle of representation must be as shortlived as it would be unjust," King warned.

This was too much for Madison. He wanted to temper majority rule, not eliminate it altogether. Madison's state had 747,000 people compared to Delaware's 59,000, and he saw no reason why they should have the same number of senators. The convention, he warned, should not "depart from justice in order to conciliate the smaller states and the minority of the people of the United States." Equal representation in the Senate, he foresaw, would only grow worse over time as sparsely populated western states were admitted into the union, allowing "a more objectionable minority than ever" to control the federal government, especially since the Senate had unique powers over the House, such as confirming ambassadors and judges.

But Bedford's extortionist tactics worked. Two weeks after the states deadlocked, the small states prevailed on a third vote, 5-4-1, with North Carolina changing sides and Massachusetts divided. Equal representation in the Senate became known as the Great Compromise, but as Daniel Wirls and Stephen Wirls wrote in *The Invention of the United States Senate*, "The Great Concession is perhaps a more apt moniker."

As a consequence, just a third of the country could now elect a majority of senators. It was the most antidemocratic outcome possible; the unelected senate would not reflect the will of the people, nor the will of the states where a majority of people lived.

"Every idea of proportion and every rule of fair representation conspire to condemn a principle, which gives to Rhode Island an equal weight in the scale of power with Massachusetts, or Connecticut, or New York; and to Delaware an equal voice in the national deliberations with Pennsylvania, or Virginia, or North Carolina," Hamilton later wrote in Federalist No. 22. "Its operation contradicts the fundamental maxim of republican government, which requires that the sense of the majority should prevail."

The new Senate made minority rule not just likely, but inevitable, at least in one body.

» » » » » »

After the small states grabbed a disproportionate share of power in the Senate, the slave states sought to do the same in the House, the only popularly elected part of the new government.

A day after Randolph proposed that the House be apportioned

according to "the number of free inhabitants," Madison, who personally opposed slavery but nonetheless owned nine enslaved people, rose and suggested that the phrase "free inhabitants" be struck out.

That laid the groundwork for Pierce Butler and Charles Pinckney of South Carolina to propose that Southern enslaved people, who could not vote and had no legal rights, be counted equally with whites for purposes of representation in order to boost the South's political clout and protect the institution of slavery.

"This was nothing more than justice," argued Pinckney, a planter and future governor of South Carolina, who owned 150 slaves. "The blacks are the labourers, the peasants of the Southern States: they are as productive of pecuniary resources as those of the Northern states. They add equally to the wealth, and considering money as the sinew of war, to the strength of the nation."

Twenty-five of the fifty-five delegates were slaveholders, but more importantly, the Southern states were outnumbered five to eight by the Northern states. The Northern states also had a much larger free population than the Southern ones, where 40 percent of the population was enslaved. The Southern states, Randolph said, demanded that "express security ought to be provided for including slaves in the ratio of Representation."

The Northern delegates balked. "Upon what principle is it that the slaves shall be computed in the representation?" asked New York's Gouverneur Morris. "Are they men? Then make them Citizens and let them vote? Are they property? Why then is no other property included?" He demanded that only free inhabitants count toward representation, as Randolph had initially proposed.

"The admission of slaves into the Representation when fairly explained comes to this: that the inhabitant of Georgia and S. C. who goes to the Coast of Africa, and in defiance of the most sacred laws of humanity tears away his fellow creatures from their dearest connections and dam[n]s them to the most cruel bondages, shall have more votes in a Govt. instituted for protection of the rights of mankind, than the Citizen of Pa or N. Jersey who views with a laudable horror, so nefarious a practice," Morris continued.

He called slavery "the most prominent feature in the aristocratic countenance of the proposed Constitution" and said that counting slaves toward representation would only encourage the Southern states to import more, "by an assurance of having their votes in the Natl Govt increased in proportion."

Yet Morris's proposal was defeated 10-1. Even many Northerners who opposed slavery and counting enslaved people toward representation were afraid of losing the Southern votes that were needed to ratify the Constitution.

Wilson proposed a compromise that the enslaved be counted as "three-fifths" of people, a figure that derived from how the Southern states were taxed in 1783. Pinckney seconded his motion.

As a month passed, however, Wilson began to have second thoughts. He "did not well see on what principle the admission of blacks in the proportion of three fifths could be explained," he said on July 11. "Are they admitted as Citizens? Then why are they not admitted on an equality with White Citizens? Are they admitted as property? Then why is not other property admitted into the computation?"

But once proposed, the three-fifths clause could not be easily rescinded.

William Richardson Davie, a future governor of North Carolina who owned 116 enslaved people, said he was sure that the state "would never confederate on any terms that did not rate at least as 3/5. If the Eastern States meant therefore to exclude them altogether the business was at an end."

Just as the small states threatened to oppose the Constitution or leave the Union if they were not given disproportionate power in the Senate, the slave states did the same with the House. The minority's extortionist tactics worked a second time. It was again called a compromise, even though the Northern majority acquiesced to virtually all of the demands of the Southern minority.

The three-fifths clause gave the Southern states a third more members in the House than if only the free population had been counted, greatly strengthening their power in the federal government. "In this one instance, the slaves' interests would have been better served if they had not been considered persons at all," wrote the historian Woody Holton. That wasn't all. The convention voted 7–3 not to consider banning slavery for at least another twenty years, during which time Georgia and South Carolina imported more enslaved people than at any other time in American history, increasing their political representation as a result. "The security the South[er]n States want is that their negroes may not be taken from them, which some gentlemen within or without doors, have a very good mind to do," said Butler of South Carolina.

Over the July 4th holiday, Tench Coxe, secretary of the Pennsylvania Society for Promotion of the Abolition of Slavery, gave Benjamin Franklin a petition asking the convention delegates to end the slave trade. Franklin was president of the society and an outspoken opponent of slavery, but he told Coxe to let the issue "lie over for the present." Franklin never presented the petition to the convention. It was the only known example of public pressure on the delegates during the convention, and it failed.

Sixty-five years later, the abolitionist Frederick Douglass commemorated the signing of the Declaration of Independence in his hometown of Rochester, New York. He delivered a biting address before the Rochester Ladies' Anti-Slavery Society denouncing the chasm between the country's founding ideals and the harsh reality of slavery. "The blessings in which you, this day, rejoice, are not enjoyed in common," Douglass said. "The rich inheritance of justice, liberty, prosperity and independence, bequeathed by your fathers, is shared by you, not by me. The sunlight that brought life and healing to you, has brought stripes and death to me. This Fourth of July is yours, not mine. You may rejoice, I must mourn."

Two years after Douglass's remarks, during a Fourth of July speech in Framingham, Massachusetts, the abolitionist William Lloyd Garrison held up a copy of the Constitution, lit it on fire, and called it "a covenant with death."

» » » » » »

On May 29, Randolph had proposed that the country's president be selected by both houses of the federal legislature, but a week later Wilson suggested the chief executive be chosen by the people instead.

This was a new experiment for America. Because of suspicions toward the British crown, the country had not had a president since independence and had given most political power in the states to the legislative branch rather than executive officials.

But the time had come for a national leader, and Wilson suggested that it be a single person, elected for three years, who could be re-elected but also impeached for misconduct. On June 1, Wilson said he was "in favor of an appointment by the people. He wished to derive not only both branches of the Legislature from the people, without the intervention of the state legislatures, but the executive also, in order to make them as independent as possible of each other, as well as of the states."

Tellingly, Wilson was the only delegate at the convention who supported popular election of both houses of the legislature and the president. As he put it, "no government could long subsist without the confidence of the people." But on this issue, like the fights over representation in the legislature, "Wilson was a minority of one," wrote Woody Holton.

Not a single delegate rose to support his proposal. Only a month and a half later did Gouverneur Morris, who led the fight against the three-fifths clause in the House, second the motion for a popular election of the president. The president "should be the guardian of the people, even of the lower classes, against legislative tyranny," Morris said. And "if he is to be the guardian of the people, let him be appointed by the people." Morris said the public would "never fail to prefer some man of distinguished character," but "if the Legislature elect[s], it will be the work of intrigue, of cabal, and of faction: it will be like the election of a pope by a conclave of cardinals."

But Wilson and Morris failed to make any new allies and their proposal was defeated 9–1, with only the Pennsylvania delegation in support of it.

A variety of arguments were made against a popular election, starting with the belief among many delegates, who unapologetically represented the country's elite, that the people were too ignorant to select a wise national leader.

"The people are uninformed, and would be misled by a few designing men," said Elbridge Gerry. "The popular mode of electing the chief magistrate would certainly be the worst of all."

Even if the public could be trusted with such an important responsibility, other delegates argued that the country was too large and information too scarce for them to make a properly informed decision. "The extent of the country renders it impossible that the people can have the requisite capacity to judge of the respective pretensions of the candidates," said Virginia's George Mason. Popular election, he said, "would be the equivalent of referring a trial of colors to a blind man."

But the same divides that marked the debates over the Congress resurfaced in the discussion of the presidency, with the small states and the slave states arguing that a popularly elected president would threaten their influence.

Roger Sherman of Connecticut, who proposed the compromise that led to equal representation in the Senate, agreed with Gerry that the "people at large will never be sufficiently informed to make a wise choice." Instead, they would "generally vote for some man in their own state," and "the largest state will have the best chance for the appointment."

Hugh Williamson of North Carolina went further, arguing that popular election would hurt both the small states and the slave states. "The people will be sure to vote for some man in their own state, and the largest state will be sure to succeed," he said. "This will not be Virginia, however. Her slaves will have no suffrage."

On July 25, a cold and rainy day, a conflicted Madison helped break the deadlock. He agreed with Wilson that "the people at large was in his opinion the fittest" way to choose the president. "It would be as likely as any that could be devised to produce an Executive Magistrate of distinguished character." But, he added, "there was one difficulty however of a serious nature attending an immediate choice by the people. The right of suffrage was much more diffusive in the Northern than the Southern States; and the latter could have no influence in the election on the score of the Negroes."

The South would be at a major disadvantage in a popular election, Madison was admitting, because its enslaved population could not vote. It was clear the small states and slave states would not give up the power they'd already won in the legislature when it came to choosing a new president.

Wilson, acknowledging that there was little support for direct election of the president, proposed a complicated alternative where "electors" selected by the voters would choose the president, although states could still determine how electors were named. Though the public would not directly elect the president, Wilson believed the electors—who would ideally be prominent men of high character—were preferable to selection of the executive by the state legislatures or Congress, which would eliminate the public's role entirely. But it still meant that the public had, at best, an indirect say in choosing the president.

Ironically it was Wilson, the great democrat of the convention, who proposed two of the most undemocratic compromises of the Constitution: the three-fifths clause and the Electoral College.

The number of electors a state received would be based on their representation in both houses of the legislature, which gave a huge boost to the small states because of equal representation in the Senate and to the slave states because of the three-fifths clause in the House. The success of both of these powerful minorities in the legislative debates fatally compromised the country's most powerful institution, the presidency. And this also skewed the third branch of government—the courts—since judges appointed for life would be nominated by a president who was not elected directly by the people and confirmed by unelected senators representing a minority of small states.

Small states like Delaware received a disproportionate number of electoral votes over large ones like Massachusetts, and slave states triumphed over free ones. Virginia and Pennsylvania had roughly equal free populations, Jesse Wegman wrote in *Let the People Pick the President*, but Virginia's 300,000 enslaved people gave the state six more House seats and presidential electors than Pennsylvania. This became known as "the Slave Power." Southern states went so far as to call their bonus electoral votes "Negro electors."

The North had double the free population of the South, but because of the combined weight of equal representation in the Senate, the three-fifths clause, and the Electoral College, slaveholders occupied the presidency for the first fifty years of the country (every president except John Adams was a Virginia slaveholder for the first thirty-six years), the speakership of the House for forty-one years, and controlled eighteen of the first thirty-one Supreme Court seats before 1850.

That wasn't all. If no candidate won a majority of electors, the House would select the president. While that was more democratic than the Senate choosing the president in such an instance, as was initially proposed, the delegates agreed that each state would get a single vote regardless of population. That meant Delaware, with its one representative, would have the same power as Virginia, with its nineteen representatives, to select the holder of the highest office in the land in such a doomsday scenario, which the delegates foresaw as likely.

And because the people would not directly choose the president, there was little incentive for them to vote in the first place. In February 1789, sixty-eight of sixty-nine electors picked George Washington as the country's first president. But because some states did not hold

a popular election and others restricted voting to white, male property owners, only 43,000 people, or 1.8 percent of the total population,
voted in the country's first true national election.

» » » » » »

Before they adjourned in Philadelphia, the delegates had to wrestle
with the thorny issue of who would be able to vote for the institutions
they were creating, even though the House of Representatives was the
only popularly elected body at the time. Every state but Pennsylvania and Vermont included property requirements for voting, which
usually amounted to fifty acres of land or fifty pounds of personal
property, a sum that excluded anywhere from a quarter to 40 percent
of white men from voting. Georgia, South Carolina, and Virginia explicitly restricted the vote to white men, though in practice the small
free Black population could vote in fewer than a half-dozen states. The
delegates had to decide whether to keep these restrictions, go further,
or eliminate them altogether.

Reflecting their oft-stated concerns about the majority's threat to
property, many delegates expressed their support for property requirements for voting in federal elections as well as state ones. Delaware's
John Dickinson called this "a necessary defense against the dangerous
influence of those multitudes without property and without principle,
with which our country like all others will in time abound."

Madison agreed that "the freeholders [property owners] of the
country would be the safest depositories of Republican liberty," because "in future times a great majority of the people will not only be
without landed, but any other sort of, property," which would threaten
"the rights of property and the public liberty."

Only a few delegates opposed property requirements altogether.
The Constitution "should not depress the virtue and public spirit of our
common people, of which they displayed a great deal during the war,"
said Benjamin Franklin, who hailed from a state where 90 percent of
white men could vote, along with free Blacks.

But regardless of ideology, there was also a practical consideration: the Constitution needed to be ratified by the states and the founders didn't want to exclude potential supporters. "The people will not readily subscribe to the Natl. Constitution," said Oliver Ellsworth of Connecticut, "if it should subject them to be disfranchised."

The delegates agreed to add property qualifications for federal officeholders but not for voters, assuming that state property requirements would apply to federal elections automatically. But the most notable aspect of the debate was the lack of any discussion about including a basic guarantee of voting rights in the Constitution. "This valuable privilege of voting by ballot, ought not to rest on the discretion of the government, but be irrevocably established in the constitution," wrote the Pennsylvania newspaper columnist Samuel Bryan, publishing under the pen name Centinel.

By failing to safeguard voting rights, the Constitution kept in place the exclusion of more than half the population from casting a ballot: a significant number of poor white men, along with African Americans and women. Leaving suffrage qualifications to the states gave them a huge amount of room to expand the franchise but also to restrict it. And, in fact, both of those things happened nearly as soon as the Constitution was approved.

In the decades after ratification, states began eliminating property requirements for white men but restricting the franchise for everyone else. Class disparities didn't disappear, but race and gender divides now took prominence. Between 1789 and 1865, the vote was restricted to white men in twenty-five out of thirty-six states. "Universal male suffrage was increasingly defined against—even predicated on— women's and blacks' exclusion from governance," wrote the historian Rosemarie Zagarri.

This was perhaps the most insidious legacy of the constitutional debates: power had to be closely guarded, and the expansion of rights for certain groups had to be done at the exclusion of others.

» » » » » »

On September 17, 1987, 250,000 Americans gathered in Philadelphia to celebrate the two-hundredth anniversary of the Constitution's signing. There were fireworks and floats depicting the revolutionary era. The US Army's Old Guard Fife and Drum Corps, dressed as members of Washington's Continental army, marched down Chestnut Street playing "Yankee Doodle Dandy." Warren Burger, who had resigned as chief justice of the Supreme Court to lead the bicentennial commemoration, rang a replica of the Liberty Bell on his eightieth birthday.

Standing in front of a statue of Washington at Independence Hall, where the Constitution had been signed, President Reagan praised "the genius of our constitutional system" and said, "in a very real sense, it was then, in 1787, that the revolution truly began."

Thurgood Marshall, the first Black justice on the Supreme Court, issued a rare public dissent to the "flagwaving fervor." The preamble to the Constitution began with the phrase "We the People," but as Marshall noted during a speech in Hawaii, "when the Founding Fathers used this phrase in 1787, they did not have in mind the majority of America's citizens."

Marshall challenged the oft-repeated platitudes about the unparalleled genius and foresight of the founders. "To the contrary," he said bluntly, "the government they devised was defective from the start, requiring several amendments, a civil war, and momentous social transformation to attain the system of constitutional government, and its respect for the individual freedoms and human rights, we hold as fundamental today."

When the delegates adjourned in September 1787 after spending an unbearably muggy summer behind closed doors in Philadelphia, the final document thirty-nine of them signed benefited small states over large ones, slave states over free ones, and the country's wealthy over the common man, collectively protecting elite white power in all three branches of government. It represented a stunning counterrevolution against the principles of the revolutionary era and set the tone for oligarchy to triumph over democracy.

Some of these objections were noted at the time. "The change now proposed," wrote New York's Melancton Smith, publishing under the pen name Federal Farmer, "is a transfer of power from the many to the few." The new Constitution would "swallow up all us little folks," predicted Amos Singletary, a gristmill owner from Massachusetts, "just as the whale swallowed up Jonah."

But most of the people excluded from the Constitution's protections were also barred from the debate over ratifying it. The Constitution, like the president, was not approved by a popular vote. Instead, the state ratifying conventions used the same voting rules that applied to state elections, which meant that a majority of people were unable to weigh in on the document that would shape their future.

Not a single woman voted for or against the Constitution. Nor did any African Americans or Native Americans, or a large number of poorer whites. Three-quarters of adult males did not vote in elections to choose the state delegates that would debate the Constitution, because they were either uninterested or unable to. The final text was approved by less than one-sixth of the country's adult male population.

The Constitution, despite its notable antidemocratic features, was still a remarkable document for its time, creating a strong central government and robust system of checks and balances that laid the groundwork for American prosperity and became a model for democracies across the globe. It prevented the country from sliding into anarchy or back into monarchy, set up durable (if flawed) governing bodies, and restored elite faith in democracy.

Yet it remains a fundamental contradiction that the nation's most important democratic document was intended to make the country less democratic, and that a system of government founded on principles of majority rule would create institutions that facilitated minority rule instead.

Even after the political system was democratized in fits and starts in the decades after the ratification of the Constitution, so that senators were directly elected by the people, the franchise was expanded for white men, and presidential electors followed the will of their state voters, the belief that popular majorities needed to be constrained

rather than encouraged, and that privileged minorities should be protected over excluded ones, remained potent ideas in American politics. The initial decision to shield much of the government from the
public would set the tone for the new republic.

But the original Constitution of 1787 also left open the possibility that it could be amended, however arduous that process might
be, requiring the agreement of two-thirds of the Congress and three-
quarters of the states (another way small minorities could block popular systemic change). And indeed, many of the rights we hold most
dear today and believe protect every American—things like freedom
of speech and the right to assembly—were only added later in response
to complaints that the Constitution was insufficiently responsive to
core democratic principles.

"The original Constitution, we now recognize, was basically a
document of governance for free, white, propertied adult males," the
Columbia University historian Richard B. Morris wrote during the bicentennial in 1987. "Left out of its text, or dealt with ambiguously, were
the forgotten people—those bound to servitude, white or black (slavery
was implicitly, rather than overtly, recognized), debtors, paupers, In-
dians, and women—most of whom were not considered a part of the
political constituency."

The effort to include these forgotten people, who comprised a
majority of the country's population, in the laboratory of American
democracy—and the ferocious pushback by the dominant white power
structure to prevent it—would be the defining political struggle of the
next two-hundred-plus years.

3

THE NEW NULLIFICATION

A few minutes past noon on March 4, 1850, John C. Calhoun, the renowned political and intellectual leader of the white South, entered a packed US Senate chamber for his last speech. At sixty-eight years old, the longtime senator from South Carolina was dying of tuberculosis, his gaunt, pale body wrapped in a black cloak. With long gray hair falling to his shoulders, he looked like a wild-eyed Old Testament prophet. Too weak to write, he dictated his forty-two-page speech to his secretary, and asked the Virginia senator James Murray Mason to read it for him as he sat and scanned the chamber.

The Senate was debating a series of bills, known as the Compromise of 1850, that sought to defuse a growing rift over slavery by admitting California as a free state and abolishing the practice in the District of Columbia while increasing penalties for Northern officials who did not return fugitive slaves to their Southern owners. But to Calhoun, the most prominent spokesman for the South's slaveholding elite, these concessions only increased the likelihood that the country would split apart.

"The Union is in danger," he warned his colleagues. "The immediate cause" was "the long-continued agitation of the slave question on the part of the North, and the many aggressions which they have made on the rights of the South."

The slaveholding South had won special concessions when the Constitution was ratified; the three-fifths clause gave Southern states a disproportionate influence in the House and Electoral College, as did equal representation in the Senate. Since 1789, political power had been concentrated in the hands of Southern slaveholders and their allies. No one better illustrated this than Calhoun himself, who had been secretary of war under James Monroe, vice president under John Quincy Adams and Andrew Jackson, secretary of state under John Tyler, and a senator from South Carolina for fifteen years.

But those specific Constitutional protections were no longer enough. The population between North and South had been roughly equal when the Constitution was adopted, but by 1850 the growth of the industrial North and the expansion of US territory in the free West meant that the North was home to four million more people than the South. The Southern states were now outnumbered in the House and, with the addition of California to the union, in the Senate as well. They had become "a permanent and hopeless minority," Calhoun proclaimed.

He proposed giving the Southern white minority veto power over the country's growing antislavery majority by letting a state nullify any federal law it deemed unconstitutional and appointing two presidents, one from the South and one from the North, with the ability to override congressional legislation. Because the North now held the country's political majority, Calhoun believed the principle of majority rule was the chief danger facing the nation. He called it a "radical error" to "confound the numerical majority with the people."

Calhoun was the first major figure, in the generation after the Founding Fathers, to develop an ideology of minority rule explicitly designed to protect white supremacy. It was a political philosophy he'd been refining for thirty-plus years. Calhoun first invoked it in 1828 when Congress passed a tariff on manufactured goods that sought to protect Northern agricultural products from foreign imports but hit the South hard by raising the costs of cotton production and limiting trade with Britain. Calhoun called it the "Tariff of Abominations," designed to redistribute wealth from South to North, and said South Carolina had a constitutional right to reject it. Four years later, when Congress passed another tariff, South Carolina convened a nullification convention, voided the federal law, and declared Charleston an open port.

President Andrew Jackson saw this as an act of war, but Congress backed down and passed a lower tariff the next year. Calhoun viewed the tariff fight as a prime example of how a determined minority could thwart the will of an oppressive majority. "It is this negative power," he wrote in his most famous work, *The Disquisition on Government*, "the power of preventing or arresting the action of the government, be it called by what term it may, veto, interposition, nullification, check, or balance of power—which in fact forms the Constitution." Instead of accepting rule by the numerical majority, Calhoun wanted "to give to each division or interest, through its appropriate organ, either a concurrent voice in making and executing the laws, or a veto on their execution."

Under his doctrine of the "concurrent majority," an act of nullification by a given state would stand unless three-quarters of the rest of the states held constitutional conventions and passed an amendment rejecting that state's nullification of federal law, at which time the state in question would be forced to stand down or secede from the Union. In practice, this allowed one state, backed by just a fourth of the country, to nullify the wishes of three-fourths of the states.

Calhoun, who was a boy when the Constitution was ratified, claimed he was merely following in the footsteps of Madison, who had imposed checks on majority rule in the Constitution. But Madison, the last of the surviving founders, strenuously disagreed with Calhoun. He wanted to refine the process of majority rule, not scrap it altogether. In August 1830, Madison, seventy-nine years old, wrote to a friend that Calhoun's doctrine of nullification would give "the smallest fraction" of the Union, "seven states out of twenty-four," the power "to give the law, and even the Constitution, to seventeen States." He conceded that in some cases the seven states might be right and the seventeen states wrong, "but to establish a positive and permanent rule giving such a power, to such a minority, over such a majority, would overturn the first principle of free government, and in practice necessarily overturn the government itself."

Yet Calhoun, with characteristic intensity, plowed ahead. After the tariff fight, which earned him the nickname "the Great Nullifier," Calhoun turned his attention to protecting the institution of slavery from the restive North. The number of enslaved people in America had increased from seven hundred thousand in 1790 to more than two million in 1830, but Calhoun maintained that Congress should not be allowed to even debate the issue of abolition.

Slavery, to Calhoun, was "the most solid and durable foundation on which to rear free and stable political institutions." Democracy could only be predicated on white supremacy. Blacks, whether free or enslaved, were "utterly unqualified to possess liberty," he said in 1848. "The whites are a European race, being masters; and the Africans are the inferior race, and slaves." While many of the founders sought to protect a propertied upper class, Calhoun was singularly focused on race. "The two great divisions of society are not rich and poor, but white and black; and all the former, the poor as well as the rich, belong to the upper class, and are respected and treated as equals," he said. Calhoun viewed South Carolina, where a white minority ruled over an enslaved Black majority, as a blueprint for the rest of the country.

Calhoun died less than a month after his last speech. "The South, the poor South, what will become of her!" he allegedly said on his deathbed. His ideas proved disastrous. Ten years after his death, South Carolina became the first state to secede from the Union. Abraham Lincoln forcefully refuted Calhoun's ideas when he became president. "A majority, held in restraint by constitutional checks, and limitations, and always changing easily, with deliberate changes of popular opinions and sentiments, is the only true sovereign of a free people," he said in his first inaugural address in 1861. "The rule of a minority, as a permanent arrangement, is wholly inadmissible."

Calhounism appeared to die with the defeat of the Confederacy. Yet Calhoun proved remarkably prescient. One year before his death, writing on behalf of forty-eight Southern members of Congress, including the future Confederate leader Jefferson Davis, Calhoun anticipated that emancipation would lead to ex-slaves being elevated "to a political and social equality with their former owners, by giving them the right of voting and holding public offices under the Federal Government."

Well before new amendments were added to the Constitution abolishing slavery and guaranteeing equal citizenship and voting rights for Blacks and other previously disenfranchised minority groups, Calhoun expressed his fear of "the sentiment of the dominant portion of the Union, that no government is republican where universal suffrage does not prevail, where the numerical majority of the whole population is not recognized as the supreme governing power."

The reconstruction of the South after the Civil War was nothing short of a "Second American Revolution," as the historian Charles Beard put it. The adoption of the Thirteenth, Fourteenth, and Fifteenth Amendments represented the first time the Constitution had been altered to include long-disenfranchised minorities in a new governing majority. It was only then that a true majoritarian political system became possible. The definition of democracy had been radically enlarged; citizenship was now tied to equality, not just whiteness. Black men won the right to vote, trailblazing Black lawmakers were elected, and the party that aligned with Black voting rights made inroads in a region dominated for a century by the party of white supremacy. Multiracial government became a fact of life where white minority rule had been the norm.

But Calhoun, described by *National Review* as "the principal philosopher of the losing side," provided the road map for how reactionary whites would overthrow the country's first, incredibly brief, attempt at multiracial democracy. After nearly a century of Jim Crow, the civil rights movement brought about a Second Reconstruction to redeem the squandered promise of the first. Once again, Calhoun inspired the policy of "massive resistance" that segregationist whites used to challenge that movement and the Southern Strategy formulated by Buchanan that mobilized a white backlash.

Nonetheless, the passage of the civil rights laws of the 1960s laid the groundwork for the country to become a durable multiracial democracy, which culminated in the election of Barack Obama in 2008. But following Obama's election, Calhoun's fears of a dispossessed white minority would rally a new conservative counterrevolution aimed at blocking the agenda of the first Black president and nullifying the will of the huge popular majorities that supported him.

» » » » » »

On November 4, 2008, as he walked on stage to address 250,000 jubilant supporters in Chicago's Grant Park, Obama framed his historic victory as a realization of the highest ideals of American democracy.

"If there is anyone out there who still doubts that America is a place where all things are possible, who still wonders if the dream of our founders is alive in our time, who still questions the power of our democracy, tonight is your answer," he said to loud cheers.

It was an altogether improbable story of the country's tortured journey to build a true multiracial democracy. Obama's African ancestors could have been brought to the United States as slaves, his parents' marriage would have been illegal in many states until 1967, and he more than likely would not have been able to vote in states in the former Confederacy, such as Florida, North Carolina and Virginia, that he had won as a candidate.

It was proof that America's Constitution and democratic institutions were not frozen in time but could evolve to become more inclusive, participatory, and reflective of the country.

"It's been a long time coming, but tonight, because of what we did on this date, in this election, at this defining moment, change has come to America," Obama said definitively.

Nearly as remarkable as the candidate was the coalition he assembled. The 2008 electorate was the most diverse in history, with people of color making up one in four voters. Obama lost white voters to John McCain by twelve points but took 75 percent of the combined Black, Hispanic, and Asian American vote, giving him a landslide victory of 365 electoral votes and 53 percent of the popular vote, the largest margin since George H. W. Bush in 1988.

Practically all the growth in the electorate had come from voters of color. Five million more people cast ballots in 2008 compared to 2004, and two million of them were Black, two million were Latino, and 600,000 were Asian American. Their turnout increased by four points from 2004, while white turnout decreased. Ronald Brownstein of the *National Journal* dubbed Obama's base of minorities, young voters, women, and college-educated whites the "coalition of the ascendant."

"Democrats are getting the growing parts of the population: Young people, minorities and states people are moving to," said the Brookings Institution demographer William Frey.

This potentially seismic political transformation reflected even broader demographic shifts. Three months before Obama's election, the Census Bureau projected that whites would become the country's minority by 2042, a full eight years sooner than they'd anticipated just a few years earlier. The main reason was the increase in immigration, which added more than a million new residents to the country each year.

"No other country has experienced such rapid racial and ethnic change," Mark Mather, a demographer with the Population Reference Bureau, told *The New York Times*.

This was the demographic and political revolution Buchanan had been warning his party about for two decades.

"What are the seemingly inevitable consequences of an America where whites are a shrinking minority?" Buchanan wrote after Obama's election. "The end of a national Republican Party that routinely gets 90 percent of its presidential votes from white America."

Obama's coalition was the future of the country. But those on the losing end—like Calhoun 160 years earlier—weren't going to give up their dominant status without a fight.

» » » » » »

Buchanan's victory in the 1996 New Hampshire primary stunned the GOP political establishment. He entered the stage at a hotel ballroom in Manchester to loud cheers of "Go, Pat, go" and joined the crowd in a spontaneous rendition of "God Bless America," his voice hoarse from round-the-clock campaigning. "This is not a victory for a man," he told his triumphant supporters. "It is a victory for a cause. It is a cause of a brand-new conservatism in American politics."

He knew his insurgent candidacy threatened more polished and palatable frontrunners like the Kansas senator Bob Dole. "They're going to come after this campaign with everything they've got," he predicted. "We need more troops. Do not wait for orders from headquarters. Mount up and ride to the sounds of the guns!" It sounded like the Civil War all over again, with Buchanan the rebel general inspiring his outnumbered men to battle.

It would be the high-water mark of Buchanan's campaign. He would win only one more state, the Missouri caucus a few weeks later. Instead of giving him a prime-time role at the convention, like in 1992, Dole called Buchanan's views "extreme" and blocked him from speaking. The *Washington Post* columnist George Will dubbed Buchanan "Pitchfork Pat." A disillusioned Buchanan left the GOP before the 2000 election, seeking the nomination of Ross Perot's Reform Party, where he briefly squared off against Donald Trump, who was considering entering the race.

"Look, he's a Hitler lover," Trump said of Buchanan on *Meet the Press* in 1999. "I guess he's an anti-Semite. He doesn't like the blacks. He doesn't like the gays. It's just incredible that anybody could embrace this guy."

Buchanan won the Reform nomination over the Transcendental Meditating physicist John Hagelin of the Natural Law Party, but received fewer than half a million votes in the general election (even that number was inflated by elderly voters in Palm Beach County, Florida, mistakenly casting their ballots for him instead of Al Gore because of a confusing ballot design). Buchanan spent the 2000s in the political wilderness, writing increasingly hyperbolic screeds about the immigrant takeover of America, such as *The Death of the West: How Dying Populations and Immigrant Invasions Imperil Our Country and*

Civilization and *State of Emergency: The Third World Invasion and Conquest of America.* He watched in horror as the white population grew by 1 percent from 2000 to 2010 while the Black population grew by 15 percent, the Hispanic population by 43 percent, and the Asian population by 46 percent.

"The people who put the GOP in power are not growing in numbers nearly as rapidly as immigrants and people of color who want them out of power," he wrote in 2006. "The fading away of America's white majority entails an existential crisis for the GOP."

These writings, mostly ignored at the time, appeared prophetic after Obama's election. As Buchanan became more marginalized, his ideas paradoxically found greater favor within the GOP, helping to inspire a new Tea Party movement that would defend the country's besieged white majority before it was too late.

» » » » » »

"Obama's election represents multiculturalism run amuck," former GOP congressman Tom Tancredo of Colorado said to loud cheers at the first major Tea Party convention in Nashville, Tennessee, in February 2010. "Because we don't have a civics literacy test to vote, people who couldn't even spell vote, or say it in English, put a committed socialist ideologue in the White House named Barack Hussein Obama."

Tancredo, who was being advised by Buchanan's sister, Bay, called on Tea Party activists to launch a "counter-revolution" that would "pass on our culture based on Judeo-Christian principles. Whether people like it or not, that's who we are," he said to a standing ovation at the Opryland Hotel.

Tancredo's call for a literacy test to vote—a Jim Crow–era device that had been used to systematically disenfranchise Black voters in the segregated South—was not an aberration but reflected the Tea Party movement's embrace of a broader antidemocratic agenda intended to curb the political power of Obama's rainbow coalition.

More than five hundred thousand people would join more than five hundred rallies, and one in five Americans—nearly 50 million people—said they supported the movement, which stood for "Taxed Enough Already" and invoked the resistance against the British at the beginning of the American Revolution. That was still a distinct minority of the country, but large enough to exert significant influence within the GOP at the state and national level. Widespread anger at the government during the economic collapse, white anxiety about Obama's election, and backing from some of the most powerful players in the conservative movement, such as Fox News and the Koch brothers, made the Tea Party far bigger than previous fringe movements like Buchanan's campaign.

The economic crisis might have provided the spark for the movement, much as the economic downturn of the early 1780s inspired Shays's rebellion, but the desire to block and nullify the agenda of the first Black president undeniably united its members, who were overwhelmingly white, male, Christian, and over forty-five, those on the losing end of the country's demographic changes. "The evidence is pretty overwhelming that it was white dispossession driving so much of the Tea Party energy," said Devin Burghart, president of the Institute for Research and Education on Human Rights, which tracked the movement from the beginning.

It began with the effort to deny Obama's citizenship and portray his presidency as fundamentally illegitimate. Just 41 percent of Tea Party supporters believed Obama was born in the United States and only 29 percent said he was Christian. Signs depicting Obama as a Muslim/Marxist/socialist and demanding to see his birth certificate were ubiquitous at Tea Party protests.

To the Tea Party, Obama's election was a symbol of how the political power of white America was under siege from minorities and foreigners. Seventy-one percent of Tea Party supporters believed that "Obama is destroying the country," while 61 percent said that discrimination against whites "is as big a problem as discrimination against blacks and other minorities." Ninety-seven percent of Tea Party supporters said illegal immigration was a serious or somewhat serious problem and 42 percent said legal immigration should be decreased.

Sometimes this ideology was couched in seemingly race-blind phrases like the need to "take our country back" that echoed Buchanan's campaigns. Other times it was stated far more directly. "The White Anglo-Saxon Protestant (WASP) population in America is headed for extinction and with it our economy, well-being and survival as a uniquely America [sic] culture," Tea Party Nation member Rich Swier wrote in an email to the group's thirty thousand members.

Buchananite notions of white displacement, which Republican leaders had tried to downplay in the 1990s and 2000s, were now being pushed into the mainstream of the party. "For the first time in our lifetimes, outside the South, white racial consciousness has visibly begun to rise," Buchanan wrote in July 2010.

Tea Party supporters didn't just want to deny Obama's citizenship, they wanted to deny the benefits of citizenship to his diverse coalition. They embraced a version of the Constitution before it had been amended to give new rights to long disenfranchised communities or updated to democratize undemocratic institutions—a world without the Reconstruction amendments and civil rights laws of the 1960s.

More than half of Tea Party supporters backed Buchanan's call to repeal a key section of the Fourteenth Amendment giving citizenship to children of undocumented immigrants born in the United States, which they said undermined the rule of law and threatened the power of the white electorate.

Prominent Tea Party supporters also called for repealing the Seventeenth Amendment of 1913, which led to the direct election of US senators by the people instead of their appointment by state legislators. Conservative author Cleon Skousen, an intellectual inspiration for the Tea Party, wrote in 1985 that the direct election of senators had left them vulnerable to the "popular pressure" of the public. Texas governor Rick Perry said the amendment had been enacted in "a fit of populist rage" and had violated the principle that "better senators" are produced by "the elect of the elected" instead of by the voters.

Tea Party Nation founder Judson Phillips, a Tennessee defense attorney who hosted the convention where Tancredo spoke, called for voting rights to once again be restricted to property owners. "The Founding Fathers originally . . . put certain restrictions on who gets the right to vote," he said on his radio show. "It wasn't you were just a citizen and you got to vote. Some of the restrictions, you know, you obviously would not think about today. But one of those was you had to be a property owner. And that makes a lot of sense, because if you're a property owner you actually have a vested stake in the community. If you're not a property owner, you know, I'm sorry but property owners have a little bit more of a vested interest in the community than non-property owners."

And at virtually every Tea Party meeting, someone brought up the Tenth Amendment, which gave states powers not reserved for the federal government and formed the basis for Calhoun's theory of nullification, to justify blocking Obama's health care reform law and limiting federal authority over immigration, gun regulation, and environmental protection. Nullification rallies were held across the country, and twenty states passed laws rejecting all or some of Obamacare. Some even called for secession. "We've got a great union," Perry said at a Tea Party rally outside the Texas capitol in April 2009. "There is absolutely no reason to dissolve it. But if Washington continues to thumb their nose at the American people, you know, who knows what may come out of that?"

"No, it is not 1860 again," Buchanan wrote approvingly in February 2010. "But with all the talk of the 10th Amendment, nullification and interposition, states rights and secession . . . one might think so."

In calling for a return to founding principles, the Tea Party movement was in essence embracing the Constitution as it had been in 1787 as opposed to how it had evolved in the 220 years since, an interpretation that all but guaranteed a government run by white Christian men instead of a multiracial majority.

The backlash to Obama's election represented a decisive turning point in American politics. After 2008, his coalition seemed to represent the new normal in American politics, which would persuade Republicans to enlarge their support and modify their policies to win over an increasingly diverse electorate. Instead, the Tea Party led a rear-guard effort to defend the past rather than adapt to the future, pushing extreme policies that appealed to a reactionary conservative base instead of a broad majority. This forced the GOP to become far more reliant on antidemocratic tactics to uphold the power of that shrinking white constituency as the country shifted demographically and politically in Obama's direction.

» » » » » »

In July 2010, the Maricopa County sheriff Joe Arpaio, who had been dubbed "America's toughest sheriff," traveled to Kansas to campaign for secretary of state candidate Kris Kobach. The "Illegal Means Illegal" rally in Overland Park, a wealthy suburb of Kansas City, could have applied to either illegal immigration or claims of illegal voting.

Inside the packed convention center ballroom, Kobach stood behind two huge banners that said "Elect Kris Kobach / Stop Voter Fraud" with stop signs next to the words.

A local talk radio host introduced Kobach as "the man behind Arizona's toughest new law." A longtime law professor, Kobach had helped write a controversial new measure in Arizona, SB 1070, which required police to ask for citizenship papers from anyone they had "reasonable suspicion" of being in the state illegally. The legislation led to fears of widespread racial profiling against Hispanics.

SB 1070 had become a rallying cry for the Tea Party, and Kobach, one of the movement's earliest proponents, bragged that "we built the law like a tank."

The NAACP was holding its convention in Kansas City at the same time and had passed a resolution that day condemning the Tea Party for "explicitly racist behavior." It cited a protest over health care reform at the US Capitol, where Tea Party supporters spit on a Black member of Congress and yelled racial epithets at the civil rights leader John

Lewis, widespread support for the birther movement, and the omnipresent racially tinged signs at protest rallies, such as one that superimposed Obama's face as the Joker over the tagline "socialism."

Outside the convention center two hundred protesters, including a contingent from the NAACP, held signs that said, "No Hate in Our State."

Kobach himself had flirted with the birther movement. "What do Obama and God have in common?" he once joked at a Kansas GOP barbecue. "Neither has a birth certificate." (He lifted the line from Rush Limbaugh.)

In Overland Park, Kobach defended the Tea Party's positions. "We're not motivated by hate. We're motivated by love," he told the crowd of two thousand, which, much like the Tea Party, was overwhelmingly white, over forty-five, and disproportionately male. A man in a black Tea Party shirt protesting Tax Day waved a giant red-and-white-striped "Don't Tread On Me" flag with the image of a rattlesnake. "We love our Constitution, we love our god and we love the rule of law. And, indeed, we even love the illegal aliens themselves, but we'd really love it if they'd consider packing their bags, going home, and try coming in legally," Kobach said to cheers.

As Kobach recited a litany of complaints against the Obama administration, which that month had sued to block Arizona's immigration law, he was interrupted by the Overland Park chief of police, who said they had found a "very suspicious" package and asked everyone to evacuate.

There were loud boos, as if the package—which turned out to be an abandoned briefcase—was part of a sinister conspiracy by the liberal establishment to censor two leaders of the right-wing resistance.

"I would encourage anyone who is even the slightest bit afraid to go," Kobach said. No one budged. The crowd chanted: "USA! USA!"

Kobach introduced Arpaio to cheers of "Joe, Joe, Joe."

The seventy-eight-year-old Arpaio described how he used the authority given to him by Kobach's legislation to round up undocumented immigrants, making them wear pink jump suits, work on chain gangs, and live in tents that reached 140 degrees in the Phoenix sun.

"I took away their cigarettes. I took away their coffee, put them on a chain gang. I'm an equal opportunity incarcerator, I put the women on a chain gang," he said to loud cheers.

Arpaio enthusiastically endorsed Kobach. "He should be running for president, but we'll take secretary of state."

Most people viewed immigration and voting as two separate issues, but Kobach saw his work cracking down on undocumented immigration in Arizona as a model for his plans in Kansas. "I want Kansas to be to stopping voter fraud what Arizona is to stopping illegal immigration," he pledged.

» » » » » »

"I can sum up my reason for running in one word—ACORN," Kobach said when he announced his secretary of state campaign. "ACORN is a criminal enterprise."

Voter fraud fears went national in 2008. Republicans seized on evidence that employees of ACORN, a community organizing group that mobilized low-income and minority voters, had registered fictitious voters like Mickey Mouse. In reality, ACORN canvassers in states like Nevada, who made eight dollars an hour, earned a bonus for submitting more than twenty-one new voter registration names a day, so they sometimes submitted fake names to make extra money. There was no evidence that Mickey Mouse or any other cartoon characters had actually voted—under the Help America Vote Act of 2002, new registrants had to provide some type of proof of identity, be it a driver's license, utility bill, or bank statement—but that didn't stop McCain from alleging in his final debate with Obama that ACORN was "on the verge of maybe perpetrating one of the greatest frauds in voter history."

After the 2008 election, one poll found that 52 percent of Republicans believed that ACORN had stolen the election for Obama. The Republican fixation with voter fraud became a "new Southern strategy," the Rutgers University political science professor Lorraine Minnite wrote in her book *The Myth of Voter Fraud*. "The reddest base of the Republican Party has been energized by the tarring of Democrats as cheaters and the association of Democrats with a radicalized crime-prone underclass."

Kobach, whose supporters wore T-shirts that had ACORN's logo crossed out, broadened these claims by fusing voter fraud paranoia with anti-immigrant hysteria. "In Kansas, the illegal registration of alien voters has become pervasive," he said on the stump. Kobach presented scant evidence of such fraud; there were only five alleged cases of noncitizens voting in Kansas over thirteen years on a report of 221 "incidents" he distributed widely. But his claims were eagerly embraced by Tea Party Republicans who already viewed Obama's presidency as illegitimate. Kobach was easily elected in 2010, part of a red wave that saw the GOP pick up nearly seven hundred state legislative seats, flip twenty state legislative chambers, and win sixty-three US House seats.

In 2011, Kansas became the first state to require proof of citizenship to register to vote, government-issued photo identification to cast a ballot, and matching signatures for absentee ballots. Kobach called it "the Cadillac of voter security measures." He wanted his "Kansas Project" to set the example for the rest of the country. "If a state enacted a model statute that was the absolute best legal framework a state could create, that would become a model for others," he said. "That's what I set out to do."

More than a dozen states, including Wisconsin, followed suit that year, passing a flurry of laws that made it more difficult to register to vote and cast a ballot. These measures ranged from new ID requirements to cutting early voting to closing polling places to adding new obstacles to voter registration. The new laws were more sophisticated and less obvious than the poll taxes and literacy tests of yesteryear, but they had the same intended effect: to control who could participate in the democratic process and to once again make voting a privilege, not a fundamental right. As the demographics of the country became younger, more diverse, and more progressive, the Republicans who took power after 2010 wanted the electorate to be older, whiter, and more conservative, as it had been in 2010, compared with 2008.

The election of the first Black president and the resurrection of new barriers to the ballot box was not a coincidence. "Of the 11 states with the highest African-American turnout in 2008, 7 have new restrictions in place," the Brennan Center for Justice reported after the 2010 election. "Of the 12 states with the largest Hispanic population growth between 2000 and 2010, 9 passed laws making it harder to vote."

No state was as aggressive as Kansas in restricting ballot access, and no elected official as dogged as Kobach. When his Secure and Fair Elections Act passed in April 2011, he compared it to landmark civil rights measures like the Nineteenth Amendment, which gave women the right to vote, and the Voting Rights Act of 1965, even though those laws dramatically expanded access to the ballot rather than constricting it. Fifty years earlier, Kobach said, Black Kansans were disenfranchised because of the color of their skin. Now, Kansans' votes were nullified by people casting "fraudulent ballots."

His initiatives quickly targeted core members of Obama's coalition. In the first major election after the SAFE Act went into effect, the voter ID provision led to a 2 percent reduction in voter turnout—enough to swing a close election—with the largest drop among African Americans, young people, and newly registered voters.

The proof-of-citizenship law had an even bigger impact, since most Americans did not carry documents like a birth certificate or passport around with them. It particularly affected minorities, young people, and low-income individuals, all of whom were more likely to be registering for the first time and less likely to have immediate access to citizenship papers, usually because they couldn't afford them or because they were more transient and didn't have copies of their documents at hand.

The measure also made it impossible for groups like the League of Women Voters to register voters at locations like farmers' markets or public gatherings. When the law went into effect, eight of nine chapters of the Kansas League of Women Voters suspended voter-registration activities; the Wichita chapter went from registering four thousand voters a year to just 465.

Half of those blocked from registering were under thirty-five and nearly all were first-time voters.

One of them was Charles Tad Stricker III. In October 2014, Stricker went to the Department of Motor Vehicles in Wichita to get a new driver's license and register to vote. Stricker, who had recently moved back to Kansas from Chicago, brought his Illinois driver's license, Social Security card, and utility bill to confirm his identity and residence. He walked out with a temporary driver's license and believed he was registered to vote.

Three weeks later, Stricker and his wife went to their polling place at Central Christian Church in northeast Wichita. When he got to the front of the line, a poll worker scanned the voter registration rolls and told Stricker he was not registered. The best she could do was give him a provisional ballot.

While his wife voted in a private booth, Stricker filled out his provisional ballot at a plastic folding table in the center of the room. "It was almost like I was on display," he said. "It was very awkward to say the least. There was a line out the door and everyone was staring at me."

After the election, Stricker learned that his ballot was not counted and he was one of thirty-five thousand voters in Kansas who had their registrations held "in suspense" by the state for failing to provide proof of citizenship. Stricker didn't know about the law nor was he asked by the clerk at the DMV to prove anything beyond attesting to his citizenship under penalty of perjury, like he'd done when he previously registered. A month after the election, he received a letter from the county informing him "under Kansas law, you are not considered a registered voter until you submit an acceptable form of proof of citizenship."

Stricker was not the type of person you would expect to be disenfranchised. He was the general manager of the nicest hotel in Wichita, the Ambassador, which had a speakeasy in the basement and a steakhouse with a $145 tasting menu. From the windows of the hotel's 1,500-square-foot "rock star suite," you could see the large black glass headquarters of Koch Industries, owned by the conservative billionaires Charles and David Koch. "If this can happen to me, it can literally happen to anybody," Stricker said. "Something is fundamentally wrong here."

He joined a lawsuit challenging the law brought by the ACLU, which argued that its real purpose was not to prevent fraud but to stop the electorate from expanding and shifting demographically. During the 2008 election, the number of registered voters had increased by 5 percent and in the twenty-nine states that recorded party affiliation, roughly two-thirds of new voters registered as Democrats. Obama won nearly 70 percent of the country's 15 million first-time voters.

Kobach was freezing the existing electorate in place, which benefited Republicans even in a red state like Kansas. But beyond helping the GOP stay in power, he had a larger project in mind. He wanted to sharply limit who could become an American citizen and who could enjoy the core values of citizenship. The question of who counted as a real American had been contested throughout US history, and Kobach brought new policies and fervor to the fight.

His plans represented a radical reordering of American priorities. They would help preserve Republican majorities. But they would also reduce the size and influence of the country's nonwhite population. For years, Republicans like Buchanan had used racially coded appeals to white voters as a means to win elections. Kobach inverted those priorities, using elections—and advocating voting restrictions that made it easier for Republicans to win them—as the vehicle for implementing policies that protected the influence of a shrinking white majority. This made him one of the leading intellectual architects of a new nativist movement that had moved far beyond Buchananism and was quickly spreading across the United States.

» » » » » »

No one represented the kind of America that Kobach wanted to preserve better than Kobach himself. He was tall and broad-shouldered and looked like John Wayne. He was born in Wisconsin and moved to Topeka, Kansas, when he was seven years old. In high school, he mowed lawns and worked at his father's Buick dealership. After becoming class president, he went on to Harvard.

At Harvard, Kobach became a protégé of Professor Samuel Huntington, then the director of Harvard's Center for International Affairs and one of the pre-eminent political scientists in America. Huntington was a hawkish old-school Democrat who had worked in the National Security Council under President Jimmy Carter and would later become known for his dire warnings about an inevitable "clash of civilizations" between Islam and the West.

In the 1980s, Huntington advised the apartheid government of South Africa, where a white minority that comprised less than 15 percent of the population brutally repressed a Black majority that represented three-quarters of citizens. "It seems likely that a minority-dominated hierarchical ethnic system will become increasingly difficult to maintain," Huntington told a conference of South African political scientists in 1981, but he cautioned against quickly giving Blacks the right to vote. Instead, he argued that a transition away from white minority rule might require a period of "enlightened despotism" to ensure stability and avoid a white backlash.

Under Huntington's guidance, Kobach wrote his senior thesis on how the movement to divest from South Africa—which was the largest protest effort at Harvard in the 1980s—was misguided because international businesses were already leading the way against apartheid.

Kobach said Huntington "touched on a lot of themes I've worked on with immigration law. He was definitely a big influence on me at Harvard."

Two of Huntington's most radical ideas played a key role in influencing Kobach and the larger reactionary movement he helped lead.

The first was that broad-based participation in a democracy was not always a good thing. "Some of the problems of governance in the United States today stem from an excess of democracy," Huntington wrote in a 1975 report called "The Crisis of Democracy." There were "potentially desirable limits to the indefinite extension of political democracy."

Huntington warned of the dangers of expanding the franchise to previously disenfranchised and marginalized groups of voters. "In itself, this marginality on the part of some groups is inherently undemocratic, but it has also been one of the factors which has enabled democracy to function effectively," he wrote. "Marginal social groups, as in the case of the blacks, are now becoming full participants in the political system. Yet the danger of overloading the political system with demands which extend its functions and undermine its authority still remains."

This view was shared by leading thinkers in the conservative movement, who used a fear of multiracial democracy to make an explicit case for white minority rule.

In 1957, as Congress debated the first civil rights bill since Reconstruction, *National Review* published an editorial by William F. Buckley titled "Why the South Must Prevail."

"The central question that emerges," Buckley wrote, "is whether the White community in the South is entitled to take such measures as are necessary to prevail, politically and culturally, in areas in which it does not predominate numerically?"

Borrowing from Calhoun's skepticism of majority rule and outdated ideas of Black inferiority, Buckley wrote "the sobering answer is *Yes*—the White community is so entitled because, for the time being, it is the advanced race . . . If the majority wills what is socially atavistic, then to thwart the majority may be, though undemocratic, enlightened. It is more important for any community, anywhere in the world, to affirm and live by civilized standards, than to bow to the demands of the numerical majority."

In 1965, as Congress debated the Voting Rights Act, *National Review* published a cover story by the Virginia newspaper columnist James Kilpatrick, who had long praised Calhoun and advocated a policy of massive resistance against the civil rights movement, opposing the law. "Over most of this century, the great bulk of Southern Negroes have been genuinely unqualified for the franchise," he wrote. "They emerged illiterate from slavery; they remained for generations, metaphorically, under the age of twenty-one."

Whites were the only safe guardians of political and economic stability, Kilpatrick maintained. "Whatever social and economic and political values have been created in the 'Black Belt' counties through the machinery of local government, the white property owner has created them," he wrote. "In those rural counties where white families have been outnumbered three and four to one by Negroes, it has been the white leadership that has kept the machinery going—paid the taxes, provided the capital, met the bills. To have yielded political control of these functions to a mass of relatively uneducated Negro voters, easily led, unequipped for public administration, would have meant total disintegration of the whole establishment."

Buckley took this position to the extreme by arguing that the solution to Jim Crow wasn't more democracy, but far less. "What is wrong in Mississippi," he said during a debate at Cambridge University with James Baldwin in 1965, "is not that not enough Negroes are voting but that too many white people are."

Over time, as opposition to Black political rights became politically untenable, conservative intellectuals saw immigration as the central threat to the country's white majority.

The second influential idea promoted by Huntington was that the changing demographics of the United States would lead to a culture war between Anglo-Protestants and newer immigrant groups, particularly Latinos. "While Muslims pose the immediate problem to

Europe," he wrote in his 1996 book *The Clash of Civilizations*, "Mexicans pose the problem for the United States."

He expanded on this view in his 2004 book *Who Are We? The Challenges to America's National Identity*, denouncing the "Hispanization" of the United States and claiming that many Mexican American immigrants "do not appear to identify primarily with the United States" and were "often contemptuous of American culture."

Huntington's central thesis was that "the large and continuing influx of Hispanics threatens the pre-eminence of white Anglo-Protestant culture and the place of English as the only national language. White nativist movements are a possible and plausible response to these trends." Huntington conferred Ivy League respectability on Buchananite nativism, helping to propel a fear of immigration into the mainstream. Writing in *Foreign Affairs*, the scholar Alan Wolfe called *Who Are We?* "Buchanan with footnotes."

In addition to Huntington's ideas, Kobach was influenced by the activism around Buchanan's campaigns. He enrolled at Yale Law School in 1992. In his final year, California voters approved Proposition 187, a sweeping law titled the Save Our State initiative, which for the first time restricted public benefits, including education and health care, for undocumented immigrants. Voters of color opposed the measure but white voters overwhelmingly supported it, helping it pass by nearly twenty points.

Prop 187 was viewed as a triumph for anti-immigration advocates. "What the vote for 187 tells us about whites is that they are now starting to vote for their own interests as a racial group, in opposition to the interests of other races," the Buchanan adviser Sam Francis wrote. "The vote for Prop 187 goes far to relegitimize the racial aspect of American identity."

But things didn't turn out as planned. The federal courts blocked the law, on the grounds that California was overstepping federal immigration authority, and it prompted a surge in naturalization from immigrants, particularly Latinos. In the decade after Prop 187's passage, California added an estimated 1.8 million new registered voters, of which two-thirds were Latino and more than 20 percent Asian American, transforming the state's electorate. California had been predominantly Republican for decades, but a backlash from the state's growing Hispanic population pushed the Republican governor, Pete Wilson, out of office and flipped the state from more-or-less red to permanently blue.

Though the law backfired politically in California, it inspired a new generation of anti-immigration activists, including Kobach, who said that Prop 187 sparked his interest in immigration law. "It was not popular at Yale Law School, but I defended it," he said. "It just struck me as obvious that a state has the right to restrict its welfare benefits only to those people who are U.S. citizens or are visiting the state legally."

Jed Shugerman, a law professor at Boston University, attended a debate at Yale as an undergraduate in which Kobach defended Prop 187. "While the other pro-187 debaters were careful to distinguish between the 'legal' and 'illegal' process, Kobach struck me even then as far more xenophobic than other Yale conservatives," Shugerman wrote. "His image at that moment is seared into my memory, because I remember thinking, This dude is really smart and really scary. Remember his name, because he'll be back with a vengeance."

» » » » » »

In 2001, Kobach took a leave of absence from his job as a law professor at the University of Missouri–Kansas City to become a White House fellow in the George W. Bush administration. He was assigned to the Justice Department a week before September 11, 2001. While much of the national security establishment regarded the attacks as an intelligence failure, Kobach viewed them as a failure of border security. Though all nineteen hijackers came to the United States legally, five overstayed their visas and four were stopped by police, who weren't authorized to check their immigration status.

Kobach wanted to rebrand Buchanan's warnings about immigration to reach a wider audience. "When Buchanan was pushing this issue, it had a nativist and protectionist flavor," he told *The New York Times* in 2004. "Today it's about national security and law enforcement."

Kobach grew close to Attorney General John Ashcroft, and when the fellowship ended a year later, he stayed on as his chief adviser on immigration and border security issues. He designed a program that required all male visa holders over the age of sixteen from twenty-four predominantly Muslim countries (and North Korea) to be finger-printed, photographed, and interviewed by immigration authorities. The ACLU said that it "mandated ethnic profiling on a scale not seen in the United States since Japanese-American internment during World War II and the 'Operation Wetback' deportations to Mexico of 1954." The program did not result in a single known conviction on terrorism charges, but it did result in deportation proceedings for nearly fourteen thousand Muslim men, many for minor immigration violations. Kobach called it a "great success."

In 2003, Kobach returned to Kansas to challenge Dennis Moore, a Democrat, for his seat in Congress. The following year, he represented a group of students who challenged a provision in state law that allowed public universities to charge undocumented residents of Kansas in-state tuition rates.

The lawsuit was sponsored by the Federation for American Immigration Reform (FAIR). The group was founded by John Tanton, who became an unlikely leader of America's anti-immigration movement. He was an ophthalmologist and avid beekeeper from rural northern Michigan who was a leader with the Sierra Club and had founded a local branch of Planned Parenthood with his wife. He initially was concerned with the impact of rising levels of population growth, fueled in part by high birth rates among immigrants, on the environment. He founded FAIR in the late 1970s as a vehicle to debate immigration without the racist connotations of the past. "We plan to make the restriction of immigration a legitimate position for thinking people," he wrote in 1978.

But Tanton soon became preoccupied by the impending minority status of white Americans. "I've come to the point of view that for

European-American society and culture to persist requires a European-American majority, and a clear one at that," he wrote in 1993. His fear of a coming culture war between whites and non-whites grew increasingly apocalyptic. "As Whites see their power and control over their lives declining, will they simply go quietly into the night?" he asked in a memo addressed to colleagues at a retreat of anti-immigration activists in 1986. "Or will there be an explosion?"

He developed a passion for eugenics, idolizing the work of John Trevor Sr., who helped write the 1924 immigration restriction law, warning of "diabolical Jewish control" of America. Tanton became friendly with Trevor's son John, who led a group started by his father, the Pioneer Fund, that sponsored research on how whites were allegedly superior to Blacks and other minorities. The Pioneer Fund gave FAIR $1.2 million in grants.

Tanton's favorite book was *Camp of the Saints*, a racist 1973 novel by a French author, Jean Raspail, depicting "the end of the white world" after a fleet of savage refugees, led by an Indian called "the turd eater," overwhelm Europe. It ridiculed white liberals, who, instead of barring the immigrants, "empty out all our hospital beds so that cholera-ridden and leprous wretches could sprawl between white sheets." Tanton republished the book in English, with a new afterword by Raspail, who wrote that "the proliferation of other races dooms our race, my race, to extinction." The book would later become a touchstone for top Trump advisers like Steve Bannon and Stephen Miller.

Like in the 1920s, FAIR promoted the distinction between "old" and "new" immigrants. But now the divide wasn't between the Nordic countries and southern and eastern Europe, but between white and nonwhite immigration. Tanton wanted to create a group called the League for European American Defense, Education, and Research, hoping that "demographic and other trends would finally bestir the sleeping majority to action." To stop the "reduction of the European-American demographic and cultural majority to minority status," Tanton wrote that "an immediate moratorium should be declared on all immigration." FAIR's work helped push Republicans away from supporting immigration reform and formed the intellectual blueprint for the campaigns of Buchanan and, later, Trump.

Kobach's connection to Tanton—in addition to representing FAIR in court, he received contributions totaling $10,000 from a political action committee run by Tanton's wife—became an issue in his congressional run. "People and groups tied to white supremacists gave Kobach thousands," said a TV ad run by Moore. "One even hired Kobach." But Kobach refused to return the donations or disavow Tanton's aggressive nativism. Instead, he made opposition to undocumented immigration the centerpiece of his campaign, criticizing Moore for supporting what Kobach described as "amnesty" and calling on the National Guard to patrol the Mexican border.

Kobach lost the race by eleven points but earned national headlines for his outspoken views. "I want to just applaud you for your courage," Fox News host Bill O'Reilly told him that year during Kobach's first of many appearances on O'Reilly's show. "You're the first former administration official to come up and really tell the folks what's going on."

Kobach became counsel to the Immigration Reform Law Institute, the legal arm of FAIR, and began drafting a series of ordinances for cities and states around the country, preventing landlords from knowingly renting to undocumented immigrants and employers from hiring them in places like Hazelton, Pennsylvania, which used to be mostly white but by then had significant immigrant communities.

Though the federal government had the exclusive power to enforce immigration laws, Kobach's cocounsel, Michael Hethmon, called the ordinances "a field study." Kobach was pioneering his own version of Calhoun's nullification doctrine, telling states and localities they had authority previously reserved only for the federal government.

Kobach's work targeting undocumented immigration led to his interest in passing new voting restrictions as Kansas secretary of state. "If you have a massive amount of immigration—both legal and illegal—into a country and you have no safeguards in effect to ensure that only citizens are being registered to vote, then you create a situation where non-citizens get on the voter rolls in a very significant number and those non-citizens can tip the outcome of elections when they're close," he said.

Though Kobach once said he wanted to reframe Buchanan's nativism, he steadily moved in that direction, particularly after Obama's election, and painted an increasingly apocalyptic picture of how white power was under siege. On a radio show he hosted as secretary of state, where he described himself as "the ACLU's worst nightmare," Kobach said that Democrats had a "strategy of replacing American voters with newly legalized aliens."

On one show, a caller asked Kobach what happens "when one culture or one race or one religion overwhelms another culture or race?"

"What protects us in America from any kind of ethnic cleansing is the rule of law, of course," Kobach responded. "And the rule of law used to be unassailable, used to be taken for granted in America. And now, of course, we have a President who disregards the law when it suits his interests. And, so, you know, while I normally would answer that by saying, 'Steve, of course we have the rule of law, that could never happen in America,' I wonder what could happen."

Kobach's vision for America included deporting all 11 million undocumented immigrants, nationalizing barriers to the ballot box, and overturning landmark civil rights laws like the Voting Rights Act. His feedback loop worked both ways; making people believe that voter fraud was rampant built public support for policies that restricted access to the ballot. And claims of illegal voting by noncitizens helped justify Kobach's hard-line anti-immigration agenda. That agenda would become increasingly influential on the right.

Perhaps more than any other leader, Kobach channeled the ideology that inspired the Tea Party and defined the backlash to the first Black president. They, in turn, pushed his views from the fringe to the center of the GOP. "For the first time in his lifetime, he had a mass movement that was dedicated to those ideas," Burghart said.

These ambitious plans for minority rule would soon transform the Republican Party.

4

THE DEATH OF THE AUTOPSY AND
THE BIRTH OF THE BIG LIE

On March 18, 2013, the Republican National Committee chairman Reince Priebus celebrated his forty-first birthday at the National Press Club by releasing the results of an autopsy.

Five months earlier, despite a slumping economy and huge GOP gains in the 2010 election, Obama had been re-elected by 5 million votes and won the Electoral College with 332 votes. The RNC interviewed more than 2,600 voters and party activists to figure out what went wrong, releasing a one-hundred-page report outlining how the party should move forward. Priebus, a Wisconsin native from the town of Twin Lakes in Van Wanggaard's district, called it "the most public and most comprehensive post-election review in the history of any national party."

Focus groups described the GOP as "narrow-minded, out of touch, and stuffy old men," Priebus said with a wince. Obama had won only 39 percent of the white vote in 2012—a lower number than Michael Dukakis in 1988—but had been re-elected by winning 80 percent of the nonwhite vote, which increased in size in every election. For the first time in US history, Black voters had voted at a higher rate than white voters, who comprised their smallest ever share of the electorate.

Democrats had won the popular vote in five of the past six presidential elections, matching the GOP's dominance from 1968 to 1988. Obama's supporters, who were 56 percent white, 24 percent Black, 14 percent Latino, and 4 percent Asian, were growing as a share of the population, while Mitt Romney's supporters, who were 88 percent white, were shrinking. "By the year 2050 we'll be a majority-minority country," Priebus noted with alarm, sharing the same statistic that Buchanan frequently cited.

Conservative commentators treated Obama's re-election as a fatal, perhaps final blow against the white America they had longed championed. "The demographics are changing," Bill O'Reilly said on Election Night. "It's not a traditional America anymore . . . The white establishment is now the minority."

A day after the election, Rush Limbaugh said on his radio show, "I went to bed last night thinking we are outnumbered. I went to bed last night thinking we've lost the country. I don't know how else you look at this."

Buchanan wrote simply: "The demographic winter of white America is at hand."

Eighteen years earlier, as he prepared to launch his 1996 campaign, Buchanan had stood on the same stage as Priebus in Washington and warned Republicans about the consequences of this demographic shift. But Priebus said Republicans had no choice but to embrace it or they would no longer be a competitive party.

"The nation's demographic changes add to the urgency of recognizing how precarious our position has become," stated the autopsy, which was formally known as the Growth and Opportunity Project. "Unless Republicans are able to grow our appeal . . . the changes tilt the playing field even more in the Democratic direction."

The report did not mince words. "Public perception of the Party is at record lows. Young voters are increasingly rolling their eyes at what the Party represents, and many minorities wrongly think that Republicans do not like them or want them in the country. When someone rolls their eyes at us, they are not likely to open their ears to us."

The RNC specifically took aim at the policies advocated by Kobach, who had been an adviser to Romney's campaign. He had persuaded Romney to adopt Arizona's immigration bill as his template, with its idea of "attrition through enforcement." Make life miserable enough for undocumented immigrants and they would leave the country on their own volition, Kobach argued. When asked in a presidential debate how he would reduce the number of undocumented immigrants in the United States, Romney replied clumsily, "I'm for self-deportation." He won only 27 percent of the Hispanic vote, the party's worst performance in sixteen years.

"If Hispanic Americans perceive that a GOP nominee or candidate does not want them in the United States (i.e. self-deportation), they will not pay attention to our next sentence," the report said, directly rebutting Kobach.

It urged Republicans to "champion comprehensive immigration reform" to court Hispanic voters and form a new Growth and Opportunity Inclusion Council to attract other minority voters. Republicans were "not generating enough angry white guys to stay in business for the long term," Senator Lindsey Graham of South Carolina said.

The report was widely embraced by the party's elite. "The reince revolution is underway," Newt Gingrich tweeted. "Todays republican national committee report is historic. It is first big step toward gop majority." The media called it "controversial and bold" (*The Washington Post*) and a "scathing self-analysis" (*The Wall Street Journal*). The recommendations—while not exactly earth-shattering—still represented a bracing change of direction for a party not known for self-reflection.

That summer, the Senate heeded Priebus's advice and leading Republicans including Graham, McCain, and Marco Rubio negotiated a wide-ranging immigration bill that provided a pathway to citizenship for eleven million undocumented immigrants, strengthened border security, and increased legal immigration. Three-quarters of Americans supported it and much of the GOP establishment believed it was a political necessity. "It's really hard to get people to listen to you on economic growth, on tax rates, on healthcare if they think you want to deport their grandmother," Rubio said.

But just as the Senate prepared to pass the bill and propel Republicans in a more inclusive direction, a counterargument to the autopsy emerged.

» » » » » »

In June 2013, a week before the Senate voted on immigration reform, the conservative writer Sean Trende wrote an analysis in *RealClear-Politics* noting that five million fewer white voters had gone to the polls in 2012 compared to 2008. He urged Republicans to focus on these "'missing' white voters" rather than "improving their vote share with the non-white electorate."

"Democrats liked to mock the GOP as the 'Party of White People' after the 2012 elections," Trende wrote. "But from a purely electoral perspective, that's not a terrible thing to be. Even with present population projections, there are likely to be a lot of non-Hispanic whites in this country for a very long time. Relatively slight changes among their voting habits can forestall massive changes among the non-white population for a very long while." To court these "downscale, blue-collar whites," the GOP "would have to be more 'America first' on trade, immigration and foreign policy; less pro-Wall Street and big business in its rhetoric; more Main Street/populist on economics," Trende wrote.

Trende echoed Buchanan's longtime arguments in two ways. He urged the GOP to become more like Buchanan on policy matters. But just as importantly, he was reaching back to Buchanan's well-worn strategy of courting white backlash voters instead of trying to win over the country's changing demographics. The countermajoritarian structure of American politics incentivized this path: working-class white voters were concentrated in battleground states like Wisconsin that enjoyed disproportionate power in the Electoral College.

Trende pushed back on the idea that demography was destiny and outlined what he called a "'racial polarization' scenario." If the white vote increased, the Black vote decreased modestly, and Hispanic and Asian voters continued voting strongly Democratic, Republicans would win every presidential election from 2016 until Texas turned blue in 2048, he projected. Republicans didn't have to win over more minority voters so long as they turned out more white voters.

Buchanan had been urging Republicans to do this for years. In his 2011 book *Suicide of a Superpower*, he called for "a strategy from which Republicans will recoil, a strategy to increase the GOP share of the white Christian vote and increase the turnout of that vote by specific appeals to social, cultural, and moral issues." Though he knew this would be controversial, "why should Republicans be ashamed to represent the progeny of the men who founded, built, and defended America since her birth as a nation?" he wrote.

Buchanan sharpened this argument as the Senate took up immigration reform, amplifying Trende's point that white voters, despite shrinking as a share of the population, still made up three-fourths of the electorate and nine out of ten GOP voters. "Is the way to increase the enthusiasm and turnout among this three-fourths of the electorate for the GOP to embrace amnesty and a path to citizenship for 12 million illegal foreign aliens?" he asked. "Or is it to demand the sealing of America's borders against any and all intruders?"

The Senate's immigration bill "will create millions of new citizens who will vote to bury the Party of Ronald Reagan forever," Buchanan predicted. "Either the Republican Party puts an end to mass immigration, or mass immigration will put an end to the Republican Party."

The Senate passed the immigration reform bill 68-32 in late June, with fourteen Republicans voting for it, but Trende's missing white voter theory soon became gospel among the party's base as the legislation moved to the GOP-controlled House.

"The people the Republicans should reach out to are the white votes—the white voters who didn't vote in the last election," said longtime conservative activist Phyllis Schlafly. "And there are millions of them."

Even those who were previously sympathetic to the recommendations of the autopsy quickly changed their tune. On Election Night, Fox News anchor Brit Hume blamed Romney's loss on his "hardline position on immigration" and said the "demographic" threat posed by Latino voters was "absolutely real." But in July 2013, he called that argument "baloney" and said the Hispanic vote was "not nearly as important, still, as the white vote."

Hume's colleague Sean Hannity said after the election that "we've got to look at some of these demographics"; he had "evolved on" the issue of immigration and now supported a "pathway to citizenship." Yet in a June 2013 column citing Trende's article, Hannity opposed the Senate bill. "Not only do I doubt the current legislation will solve the immigration problem," he wrote, "but it also won't help the GOP in future elections."

Around the same time, the editors of the two largest conservative magazines, Rich Lowry of *National Review* and Bill Kristol of the *Weekly Standard*, who often spoke for the GOP establishment, wrote a rare joint editorial entitled "Kill the Bill."

"At the presidential level in 2016, it would be better if Republicans won more Hispanic voters than they have in the past—but it's most important that the party perform better among working-class and younger voters concerned about economic opportunity and upward mobility," they wrote. "Passing this unworkable, ramshackle bill is counterproductive or irrelevant to that task."

The debate over immigration reform quickly crystallized the central question facing Republicans: Would they embrace the changing demographics of the country or fight a rear-guard effort to counteract them? Once Republicans convinced themselves that outreach to minority voters could hurt their pursuit of white voters, the bill was effectively dead. "It's the defining struggle for the Republican Party, and right now the good guys are losing," said John Feehery, a former top aide to House Republicans.

Anti-immigration hard-liners quickly gained the upper hand in the House. Kobach testified against the bill a week after the Boston Marathon bombings, arguing that it would grant amnesty to future terrorists, and ridiculed the notion it would help the GOP's electoral prospects. "Any politician who thinks, 'Oh, we just cast one vote, and then all of a sudden this demographic group comes flocking to us,' they're being superficial Washington idiots," he said.

With Kobach's urging, Republicans on the House Judiciary Committee instead drafted a bill modeled after Arizona's SB1070 that would criminalize the presence of undocumented immigrants in the United States and give state and local police the authority to enforce federal immigration laws.

The Iowa GOP congressman Steve King, a Kobach ally, led the revolt against the Senate bill, which he said would taint "American civilization and culture into perpetuity." King had long portrayed immigration as a threat to "Judeo-Christian values." Like John Tanton, he praised the French novel *The Camp of the Saints* and spoke of "the Great Replacement," arguing that minority groups were systematically taking the place of whites in Europe and the United States.

"Culture and demographics are our destiny," King argued. "We can't restore our civilization with somebody else's babies." When asked to clarify his statement, he said: "I'd like to see an America that's just so homogenous that we look a lot the same."

King's views on immigration were not an extreme outlier within the GOP caucus precisely because so many Republicans represented districts that were far more homogenous than the country as a whole.

Ninety percent of the nation's population growth from 2000 to 2010 had come from nonwhite residents, yet the average Republican congressional district went from 73 percent white to 75 percent white when state-level Republicans drew new districts in many key swing states after the 2010 census. In part due to gerrymandering that sought to insulate them from competitive elections, nearly two-thirds of House Republicans represented districts where Hispanics made up less than one-tenth of the population, giving them little incentive to compromise on immigration or reach out to minority voters.

House rules exacerbated this problem. Speaker of the House John Boehner, who supported immigration reform, would only take up the bill if it had the support of a majority of the GOP caucus, a tradition dating back to his predecessor Dennis Hastert. There were 234 Republicans in the House compared to 201 Democrats, which meant that 118 Republicans—just over a quarter of the overall House—could block legislation supported by broad majorities in Congress, so long as half of House Republicans stood their ground.

Things came to a head in June 2014, when the House majority leader Eric Cantor—whose district was redrawn by Republicans after 2010 to make it more conservative—lost in a shocking primary upset to a little-known Tea Party challenger named David Brat, who ran against "amnesty for illegal immigrants." Boehner pulled the plug on immigration reform after that. The best chance in three decades to rewrite the country's immigration laws and moderate the policies and perception of the GOP had come and gone.

» » » » » »

In August 2014, two months after Cantor's loss, the GOP pollster Kellyanne Conway released polling showing that white voters who were unhappy about demographic change would turn out in higher numbers if a candidate emphasized "enforcement of current [immigration] law" and demanded that "illegal immigrants . . . return to their home countries." As Donald Trump prepared to launch a seemingly quixotic bid for the presidency, his chief strategist Steve Bannon called Trende's "missing whites" theory and Conway's polling on immigration "the intellectual infrastructure" of Trump's presidential campaign.

Three years after the party's autopsy, Republicans nominated a candidate who had questioned the citizenship of the first Black president, called Mexicans "rapists" and murderers, pledged to ban Muslim immigrants from entering the United States, and bragged of grabbing women "by the pussy." Just as Buchanan had taken David Duke's ideas and made them palatable to a sizable chunk of the GOP base, Trump adopted Buchanan's "America First" platform and marketed it to a much wider audience.

Many Republicans put aside their personal or policy qualms with Trump because they viewed his election as the last, best chance to preserve the power of a conservative white America they saw slipping away.

This view was best expressed in a widely read essay by the conservative writer Michael Anton in the *Claremont Review of Books* in September 2016.

Writing under the pseudonym of Publius Decius Mus, a Roman consul who sacrificed himself to win victory in the Battle of Vesuvius in 340 BC, Anton called 2016 "the Flight 93 election: charge the cockpit or you die."

Mixing metaphors, Anton wrote that "a Hillary Clinton presidency is Russian Roulette with a semi-auto. With Trump, at least you can spin the cylinder and take your chances."

Anton painted an apocalyptic picture of the future of the country and wrote that Trump, despite being "worse than imperfect," had been right on the one issue that mattered above all others: "Most important, the ceaseless importation of Third World foreigners with no tradition of, taste for, or experience in liberty means that the electorate grows more left, more Democratic, less Republican, less republican, and less traditionally American with every cycle."

In January 2019, a prophetic Buchanan wrote a column endorsing Trump's plan to build a wall along the US–Mexico border, an idea first proposed by Buchanan in 1992. "The more multiracial, multiethnic, multicultural, multilingual America becomes—the less it looks like Ronald Reagan's America—the more dependably Democratic it will become," he wrote.

Trump tweeted Buchanan's column to his 58 million followers.

So complete was the transformation of the party that none other than Reince Priebus became Trump's chief of staff.

» » » » » »

On November 8, 2016, Andrea Anthony, a thirty-seven-year-old Black woman with an infectious smile, went to the Clinton Rose Senior Center, her polling site on the predominantly Black north side of Milwaukee, to cast a ballot for Hillary Clinton. She'd voted in every major election since she was eighteen years old and had voted at this location during the 2016 primary and 2012 presidential election. "Voting is important to me because I know I have a little, teeny, tiny voice, but that is a way for it to be heard," she said. "Even though it's one vote, I feel it needs to count."

She'd misplaced her driver's license a few days earlier, but came prepared with an expired Wisconsin state ID and proof of residency. A poll worker recognized her and confirmed she was registered to vote at her current address. But this was Wisconsin's first major election that required voters—even those who were already registered—to present a current driver's license, passport, or state or military ID to cast a ballot, a policy that was a top priority for Wisconsin Republicans after they took over the state in 2010. Walker had been advocating for a strict voter ID law since 2000, when he was a state representative from suburban Milwaukee and chair of Bush's presidential campaign in Wisconsin. He wrote the first version of the bill in the legislature after Bush narrowly lost the state, alleging without proof that "many dishonest people undermined the integrity of Wisconsin's election system."

Anthony didn't have the right documents, and so she wasn't able to vote. The poll worker gave her a provisional ballot instead. It would be counted only if she went to the Department of Motor Vehicles to get a new ID and then to the city clerk's office to confirm her vote, all within seventy-two hours of Election Day. But Anthony couldn't take time off from her job as an administrative assistant at a housing management company, and she had five kids and two grandkids to look after. For the first time in her life, her vote wasn't counted.

"This particular election was very important to me," she said, citing her strong aversion to Trump. "I felt like the right to vote was being stripped away from me."

Anthony said her nineteen-year-old daughter and twenty-one-year-old nephew, who didn't drive regularly and had misplaced their licenses, were also stymied by the state's voter ID law, which after initially being blocked for violating the Voting Rights Act went into effect in 2016 after a conservative appeals court approved it. "It was their first election, and they were really excited to vote," she said. But they didn't go to the polls because they knew their votes wouldn't count. Both had planned to vote for Clinton.

On election night, Anthony was shocked to see Trump carry Wisconsin by nearly twenty-three thousand votes. The state, which ranked second in the nation in voter participation in 2008 and 2012, saw its lowest turnout since 2000. More than half the state's decline in turnout occurred in Milwaukee, which Clinton carried by a 77-18 margin, but where almost 41,000 fewer people voted in 2016 than in 2012. Turnout fell only slightly in white, middle-class areas of the city but plunged in Black ones. In Anthony's district, where aging houses on quiet tree-lined streets were interspersed with boarded-up buildings and vacant lots, turnout dropped by 23 percent from 2012. This is where Clinton lost the state and, with it, the election.

While Trump fixated on courting reactionary white voters, an equally important part of the GOP's strategy relied on making sure Black voters wouldn't—or couldn't—show up at the polls. In 2013, Trende, as part of his "racial polarization" scenarios, had projected that if the Black vote decreased, a Republican could win the presidency in 2016 without increasing turnout among white voters or improving their vote share with Hispanic and Asian voters. That's exactly what Trump did.

Nationwide, Trump won white voters by nearly the same margin as Romney, and white turnout increased by only a point, but Black turnout fell by seven points from 2012, the first time it had declined in twenty years. Wisconsin saw a 3.3 percent drop in turnout, the largest decrease in voting of any state other than Mississippi. Black turnout dropped by 19 percent in the state, more than four times the national decline among Black voters.

This is what Wisconsin Republicans hoped would happen when they argued for the voter ID law behind closed doors in 2011, singling out "neighborhoods around Milwaukee"—a widely understood euphemism for Black neighborhoods—and "college campuses around the state." Seemingly by design, Republicans who controlled the state never made it easy for those constituencies that needed new IDs—who disproportionately leaned toward the Democratic Party—to get them. Voters who tried to obtain a free ID at the DMV were repeatedly told that they had to pay for underlying documents, like a birth certificate. Eighty-five percent of those denied IDs were Black or Latino, the US district court judge James Peterson noted in a September 2016 ruling. The roster of people unable to comply with the law bordered on the surreal: a man born in a concentration camp in Germany who'd lost his birth certificate in a fire; a woman who'd lost use of her hands but was not permitted to grant her daughter power of attorney to sign the necessary documents at the DMV; a ninety-year-old veteran of Iwo Jima who could not vote with his veteran's ID card. One woman who died while waiting for an ID was listed as a "customer-initiated cancellation" by the DMV. Peterson called the state's process for issuing IDs a "wretched failure" that had "disenfranchised a number of citizens who are unquestionably qualified to vote."

There was plenty of evidence that Wisconsin's shoddy implementation of the law was a feature, not a bug. After the measure passed, the GOP-controlled legislature disbanded the nonpartisan agency tasked with overseeing state elections, replacing it with a commission of partisan appointees. When voting rights groups sued in the run-up to the presidential election to make the law less restrictive, Walker said his "primary focus" was "on making sure that a strong form of Voter ID is in place." The governor, who campaigned with Trump in Wisconsin, opposed spending state money to educate the public about the law, and the legislature didn't allocate any funds for voter ID advertising until June 2016, just months before the general election. The reconfigured state election board, with a small $250,000 budget, belatedly ran ads about the law in fifty-two movie theaters across Wisconsin, but none were in Milwaukee, where nearly 70 percent of the state's Black population lived. Though Walker's own presidential campaign flamed out in 2015, the policies he'd implemented in Wisconsin laid the groundwork for Trump's surprise victory.

Some even said the quiet part out loud. On the night of Wisconsin's 2016 primary, the GOP representative Glenn Grothman, a who'd argued for the law in the state senate over Dale Schultz's objections and had sponsored legislation cutting early voting, predicted that a Republican would carry the state in November, even though Wisconsin had gone for Obama by seven points in 2012. "I think Hillary Clinton is about the weakest candidate the Democrats have ever put up," he told a local TV news reporter, "and now we have photo ID, and I think photo ID is going to make a little bit of a difference as well."

Despite these comments, Clinton's stunning loss in Wisconsin was blamed on her failure to campaign in the state, and the depressed turnout was attributed to a lack of enthusiasm for either candidate. "Perhaps the biggest drags on voter turnout in Milwaukee, as in the rest of the country, were the candidates themselves," Sabrina Tavernise of *The New York Times* wrote in a postelection dispatch that typified this line of analysis. "To some, it was like having to choose between broccoli and liver."

The impact of Wisconsin's voter ID law received almost no attention. When it did, it was often dismissive. Walker said it was "a load of crap" to claim that the law had led to lower turnout. When Clinton, in an interview with *New York* magazine, said her loss was "aided and abetted by the suppression of the vote, particularly in Wisconsin," the *Washington Examiner* responded, "Hillary Clinton Blames Voter Suppression for Losing a State She Didn't Visit Once During the Election."

As the months went on, pundits on the right and left turned Clinton's loss into a case study for the Democratic Party's abandonment of the white working class. As the media spent countless hours interviewing white Trump supporters, stories like Anthony's were largely invisible. During the 2016 campaign cycle, there were twenty-five presidential debates during the primaries and general election but not a single question about efforts to keep Black voters from the polls in states like Wisconsin.

A year after the election, the University of Wisconsin political scientist Ken Mayer tried to quantify precisely what role the ID law played

in reducing turnout in a state that was once known for its high participation. He asked registered voters in Milwaukee County and Madison's
Dane County—two Democratic strongholds—who did not show up in
2016 why they didn't cast a ballot. Eleven percent cited the voter ID law
and said they didn't have an acceptable ID; of those, more than half
said the law was the "main reason" they didn't vote. That implied that
between twelve thousand and twenty-three thousand registered voters in Madison and Milwaukee—and as many as forty-five thousand
statewide—were deterred from voting by the ID law. "We have hard
evidence there were tens of thousands of people who were unable to
vote because of the voter ID law," he said.

The study also found striking socioeconomic and racial disparities
among those most impacted. "The burdens of voter ID fell disproportionately on low-income and minority populations," Mayer wrote. More
than 20 percent of registrants coming from homes with incomes less
than $25,000 said they were kept from voting by the law; 8.3 percent of
white voters surveyed were deterred from voting, compared with 27.5
percent of African Americans.

The law's impact was particularly acute in Milwaukee, where nearly
two-thirds of the state's Black population lived, 37 percent of them below the poverty line. Milwaukee was the most segregated city in the nation, divided between low-income Black areas and middle-class white
ones. It was known as the "Selma of the North" in the 1960s because
of fierce clashes over desegregation. George Wallace once said that if
he had to leave Alabama, "I'd want to live on the south side of Milwaukee." When white voters fled to the suburbs, Milwaukee became the
favorite target of Republicans in the state. "We don't want Wisconsin to
become like Milwaukee," Walker said during his recall election.

Neil Albrecht, Milwaukee's election director, believed that the voter
ID law and other changes passed by the Republican legislature, such
as cuts to early voting and restrictions on voter registration drives,
contributed significantly to lower turnout in 2016. Albrecht was fifty-
five years old but seemed younger, with bookish tortoise-frame glasses
and a salt-and-pepper stubble. "I looked 12 until I became an election

administrator," he joked. At his office in City Hall with views of the Milwaukee River, Albrecht had a color-coded map of the city's districts showing the areas where turnout had declined the most, such as Anthony's. "It is very probable that between the photo ID law and the changes to voter registration, enough people were prevented from voting to have changed the outcome of the presidential election in Wisconsin," he said.

Wisconsin was a microcosm of the broader rollback of voting access in the United States. From the passage of the Voting Rights Act to the election of the first Black president, the country saw a gradual expansion of voting rights. But the GOP's takeover of key state governments like Wisconsin in 2010 reversed that trend. Trump, for all the ways he pushed the GOP to the extremes, wouldn't have been a viable candidate if the party hadn't already committed to minority rule and embraced oligarchy over democracy well before he rode the golden escalator down Trump Tower.

"We're moving into a pre–Voting Rights Act era, where there isn't any real watchdogging of elections and changes to election laws," said Albrecht. "States, including Wisconsin, are making maverick changes that have a significant impact on populations that have been historically disenfranchised."

From the beginning, Walker wanted to show that his Wisconsin model could succeed nationally. Trump's win in 2016 was the clearest evidence of that.

"Whoever comes next, this is not going to end," Clinton predicted after the election. "Republicans learned that if you suppress votes, you win."

» » » » » »

Two weeks after the election, Kobach met with Trump at his golf club in Bedminster, New Jersey. The president-elect was auditioning prospective members of his cabinet, and Kobach was under consideration to run the Department of Homeland Security. They smiled for the cameras as Trump pointed at Kobach with a sheepish grin. Kobach was photographed holding a one-page white paper outlining his "Kobach Strategic Plan for First 365 Days."

Though partly obscured, what could be read of the document was a bullet-pointed wish-list of right-wing policies that included "extreme vetting" and tracking of "all aliens from high-risk areas," reducing the "intake of Syrian refugees to zero," deporting a "record number of criminal aliens in the first year" and the "rapid build" of a wall along the US–Mexico border. These policies would form the basis for much of Trump's governing agenda and the largest curbs on immigration since the 1920s.

At the bottom of the document was a section called "Stop Aliens From Voting," where Kobach recommended the administration "draft Amendment to National Voter Registration Act to promote proof-of-citizenship requirements." Kobach wanted his proof-of-citizenship law in Kansas—which had blocked one in seven people from registering to vote—adopted in every state. When they went inside, he and Trump discussed "the problem of noncitizens voting illegally in U.S. elections," Kobach said.

A week after their meeting, Trump tweeted, "I won the popular vote if you deduct the millions of people who voted illegally."

It was a staggering assertion; a president-elect had never before alleged fraud on such a massive scale, let alone in an election he won.

When asked in an ABC News interview where Trump got that information, his senior adviser Kellyanne Conway named Kobach as a source of the claim.

Three days after Trump's tweet, when Kobach certified the results of the 2016 election in Kansas as a member of the state board of canvassers, he told reporters, "I think the president-elect is absolutely correct when he says the number of illegal votes cast exceeds the popular-vote margin between him and Hillary Clinton."

As evidence, Kobach pointed to a 2014 study whose lead author was an Old Dominion University political scientist, Jesse Richman. It estimated that "6.4 percent of noncitizens voted in 2008." That finding was quickly picked up by Breitbart ("Study: Voting by Non-Citizens Tips Balance for Democrats") and *National Review* ("Jaw-Dropping Study Claims Large Numbers of Non-Citizens Vote in U.S.") and cited by Trump on the campaign trail.

"If we apply that number to the current presidential election," Kobach said while standing in front of a wall of law textbooks in the secretary of state's office, "you'd have 3.2 million aliens voting in the presidential election, and that far exceeds the current popular vote margin between President-elect Trump and Secretary Clinton." Kobach had no way of knowing which candidate won these alleged millions of illegal votes, but he said, "You could probably conclude that a very high percentage voted for Hillary Clinton given the diametric opposite positions of the two candidates on the immigration issue."

The Kansas statehouse reporters aggressively pushed back on Kobach's claims.

"You don't have any hard, physical evidence that this happened," responded John Hanna of the Associated Press. "You're pulling these numbers out of the air."

"That's incorrect," Kobach said. "We have hard physical evidence in Kansas . . ."

"A handful," Hanna said.

"In one county, thirty aliens registered or attempted to register, and some of those aliens voted," Kobach said.

"Only three of them voted over a decade," added Bryan Lowry of *The Wichita Eagle.*

Richman's study was soon contested by other political scientists. Richman had found 489 noncitizens in a much larger Harvard survey of 55,400 American adults called the Cooperative Congressional Election Study. In 2012, three political scientists who coordinated the original CCES study went back and reinterviewed 19,000 of the respondents. They found only 85 who said they were noncitizens in the survey, and none of them could be matched to a valid voting record. "Thus the best estimate of the percentage of noncitizens who vote is zero," they wrote.

In January 2017, nearly two hundred leading political scientists signed an open letter criticizing Richman's study. Even Richman conceded, "the claim Trump is making is not supported by our data."

But when it came to illegal immigration and illegal voting, Kobach, who had been an early endorser of Trump and was brought into his inner circle by Donald Trump Jr., told the president-elect what he wanted to hear. At his first official meeting with congressional leaders at the White House on January 23, 2017, Trump once again brought up his popular vote loss to Clinton and asserted that three to five million undocumented immigrants had voted in 2016.

Trump was widely criticized for these claims, including by top Republicans. "It's the most inappropriate thing for a president to say without proof," said Lindsey Graham. "He seems obsessed with the idea that he could not have possibly lost the popular vote without cheating and fraud." Added House Speaker Paul Ryan: "I have seen no evidence. I have made this very, very clear."

But Kobach kept defending him. When asked by MSNBC if he believed Clinton had won the popular vote, he responded, "We may never know the answer to that."

Kobach did not get the job he wanted in the Trump administration. John Kelly, a former top general, was named DHS secretary and subsequently blocked Kobach from becoming his deputy, even as Kobach helped the administration draft a flurry of anti-immigration executive orders.

But he was still rewarded by the president. On May 11, two days after Trump fired FBI director James Comey, who was investigating Russian interference in the 2016 election and possible collusion with the Trump campaign, the president announced the creation of a new Presidential Advisory Commission on Election Integrity, led by Vice President Mike Pence, and he named Kobach its vice chair. The commission was tasked with examining "improper voter registrations and improper voting," issues that Kobach had almost single-handedly put on the Trump administration's radar. His state-based efforts to investigate fraud and tighten access to the ballot had gone national. "This is a first of its kind nationwide effort to actually look at all 50 states," Kobach said.

Trump called it his "VOTER FRAUD PANEL" and tweeted, "depending on results, we will strengthen up voting procedures!"

» » » » » »

At the commission's first public meeting at the White House in July 2017, as Trump spoke of "voter inconsistencies and irregularities . . . in some cases, having to do with very large numbers of people in certain states," Pence maintained that "this commission has no preconceived notions or preordained results."

But the first major action of the commission a few weeks earlier had quickly confirmed the worst fears of its critics.

On June 28, 2017, the commission sent a letter, drafted by Kobach, to all fifty states asking them to provide sweeping voter data including "the full first and last names of all registrants, middle names or initials if available, addresses, dates of birth, political party (if recorded in your state), last four digits of social security number if available, voter history (elections voted in) from 2006 onward, active/inactive status, cancelled status, information regarding any felony convictions, information regarding voter registration in another state, information regarding military status, and overseas citizen information." While the letter asked for "publicly-available voter roll data," much of this information was, in fact, private. Never before had a White House asked for such broad data on voters, which Kobach said would be "very helpful in the Commission's work identifying fraudulent registrations and other forms of voter fraud."

At first, only a few states said no, denouncing the request as "a waste of taxpayer money and a distraction from the real threats to the integrity of our elections today" (California) and "a pretext to validate Donald Trump's alternative election facts" (Virginia). But over the July 4th weekend, opposition to Kobach's letter exploded, including from Republican secretaries of state in deep red states.

Mississippi's Delbert Hosemann told Kobach to "go jump in the Gulf of Mexico." Louisiana's Tom Schedler said, "the President's Commission has quickly politicized its work by asking states for an incredible amount of voter data that I have, time and time again, refused to release." Arizona's Michele Reagan blasted "this hastily organized experiment."

Even Kobach, as Kansas secretary of state, couldn't hand over voters' Social Security numbers because they weren't publicly available in Kansas, nor could secretaries of state from Indiana, Maine, and New Hampshire, who also served on the commission. Twenty-one states refused to provide any data while the rest only partially complied.

"I've been studying America's election administration since 2000, and I've rarely seen a firestorm like this," wrote the MIT political scientist Charles Stewart III. By July 3, the Electronic Privacy Information Center filed the first lawsuit against the commission, calling the data request "both without precedent and crazy." Similar suits from civil rights groups like the ACLU and NAACP Legal Defense Fund soon followed.

Kobach's efforts in Kansas offered a clue for why he wanted so much data on voters and what he planned to do with it.

In 2005, Kansas joined with three other midwestern states in a regional compact called the Interstate Voter Registration Crosscheck Program. The program compared state records to find people registered to vote in more than one place. On taking office, Kobach championed it to election officials around the country, rapidly expanding its reach to include more than thirty states.

Crosscheck appeared to offer an appealing scientific certainty to the hunt for voter fraud. But its deeply flawed methodology could also be used to suppress the vote. The program searched for double registrations using only voters' first and last names and dates of birth, and thus generated thousands of false matches: John Smith in Kansas could easily be confused with John Smith in Iowa. These false matches had in several instances led to people being wrongly removed from voter rolls. In 2013, after Virginia joined Crosscheck, in the midst of a hotly contested governor's race the state board of elections sent counties a list of more than fifty-seven thousand voters to purge because they were supposedly registered in other states. The data was littered with errors: Lawrence Haake, the registrar in Chesterfield County, told the *Richmond Times-Dispatch*, "We do need an interstate checking mechanism, but I'm not real impressed with this one."

Crosscheck led to outrageous headlines that made double voting seem far more common than it actually was. In 2014, after North Carolina joined Crosscheck, the head of the state board of elections reported that in the 2012 general election there were 35,750 voters in the state whose first and last names and dates of birth matched those of individuals who voted in the same election in a different state. Republican leaders of the North Carolina legislature called it "alarming evidence of voter fraud," and the conservative political strategist Dick Morris told Hannity it was "the first concrete evidence we've ever had of massive voter fraud." But when North Carolina investigated the numbers using additional data like the last four digits of voters' Social Security numbers, only eight cases of potential double voting were referred to prosecutors, and two people were convicted.

In a 2016 paper, researchers at Stanford, Harvard, Yale, and the University of Pennsylvania analyzed the lists of potential duplicate voter registrations that Crosscheck sent to the state of Iowa before the 2012 and 2014 elections and found that "200 legitimate voters may be impeded from voting for every double vote stopped."

Voting rights advocates suspected Kobach wanted to use the state voter data to do Crosscheck on a national scale, searching not just for double voting, but using other federal databases to hunt down alleged cases of noncitizen voting as well. (In Texas, the commission had asked the state to identify all voters with Hispanic surnames.) "The Commission may compare voter rolls to federal databases of known noncitizens residing in the United States to identify ineligible noncitizens," Kobach wrote.

The databases Kobach wanted access to were not designed for that purpose. The DHS Systematic Alien Verification for Entitlements database, for example, did not automatically reveal the status of immigrants who became US citizens, which meant that thousands of noncitizens who subsequently naturalized could mistakenly be tagged as illegal voters.

But that seemed to be the point. Generating sensational cases of noncitizens who allegedly registered and voted based on shoddy data—even if it turned out on closer inspection not to be true—would help validate Trump's claims and build support for policies like voter ID laws and proof-of-citizenship requirements that Kobach had long championed.

"He already has policy recommendations," said Dale Ho of the ACLU. "They're the Kansas experiment. It seems like this commission is just a fig leaf of a process."

» » » » » »

Despite the commission's lack of success in obtaining state voter data, Kobach and a small circle of conservative ideologues kept doggedly trying to prove Trump's fraud claims.

In a meeting with senators in February 2017, Trump had made a new assertion: "thousands" of people from Massachusetts were "brought in on buses" to "illegally" vote in New Hampshire in 2016, costing Trump the state and the GOP senator Kelly Ayotte her re-election.

In September 2017, days before the commission was set to have its second meeting, in New Hampshire, Pence aide Andrew Kossack, the commission's top staffer, sent Kobach data from the New Hampshire secretary of state's office showing that more than five thousand voters who had registered on Election Day with an out-of-state-license had yet to obtain a state driver's license. "To put the 5,526 figure in context, the vote margin between President Trump and Hillary Clinton was 2,732," wrote Kossack. "Senator Kelly Ayotte lost by 743 votes to Maggie Hassan."

That afternoon, Kobach wrote an "exclusive" column for *Breitbart News* citing the numbers as "proof" that "a pivotal, close election was likely changed through voter fraud."

It turned out there was a far simpler and less nefarious explanation for what happened: it was legal to use an out-of-state driver's license as an ID at the polls in New Hampshire. The people who did so didn't drive in New Hampshire or own a car there or plan to reside permanently in the state. College students quickly came forward to say they'd voted using out-of-state licenses, viewing the state as their home since they spent most of the year there.

When the commission met at Saint Anselm College in Manchester on September 12, however, Kobach doubled down on his claim. He said voters from other states were "flooding across borders" to cast ballots in New Hampshire, and the five thousand people who used out-of-state licenses were likely nonresidents. "We will never know the legitimacy of the election" in New Hampshire, he stated.

That prompted a rare rebuke from New Hampshire secretary of state Bill Gardner, who hosted the meeting. "The result, as we have recorded it, is real—it is real and valid," Gardner said to cheers from the crowd. Though a Democrat, Gardner often sided with Republicans on ballot access issues. He told Kobach that "it's not right to come to conclusions" based on those numbers, and "those facts don't create proof."

The Maine secretary of state Matt Dunlap, one of the few other Democrats on the commission, had his own doubts about the data presented by Kobach. Despite his resemblance to a 1950s accountant, with a balding head and nerdy retro glasses, Dunlap was an avid hunter who had killed a black bear that became a rug in his office and a moose whose head was on the wall. He and Kobach met through the secretaries of state association and bonded over guns.

"Politically and philosophically he and I could not be more diametrically opposed but I always got along with him pretty well," Dunlap said. "I've hunted everything in Maine with some degree of success. We'd talk about firearms. We'd discuss the distinct virtues between the 150 grain bullet and the 220 grain bullet. He was like, I'm having a conversation with a Democrat about guns and we're not arguing."

Dunlap had taken heat from many Democrats for joining the commission on Kobach's invitation, but he figured he could do more good from the inside. As one of his staffers told him, "If you're not at the table, you're probably on the menu."

He'd tried to keep an open mind, but he knew that Maine had used Election Day registration since 1973 and had uncovered few cases of fraud. "One of the things I learned in 14 years as secretary of state is that voter originated fraud is vanishingly rare," Dunlap said.

At the meeting in Manchester, Dunlap went public with his critique. "You have a right to vote; driving is a privilege," he told Kobach. "Making the equation that failing to update your driver's license is proof of voter fraud would be almost as absurd as saying that if you have cash in your wallet, it's proof that you robbed a bank."

In the weeks that followed, Dunlap began to suspect that Kobach had frozen him out of the commission's work. Walking into church one Sunday in October, he saw a story in *The Washington Post* that a researcher for the commission had been arrested on child pornography charges. Dunlap didn't even know the commission had a researcher on staff. Shortly thereafter, Dunlap was told by the secretary of state of Minnesota that a conservative group there had been invited to a December meeting of the commission. That was the first Dunlap had heard of another meeting.

He sent a letter to Kossack asking basic questions: "What are we working on? Who are we talking to? What is our schedule?"

Kossack responded that he was reviewing the request with legal counsel. Dunlap found it odd that he couldn't get answers to simple questions as a member of the commission. Then, while straightening his yard on a fall day, he received a call from Kay Rand, the chief of staff to the Maine senator Angus King, who passed on a message from another senator who wanted to remain anonymous. "Matt, you should get a lawyer," Rand told him. "You can't take on the Trump White House and the Department of Justice by yourself. These people are coming after you."

Suddenly, everything felt very cloak and dagger. "I was really rattled," Dunlap said.

He connected with a liberal watchdog group, American Oversight, who filed a lawsuit against the commission on Dunlap's behalf demanding that he be allowed "to participate meaningfully in the work of the Commission."

It was the fifteenth lawsuit against the commission but the first from the inside. As the commission's legal woes piled up, Trump chief strategist Steve Bannon sent Kobach an email that read, simply: "WTF?"

» » » » » »

On December 23, 2017, a federal judge ruled in Dunlap's favor, writing that the commission's "indefensible" position excluding him "ignores the law."

Twelve days later, as the new year began, the administration decided to abruptly dissolve the commission "rather than engage in endless legal battles at taxpayer expense."

Kobach portrayed it as "a tactical shift where the mission of the commission is being handed off to Homeland Security without the stonewalling by Democrats," and he said, "I'll be working closely with the White House and DHS to ensure the investigations continue."

But the White House said that "no Commission records or data will be transferred to the DHS or another agency," and a DHS spokesman said, "Mr. Kobach is not advising DHS in a formal or informal manner."

In August 2018, Dunlap received eight thousand pages of records that revealed the inner workings of the commission. It confirmed many of his suspicions. Some of it even shocked him.

On November 18, 2017, after just two meetings of the commission, Kossack had written a draft "Staff Report" of its findings. It had a section called "Evidence of Election Integrity and Voter Fraud Issues" that included proposed entries on "improper voter registration practices" and "instances of fraudulent or improper voting."

The commission's goal, from the beginning, had finally become obvious to Dunlap. "They wanted to have a federal committee report with the imprimatur of the White House that showed we needed to save our elections from illegal immigrants, voter fraud at the college student level, whatever," Dunlap said.

But the evidence section was left blank. As Dunlap noted in a letter to Pence, "the sections on evidence of voter fraud are glaringly empty." (Pence never responded.)

The demise of the commission should have debunked the myth of widespread voter fraud once and for all. Kobach and his allies were given unprecedented resources and a presidential platform to finally produce real proof of illegal voting and they had found nothing.

"I thought this was finally a chance to exorcise the monster under the bed, to lay out what actually happened and we could put a lot of it to rest," Dunlap said. "That was incredibly naive of me. I thought you could argue with these people."

After the committee disbanded, Trump kept tweeting, "Many people are voting illegally. System is rigged, must go to Voter I.D." Polling showed that more than a third of his supporters believed three to five million people had voted illegally in 2016.

Even though the facts refuted Trump's lies, the commission had laid the groundwork for even bigger falsehoods to spread.

"The narrative," as Dunlap called it, had already been established. "When you lose an election that's because it was stolen—not because more people voted for the other guy."

The conspiracy theories spread by Trump and his acolytes had a deeper purpose: they sowed doubt about the legitimacy of the vote, government institutions, the media, and democracy itself. Unfounded claims of widespread fraud became a new form of nullification, opening the door for Trump and his allies to dismantle or transform whatever institutions were perceived to be preventing a shrinking white minority from maintaining its hold on power.

5

—

THE MOST DANGEROUS BRANCH

On December 18, 2019, as the House of Representatives prepared to impeach President Trump for pressuring Ukrainian president Volodymyr Zelensky to investigate Hunter Biden in exchange for receiving $400 million in military aid, the GOP representative Bill Johnson of Ohio called for a moment of silence on the House floor to recognize the Trump voters that "this partisan impeachment sham seeks to disenfranchise."

Johnson and his colleagues—nearly all older white men—stood for a minute to "remember the voices of the 63 million American voters the Democrats today are wanting to silence."

But when it came to popular support, House Republicans didn't mention that Hillary Clinton had won 66 million votes in 2016 or that Democratic House candidates won nine million more votes than their GOP counterparts in 2018, picking up forty-one seats in an anti-Trump wave to retake the chamber. The next day, the House impeached Trump—who described his call with Zelensky as "perfect" despite telling him "I would like you to do us a favor"—for obstruction of Congress and abuse of power.

It was a different story, however, when the House delivered the articles of impeachment to the Senate. On February 5, 2020, before the Senate voted to acquit Trump, Senate majority leader Mitch McConnell said the body was performing the function envisioned by the founders of checking the excesses of democracy. "The framers predicted that factional fever might dominate House majorities from time to time," he said. "They knew the country would need a firewall to keep partisan flames from scorching the republic. So they created the Senate."

But McConnell ignored Madison's critique of the consequences of small-state domination of the Senate, which he predicted in 1787 would become "a more objectionable minority than ever." Indeed, Democratic Senate candidates had won nearly 20 million more votes in 2018 than their GOP opponents, but Republicans picked up two seats in the chamber, giving them a 53–47 majority.

The GOP's advantage in sparsely populated, overwhelmingly white, rural states, which had become more pronounced over time, meant that the 2018 election results were hardly a one-off. Republicans had controlled the Senate more than half the time from 1980 to 2020 but represented a majority of Americans only once during that period, from 1997 to 1998. The structure of the US Senate benefited conservative voters more than any other upper chamber among democratic countries.

Polls showed that the country favored impeaching Trump and overwhelmingly wanted the Senate to call more witnesses during its trial, but only one Republican senator, Mitt Romney, joined Democrats in finding the president guilty of abusing his power. "Corrupting an election to keep oneself in office is perhaps the most abusive and destructive violation of one's oath of office that I can imagine," Romney said. But his GOP colleagues ignored his impassioned plea and the views of the broader public. The forty-eight senators who voted to convict Trump represented eighteen million more Americans than the fifty-two senators who voted to acquit him.

After Chief Justice John Roberts read the results of the trial, McConnell said, "the Senate can now get back to the business of the American people."

Thirty minutes later, when the TV cameras except for C-Span had left the Senate chamber, McConnell returned to the floor and made it clear what that business was: confirming Trump's 188th federal judge. "My motto for the year is 'leave no vacancy behind,'" he said.

The Electoral College handed Trump the presidency. The Senate

protected him and the Republican majority. The GOP's countermajoritarian advantages in these two branches allowed them to entrench
their power in the third branch of government: the courts.

Trump and McConnell were quickly confirming judges who would
tip the scales of democracy to favor the GOP and their wealthy backers. The judge whose nomination the Senate advanced that day, Andrew Lynn Brasher from Alabama, was the perfect foot soldier for the
Trump judicial revolution.

» » » » » »

In 2013, while Brasher served as deputy solicitor general in Alabama,
the state filed a brief asking the Supreme Court to strike down a key
provision of the Voting Rights Act that required states with a long
history of voting discrimination, mostly in the South, to approve
their voting changes with the federal government. Alabama was the
birthplace of the VRA; the brutal beating of civil rights marchers on
Bloody Sunday in Selma inspired Lyndon Johnson to introduce the
landmark civil rights law. "The Voting Rights Act is Alabama's gift
to our country," the civil rights lawyer Debo Adegbile once said. But
Shelby County, Alabama, outside of Brasher's hometown of Birmingham, was challenging the constitutionality of the law after eliminating
the only Black city council district in the town of Calera, and the state
was backing them up.

"Things in the South have, indeed, changed," said Alabama's brief,
which Brasher helped write. "The Alabama of 2013 is not the Alabama
of 1965—or of 1970, 1975, or 1982."

Even though Alabama had the second most violations of a key
section of the law since 1982, trailing only Mississippi, and ranked
last nationally in voter access according to a report by the Center for
American Progress, the state argued that the effects of "the tragic
events of 1965 . . . on voting and political representation have now,
thankfully, faded away."

The brief called the VRA "a necessary and appropriate exercise of emergency federal power" but said, "it is time for Alabama and the other covered jurisdictions to resume their roles as equal and sovereign parts of these United States."

These arguments were evidently persuasive to Chief Justice Roberts, whose majority opinion in *Shelby County v. Holder* used strikingly similar language to Alabama's brief. "Nearly 50 years later, things have changed dramatically," wrote Roberts, who had been trying to weaken the law since he was a young lawyer in the Reagan Justice Department. Responding to Alabama's call to be freed from federal oversight, which had echoes of the post-Reconstruction era, Roberts said the VRA violated the "fundamental principle of equal sovereignty" among the states. In the contested battle for freedom throughout US history, Roberts was favoring states with a history of discrimination over those groups who had been subject to discrimination for so many years.

The *Shelby* decision was radical in scope and practice, with a notably aggressive conservative majority gutting a law that was passed and reauthorized by Congress with broad bipartisan support, upheld by the courts on numerous occasions, and remarkably successful in increasing turnout and representation among previously disenfranchised minority groups. It was the first time the Supreme Court had overturned a federal voting rights statute in modern times. The ramifications were immediate.

Within hours after the decision, Texas implemented a voter ID law that allowed someone to vote with a gun permit but not a student ID; a federal court later called it an "unconstitutional poll tax" that was passed "because of and not merely in spite of the voter ID law's detrimental effects on the African-American and Hispanic electorate."

A month after the decision, North Carolina passed a sweeping rewrite of its election laws that required strict voter ID, eliminated same-day voter registration, and cut early voting, including Sunday voting, when Black churches held "Souls to the Polls" voter mobilization drives; the Fourth Circuit Court of Appeals found that it targeted Black voters "with almost surgical precision."

Alabama implemented its own voter ID law after *Shelby*, then promptly closed thirty-one DMV offices where people were most likely to obtain the identification now required to vote. Offices were closed in eight of eleven majority-Black counties but only fifteen of fifty-five majority-white counties; the Department of Transportation later concluded that the closures violated the Civil Rights Act of 1964.

At Brasher's hearing before the Senate Judiciary Committee on December 4, 2019, the Delaware Democratic senator Chris Coons, who had traveled to Selma on three occasions with the civil rights icon John Lewis, brought up the *Shelby* ruling and Brasher's role in it.

"Can you give an example of a discriminatory voting restriction that's been instituted after *Shelby County*?" Coons asked.

Brasher, his small, deep-set eyes blinking rapidly, attempted to explain Alabama's position in the case. The VRA "needed to be updated in a way that was more consistent with the facts on the ground," he said with a pained expression on his face.

"Can you give an example of a discriminatory voting restriction instituted after *Shelby County*?" Coons asked again.

"Senator, I have not researched that issue," Brasher responded.

Brasher was just thirty-eight years old, emblematic of the type of judge Trump was putting on the bench: young, male, white, extremely conservative, and active in right-wing causes. After serving as a top lawyer in the Alabama attorney general's office for nearly a decade, when he was also vice president of the Montgomery chapter of the Federalist Society, Brasher was confirmed to a district court seat in 2019 that Republicans had blocked the Obama administration from filling. After just seven months on the bench, he was nominated, with unusually rapid speed, to the powerful Court of Appeals for the Eleventh Circuit, overseeing Alabama, Florida, and Georgia. Since the Supreme Court heard only about eighty cases a year, the appellate courts were essentially the country's regional Supreme Courts, deciding thousands of cases a year that would become the final word on the law.

"He's someone with a lot of promise," said his chief sponsor, the Alabama GOP senator Richard Shelby, who was already floating Brasher for a future Supreme Court vacancy. "He'll make a distinguished appellate judge and you never know what he'll do from then, he might come before you again someday. I hope so."

"It sounds like it," said Judiciary chair Lindsey Graham.

Brasher dressed like a college Republican, with a dark blue suit, navy tie, and a swoop of blond hair reminiscent of a young Brett Kavanaugh. He was polite and well-mannered, tearfully thanking his parents for the sacrifices they'd made so he could become the first lawyer in his family. But he grew flustered when Coons pressed him on voting rights, a major issue in the three Southern states he would oversee as an appellate judge.

Coons noted that Brasher had been nominated to fill the seat on the Eleventh Circuit of "the legendary" Judge Frank Johnson, who had authorized the Selma-to-Montgomery voting rights march, ruled in favor of Rosa Parks during the Montgomery bus boycott, ordered the KKK to stop assaulting the Freedom Riders, struck down literacy tests in Alabama, and desegregated the state's public schools. The journalist Jack Bass called Johnson and a handful of other pioneering Southern judges in the 1960s "the institutional equivalent of the civil rights movement."

"What do you see as the most important voting rights decision, either in Alabama or in the 11th Circuit history?" Coons asked Brasher.

There was an awkward silence. "You know, I think there are so many important decisions in that area," Brasher responded.

"Pick one," Coons said.

"I don't think I really can, honestly," Brasher said. He began to speak in generalities. "The Supreme Court has recognized that one reason the vote is fundamental is because at the root of it it protects our other rights."

"Judge, I agree with you that it's our most foundational right in a democracy, could you please just name one case for me from the 11th Circuit or Alabama that's an important voting rights decision. Just name one for me," Coons said, throwing up his hands.

"You want me to name a case?" Brasher asked.

"Yes, just tell me any case that you think was significant in 11th Circuit history on voting rights," Coons repeated.

After hemming and hawing, Brasher eventually named *Gomillion v. Lightfoot*, a major redistricting case in the early 1960s where Johnson, on the orders of the Supreme Court, struck down a racial gerrymander in Tuskegee, Alabama, that excluded nearly all Black residents from legislative representation by drawing a twenty-eight-sided district encompassing only white areas. "That was a landmark voting rights case," Brasher said.

"Thank you, judge," Coons responded tersely.

In years past, Brasher's advocacy and testimony might've disqualified him from a seat on the bench. In addition to cowriting the *Shelby* brief, he'd argued in favor of racial gerrymandering before the Supreme Court, filed a brief with officials from Georgia, Kansas, and Texas supporting proof-of-citizenship laws to register to vote, and defended an Alabama law stripping voting rights from hundreds of thousands of people with past felony convictions. The NAACP said Brasher had "the worst voting rights record of any Trump appellate nominee."

» » » » » »

In 2011, the same year Brasher became deputy solicitor general in Alabama, Kobach helped draft an immigration bill for the state that became known as "Arizona on steroids." Kobach edited the final version of the bill while hunting turkeys in Kansas. "A bad day for turkeys turned out to be a good day for constitutional law," he said.

The law included an Arizona-style provision authorizing state and local police officers to ask about the immigration status of anyone they believed had a "reasonable suspicion" of being undocumented. But it went much further, requiring schools to check students' citizenship status, preventing undocumented immigrants from enrolling in public colleges, barring landlords from renting to undocumented residents, and even making it a crime to give an undocumented person a ride.

"Alabama is now the new No. 1 state for immigration enforcement," Kobach said after the law passed. "The untold story is how successful it has already been."

But the law immediately turned into a debacle. Farm workers abandoned their crops before the autumn harvest. Thousands of Latino students stayed home from school. Church soup kitchens shut down. Lines stretched out the door at the DMV as workers were forced to check citizenship status for routine transactions. Utility companies shut off water and power to customers. Executives from Mercedes-Benz and Honda were detained during routine traffic stops. Though Alabama was home to just 1 percent of the country's undocumented residents, one economist estimated the state could lose billions of dollars if thousands of people fled the state.

Brasher's office defended the law before the Eleventh Circuit, which struck most of it down. "We are convinced that Alabama has crafted a calculated policy of expulsion, seeking to make the lives of unlawfully present aliens so difficult as to force them to retreat from the state," the court wrote. Brasher then asked the Supreme Court to reverse the ruling, but it refused after striking down the bulk of Arizona's law. The Kobach-inspired bill reflected the types of laws Brasher would defend while serving as deputy solicitor general and then solicitor general of Alabama.

After attending Samford University, a private Christian school in suburban Birmingham, and then Harvard Law School, Brasher got his start in 2006–2007 clerking for Eleventh Circuit judge William Pryor, one of the most outspoken conservatives on the bench. He called *Roe v. Wade* "the worst abomination in the history of constitutional law" that had "led to the slaughter of millions of innocent unborn children." He said that a constitutional right to sodomy adopted by the Supreme Court in *Lawrence v. Texas* "must logically extend to activities like prostitution, adultery, necrophilia, bestiality, incest and pedophilia."

He testified before Congress that the Voting Rights Act was "an affront to federalism and an expensive burden that has far outlived its usefulness."

Brasher amplified Pryor's ideology when he joined the Alabama attorney general's office. He defended a series of antiabortion laws designed to undercut *Roe v. Wade*, including one allowing a judge to appoint an attorney for the fetus when a young woman sought an abortion without parental consent. In another case, Brasher said women in Alabama could just travel to Georgia if abortion clinics closed in the state, and he relied on an expert witness who claimed that abortion led to mental illness. "The ACLU and Planned Parenthood want a fight and we will give them one," Brasher said at an antiabortion rally in front of the Alabama statehouse in 2014.

Brasher didn't just defend extreme Alabama laws, but actively recruited other states to join hard-line briefs before the Supreme Court on hot button issues. In *Obergefell v. Hodges*, he urged the court not to recognize marriage equality, writing, "Sexual relationships between men and women—and only such relationships—have the ability to provide children with both their biological mother and their biological father in a stable family unit."

After the shooting at Sandy Hook Elementary School that killed twenty children in 2012, he asked the Supreme Court to strike down bans on automatic weapons passed in Connecticut and New York, writing that they had "little effect on gun violence and public safety."

These stances put Brasher well to the right of the general public. "He's not just unqualified," the Senate Democratic leader Chuck Schumer said when Brasher was nominated to the Eleventh Circuit. "Maybe the fact that they're promoting him so quickly is that they love the fact that his views are so wildly out of the mainstream. As Alabama's solicitor general, Brasher fought against reproductive rights that three-quarters of Americans believe in, common-sense gun safety laws which 90 percent of Americans believe in and marriage equality, which a majority of Americans believe in."

But it was precisely these positions that put Brasher on the radar of national Republicans and made him stand out among members of the Federalist Society, the powerful conservative legal organization created in 1982. Carrie Severino, the president of the Judicial Crisis Network—a sister group of the Federalist Society that raised tens of millions of dollars from large, anonymous donors to reshape the federal courts and state courts in places like Wisconsin—praised Brasher when he became solicitor general in 2014. "He is known as a strong supporter of limited constitutional government, and he joins a great group of like-minded SGs from all across the country," she wrote in *National Review*. "We look forward to seeing the results of Brasher's advocacy."

When Trump announced Brasher's judicial nomination, Severino, a former law clerk to Clarence Thomas, wrote that she "couldn't be more thrilled."

Brasher's nomination showed how Republicans were increasingly looking to the courts to try to dismantle popular policies that they couldn't block through the regular political process, which represented a major shift not only for conservatives, who used to speak of judicial restraint, but for the judiciary as well.

» » » » » »

The courts were designed to protect minority rights from the other branches of government. Hamilton wrote in Federalist No. 78 that an independent judiciary was intended to "guard the Constitution and the rights of individuals" and prevent "serious oppressions of the minor party in the community." Thurgood Marshall wrote that the court's legitimacy stemmed from its reputation as "a protector of the powerless." The countermajoritarian structure of the courts was intended, in a good way, to defend the groups who were most at risk of having their rights violated by an intemperate majority.

Yet for much of US history the courts defended powerful minorities instead of vulnerable ones. The Supreme Court famously upheld the institutions of slavery and Jim Crow in decisions like *Dred Scott v. Sandford* and *Plessy v. Ferguson* and sided with wealthy economic interests during the late 1800s and early 1900s.

That began to change in 1938, when the Court issued a footnote in an obscure case concerning the regulation of imitation milk products, specifying that it would defer to most state and federal laws, but that laws imposing a special burden on "discrete and insular minorities," including religious and racial minorities, would be subject to a "more searching judicial inquiry." Justice Hugo Black elaborated on this theme in 1940, writing that courts should be "havens of refuge for those who might otherwise suffer because they are helpless, weak, outnumbered, or because they are non-conforming victims of prejudice and public excitement."

Beginning in 1953, the Court led by Chief Justice Earl Warren embarked on a "minority rights revolution" that embraced a broad conception of equal protection expanding civil rights and civil liberties, from *Brown v. Board of Education* to the "one person, one vote" cases to proclaiming a right to counsel, privacy, and reproductive choice.

But the victories of the Warren Court led to an equally potent backlash among aggrieved white conservatives. "Impeach Earl Warren" bumper stickers appeared across the South after the *Brown* decision and inspired a policy of massive resistance by the Southern states.

Nixon campaigned in 1968 against the Warren Court. In a speech before the election written by Buchanan, he pledged to appoint "strict constructionists" as judges who would "see their duty as interpreting the law, rather than making law."

A pivotal turning point came in 1971 when the corporate lawyer Lewis Powell wrote a memo for the Chamber of Commerce declaring that the "American economic system is under broad attack" and urging corporations to counterattack through "a broader and more vigorous role in the political arena." Powell identified the courts as a "vast area of opportunity" and urged corporate interests to invest in swaying the judiciary through amicus briefs and training "highly competent" lawyers. "Under our constitutional system," Powell wrote, "especially with an activist-minded Supreme Court, the judiciary may be the most important instrument for social, economic and political change."

Two months after submitting his memo, Nixon nominated Powell to the Supreme Court, though the memo was not disclosed at the time.

Two years later, the court he sat on decided *Roe v. Wade*, which mobilized evangelical Christians against a constitutional right to abortion in the same way that *Brown* activated Southern conservatives.

Before the early 1980s, there had been three major strands of conservatism—racial, corporate, and evangelical—that were sometimes at odds. These forces came together with the founding of the Federalist Society, sharing a joint goal of taking control of the courts. Dedicated to "the virtues of individual freedom and limited government," it was started by a small group of conservative law students at Yale and the University of Chicago whose advisers were Robert Bork at Yale and Antonin Scalia at Chicago. They defined freedom in a way that was beneficial to their cause.

Bork and Scalia preached a new doctrine of originalism—which held that the Constitution and its amendments should be interpreted as written or intended at the time—as a way to overturn the decisions of the Warren Court and the civil rights laws of the 1960s. In so doing, they largely ignored or attempted to rewrite the meaning of the Reconstruction amendments. Scalia would call the Voting Rights Act a "racial entitlement" while Bork wrote that the Warren Court's decision striking down the poll tax in Virginia turned the Fourteenth Amendment's Equal Protection Clause into an "Equal Gratification" clause. Originalism became a more scholarly version of nullification, freezing the Constitution and its amendments in time to justify rolling back existing rights or to prevent the establishment of new ones by striking down congressional laws and overturning court precedents.

The debate over originalism dated back to the *Brown* decision, when the Supreme Court considered the meaning of the Fourteenth Amendment as it related to segregated schools.

"In approaching this problem, we cannot turn the clock back to

1868, when the Amendment was adopted, or even to 1896, when *Plessy v. Ferguson* was written," Warren wrote. "We must consider public education in the light of its full development and its present place in American life throughout."

Many conservatives were furious at this reasoning. "The original Constitutional does not mention education," declared the Southern Manifesto signed by 101 members of Congress in 1956. "Neither does the Fourteenth Amendment nor any other amendment. The debates preceding the submission of the Fourteenth Amendment clearly show that there was no intent that it should affect the systems of education maintained by the states."

After the Brown decision, the conservative journalist James Kilpatrick wrote to the *National Review* editor William F. Buckley that in "constitutional cases clocks must always be turned back"; we must accept "the Constitution as we find it."

Key members of the Federalist Society used originalism to aggressively reorient the judiciary from safeguarding the rights of powerless minorities to once again protecting the priorities of powerful ones, such as wealthy GOP donors and partisan political interests that favored white conservatives.

"They needed a way to dress up their judicial philosophy," said Nan Aron, the longtime head of the liberal group Alliance for Justice. "They couldn't come out and say we oppose clean air, clean water, civil rights. They needed a philosophy to articulate and so they landed on originalism."

In a 1986 memo to the Reagan attorney general Edwin Meese, the Justice Department lawyer Steven Calabresi, a cofounder of the Federalist Society, criticized the DOJ for "not acting as an agent of counterrevolutionary change." He urged Republicans to abandon "judicial restraint" and refrain from praising the courts for not striking down federal laws. "The *courts* and the executive must start using their constitutional powers to hold the Congress within its proper constitutional sphere," he wrote.

Thanks to millions of dollars in sustained funding from the likes of the Kochs and Bradleys, the Federalist Society took over the GOP legal establishment. From 2014 to 2020, the group's president, Leonard Leo, raised $580 million through a shadowy network of a dozen dark money nonprofit groups to put his preferred judges on the bench. "We're going to have great judges, conservative, all picked by Federalist Society," Trump pledged in 2016.

Whereas the group had advised previous GOP administrations, it was essentially in charge of judicial selection during the Trump administration. "We have seen our views go from the fringe, views that in years past would inhibit someone's chances to be considered for the federal bench, to being the center of the conversation," the White House counsel Don McGahn said at the group's national convention in 2017 at the Mayflower Hotel in Washington. Members of the Federalist Society represented just 4 percent of all lawyers but comprised 85 percent of Trump's judicial appointees.

"Our opponents of judicial nominees frequently claim the president has outsourced his selection of judges," McGahn continued. "That is completely false. I have been a member of the Federalist Society since law school. Still am. So, frankly, it seems like it's been insourced," he said to applause and cheers.

» » » » » »

The work of the Federalist Society dovetailed perfectly with the ideological crusade of Mitch McConnell. The most important issue to McConnell had always been money, which he viewed as integral to his own career and that of his party.

"I never would have been able to win my race if there had been a limit on the amount of money I could raise and spend," he wrote of his first Senate election in 1984. When Republican John McCain and Democrat Russ Feingold proposed a ban on unlimited donations to political parties, he told his GOP colleagues in 1997, "If we stop this thing, we can control the institution for the next twenty years."

As he strenuously opposed campaign finance reform, McConnell also fought efforts to increase voter participation. "Low voter turnout is a sign of a content democracy," he wrote in 1991, when Congress took up a bill to allow people to register to vote at DMVs and other public agencies. "It is not indicative of a nation in decline or democracy imperiled."

After McCain-Feingold passed in 2002, McConnell challenged it before the Supreme Court. The Court ruled against him 5-4, with Sandra Day O'Connor siding with the liberal justices that the federal government had a compelling interest in regulating "the corrosive and distorting effects of immense aggregations of wealth." McConnell called it the "worst Supreme Court decision since the Dred Scott case" that upheld slavery.

But four years later, after Samuel Alito replaced O'Connor, the court's conservative majority successfully gutted McCain-Feingold by authorizing corporate issue ads—such as the barrage of spending by Wisconsin Club for Growth supporting Scott Walker—as long as they didn't explicitly endorse or oppose a candidate. That paved the way for the *Citizens United* decision.

Thus began a trend: GOP-appointed judges reliably supported Republican efforts to tilt the rules and institutions of democracy in their favor in cases like *Citizens United* and *Shelby County*, which in turn helped Republicans win more elections and appoint more judges, with one undemocratic feature of the system augmenting the other.

That's why McConnell went to such great lengths to block Obama's judicial nominees.

Before Merrick Garland, there was Abdul Kallon.

On February 11, 2016, Obama nominated Kallon, who had clerked for Alabama's first Black judge, E. W. Clemon, to a seat on the Eleventh Circuit. If confirmed, Kallon, an immigrant from Sierra Leone, would be the first Black judge from Alabama to sit on the court of appeals. For seven years, the administration had negotiated with Alabama's GOP senators, Jeff Sessions and Richard Shelby, to fill a half-dozen judicial vacancies in the state, but had confirmed only Kallon to a district court seat.

"Judge Kallon has a long and impressive record of service and a history of handing down fair and judicious decisions," Obama said. "He will be a thoughtful and distinguished addition to the 11th Circuit, and I am extremely pleased to put him forward."

That night, however, Sessions and Shelby, despite supporting Kallon for the district court, said it was "too late now" to confirm him as an appellate judge. When he returned to Alabama, Shelby told a local Republican group: "a Republican President will do a lot better job. I don't want somebody selected by President Obama getting a lifetime appointment here in Alabama."

Two days later, when Scalia unexpectedly passed away, McConnell invoked the same argument to prevent Obama from filling his seat and flipping the Supreme Court from a 5–4 conservative majority to a 5–4 liberal one for the first time since the Warren Court era.

There was no precedent or constitutional principle to justify McConnell's actions. In February 1988, Anthony Kennedy had been confirmed by a Democratic Senate during the last year of Reagan's presidency.

McConnell was simply doing the bidding of conservative groups who prioritized the judiciary above all else. Even before Scalia's death, powerful interests had urged Senate Republicans not to confirm any more Obama judicial nominees. "Granting any more lifetime appointments to federal judges whose views align with this president's radical ideological agenda is indefensible," said a memo from Heritage Action, the sister group of the Heritage Foundation, on January 15, 2016.

McConnell called "the decision not to fill the Scalia vacancy . . . the most consequential thing I've ever done" and credited his 293-day filibuster of Merrick Garland, the longest in Supreme Court history, with electing Trump. "The Supreme Court ended up being the single biggest issue in leading Trump to get ninety percent of the Republican vote," McConnell said after the election. "It ended up helping him win the election." Twenty-one percent of voters in 2016 said that Supreme Court appointments were their most important issue, and they backed Trump over Clinton by 56 to 41 percent.

McConnell's unprecedented blockade extended to the lower courts. In their last two years in office, Presidents Reagan, Clinton, and Bush II all faced a Senate controlled by the other party but got eighty-three, seventy-three, and sixty-eight district and appellate judges confirmed respectively. McConnell's Senate, in contrast, confirmed only twenty Obama nominees in the last two years of his presidency, including just two appellate judges, the lowest number since Harry Truman denounced the "do-nothing Congress" in 1948. None of the seven circuit nominees—including Kallon—that Obama submitted in 2015 or 2016 were confirmed.

McConnell held open 105 judicial vacancies during the Obama era and then pledged "to move judges like they are on a conveyor belt" after Trump was elected. He took away the right to appoint judges from a president who won five million more votes and gave that power to a president who received three million fewer votes and a Senate GOP caucus that represented fifteen million fewer people than Democrats.

When he was confirmed to replace Scalia, Neil Gorsuch not only occupied a seat that Obama should have filled, but he had the distinction of being the first Supreme Court justice nominated by a president who lost the popular vote and confirmed by senators representing a minority of Americans. That "super-minoritarian" exception soon became the norm, as Trump would go on to appoint a third of the Supreme Court and one-fourth of the federal judiciary. Sixty percent of Trump's appellate picks—including Brasher—were confirmed by senators receiving fewer votes or representing fewer people than the senators opposing them. These products of minority rule brought an ideology of minority rule with them to the bench.

Trump would confirm as many appellate judges in four years (fifty-four) as Obama had in eight (fifty-five). When Brasher was confirmed five days after Trump's acquittal, Trump appointees comprised half of all judges on the Eleventh Circuit. Brasher's mentor Bill Pryor became its chief judge. The circuit had the largest percentage of Black voters of any appellate region in the country, but just one of its twelve judges was Black. The demographics and ideology of the country were moving in one direction and the courts in another, setting up an inevitable clash between those subject to the law and those who made it.

The impact of Brasher's appointment would soon become clear in one of the states he would oversee as an appellate judge: Georgia.

6

THE NEW AMERICAN MAJORITY

Two months after the *Shelby* decision, civil rights leaders gathered at Martin Luther King Jr.'s old church in Atlanta, Ebenezer Baptist, to launch a fifty-state effort to protect voting rights. One of the attendees was Stacey Abrams, the minority leader of the Georgia House of Representatives. "[We want to] call out in a nationwide level those laws that are suppressing voting rights," she said in front of the famed gothic revival church on Auburn Avenue, its red brick the color of Georgia clay.

Joining Abrams that afternoon was Ebenezer's pastor, Rev. Raphael Warnock. In many ways they were kindred spirits.

They were both born in the immediate aftermath of the civil rights movement, Warnock in 1969 and Abrams in 1973, to large families—Abrams the second of six, Warnock the eleventh of twelve—and parents who were ministers. They grew up along the Southern coast, Abrams in Gulfport, Mississippi, and Warnock in Savannah, Georgia. Their families had little money; Abrams's father also worked as a shipyard worker while Warnock's father salvaged junk cars. They described their upbringings in similar ways. "We were short on money, but long on love and faith," Warnock said. Abrams jokingly called her family the "genteel poor," saying, "We had no money, but we had class. We watched PBS and read books."

Inspired by King, they both went to historically Black colleges in Atlanta, Warnock to King's alma mater, Morehouse, and Abrams to its sister college, Spelman. They each made history, Warnock as the youngest senior pastor at King's church and Abrams as the first woman and Black person to lead a major party in the Georgia legislature.

Abrams gave her first major speech in 1993 as a nineteen-year-old college student at the thirtieth anniversary of the March on Washington, where King had delivered his "I Have a Dream" speech. "We ask you to let us come forth with you, not behind you, not in front of you, but together on that road to jobs, justice, and peace," she said to the elders of the civil rights movement before seventy-five thousand people gathered on the National Mall.

Twenty years later, as the country prepared to celebrate the fiftieth anniversary of the March on Washington, Warnock signed a letter with more than one hundred religious leaders arguing that "the present initiatives around the country to restrict voting rights are a retreat from the promise of [King's] dream."

He noted that Trayvon Martin had been murdered in Florida a month after the Supreme Court gutted the Voting Rights Act and brushed aside fears of racial discrimination in the South. "The last few weeks have been pivotal to the consciousness of black America," he said.

Warnock and Abrams shared a belief that voter mobilization was the antidote to voter suppression, but they were struggling to get Democrats and national organizations to take notice of the importance of Georgia and the South.

A critical turning point came on another historic occasion, the fiftieth anniversary of Freedom Summer in Mississippi, when civil rights activists had launched a huge voter registration drive in 1964 to challenge Jim Crow, and three young civil rights activists were murdered by the KKK. To mark that date, in the summer of 2014 the Center for American Progress released a striking report authored by former NAACP president Ben Jealous on the changing demographics of the South.

Though long a bastion of white Republicanism, the region was now home to 57 percent of African Americans in the United States, the highest number since 1960, part of a reverse migration from North to South, along with nine of the twelve states with the fastest-growing Latino populations. These profound yet politically unrealized changes provided a blueprint for challenging a recalcitrant white power structure. "The first and most important lesson is that massive voter registration can overcome massive voter suppression," Jealous wrote.

The report featured Georgia, which was shifting faster than nearly any other state, as a case study. Its population had increased by nearly 30 percent over the past two decades, with African Americans making up half of that growth. Georgia was 45 percent nonwhite by the 2010 census, and on track to become a majority-minority state as early as 2025.

These changes posed an opportunity but also a challenge for Democrats in the state, which hadn't voted for a Democratic president since 1992 or elected a Democratic governor since 2002. They needed to convert new residents into new voters.

The CAP report found there were seven hundred thousand unregistered Black voters in the state and nine hundred thousand unregistered Black, Hispanic, and Asian voters combined. Registering 60 percent of them would "upset the balance of power in the state," Jealous wrote.

Abrams had been traveling the country with a twenty-page PowerPoint presentation making many of the same points. Jealous, who had first met Abrams when they were student organizers in 1993, invited her to give the keynote speech at a launch event for the report at the CAP office a few blocks from the White House. They saw the state as a test case for whether a new generation of Black activism could transform the South.

"If you change Georgia, you begin to change the South," Abrams said. "And if you change the South, you change the nation."

In 2013, Abrams had founded a group, the New Georgia Project, to sign up Georgia residents for the Affordable Care Act after the GOP governor Nathan Deal rejected Medicaid expansion. As the midterm election approached, the group pivoted to launching the largest voter registration drive in the state since the civil rights era, with a mission to "civically engage the rising electorate in our state." Warnock became the group's chair.

By the summer of 2014, Abrams's group had submitted tens of thousands of new registrations, 60 percent from voters under thirty-five. This alarmed Georgia Republicans, who were locked in close races for governor and senator. "Democrats are working hard registering all these minority voters that are out there and others that are sitting on the sidelines," warned Georgia's Republican secretary of state Brian Kemp, a close ally of Kobach's. "If they can do that, they can win these elections in November."

Kemp, who was also running for re-election in 2014, took a page from Kobach, turning an office that was supposed to encourage people to vote into a weapon to curb voter participation.

In September, Kemp, a wealthy developer and former state senator from Athens, announced his office was investigating Abrams's group for "significant illegal activities" including forged voter registration applications. His probe drew national headlines. Abrams called it a "fishing expedition" meant to "suppress our efforts."

As the state's voter registration deadline approached in early October, Abrams and Warnock held a press conference outside the state capitol with thirteen plastic bins filled with copies of thousands of voter registration applications they claimed the state had not processed while Kemp scrutinized the group for minor technicalities.

"You don't have to wear a hood or be a member of the Ku Klux Klan to be engaged in voter suppression," Warnock said.

Kemp's office ultimately identified only fifty-three registration applications as possibly fraudulent, submitted by outside canvassers hired by the New Georgia Project. No charges were filed against the group and Abrams was cleared of wrongdoing.

Yet of the eighty-seven thousand registration forms submitted by the New Georgia Project, only forty-six thousand people made it on the rolls by Election Day. Another eighteen thousand people were added *after* the election, once Republican candidates for governor and senator—along with Kemp—had been easily elected.

The clash between Abrams and Kemp was a prelude to 2018, when they faced off in a historic race for governor.

» » » » » »

The 2018 governor's race pitted two candidates with wildly divergent visions for the South and the country.

Kemp unabashedly tailored his message to conservative white Georgians, running a throwback campaign to the racially charged elections of the 1960s. He called himself a "politically incorrect conservative" and touted his endorsement from Trump. "I'm so conservative," he said in one TV ad, "I got a big truck, just in case I need to round up criminal illegals and take 'em home myself. Yep, I just said that."

Abrams, who was running to become the first Black woman governor in US history, rejected the longtime strategy of white Democrats in Georgia, who often echoed GOP positions on issues like guns and abortion in an attempt to woo conservative white voters back to the party.

"The approach of trying to create a coalition that is centered around converting Republicans has failed Democrats in the state of Georgia for the last 15 years," she said.

Instead, she wanted to activate a "New American majority" of young people, women, people of color, and moderate and progressive whites.

The race became a battle between one candidate who wanted to expand democracy and another who wanted to constrict it.

Kemp had one major advantage that Abrams did not: as secretary of state, he oversaw voting laws and could shape them to his advantage. He refused to recuse himself as the state's top election official while he ran for higher office, even though he was essentially overseeing his own election. Former president Jimmy Carter, who had monitored elections all over the world, said that Kemp's position ran "counter to the most fundamental principle of democratic elections—that the electoral process be managed by an independent and impartial election authority."

Kemp oversaw a series of restrictive voting laws passed or implemented in the wake of the *Shelby* decision that allowed him, as both a player and referee in the election, to "tilt the playing field in his favor," Abrams said.

In May 2014, a worker with the New Georgia Project knocked on the door of Amos Amoadu Boadai, a naturalized US citizen from Ghana who served in the US Army, and asked if he wanted to register to vote. Boadai had become a citizen in 2011 and had registered to vote in Virginia before moving to Columbus, Georgia, in 2013. He switched his registration to Georgia, and the New Georgia Project submitted the form to local election officials in Muscogee County.

Yet Boadai never received a voter registration card in the mail, and his registration application was canceled by the county two weeks before the election. Believing he was not eligible to vote, Boadai never went to the polls. "As a naturalized United States citizen who is proud to serve my country in the United States Army, I cherish my right to vote and was disappointed to learn . . . that my application had been canceled," he said after the election.

Boadai had been flagged by a Georgia policy called "exact-match" that required information on a voter registration application to perfectly match that voter's data in Georgia Department of Driver Services or Social Security Administration databases. Something as small as a missing hyphen or apostrophe in someone's name could lead to a canceled registration. Though Boadai had correctly filled out his application, Georgia's voter registration database wrongly said his information did not match the federal Social Security database. He was never told why his application was rejected.

This "no match, no vote" policy—which essentially served as Georgia's version of Kobach's Crosscheck—disproportionately hurt

minority voters, who were far more likely to have names like Boadai's that were unfamiliar to Georgia's predominantly white election
officials. The Justice Department had blocked Georgia's exact-match
program in 2009, when the state still had to approve its voting changes
under the Voting Rights Act, finding it was a "flawed system [that]
frequently subjects a disproportionate number of African-American,
Asian, and/or Hispanic voters to additional and, more importantly,
erroneous burdens on the right to register to vote."

But when Kemp became secretary of state in 2010, he sued the DOJ
and threatened to challenge the constitutionality of the VRA if the
government didn't approve the program. The department agreed after
Kemp promised to make tweaks to it. But he never did, and between
2013 and 2016, thirty-five thousand voters—more than three-quarters
of them people of color—had their registrations canceled because of
exact-match.

Civil rights groups, including the New Georgia Project, sued in the
run-up to the 2016 election on behalf of voters like Boadai, and Kemp
agreed to suspend the program as part of a legal settlement in February 2017. But just two weeks later, he persuaded the Georgia legislature
to pass a nearly identical law resurrecting exact-match in early 2017,
and it took effect immediately since Georgia no longer needed to get
federal approval for its voting changes.

Abrams was astonished.

"I've become very familiar with voter registration in the state of
Georgia, almost painfully so," she said dryly on the House floor on
February 23, 2017. "The right to vote should not be taken away because
of clerical error and this is what this bill seeks to restore."

Georgia Republicans, emboldened by Trump's election, said they'd
take their chances in court. "Sometimes we parachute in to the right
judge," said the GOP representative Earl Ehrhart. "We'll see what the
next federal judge says. We have that right."

"I like some of the federal judges in this state very much but I
wouldn't say that's a reason to pass a law that we know is in violation
of federal law," said Abrams.

Weeks before the 2018 election, the Associated Press reported that the revived exact-match policy was working as Democrats feared: Kemp's office had put the registrations of fifty-three thousand people on hold because information on their forms did not exactly match state databases. Seventy percent of them were Black and 80 percent were voters of color. Suddenly, tens of thousands of people among Abrams's core base who thought they were correctly registered were unsure if they were able to vote.

But that was just one facet of Kemp's suppressive strategy. He began by shrinking the electorate. Under his watch, Georgia purged 1.5 million voters from 2012 to 2016, twice as many as during the previous four years, and removed an additional 735,000 voters from the rolls over the next two years. On one evening in July 2017, Georgia removed 500,000 voters, in an act *The Atlanta Journal-Constitution* said "may represent the largest mass disenfranchisement in US history." Some voters were removed for sound reasons, because they had died or moved, while others were purged based on more suspect criteria, such as not having voted in the previous six years. More than 130,000 of those purged had registered to vote in 2008, when Obama first ran for president, and nearly half of them were voters of color.

Those who were able to successfully register still experienced problems when they went to the polls. Georgia had closed 214 polling places since 2012, with one-third of the counties having fewer voting precincts than they did in 2012. More than half of the counties with closed voting locations had Black populations of 25 percent or higher. Kemp had advised local counties on how to close polling locations shortly after the *Shelby* decision.

Fewer polling places led to longer lines. At one largely African American precinct in Snellville, Georgia, in a county outside of Atlanta that had recently become majority-minority, voters waited for four and a half hours because voting machines malfunctioned. "This was definitely foreseeable," said the Democratic congressman Hank Johnson. "It's part of the last gasp attempts by Republicans to maintain their positions of privilege." The average wait time in metro Atlanta was three hours. There were few similar reports of long lines in Republican-leaning areas.

Georgia had the longest wait times in the country in 2018, two and a half times the national average. Fewer polling places and longer distances to travel to vote kept an estimated fifty-four thousand to eighty-five thousand people from casting ballots, found *The Atlanta Journal-Constitution*, and reduced overall turnout by up to 2 percent. "Maybe the South hasn't changed as much as one would have hoped," said former Obama administration solicitor general Donald Verrilli, who had defended the VRA before the Supreme Court in 2013.

Perhaps the most stunning move was Kemp's announcement seventy-two hours before the election, as Trump prepared to campaign in the state on his behalf, that his office was investigating the Democratic Party of Georgia for "possible cyber crimes."

There was no evidence to support these charges. Georgia was one of only five states that used electronic voting machines with no paper backups, and Kemp had firmly resisted efforts to secure his state's voting system, accusing the federal government of trying to "subvert the Constitution" when it offered to help safeguard against Russian hacking in 2016.

It later came out that what Kemp called a "failed hacking attempt" was actually a Department of Homeland Security scan of the state's voting system, which Kemp's office had agreed to ahead of time. And when a Georgia Democratic activist had noticed vulnerabilities in the state's My Voter Page and notified the secretary of state's office that confidential voting information could be accessed, Kemp attacked Democrats instead of trying to fix it. Thus, when Georgians went to check their voting information on the secretary of state's website days before the election, they saw a press release from Kemp's office falsely blaming his opponent for compromising the state's election integrity.

The election law expert Rick Hasen called it "perhaps the most outrageous example of election administration partisanship in the modern era."

>> >> >> >> >> >>

There was a through line to Kemp's strategy: like Kobach, he justified his unprecedented intrusions into the electoral process by claiming he was stopping noncitizens from voting, which played on Republican fears of Georgia's changing demographics. He said Abrams wanted to allow "illegals to vote" after she had voted against a Kansas-style proof-of-citizenship law in the state legislature. "Hard-working Georgians should decide who their governor is, not people here illegally like my opponent wants."

But it was US citizens—not undocumented immigrants—who were kept from the polls. Phoebe Einzig-Roth, an eighteen-year-old freshman at Emory, moved to Georgia in August 2018 and was "so excited to vote" in her first election. Her parents had always taken her to the polls, just like Abrams's parents had, and she couldn't wait to cast a ballot of her own. But when she went to her polling location near campus on Election Day, election officials scratched their heads and told her she'd been flagged as a noncitizen. Even though she'd brought three forms of identification—her driver's license, passport, and student ID—she was forced to cast a provisional ballot.

Three days later, she went to confirm her citizenship at the local election office, where she was assured her vote would be counted. But she kept checking Georgia's online My Voter Page and there was no record it had been. She posted a picture of herself on Facebook wearing an "I'm a Georgia Voter" sticker with a peach on it and wrote, "The thing that infuriates me the most about voter suppression is not that it happened to me, but that it happened, and is continuing to happen to thousands of people all over the country, and most of the time, nothing is done to stop people from being turned away at the voting polls."

Even Abrams had trouble voting. When she went to cast her ballot at the South DeKalb Mall in Decatur two weeks before the election, trailed by reporters at the busy polling location, a poll worker said she couldn't vote in person because she had already requested an absentee ballot. But Abrams had always voted in person and quietly asked to talk to a polling place manager out of the earshot of the press, not wanting to publicize her difficulties. She was able to cast a ballot that day, but many other Georgians weren't so adept at navigating the state's patchwork voting system.

The number of disputed provisional ballots cast by voters like Einzig-Roth skyrocketed from twelve thousand in 2014 to twenty-two thousand in 2018. Nearly half were not counted. The Abrams campaign received eighty thousand calls from people who encountered problems voting; she fell short of forcing a runoff against Kemp by eighteen thousand votes.

Despite these obstacles, in many ways Abrams had succeeded. She won more votes than any Democrat in Georgia history and forced the closest gubernatorial election since 1966. Democrats picked up eleven seats in the Georgia state house and two in the state senate, and Lucy McBath, a gun control activist, became the first Black woman to hold Newt Gingrich's former congressional seat in suburban Atlanta. The winning multiracial coalition Abrams envisioned was closer than ever to taking over the state.

"We are seeing unfold before our very eyes a new South that is progressive and inclusive and increasingly embracing of the future," said Warnock, who remained chair of the New Georgia Project during the election. "Georgia will never be the same because of her candidacy."

But Abrams was ultimately unable to overcome the barriers Kemp placed in her way. She had a plan, but he did too, using control of democratic institutions to undermine democracy.

Ten days after the election, with deep frustration, she acknowledged Kemp's victory while refusing to give a typical concession speech. "To watch an elected official—who claims to represent the people of this state—baldly pin his hopes for election on the suppression of the people's democratic right to vote has been truly appalling," she said at her campaign headquarters in east Atlanta.

Abrams urged her supporters "to not give in to that anger or apathy but instead turn to action." She announced she was launching a new voting rights group, Fair Fight Action, and "filing a major federal lawsuit against the state of Georgia for the gross mismanagement of this election and to protect future elections from unconstitutional actions."

Abrams's words after the *Shelby* decision had proved prophetic: the conservative effort to restrict democracy had inspired an equally motivated movement to defend it. "Voting is not a right for some," she said. "It is a right for all." Those words would be tested like never before in the next election.

7

THE INSTITUTIONAL COUP

In April 2017, Steve Bannon, Trump's chief strategist, asked Commerce Secretary Wilbur Ross, who oversaw the Census Bureau, to "talk to someone about the census" and suggested he speak to Kris Kobach. Three months later, Kobach, who'd just been named vice chair of the administration's voter fraud commission, wrote to Ross "at the direction of Steve Bannon" and said it was "essential" that "one simple question" be added to the census form.

The seemingly innocuous nine-word question proposed by Kobach—"Is this person a citizen of the United States?"—which had not been asked since 1950, threatened to derail the entire 2020 census.

The census was America's oldest and largest civic event, the only one that involved everyone in the country, young and old, citizen and noncitizen, rich and poor. It had been conducted every ten years since 1790, when 650 US marshals and their assistants swore an oath to undertake "a just and perfect enumeration" of the population, traveling across the Eastern seaboard on horseback for nine months to count 3.9 million people. The founders considered the census so important—providing the basis for both taxation and representation—that it was mentioned in the sixth sentence of the Constitution as the first responsibility of the new federal government, before instructions on how to elect members of Congress or select the judiciary.

In the modern day, the census determined how $1.5 trillion in federal funding was allocated to states and localities each year for things like health care, schools, public housing, and roads; how many congressional seats and electoral votes each state received; and how states redrew local and federal voting districts. It laid the groundwork for the core infrastructure of American democracy, bringing a measure of transparency and fairness to how representation and resources were distributed across the country. The census determined—quite literally—who counted as a resident of the country and what benefits they received.

But the Trump administration wanted to radically change how the census was conducted and who it counted. The question about citizenship was likely to scare away immigrants who were terrified by the administration's nativist policies and worried that giving their citizenship status to the federal government could be used to initiate deportation proceedings against them or their families. An undercount of immigrant communities, particularly among Latinos, would shift economic and political power to whiter and more Republican areas that were more likely to be counted by the census; the 2010 census, the most accurate to date, still overcounted white residents by nearly 1 percent while failing to count 1.5 percent of Hispanics, 2.1 percent of Blacks, and 4.9 percent of Native Americans on reservations.

The fear of census information being misused had precedent. During World War II, the Census Bureau had given the names and addresses of Japanese Americans to the Secret Service, which used the information to send them to internment camps. That abuse led to strict confidentiality standards for the bureau, but many immigrants didn't trust the Trump administration with their personal information.

"Immigrants and their families all feel under attack, under siege, by the federal government," said Arturo Vargas, executive director of the National Association of Latino Elected Officials Educational Fund, who served on a Census Bureau advisory committee. "And then we have to turn around and tell these same people, 'Trust the federal government when they come to count you.'"

Demographers expected the 2020 census to show that the white share of the population had fallen below 60 percent for the first time. Trump, who won the white vote by 20 points in 2016, would benefit politically if the census were manipulated to slow that shift. If immigrant and minority communities weren't accurately counted in the census, it would slow the emergence of a majority-minority country and electorate. Those uncounted communities would not disappear, but they would be invisible when it came to economic and political representation.

This was Bannon and Kobach's most ambitious attempt yet to preserve white conservative political power. The census formed the DNA of America's democratic system. If it were corrupted, then many of the country's other democratic institutions, which relied on census data, would be too. Of all the ways democracy was threatened under Trump, an unfair and inaccurate census could have the most dramatic long-term impact.

» » » » »

Wilbur Ross, an eighty-one-year-old billionaire known as the King of Bankruptcy, had served as a census worker while attending Harvard Business School, but he nonetheless sided with Bannon and Kobach and embarked on a furious lobbying campaign to add the citizenship question to the 2020 form.

"I am mystified why nothing has been done in response to my months old request that we include the citizenship question," Ross wrote in May 2017 to two Commerce Department aides. Ross spoke that spring to Kobach and Attorney General Jeff Sessions, who had been a foremost critic of immigration when he represented Alabama in the Senate and was the first US senator to endorse Trump in 2016.

"We need to work with Justice to get them to request that citizenship be added back as a census question," responded Ross's senior adviser Earl Comstock.

Ross couldn't simply order the Census Bureau to add the question; any proposed changes to the census form underwent years of testing and scientific scrutiny. He had to convince another agency to request it, so it didn't seem like the edict came from him or anti-immigration hard-liners like Bannon and Kobach.

By the summer, Ross was getting impatient.

"Where is the DoJ in their analysis?" he asked Comstock in August 2017. "If they still have not come to a conclusion please let me know your contact person and I will call the AG."

"Since this issue will go to the Supreme Court we need to be diligent in preparing the administrative record," Comstock responded the next day.

A month later, Comstock told Ross he'd asked multiple federal agencies if they would request the question, but hadn't had any luck.

"Justice staff did not want to raise the question given the difficulties Justice was encountering in the press at the time (the whole Comey matter)," he wrote on September 8.

But five days later, an aide to Sessions wrote to Ross's chief of staff and said, "The AG is eager to assist." This was the breakthrough Ross needed.

That December, the Justice Department sent a letter to the acting head of the Census Bureau, Ron Jarmin, formally requesting that the citizenship question be added to the 2020 census.

The Census Bureau strenuously opposed the new question. A citizenship question "is very costly, harms the quality of the census count, and would use substantially less accurate citizenship status data than are available from administrative sources," the bureau's top scientist, John Abowd, wrote to Ross in January 2018. Census Bureau researchers predicted it could lead to nine million people not filling out the census form, making it the most inaccurate census in decades.

Jarmin requested a meeting with the Justice Department to explain the bureau's opposition. But Sessions told staff in the Civil Rights Division not to take the meeting.

In March 2018, Ross overruled the career professionals at the bureau and publicly announced the addition of the citizenship question, which he claimed the Justice Department needed for "more effective enforcement" of the Voting Rights Act. Ross testified before Congress that he had added the citizenship question "solely" at the DOJ's urging. In fact, he had orchestrated the DOJ's request and provided the chief argument for it, with a Commerce Department lawyer telling a top DOJ official in the fall of 2017 that "Sec Ross has reviewed concerns and thinks DOJ would have a legitimate use of data for VRA purposes."

Voting rights advocates viewed this rationale as pure farce, given that the architects behind the policy, like Kobach, had spent their careers trying to restrict voting rights. The Trump administration hadn't filed a single lawsuit to enforce the Voting Rights Act and the citizenship question hadn't been on the census form since the act had passed in 1965.

"Voting rights enforcement has never depended on having that question on the [census] form since the enactment of the Voting Rights Act," said Vanita Gupta, who led the Justice Department's Civil Rights Division under Obama and then served as president of the Leadership Conference on Civil Rights. "That's plainly a ruse to collect that data and ultimately to sabotage the census."

The administration had turned one of the oldest and most important constitutional acts into a political weapon.

» » » » » »

The likes of Kobach didn't want to simply reduce the count of immigrant and minority communities. They wanted to exclude noncitizens from counting altogether toward political representation. That would give the GOP a major boost, since most Republicans represented areas with few immigrants. After the 2018 election, Democrats in the House of Representatives represented 137 of the 155 House districts with more immigrants than the national average.

Kobach wrote to Ross in July 2017 that the absence of a citizenship question "leads to the problem that aliens who do not actually 'reside' in the United States are still counted for congressional apportionment purposes." As he further explained in a column for *Breitbart News*: "A person [whose] very presence in the United States is illegal—and who may return home or be deported at any time—cannot be considered a resident of the district in any meaningful sense."

Kobach's plan would have redefined the very nature of how representation was determined in the United States dating back to the country's founding. Fair representation had been one of the core principles of the new republic. "No taxation without representation" was a leading rallying cry of the revolution, which was followed in Great Britain by a revolt against the "rotten boroughs" of the British Parliament, where absentee lords representing as few as a dozen people received more seats than growing industrial cities like Manchester and Birmingham.

Though most of the newly formed states denied the vote to women, Black people, and propertyless white people, the leading founders believed everyone was entitled to political representation, even if the institutions they created often fell short of democratic ideals. "There can be no truer principle than this—that every individual of the community at large has an equal right to the protection of government," Hamilton said at the Constitutional Convention.

When the post–Civil War slate of constitutional amendments was being debated in 1865 and 1866, some radical Republicans, led by Representative Thaddeus Stevens, proposed apportioning House seats based on "legal voters" instead of total population. They predicted—correctly—that newly emancipated African Americans would be disenfranchised yet still counted by former slave states seeking to grab even more power than they'd had under the three-fifths clause. But other pro-Reconstruction Republicans argued that despite this prediction, nonvoters such as women and children were entitled to representation even if they could not vote. "No one will deny that population is the true basis of representation; for women, children, and other nonvoting classes may have as vital an interest in the legislation of the country as those who actually deposit the ballot," said the representative James Blaine of Maine.

In the end, the Fourteenth Amendment stated that "Representatives shall be apportioned . . . counting the whole number of persons in each State." That settled the issue at the federal level for a while, until immigration surged at the turn of the twentieth century and the census became a political battleground at a time of rising nativism and demographic tension.

Between 1905 and 1914, nearly ten million immigrants entered the United States, the highest rate in the country's history. By 1921, there was such a backlog at Ellis Island that New York–bound ships were re-routed to Boston.

The 1920 census showed that 70 percent of the immigrant population lived in urban areas while only 40 percent of native-born people did. In cities like New York, Chicago, Boston, Cleveland, and Detroit, immigrants and their children constituted three-fourths of residents, crowding in tenements and bringing exotic new languages and cultures.

This sparked a fierce backlash among Anglo-Saxon whites, who welcomed the "old" immigrants from northwest Europe but demonized the "new" arrivals from southern and eastern Europe as a lesser race more akin to Blacks or Chinese. "We have admitted the dregs of Europe until America has been Orientalized, Europeanized, Africanized, and mongrelized to that insidious degree that our genius, stability, greatness and promise of advancement and achievements are actually menaced," said the Democratic representative John Tillman of Arkansas.

Albert Johnson, the Republican chair of the House Immigration Committee, introduced a new law in 1924 to institute strict quotas on immigration from everywhere but northwest Europe. It capped immigration at one-tenth of current levels and limited arrivals from any country to 2 percent of its foreign-born population in the United States, basing these numbers not on the 1920 census but from 1890, before most immigrants from southern and eastern Europe had arrived. "It is hoped to guarantee, as best we can at this late date, racial homogeneity in the United States," Johnson said.

Johnson's bill passed with ease: 308-62 in the House, 69-9 in the Senate, supported by large majorities of both parties. "America must be kept American," said President Calvin Coolidge, who signed the law in May 1924.

"AMERICA OF THE MELTING POT COMES TO END" read a

full-page *New York Times* editorial by Senator David Reed of Pennsylvania, who sponsored the bill with Johnson. It showed two maps, one with current levels of immigration, the other with the new plan. In the second map, much of the immigration from southern and eastern Europe simply disappeared. "The racial composition of America at the present time thus is made permanent," Reed wrote.

The law worked with precision. Immigration fell from 1.2 million in 1914 to just 150,000 by the end of the 1920s, and nearly 90 percent of visas went to northwest Europe instead of southern and eastern Europe, a complete reversal from earlier in the decade. The law established the country's first numerical limits on immigration and a clear racial and ethnic hierarchy.

A year after its passage, Adolf Hitler credited America as the "one state in which one can observe at least weak beginnings of a better conception" of citizenship. The Nazi Handbook would cite Johnson-Reed as a model for Germany. "It was America," Hitler said a year before becoming chancellor, "that taught us a nation should not open its doors equally to all nations."

» » » » » »

As the Congress passed new immigration restrictions, the House refused to redraw its districts based on the new population estimates from the 1920 census, as it had done every ten years prior, since that would've shifted eleven seats from rural to urban areas. "It is not best for America that her councils be dominated by semicivilized foreign colonies in Boston, New York, and Chicago," said the Republican representative Edward Little of Kansas.

Throughout the 1920s, rural legislators sought to pass a constitutional amendment excluding noncitizens from congressional apportionment. Representative William Vaile of Colorado said he wanted to count a "more distinctly American population," since at the time of the Fourteenth Amendment, the number of immigrants "had not become sufficiently noticeable to be recognized as a danger or an evil."

But liberals like Representative Fiorello LaGuardia of New York argued persuasively that all inhabitants were entitled to equal representation. "The exclusion of aliens is only the first step in getting away from a popular and constitutional government of free men," LaGuardia said on the House floor. "Perhaps this is only the entering wedge—first to exclude aliens from the count. And then the next step will be to exclude those who do not own property; and then the next step will be to exclude all those who do not own real property, until the government will be controlled entirely by a small, privileged class, as it was in England at the time of the American Revolution."

Still, the House didn't adopt a new congressional map that reflected the changing population until 1929. It protected rural, native-born interests by removing existing language that House districts "be composed of contiguous and compact territory and contain as nearly as practicable the same number of individuals." That led to widespread malapportionment: in New York state, the largest urban House district in New York City contained 799,407 people while the smallest rural one upstate had just 90,671 people.

This conservative rural overrepresentation was already the norm in state legislatures across the country, who locked in an advantage by amending state constitutions or by simply ignoring the constitutional requirement to redraw legislative districts every ten years to account for population change. This was another form of nullification, designed to limit the impact of demographic changes that were taking place nationwide.

In the 1930s, "in the typical state, just 37 percent of the population elected a majority of seats in at least one chamber," wrote political scientists Stephen Ansolabehere and James M. Snyder Jr. in *The End of Inequality: One Person, One Vote and the Transformation of American Politics.* A 1926 amendment to California's constitution specified that no county could have more than one state senator, which meant that by 1960 the six million people of Los Angeles County had the same number of senators—one—as a district with fourteen thousand residents east of the Sierras. The distribution of representation became so skewed that it was possible for just 10 percent of Californians to elect a majority of the state senate.

The Supreme Court struck down this system of rural minority rule in a series of "one person, one vote" cases in the early 1960s, holding that state legislative and congressional districts must be roughly equal in population and "apportioned on a population basis." This shifted power from sparsely populated areas to the urban and suburban population centers where Americans increasingly lived.

"The fundamental principle of representative government in this country is one of equal representation for equal numbers of people, without regard to race, sex, economic status, or place of residence within a State," Chief Justice Earl Warren wrote in *Reynolds v. Sims* in 1964. As he pithily put it, "Legislators represent people, not trees or acres." In tandem with the Voting Rights Act, the "one person, one vote" cases led to "the greatest peace-time change in representation in the history of the United States," wrote Ansolabehere and Snyder. Of all his landmark rulings, Warren considered this democratic transformation his most important achievement on the Court.

But gerrymandering would soon replace malapportionment as the leading threat to fair representation, thanks largely to the work of one GOP strategist who would play an unexpectedly large role in Trump's efforts to rig the 2020 census.

On May 30, 2019, just weeks before the Supreme Court was set to rule on the constitutionality of the citizenship question after New York and sixteen other states had challenged it, bombshell news broke: a legal filing from the ACLU showed that Thomas Hofeller, the longtime redistricting coordinator for the Republican National Committee, was behind the administration's push for the question. Hofeller, who drew heavily gerrymandered maps for the GOP in key swing states after the 2010 census, wrote that the question would allow Republicans to craft new political districts that "would clearly be a disadvantage to the Democrats" and "advantageous to Republicans and Non-Hispanic Whites." It was the clearest evidence yet showing why Republicans wanted to change the census.

» » » » » »

A few years earlier, the Project on Fair Representation, a conservative legal organization that had recruited Shelby County, Alabama, to challenge the Voting Rights Act, had filed a new lawsuit, *Evenwel v. Abbott*. It demanded that the state of Texas draw state legislative districts based on eligible voters instead of on the total population, which had been the standard since the 1960s. The group claimed in 2015 that the current system denied "eligible voters their fundamental right to an equal vote."

The lawsuit went even further than Kobach's plans by arguing that all nonvoters, not just undocumented immigrants but also lawful permanent residents and children, should be excluded from state-level political representation. Such a move would deny representation to 55 percent of Latinos, 45 percent of Asian Americans, and 30 percent of African Americans, according to a legal filing by the Leadership Conference on Civil Rights. "This would amount to a massive shift in political power away from groups that are already disadvantaged in the political process and further concentrate power in the hands of a white plurality that does not adequately represent the full diversity of the total population," the group wrote.

In August 2015, Hofeller was hired by *The Washington Free Beacon*, a conservative news outlet bankrolled by New York hedge fund billionaire Paul Singer, one of the party's largest donors, to conduct a study that would "inform our principal's decision whether or not to fund a group handling the Evenwel lawsuit." (Hofeller was notoriously secretive but his study came to light after his estranged daughter turned over his hard drives following his death in 2018 to Common Cause as part of a lawsuit challenging gerrymandered maps he'd drawn in North Carolina.)

Hofeller's analysis of Texas state legislative districts found that drawing seats based on eligible voters instead of total population would be a "radical departure from the federal 'one person, one vote' rule presently used in the United States." It would reduce representa-

tion for Hispanics, who tended to vote Democratic, and increase representation for white Republicans. Democratic districts with a high
number of nonvoters would have to add population to include more
eligible voters, which would lead to fewer Democratic seats in places
like Houston, Dallas, and south and west Texas, with their electoral
power redistributed to white strongholds. "Democratic districts could
geographically expand to absorb additional high Democrat precincts
from adjacent Republican districts, strengthening the adjoining GOP
districts," Hofeller wrote.

In Texas, such a shift would leave 2.7 million noncitizens and
7 million children without political representation. The Texas legislature would see its lowest level of Latino representation since the 1980s,
undoing decades of progress for minority lawmakers. The new districts
drawn by Republicans would make the gerrymandering undertaken by
states like Wisconsin after the 2010 election look tame by comparison,
returning state-level politics to an era of severe malapportionment
that the Supreme Court had outlawed in the 1960s.

The Supreme Court ultimately ruled unanimously against the *Evenwel* plaintiffs in April 2016, finding that Texas did not have to draw
districts based on citizenship instead of total population if it didn't
want to. "As the Framers of the Constitution and the Fourteenth
Amendment comprehended, representatives serve all residents, not
just those eligible to vote," wrote Justice Ruth Bader Ginsburg.

However, Ginsburg stopped short of banning states from counting
only eligible voters, which the Obama administration had advocated
for during oral arguments. In a concurring opinion, Justice Thomas
said the Constitution "leaves States significant leeway" to draw districts as they see fit. And Justice Samuel Alito wrote that the court
might finally answer the "important and sensitive question" of the
constitutionality of drawing districts based on eligible voters when a
state drew a map to that effect.

During the case, the *Evenwel* plaintiffs faced a practical problem:
the Census Bureau didn't possess the citizenship data needed for
states to draw districts counting only citizens. "Without a question on

citizenship being included on the 2020 Decennial Census questionnaire, the use of citizen voting age population is functionally unworkable," Hofeller wrote.

After Trump's election, Hofeller saw his opening. He contacted Trump's transition team and urged them to add the citizenship question to the 2020 census, telling them to argue that it was needed to better enforce the Voting Rights Act, even though his own study had concluded it would harm the minority groups that the law was intended to protect.

In August 2017, Hofeller created a document detailing how the question could help VRA enforcement and gave it to Mark Neuman, the Trump transition official in charge of census issues, who became a key outside adviser to Ross.

Neuman incorporated Hofeller's memo in a letter he was drafting for the Justice Department requesting the citizenship question and asked him to review it.

"Please make certain that this language is correct," Neuman wrote to Hofeller on August 30, 2017.

"It is fine as written," Hofeller responded later that day.

Two months later, Neuman sent his draft to the assistant attorney general John Gore, who included Hofeller's ghostwritten language in the official Justice Department letter requesting the citizenship question. Hofeller's role was never disclosed when the Commerce Department unveiled the change to the census.

Despite the administration's public claim that the question was intended for Voting Rights Act enforcement, Neuman said Hofeller wanted to use it to gather "block level citizen voting age population data," precisely what Republicans needed to draw districts based on eligible voters instead of total population.

» » » » » »

Though the "one person, one vote" cases were supposed to lead to a new era of political equality, Hofeller grasped before nearly anyone in modern American politics how district lines could be manipulated for partisan ends.

While working on his PhD in government from Claremont Graduate University in Southern California, Hofeller created the first computerized mapping system for the California State Assembly in the early 1970s. The speaker of the California House called Hofeller "the kid with the shit-eating grin."

Hofeller got an early firsthand lesson in the power of gerrymandering. California had been a reliably Republican state, but after Democrats took control of state politics when Ronald Reagan left the governor's office to run for president, they drew maps that shifted the state's congressional delegation from nearly evenly divided to a 28-17 Democratic edge. Hofeller's alternative maps drawn for California Republicans were rejected; he said the Democrats' plan should win the "Gerrymander of the Year Award."

At the time, Democrats had dominant control of the US House and state capitals. They outnumbered Republicans two-to-one in state legislatures in the mid-1970s. When Hofeller went to work for the National Republican Congressional Committee ahead of the 1990 redistricting cycle, Republicans had full control over the redistricting process in states accounting for just five US House seats, compared to 172 seats for the Democrats.

Yet Hofeller saw an unexpected opportunity. As white Democrats ruled over statehouses in the 1980s and early 1990s, he pushed Republicans to support new majority-minority districts for Black and Latino Democrats, arguing that they were required under the Voting Rights Act. With minority voters concentrated in fewer areas, Republicans found it easier to target white Democrats for extinction.

"It's a paradox, but if you build a black district, you often take black votes away from an adjoining district, enabling you to elect more Republicans," Hofeller explained. Ben Ginsberg, a prominent GOP election lawyer who worked closely alongside Hofeller, memorably termed the strategy "Project Ratfuck."

Twenty new Black and Hispanic congressional districts were created during the post-1990 redistricting cycle, a landmark victory for minority representation that also helped Republicans knock off vulnerable white Democrats during their landslide victories in 1994, when the party picked up fifty-four seats and retook the House for the first time in forty years.

Hofeller, who had a monk-like devotion to his profession and few hobbies other than singing in a church choir at the National Cathedral, was remarkably blunt about the impact of his work. "The gerrymander overcometh all," he said. "What demographics give, legislatures can take away in the dead of the night." He called the maps he drew "the only legalized form of vote-stealing left in the United States."

The GOP aggressively targeted state-level races in 2010 through the Republican State Leadership Committee's REDMAP plan. That year Republicans picked up 680 state legislative seats, their largest number since 1928. This allowed them to draw four times as many federal and state legislative districts as Democrats. After the election, the RSLC and RNC urged GOP state legislatures to hire Hofeller to draw their new maps. "Now that we had a spectacular election outcome, it's time to make sure the Democrats cannot take it away from us in 2011 and 2012," the RNC wrote to state parties.

Hofeller worked on redistricting in a half-dozen states after the 2010 election, but he was most intimately involved in North Carolina, eventually moving from northern Virginia to Raleigh. He said he was instructed by North Carolina Republicans "to minimize the number of districts in which Democrats would have an opportunity to elect a Democratic candidate." The maps he drew transformed a purple state carried by Obama, where Democrats had a seven-to-six advantage in the congressional delegation after the 2010 election, into a deeply red one where Republicans held ten of thirteen districts after redistricting occurred, the largest shift for Republicans at the congressional level in any state.

Hofeller accomplished this remarkable feat by drawing half of the state's Black population of 2.2 million people, who voted overwhelmingly for Democrats, into a fifth of all congressional and state legislative districts. He claimed this was required by the Voting Rights Act—echoing his justification for the census citizenship question—but this time civil rights groups disagreed, challenging the maps for reducing the influence of Black Democrats by unnecessarily increasing the number of minority voters in existing majority-minority districts.

The Supreme Court struck down the maps as illegal racial gerrymandering and ordered the state to draw new congressional districts. North Carolina Republicans once again retained Hofeller, telling him "to change as few" districts as possible. "I propose that we draw the maps to give a partisan advantage to ten Republicans and three Democrats, because I do not believe it's possible to draw a map with eleven Republicans and two Democrats," admitted the GOP state representative David Lewis, who oversaw the redistricting process. "I acknowledge freely that this would be a political gerrymander, which is not against the law."

But a federal court once again disagreed, striking down the new lines in August 2018, this time as partisan gerrymandering. "The process Dr. Hofeller followed in drawing the 2016 Plan," wrote a federal court panel, "reflected the General Assembly's intent to discriminate against voters who were likely to support non-Republican candidates." North Carolina's congressional maps were more skewed toward Republicans than those of any other swing state: in 2018, Democratic candidates for Congress won 49 percent of the vote in North Carolina, but Republicans retained 75 percent of House seats.

On the morning of June 27, 2019, the Supreme Court decided two cases, within minutes of each other, that determined Hofeller's legacy.

In the first 5–4 decision, Chief Justice John Roberts blocked the administration from adding the citizenship question to the 2020 census. He ruled that Ross possessed the authority to include the question but found that the administration's argument that it was needed to better enforce the VRA, which had been concocted by Hofeller, "seems to have been contrived."

"The record shows that the Secretary began taking steps to reinstate a citizenship question about a week into his tenure, but it contains no hint that he was considering VRA enforcement in connection with that project," Roberts wrote. "Altogether, the evidence tells a story that does not match the explanation the Secretary gave for his decision."

Yet ten minutes later, in another 5-4 decision by Roberts, the Court upheld the gerrymandered maps drawn by Hofeller in North Carolina. But the conservative majority went much further, ruling that partisan gerrymandering presented "political questions beyond the reach of the federal courts" and could not be reviewed, let alone overturned, by the federal judiciary.

Two years earlier, voting rights advocates had been hopeful that the court would finally strike down partisan gerrymandering in a landmark case challenging Wisconsin's heavily skewed state legislative districts. But the court punted, refusing to decide the merits of the case, and after Brett Kavanaugh replaced Anthony Kennedy—who in the past had expressed an openness to curbing gerrymandering—the Court shut the door once and for all to future partisan gerrymandering challenges. The conservative justices had intervened to boost GOP political interests in cases like *Citizens United* and *Shelby County*, but now claimed it was impossible for them to uphold fair representation, adopting much the same argument that courts had used to sustain malapportioned legislative districts before the "one person, one vote" cases.

"Of all times to abandon the Court's duty to declare the law, this was not the one," Justice Elena Kagan dissented. The maps drawn by Hofeller "imperil our system of government," she continued. "Part of the Court's role in that system is to defend its foundations. None is more important than free and fair elections."

Hofeller wasn't around to read the rulings. He passed away at seventy-five in August 2018. But the North Carolina decision all but ensured that the next generation of GOP mapmakers would have a green light to draw extreme lines undermining representative democracy, accomplishing the ultimate goal of the citizenship question through other means.

» » » » » »

On July 11, 2019, a visibly agitated Trump appeared in the White House Rose Garden on a rainy Friday afternoon to announce that his administration was dropping its bid to add the citizenship question to the census. For two weeks after the Supreme Court's decision, the administration had scrambled to find a "new rationale" for the question that would satisfy the judiciary, at the urging of top figures in the conservative legal movement, including Leonard Leo of the Federalist Society. They hadn't succeeded, but Trump said defiantly, "I'm here to say we are not backing down on our effort to determine the citizenship status of the United States population."

In lieu of the citizenship question, Trump announced an executive order directing the Commerce Department to obtain existing citizenship data from the administrative records of federal agencies. "Some states may want to draw state and local legislative districts based upon the voter-eligible population," Trump explained, endorsing Hofeller's plan. The Court's North Carolina gerrymandering decision "could encourage states to make such decisions based on voter eligibility," the president added.

Conservative activists urged Republican state legislators to take advantage of Trump's order. At the annual meeting of the American Legislative Exchange Council, the influential group that paired state officials with corporate interests to write model legislation, Heritage Foundation senior fellow Hans von Spakovsky, who served on Trump's voter fraud commission, told two hundred GOP state legislators: "All of you need to seriously consider using citizen population to do redistricting." He explained why at the group's panel on redistricting in Austin in August 2019: "The higher the number of noncitizens in a district, the greater the chances they're going to vote for a liberal. The higher the number of citizens in a district, the higher the chances they're going to vote for a conservative." Cleta Mitchell, a GOP elections lawyer who spoke alongside von Spakovsky, urged the lawmakers to destroy their notes from the conference so they couldn't be cited in future lawsuits.

In July 2020, in the heat of his re-election campaign, Trump issued another executive action on the census, ordering the Commerce

Department to exclude undocumented immigrants from the apportionment of US House seats, which Kobach and groups like FAIR had long urged the administration to do. "States that welcome illegal immigration should not be rewarded," Kobach wrote approvingly.

Such a move would shift House seats from blue states like California that had a large undocumented immigrant population to red states like Alabama that had fewer immigrants. In 2018, Alabama had filed a lawsuit against the Commerce Department to remove undocumented immigrants from the apportionment count, which Andrew Brasher worked on before Trump nominated him as a federal judge.

At the same time Trump pushed to exclude immigrant communities from political representation, he railed against the expansion of voting by mail during the COVID-19 pandemic, accusing Democrats of "using covid to steal an election."

That spring, the US Postal Service's Board of Governors—under heavy lobbying from the administration—had overlooked more qualified candidates and installed as postmaster general Louis DeJoy, a GOP megadonor who had donated $2.5 million to the party since 2016 and served as finance chairman for the Republican National Convention. In record time, DeJoy, who ran a logistics company in North Carolina, instituted a dizzying array of changes—eliminating overtime, reassigning twenty-three top executives, reducing post office hours—that led to major mail delays. These moves seemed designed to further both the GOP's long-term goal of privatizing the post office and its short-term goal of suppressing mail-in votes cast disproportionately by Democrats during the pandemic.

Like the census, the post office dated back to the country's founding. In 1775, a year before the Declaration of Independence, the Continental Congress created the Post Office Department and named Benjamin Franklin the first postmaster general. American democracy expanded with the postal system, one of the only institutions that bound the new nation together and aimed to serve the many rather than the few. Winifred Gallagher, author of *How the Post Office*

Created America, called it "the central nervous system of American democracy."

Both the post office and the census had been politicized before, but no president prior to Trump had sought to sabotage the USPS to win an election or manipulate the census count for partisan benefit.

Though the Fourteenth Amendment required the counting of the "whole number of persons in each state" for apportionment purposes, Trump said that his census memorandum in July 2020 removing undocumented immigrants from the apportionment count reflected "a better understanding of the Constitution."

What it really reflected was an emphatic repudiation of the Constitution. Over the past decade, Republicans had passed laws making it more difficult to vote and employed other aggressive efforts to distort the political process, but Trump's attacks on the USPS and the Census Bureau represented a dramatic escalation of his party's antidemocratic agenda; rather than pursuing the disenfranchisement of people of color and Democrats within the bounds of the Constitution, he was seeking to eviscerate those limits altogether. The goal was to transform long-standing nonpartisan institutions into explicitly partisan ones, shifting their core mission from serving all Americans to furthering only the interests of a conservative white minority.

At a hastily planned hearing before the House Oversight Committee on July 29, 2020, four former Census Bureau directors said that Trump's memorandum excluding undocumented immigrants from congressional apportionment was unconstitutional and another attempt to dissuade immigrant communities from responding to the census.

"I am very concerned that the release of this memorandum will increase the fears of many in the hard-to-count community that their data will not be safe," testified John Thompson, who led the Census Bureau from 2013 to 2017. "The end result will most likely be increased nonparticipation and increased undercounts of these populations."

The only witness to testify in favor of Trump's order was John

Eastman, a former law clerk to Clarence Thomas who served as chairman of the Federalist Society's Federalism and Separation of Powers Practice Group. "I actually think President Trump's directive is not only good policy, but perfectly constitutional," Eastman testified over Zoom from his home in California. "To continue to count total population for apportionment purposes is to give an undue weight to states that have large numbers of noncitizens living within their borders." (An August 2017 draft memo to Ross from the Commerce Department attorney James Uthmeier had reached the opposite conclusion, stating that "over two hundred years of precedent, along with substantially convincing historical and textual arguments suggest that citizenship data likely cannot be used for purposes of apportioning representatives.")

Eastman, a sixty-year-old law professor with white hair and bushy eyebrows, had founded the Center for Constitutional Jurisprudence at the Claremont Institute, the pro-Trump think tank that published Michael Anton's "Flight 93" manifesto. It was started in 1979 by conservative political philosopher Henry Jaffa, who promoted an originalist interpretation of America's founding that opposed the Progressive Era and New Deal and cited Barry Goldwater's famous phrase at the 1964 Republican convention: "extremism in defense of liberty is no vice."

Eastman had filed twenty briefs before the Supreme Court, urging it to strike down campaign finance laws, oppose gay marriage, and overturn *Roe v. Wade*. Just as slavery and polygamy were "twin relics of barbarism" in the nineteenth century, he wrote in 2000, "two new indicia of barbarism arose during the 20th century: abortion and homosexuality."

Eastman was skilled at challenging long-established views of the Constitution to fit Trump's goals. He was best known for arguing that the Fourteenth Amendment did not grant citizenship to children born in the United States to noncitizen parents, which would have stripped citizenship from millions of Americans who were disproportionately nonwhite. Though the first sentence of the Fourteenth Amendment clearly stated that "all persons born or naturalized in the United States and subject to the jurisdiction thereof, are citizens of the United States and of the state wherein they reside," Eastman claimed that undocumented immigrants were not subject to the jurisdiction of the United States.

Eastman caught Trump's attention in 2019 after he criticized the former FBI director Robert Mueller's investigation into Russian interference in the 2016 election as a "show trial" on Fox News. Two months later he was meeting with the president in the Oval Office, urging him to issue an executive order revoking birthright citizenship, which few legal scholars believed Trump had the power to do.

In the hearing on Capitol Hill, Eastman argued that the census's "asserted obligation to 'count every person' [was] demonstrably false," since the framers of the Constitution and the Fourteenth Amendment had no conception of illegal immigration at the time. Though Eastman was a committed originalist, he attempted to rewrite how the census and its connection to political representation was understood in 1787 and 1868.

Democratic Representative Gerry Connolly of Virginia likened Eastman's position to the Dred Scott ruling in 1857, which held that Blacks were not entitled to the same citizenship rights as whites. "We would've had millions of Americans declared noncitizens under Dr. Eastman's logic, not counted in a census," he said.

Eastman called the comparison "slanderous," but a month later he would publish a *Newsweek* editorial arguing that Kamala Harris, who was born in California to immigrant parents who had not yet naturalized, was not a US citizen and thus ineligible to run as Joe Biden's running mate. Trump, who called Eastman "brilliant," quickly amplified his much-criticized claim, saying of Harris: "she doesn't meet the requirements."

» » » » » »

Producing citizenship numbers to entrench GOP political representation became the administration's overarching goal for the 2020 census, even as the Census Bureau faced the unprecedented challenge of counting every person in America in the middle of a deadly pandemic.

The timing of the 2020 census could hardly have been worse: its long-planned nationwide rollout on March 12 occurred the day after the World Health Organization officially declared COVID-19 a pandemic. Trump called for "a major delay" in census operations, and the bureau suspended field operations until the summer of 2020. It was granted a 120-day extension to complete the enumeration, pushing back the deadline to end door knocking from July 31 to October 31. The apportionment numbers would be released on April 30, 2021, instead of by the end of the year.

But in early August, as the Census Bureau was finally dispatching workers to knock on doors in hard-to-count areas after months of delay, the administration abruptly announced that it was cutting census operations short by a month. That gave enumerators less than eight weeks to track down the 40 percent of households that had not yet filled out the census form, which were disproportionately in communities of color. Shortening the time period for counting, the bureau warned in an internal memo, "will result in a census that has fatal data quality flaws that are unacceptable for a Constitutionally-mandated national activity."

Trump then reinstated the end-of-the-year deadline for finalizing the apportionment count that existed before the pandemic so that he could obtain the data excluding undocumented immigrants from political representation before he left office in the event he lost re-election. The bureau said this was impossible. "Any thinking person who would believe we can deliver apportionment by 12/31 has either a mental deficiency or a political motivation," wrote Timothy Olson, the bureau's associate director for field operations.

Yet the administration, in another break from established norms, installed four political appointees at the bureau to make sure Trump got what he wanted.

One of them, Benjamin Overholt, was a statistician at the voting section of the Department of Justice who had asked Kobach to hire him as a researcher for Trump's voter fraud commission. "Since the first time I heard the President was planning to establish an Election Integrity Commission, I wanted to be a part of it," he wrote to Kobach, citing "my heart-felt concerns about voter fraud."

Christy McCormick, a Justice Department lawyer under George W. Bush who served on the election integrity commission with Kobach, recommended Overholt. "When I was at DOJ, we had numerous discussions that make me pretty confident that he is conservative (and Christian, too)," she wrote to an aide to Vice President Pence.

Kobach told Pence's aides that "I really would like to get [Overholt] on board." When he learned that the Justice Department had refused to transfer Overholt to the commission, Kobach said, "I would like to personally elevate the request to AG Sessions's office."

Instead, Overholt arrived at the Census Bureau in August 2020 to fill the newly created position of deputy director for data. He was joined by a new deputy director for policy, Nathaniel Cogley, a professor of political science at Tarleton State University, a little-known college in rural Texas, who specialized in African studies and had criticized Trump's impeachment trial in media appearances. Cogley was paired with a senior adviser, Adam Korzeniewski, who had been a political consultant to a Republican US House candidate in Staten Island, Joseph Saladino, who performed politically incorrect prank videos on YouTube under the name of Joey Salads.

These political appointees had little expertise with the census. In a highly unusual departure from protocol, the Federalist Society went so far as to recruit prospective hires for the Commerce Department. "We have come up with the five people below as good mid level prospects," Deecy Gray, a government affairs specialist representing the Federalist Society, wrote to Ross and his chief of staff in April 2020. "We hope you can use any, or all, of them."

One of the people recommended, a conservative lawyer named Earl "Trey" Mayfield, was hired in September 2020 as counselor to the Census Bureau's new director, Steven Dillingham.

These hires, who briefed White House chief of staff Mark Meadows on a weekly basis, set off alarm bells within the Census Bureau, which was renowned for its expertise and independence. "The [Commerce] department is demonstrating an unusually high degree of engagement in technical matters, which is unprecedented relative to the previous censuses," Jarmin, the bureau's deputy director, wrote to colleagues in September.

Jarmin told Overholt and Cogley that the bureau had been "consistently pessimistic" on the feasibility of removing undocumented immigrants from the apportionment count. There was no master database of undocumented immigrants in the United States, and the records that did exist from other federal agencies were often inaccurate, but the political appointees at the bureau aggressively tried to obtain the data, much as Trump's voter fraud commission had sought to find evidence of illegal voting.

They asked for records on food stamps, financial assistance for needy families, driver's license data, and other sources from the states that could be used to estimate the noncitizen population. Ross called state officials, including governors, "who were slow or reluctant to share data with us."

The effort hit a snag, however, when the bureau discovered "processing anomalies" in November due to the pandemic, such as where to count college students and seasonal agricultural workers, who would normally be counted where they studied or worked but had relocated during COVID. These errors would take time to resolve and the bureau said it could not deliver the census data until the end of January 2021.

But once it became clear that Trump had lost the election, Dillingham rushed ahead to obtain the citizenship data before Trump left office, setting a new deadline of January 15. He offered cash bonuses to anyone working on the project. Cogley floated the idea of taking computers from other federal agencies to speed up the work.

That was the last straw for Census Bureau employees. Several whistleblowers contacted the Commerce Department's inspector general and told her that Dillingham's "number one priority" was a report on the noncitizen population, which the bureau was under "significant pressure" to produce by January 15. They called Cogley and Over- holt "the driving forces behind this work" and said the release of any citizenship data, before thoroughly vetted, would be "statistically indefensible."

Jarmin had finally had enough. He ordered the career professionals at the bureau to stop working on the project. When the whistleblower complaints to the inspector general's office about Dillingham became public, he resigned two days before Trump left office. "In my opinion, politics, not the pandemic, was the greatest challenge to the 2020 Cen- sus," Dillingham said after leaving.

President Biden revoked Trump's executive orders on the census as one of his first actions upon taking office. His domestic policy adviser Susan Rice called them "inconsistent with our nation's history and our commitment to representative democracy."

» » » » » »

The release of the census count in August 2021 showed what the Trump administration had been so afraid of.

The white share of the country had fallen to 57.8 percent, the lowest in US history, with the white population declining for the first time on record since 1790. The country was more diverse than ever before: of the 23 million new residents counted over the past decade, all the growth had come from people who identified as Hispanic, Asian, Black, or more than one race.

"Our analysis of the 2020 Census results show that the US popula- tion is much more multiracial, and more racially and ethnically diverse than what we measured in the past," said Nicholas Jones, the director of race and ethnic research in the Census Bureau's population division.

Georgia was on the verge of becoming a majority-minority state years earlier than expected, and whites had become the minority in six new metropolitan areas: Atlanta, Austin, Dallas-Fort Worth, New Orleans, Orlando, and Sacramento. Similarly, the white population decreased in Wisconsin but nearly all of the state's growth came from communities of color.

Sixty percent of US residents lived in the 539 counties that voted for Biden, which accounted for 65 percent of the country's population growth over the past decade. Huge swaths of rural America lost population while urban areas boomed. This "diversity explosion," as Brookings Institution demographer William Frey called it, was exactly what the likes of Kobach, Bannon, and Eastman had been trying to stop.

Yet seven months later, when the bureau released a deeper analysis of the count, it became clear that Trump's efforts to sabotage the census had at least partially succeeded.

The 2020 census had failed to count 18.8 million people—more than twice the size of New York City—the largest undercount in three decades. Blacks, Latinos, and Native Americans were all missed at higher rates than the 2010 census, while white residents were overcounted at double the rate. The repeated attempts to obtain citizenship information had indeed skewed the final count: the Latino undercount tripled in 2020 from 2010, depriving these communities of critical economic and political resources for the next decade. Marc Morial of the National Urban League called it "population suppression."

"Today we learned that the 2020 Census was a five-alarm fire," said NALEO's Arturo Vargas.

By that time, the key figures who had led the fight to undermine one of the institutional pillars of American democracy had moved on to an even more frightening effort to overthrow the country's electoral system.

8

THE ELECTORAL COUP

On December 3, 2020, the Georgia state senator William Ligon, a Republican lawyer from the southeast coast, convened a hearing in a packed meeting room on the fourth floor of the state capitol. It had been a month since the presidential election and Ligon said GOP members of the legislature had been "flooded with reports from citizens about voting irregularities and potential fraud." A special subcommittee of the Judiciary Committee was meeting because "these complaints deserve full investigation, even though those in the national and state media are pretending there's nothing to see here."

Ligon introduced Rudy Giuliani, the bombastic former New York City mayor whom Trump had put in charge of his efforts to contest the 2020 election results, as the first witness. Over the course of the next six hours, Giuliani and members of his team would spin a lurid tale of how Trump was cheated out of victory in Georgia and other battleground states. Tens of thousands of "phantom votes" had been produced by voting machines tied to Venezuelan autocrat Hugo Chavez, Giuliani claimed, and thousands more illegal votes were cast by people who were dead, underage, felons, lived out of state, or were otherwise ineligible.

Though Georgia had conducted three recounts affirming Biden's 11,779-vote victory and had found no evidence of irregularities, and Governor Brian Kemp had certified the results two weeks earlier, Giuliani told the legislature, "It's clear that the count you have right now is false."

Giuliani claimed the fraud in Georgia was one facet of a multistate conspiracy to deprive Trump of re-election. "It was part of a concerted plan," he testified. "Certain cities were picked in order to carry this out where they thought they could get away with it. They didn't do it everywhere. It's not accidental they picked Detroit and Pittsburgh and Philadelphia and Milwaukee and Phoenix and Las Vegas—what do they have in common? They're controlled by one political party."

It was impossible to ignore how the Trump campaign—whose supporters were overwhelmingly white—had alleged widespread fraud in cities with large minority populations. The effort to overturn the 2020 election—more so than any other event in modern American history—would reveal the extraordinary tactics the country's conservative white minority would employ to attempt to prevent a new multiracial governing majority from taking power.

Trump trailed by seven million votes nationwide but needed just forty-five thousand votes in the three closest battleground states, Georgia, Arizona, and Wisconsin, to win the Electoral College. That gave him at least a theoretical opening to challenge the outcome. Still, what he was attempting to do was unprecedented. There had been contested elections before in US history, but they usually involved a dispute over a few hundred ballots, such as George W. Bush's 537-vote margin of victory in Florida in 2000. Never before had a losing candidate tried to throw out so many votes, in such an aggressive fashion, based on such flimsy evidence of fraud.

The claims made by Giuliani in Georgia and other key swing states had already been rejected by courts in more than thirty lawsuits, so now Trump's team was adopting a new strategy: lobbying Republican-controlled legislatures to override the popular vote winners in their states and appoint new electors for Trump. Giuliani claimed he had powerful new evidence that he believed would persuade the Georgia legislature to take this dramatic step.

He introduced Jackie Pick, a major Republican donor from Texas who was helping Trump's legal team in Georgia. Pick showed excerpts of surveillance footage from State Farm Arena in Atlanta's heavily Democratic Fulton County, where ballots were tallied on Election

Night. At 10:20 on Election Night, Pick said, an election official told Fox News and two Republican poll monitors to leave the carpeted room where ballots were being counted. Once they left, two women Pick referred to as "the ladies in yellow" began to "spring into action," she asserted, pulling out "suitcases of ballots [from] under a table" and "counting [them] unobserved, unsupervised, not in public view," until 1 a.m. The number of ballots counted during that time was "certainly beyond the margin of victory in this race," Pick claimed.

Giuliani, in typically over-the-top fashion, called the video "a powerful smoking gun" and said, "I don't have to be a genius to figure out that those votes are not legitimate votes." He tweeted a ninety-second clip that evening that immediately went viral, receiving thirty-five thousand retweets and millions of views on social media. "Wow! Blockbuster testimony," Trump tweeted. "This alone leads to an easy win of the State!" When the ladies in yellow were identified days later by a right-wing website as Shaye Moss, a clerical worker in Fulton County, and her mother, Ruby Freeman, who volunteered as a temporary worker to help count ballots during the pandemic, the two Black women were subject to death threats and racial slurs and forced to go into hiding.

The video did not actually show what the Trump campaign claimed it did. In reality, election workers who had been on the job for eighteen hours had packed up for the night around 10 p.m., but were told by county officials to keep counting ballots until the early morning to produce a faster result. That's why they reopened the sealed containers, whose ballots had been opened and prepped for counting earlier in the day, in full view of members of the media and GOP election observers. The Republican election monitors and members of the press had left voluntarily and state officials were present the entire time.

"The President's team is intentionally misleading the public about what happened at State Farm Arena on election night," tweeted Gabriel Sterling, a top official in the Georgia secretary of state's office. Referencing the threats made against election workers, he warned, "Someone's going to get hurt. Someone's going to get shot. Someone's going to get killed."

But even as disinformation spread among Trump's base, hardening their view that the election had been stolen, Georgia law prevented the legislature from overturning the popular vote winner in the state. So Giuliani invited John Eastman to testify as the next witness to present a novel legal theory. He appeared over Zoom, sitting on a tufted leather couch surrounded by old books, with the air of a medieval historian.

In a remarkably short period of time Eastman had gone from a little-known law professor and member of the conservative legal establishment to the leading constitutional theorist behind Trump's effort to overturn the election. "With all due respect," he told members of the Georgia legislature, "you don't have a valid election." That gave them the unique power to override state law and appoint their own electors for Trump, he argued. "You have a duty to do that to protect the integrity of the election in the state of Georgia."

Trump, Giuliani, and Eastman, along with sixteen other Trump associates, would later be indicted by the district attorney in Atlanta's Fulton County for participating in a "criminal enterprise" that tried to "unlawfully change the outcome of the election in favor of Trump." Giuliani was also found liable in federal court for defaming Freeman and Moss.

Five days after the state senate hearing, the claims made in Georgia would become a central piece of evidence in a new lawsuit filed before the Supreme Court that Trump called "the big one."

» » » » » »

On November 24, 2020, two days before Thanksgiving, Kris Kobach sent an email to the Louisiana attorney general, Jeff Landry, who led the Republican Attorneys General Association and was one of nine attorneys general in Lawyers for Trump.

"I have been watching from Kansas, and I'm happy to see you have continued to fight the good fight!" Kobach wrote. He asked if Landry would have "a moment to talk" about a "presidential election suit" he was working on with a few other lawyers, including a former conservative justice on the North Carolina Supreme Court.

Louisiana solicitor general Elizabeth Murrill responded to Kobach and said, "Jeff is reviewing all of it and Texas is too."

The next day, Kobach wrote back and asked her to review a "revised and streamlined" template of a lawsuit. Previously, the Trump campaign had challenged the election results state by state. In Wisconsin, for example, it had sought to throw out more than 221,000 votes in the Democratic strongholds of Madison and Milwaukee. The lawsuit was filed by a prominent GOP lawyer in Madison, James Troupis, who had helped legislative Republicans draw the 2011 redistricting maps that cemented their power and was later appointed as a county judge by Scott Walker. Walker had served as chairman of Trump's re-election campaign in Wisconsin. Despite Trump's losses piling up in court and the unusual attempt to challenge ballots cast only in two heavily Democratic counties, Walker tweeted that "Trump's lawyers have a valid case in WI."

Kobach, who had pushed claims of widespread voter fraud earlier and more insistently than practically anyone in the GOP, proposed that one state challenge the results in all the key battleground states won by Biden and file it directly before the Supreme Court, where conservatives had a supermajority thanks to Trump's three appointees.

"Using the COVID-19 pandemic as a justification," the lawsuit stated, "a few government officials in the defendant States Georgia, Michigan, Minnesota, Nevada, Pennsylvania, and Wisconsin usurped their legislatures' authority and unconstitutionally revised their State's election laws." He wanted Louisiana to petition the Supreme Court to reverse the election results in these six states, which would hand the election to Trump.

It was highly unusual for one state to challenge the voting procedures and election results of another. But Kobach claimed that changes to voting laws due to the pandemic—such as easing the rules for voting by mail—in states won by Biden had violated the rights of voters in states that were carried by Trump (even though voting laws were modified in many of those states too). "If one player in a game commits a penalty and no penalty is called by the referee, that is not fair," he said.

"Have you been in touch with Texas?" Murrill responded. The Texas attorney general, Ken Paxton, was known for his aggressive prosecutions of alleged voter fraud and led the advisory board of Lawyers for Trump.

"Someone else in our group has," Kobach wrote. "But if you want to forward this version to your counterpart in TX, please do so."

On December 8, Texas filed a lawsuit before the Supreme Court using nearly identical language to the draft circulated by Kobach, but updating it to reference "suitcases full of ballots being pulled out from underneath tables after poll watchers were told to leave" in Georgia and other outlandish claims made by the Trump campaign. It asked the Court to void the Electoral College results in Georgia, Michigan, Pennsylvania, and Wisconsin and have the Republican-controlled legislatures in those states appoint new electors for Trump. That would erase 10.3 million votes cast for Biden in those states, representing the largest act of electoral nullification in US history.

Texas drew support from seventeen other states, including Louisiana, 126 GOP members of the House, nearly half of the members of the Georgia state senate, and Georgia's two US senators, a startling indication of how many Republicans were willing to topple basic democratic norms. Kobach called the lawsuit "far more important than all of the others." Eastman filed a supporting brief for Trump, which claimed that "a large percentage of the American people know that something is deeply amiss."

But the extreme nature of the lawsuit was too much even for the conservative-dominated Supreme Court. Four days later, it unanimously dismissed the case, ruling that Texas did not have standing to challenge "the manner in which another State conducts its elections."

With the legal paths for challenging the election seemingly closed, Republicans in Georgia and elsewhere began developing a new plan for the coming year. If they couldn't overturn the election results, they would eliminate or roll back the voting methods used most often by Democratic constituencies to gain an advantage for the GOP in future elections.

Georgia's Senate Republican caucus released a statement the same day the Texas lawsuit was filed. "We have heard the calls of millions of Georgians who have raised deep and heartfelt concerns that state law has been violated and our elections process abused in our November 3, 2020 elections," it read. "We will fix this."

Though Georgia law provided "no avenue for us to retroactively alter the results from November 3, 2020," the GOP state senators pledged that "as soon as we may constitutionally convene, we will reform our election laws to secure our electoral process."

» » » » » »

The lies spread during and after the 2020 election—and the call to "fix" the country's voting system that followed—were a direct response to the expansion of the electorate that had occurred in battleground states, most notably in Georgia.

On the eve of the election, Obama arrived in Georgia for one last rally for the Biden-Harris ticket. It was an unexpected place for him to be—a state that had not voted for a Democratic presidential candidate since 1992, where white voters had abandoned the Democratic Party and launched the careers of conservative firebrands like Newt Gingrich.

"Georgia could be the state," Obama told a large crowd of cars that had assembled outside the former Olympic stadium in Atlanta for a socially distanced drive-in rally. "Georgia could be the place where we put this country back on track and not just because Joe Biden and Kamala Harris have a chance to win Georgia, but you've got the chance to flip two Senate seats. This is a big deal."

Polls showed the presidential race neck-and-neck. Raphael Warnock had decided to run for the Senate after Abrams chose not to and was joined on the ticket by Jon Ossoff, a young documentary filmmaker who had run for Gingrich's former congressional district in 2017. If elected, they would become the state's first Black and Jewish senators.

Few aside from Abrams saw this coming. "I don't know if you guys heard, but tomorrow we're making history," she said before Obama took the stage. Cars honked in support.

It had been a tumultuous summer in America, and not just because of the pandemic. The death of George Floyd in late May led to widespread protests against police brutality across the country. A few weeks before Floyd's murder, a video was released showing three white men murdering another Black man, Ahmaud Arbery, while he was running in coastal Georgia. That July, the longtime civil rights leader John Lewis, who had represented Atlanta in the US House for three decades and was known as the "conscience of the Congress," passed away from cancer.

"Protesting is the diagnosis," Abrams told the crowd. "Voting is the medicine. It's how we start to treat our ills."

At a moment when the country was reckoning with its legacy of racial discrimination like never before, the "new American majority" that Abrams foresaw when she ran for governor in 2018 was on the verge of becoming a reality.

In September 2019, less than a year after her defeat, she'd written a sixteen-page memo for party donors and strategists that she called "the Abrams playbook." She predicted that "next year, Georgia will be the premier battleground state in the country." She noted the rapid transformation of the state, with people of color making up nearly half the population, writing that "Georgia is not the only state poised to take advantage of demographic changes; but we are uniquely positioned for effectiveness." With many in the national party skeptical, however, that the state was a true battleground, she warned that "any less than full investment in Georgia would amount to strategic malpractice."

Still, during the state's disastrous presidential primary in June 2020, it was hard to see how Abrams's prophecy would come into being. The voting problems that had marred her race in 2018 had only gotten worse. Eighty polling places were closed in metro Atlanta—on top of the 214 that had already been closed across the state after the Supreme Court had gutted the Voting Rights Act—as urban counties hit hard by COVID-19 struggled to find locations and recruit poll workers. New voting machines purchased by the state malfunctioned during their trial run, contributing to long lines. Thousands of mail-in ballots requested by voters never arrived. This impacted some communities much more than others: wait times at predominantly Black and Latino precincts were more than six times longer than in majority-white areas.

Lucille Anderson, a seventy-one-year-old Black woman from Fulton County, had arrived at 9 a.m. to vote at the Christian City Welcome Center in Union City, a predominantly Black area in southwest Atlanta, but "the line was already too long," she said, and she needed to go to work. Nine thousand voters had been assigned to a single polling site—more than triple the state average—at a housing complex attached to a nursing home, the type of facility where one-third of all COVID deaths nationwide had occurred. She returned at 4 p.m., "only to see that the line to vote now stretched out the door, around the building, down the street, and up the next street." She waited for an hour and the line hadn't moved. There was little shade and she thought she might pass out amid the scorching humidity, so she went home to rest. She returned at 6:30 for a third time, but "the line was even longer than before." She gave up on voting that day.

LaTosha Brown, cofounder of the voting rights group Black Voters Matter, which worked to mobilize Black voters in the South, arrived in Union City at 9:30 p.m. to find more than three hundred voters still in line. The last voter cast a ballot at 12:37 a.m., nearly six hours after polls closed.

As Brown and her colleagues handed out masks, water, and hand sanitizer to exhausted voters, a security guard called the police and six squad cars arrived, lights flashing, telling them to leave because they were on private property. "2018 was the cake, the primary of 2020 was the icing in terms of the problems," Brown said.

The *Atlanta Journal-Constitution* cartoonist Mike Luckovich drew a sticker of a peach that said, "I tried to vote in Georgia." The newspaper's front page proclaimed: "Complete Meltdown."

It would have been easy for voting rights activists to give up at that point, but the widespread voting problems motivated them to work even harder as November approached.

First, they expanded the electorate. Between 2016 and 2020, one million new voters were added to the rolls through Georgia's system of automatic voter registration at motor vehicle offices and through registration drives by grassroots groups such as Abrams's Fair Fight. Two-thirds of them were people of color. The number of eligible but unregistered Georgians fell from 22 percent in 2016 to just 2 percent in 2020.

Second, they encouraged voters to cast their ballots early to prevent another Election Day meltdown. "VOTE EARLY" billboards went up along busy highways like I-85 and I-20 in metro Atlanta. Fair Fight contacted one million voters a week in the run-up to Election Day, urging them to make a plan to vote early, either in person or by mail. "When I would go to the polls, I would hear, 'We're not going to let them steal this one,'" said Brown. "That's why I think you had so many people vote early." Eighty percent of Georgians voted early, leading to many fewer problems on Election Day. There were still long lines—up to eleven hours on the first days of early voting in Atlanta—but they steadily decreased as the election got closer.

Third, they reformed Georgia's voting laws to make sure ballots were properly counted. In 2020, following a settlement between voting rights groups and the secretary of state's office, it was harder for election officials to throw out mail ballots for mismatched signatures, and voters had a chance to fix problems with their ballots after Election Day. The rejection rate for mail ballots fell from 3.4 percent in 2018 to just 0.2 percent in November.

Counties in metropolitan Atlanta processed absentee ballots more quickly and made their designs less confusing. When in 2019 the secretary of state removed from the rolls three hundred thousand voters who he claimed had died or moved, Fair Fight sued and reinstated twenty-two thousand voters who were still eligible to vote. A law restricting early voting locations to government buildings was repealed, allowing the Atlanta Hawks' arena to become a massive polling place in downtown Atlanta.

The electorate in 2020 was the one Abrams envisioned in 2018. The state saw its highest turnout in forty years. People of color made up nearly 40 percent of all voters, and Biden won roughly 70 percent of their votes. He improved on Abrams's margin in eight counties in metro Atlanta, building a remarkably diverse coalition of new voters, young voters, people of color, and moderate white suburbanites. Asian American turnout increased by 91 percent from 2016 to 2020, Latino turnout by 72 percent, and Black turnout by 20 percent, while white turnout grew by just 16 percent.

Abrams had argued for a decade that a diversifying electorate would allow Democrats to be competitive in Georgia, but numerous barriers to the ballot box had kept that electorate from fully forming. Now, years of determined organizing against voter suppression—which began with the founding of the New Georgia Project in 2013, accelerated with Abrams's campaign in 2018, and culminated in 2020—had created the conditions for Biden's upset victory.

Trump led in Georgia by eighty-seven thousand votes on Election Night, but his lead dwindled as absentee ballots were counted, with the president angrily tweeting, "STOP THE COUNT." Biden finally took the lead at 4 a.m. Friday morning as the remaining absentee ballots were tallied in Clayton County south of Atlanta, in a squat concrete building known as "the bunker."

Black Georgians found it poetic that the congressional district of the late John Lewis, which Trump had attacked in 2017 as "crime-infested" and "horrible," had put Biden over the top. "Could this be John Lewis looking down and giving Trump 'Good Trouble'?" tweeted the civil rights lawyer Ben Crump, who represented the family of George Floyd.

The next morning, after the networks officially called the race for

Biden, a jubilant crowd assembled at Freedom Park outside downtown Atlanta, near the John Lewis Freedom Parkway.

A "count every vote" rally became an impromptu Biden-Harris victory party, as voting rights activists danced the electric slide.

"Yesterday we were helping Georgians chase and cure their provisional ballots, all the way up until the deadline," said Nsé Ufot, the executive director of the New Georgia Project. "And tomorrow we're going to be knocking on doors and telling people how important the Senate race is and how important Georgia voters are to it. But today, today we celebrate."

The results weren't just a victory for Democrats in Georgia. They were a vindication of democracy in America. In the middle of an unprecedented pandemic, the country saw the highest turnout in a presidential election since 1900.

Just over a month later, Georgia's sixteen presidential electors gathered at the state capitol to finalize the outcome.

Nikema Williams, who had been elected to replace her mentor Lewis in Congress after serving as the first Black woman to lead the state Democratic Party, opened the meeting in the regal state senate chambers. Two years earlier, she had been arrested during a protest at the state capitol that challenged voter disenfranchisement in Abrams's race. Now she paid tribute to the voters who overcame hurdles to cast a ballot in 2020. "This moment," she said, "is for those voters who applied early for mail-in ballots or who waited in line for hours to make sure their voices were heard."

She called up Abrams to preside over the meeting. "This is a moment for me that I have dreamed about," she said.

The electors sat down and filled out their certificates. "I am pleased to announce that Joseph R. Biden has received 16 votes for president of the United States," Abrams said to cheers.

As she read the roll call for vice president, making Kamala Harris the first woman to hold the office, State Representative Calvin Smyre, the longest serving member of the Georgia legislature at seventy-three, called out, "I cast my vote for history."

It was one of those days that felt like a historical hinge point. The Electoral College results were finalized as the death toll from the pandemic topped three hundred thousand and the first COVID-19 vaccinations were given to frontline health care workers. Attorney General William Barr announced he would resign after challenging Trump's election fraud claims, and the Michigan congressman Paul Mitchell said he was leaving the Republican Party because he feared "long-term harm to our democracy." The Wisconsin Supreme Court rejected one of the last remaining legal challenges to the election results, blocking Trump's attempt to throw out votes cast solely in Madison and Milwaukee.

Biden spoke to the nation that evening. "In this battle for the soul of America, democracy prevailed," said the president-elect. "We the people voted, faith in our institutions held, the integrity of our elections remains intact."

But in the coming weeks, the legitimacy of those institutions would be tested like never before.

» » » » » »

The day after the Electoral College votes were certified, Biden traveled to Georgia to campaign for Warnock and Ossoff in runoff elections taking place on January 5. The state had helped deliver him the presidency. Now it would determine whether Democrats would control the Senate and could advance his ambitious agenda.

"You voted like your lives depended on it," Biden said at a train yard outside Atlanta that once housed the Brotherhood of Sleeping Car Porters, the nation's first Black-led labor union. "Well, guess what? Now you're going to have to do it again."

The Democratic candidates emphasized the high stakes of the races. "With these two Senate runoff elections to determine control of the United States Senate," said the thirty-three-year-old Ossoff, "you've got the young Jewish son of an immigrant mentored by John Lewis, running alongside a Black preacher who holds Dr. King's pulpit at Ebenezer Baptist Church, who pastored John Lewis." Warnock called their alliance, which harked back to the Black–Jewish civil rights coalition of the 1960s, "the new Georgia."

Although Democrats had the momentum after November, runoff elections in Georgia were designed specifically to prevent candidates like Warnock and Ossoff from being elected.

In 1917, after Georgia had instituted a poll tax, literacy test, grandfather clause, property qualification, and an all-white primary to disenfranchise Black voters, the state added an additional protection to maintain white supremacy. It created an arcane Electoral College–type system where statewide and congressional elections were decided not by the popular vote, but by the number of county units a candidate received. Each county in Georgia received twice as many unit votes as it had representatives in the lower state house. This system gave conservative rural areas far more power over state politics than more diverse and moderate urban areas.

Out of Georgia's 159 counties, 121 counties containing a minority of the population controlled nearly 60 percent of unit votes. By 1950, Georgia's three least-populous counties, containing 9,267 residents, had the same number of unit votes as Atlanta's Fulton County, with 473,572 residents. This empowered a series of white supremacist rural demagogues, such as Governor Eugene Talmadge, who declared in 1946, "this is a white man's country and we must keep it so." When asked how he would keep Blacks from the polls after a federal court struck down the state's all-white primary, Talmadge responded, "Pistols." Talmadge lost the popular vote in Georgia's Democratic primary that year to a more moderate white businessman from Atlanta by nearly three points but won the county unit vote by twenty-four points.

In 1963, however, the Supreme Court struck down the county unit system as part of its "one person, one vote" cases. State Representative Denmark Groover, a staunch segregationist from Macon, fretted that "all we have to have is a plurality and the Negroes and the pressure groups and special interests are going to manipulate this State and take charge." Groover had lost an election in 1958 when he carried the white vote but his opponent won Black ballots by a five-to-one margin. After returning to office four years later, he introduced a new system where no candidate could win without an outright majority of the vote, which would prevent the state's white majority from splintering. If no candidate reached 50 percent, a runoff would ensue, "as a means," Groover said, "of circumventing what is called the Negro bloc vote."

Ever since, the electorate in runoffs had been smaller, older, whiter, and more Republican than in the general election. Since the 1990s, Democrats had won only one of seven statewide runoffs in Georgia. In 1992 and 2008, Democratic US Senate candidates lost when turnout dropped more than 40 percent from the general election. In 2018, in the secretary of state race to replace Kemp, Democrat John Barrow trailed Republican Brad Raffensperger by just sixteen thousand votes in the general election. He lost the runoff by fifty-five thousand votes, with turnout only a third of that in November.

But after Biden's surprise victory, far more money, resources, and organizing power poured into Georgia than in past runoffs, with the specific goal of getting communities of color back to the polls. The New Georgia Project, which had registered five hundred thousand new voters since Abrams founded it, knocked on two million doors, texted three million voters, and made five million phone calls by the end of the runoff. Fair Fight recruited more volunteers for the runoff than it had in November and gave $22 million to grassroots groups working to register and mobilize voters of color. LaTosha Brown and her cofounder Cliff Albright traveled across the state in the "Blackest Bus in America" handing out voter registration and turnout materials in Black neighborhoods, alongside Thanksgiving turkeys and Christmas presents.

While young and Black voters were particularly deflated after Abrams's loss in 2018, Ufot said the November election had motivated them to turn out again. "Having the entire country wait with bated breath while Georgia's returns came in, having the margin be so small, and then confirmed in recount after recount, has done more than anything to combat the narrative that my vote doesn't matter," she said.

The Georgia Republican Party, meanwhile, was in a full-scale civil war. Trump began attacking Brian Kemp, who had been one of his closest allies in 2018 when the governor employed a series of voter suppression tactics against Abrams, almost immediately after the election for refusing to overturn the results, which the governor almost apologetically said he didn't have the power to do. "The governor's done nothing," Trump told Fox News. "He's done absolutely nothing. I'm ashamed that I endorsed him." He denounced Kemp on Twitter as "the hapless Governor of Georgia."

Georgia's two GOP senators, Kelly Loeffler and David Perdue, called on Secretary of State Raffensperger, who oversaw the count, to resign, and they backed the Texas lawsuit that sought to throw out the state's electoral votes. Fellow Republican senators, such as GOP leader Mitch McConnell, had refused to urge Trump to concede to Biden because they didn't want to alienate his red-meat base in Georgia during the runoffs. But that strategy backfired when Trump-allied lawyers Lin Wood and Sidney Powell, who worked closely with Giuliani, told Republicans not to vote for Perdue and Loeffler in the runoffs because the general election had been rigged.

"They have not earned your vote," Wood said at a rally in suburban Atlanta on December 2, where Trump voters chanted "lock him up" about Kemp. "Don't you give it to them. Why would you go back and vote in another rigged election, for god's sake?"

On January 5, 114,000 core GOP supporters who had voted in November skipped the runoffs. Warnock and Ossoff not only held their base, but expanded it.

Nearly fifty thousand Black voters who didn't vote in November cast their ballots during the runoffs. Turnout reached 92 percent of general election levels in precincts carried by Biden in November, compared with 88 percent in precincts carried by Trump, a record turnout for a runoff.

Once again it was Lewis's former congressional district that put Democrats over the top when the majority-Black DeKalb County in metro Atlanta reported its results, giving Warnock the lead around

11 p.m. and inching Ossoff ahead in the early hours of Wednesday morning.

When the networks called his race that night, Warnock had defeated a system designed to preserve white supremacy and had achieved a series of firsts: the first Black senator from Georgia, the first Black Democratic senator from the South, and the first Black senator to be elected with a majority-Black coalition.

Speaking from his home in Atlanta, Warnock paid tribute to his mother, Verlene, who had picked cotton in the summers in Waycross, Georgia, before raising twelve kids and becoming a preacher. "Because this is America," he said shortly after midnight, "the 82-year-old hands that used to pick somebody else's cotton went to the polls and picked her youngest son to be a United States senator."

He closed by remembering his father, Jonathan, who served in World War II and came home to Savannah in a public bus, dressed in his uniform, only to be told to give up his seat for a white teenager and move to the back of the bus. "He used to wake me up every morning at dawn," Warnock told his supporters. "It was morning. But it was still dark. It's dark right now. But morning comes."

Despite the jubilation Warnock experienced in the wee hours of the morning, there would be far more darkness than light as the day went on.

» » » » » »

January 6, 2021, was only the third day in Congress for Nikema Williams, but it was shaping up to be a busy one. She'd slept just two hours the night before, celebrating Warnock's win and doing countless media interviews.

Now she was preparing to give her first speech on the floor of the House of Representatives. Republican members of Georgia's congressional delegation were planning to challenge the certification of the state's Electoral College votes when Congress officially counted them, just days after Trump demanded in a phone call with Raffensperger that he "find 11,780 votes" to reverse Biden's victory. Williams was slated to rebut them. She wore blue for the occasion.

As one of those electors, this was personal for Williams. She was raised by her grandparents in rural Alabama, in a home with no indoor plumbing or running water. Her great-aunt Autherine Lucy had been the first Black student to attend the University of Alabama in 1956, where she was expelled after three weeks following white riots. The man she had replaced in Congress, John Lewis, had been brutally beaten while marching for voting rights in Selma, Alabama.

Williams planned to argue that the challenge to certifying Biden's victory in Georgia was the latest in a long line of voter suppression tactics targeting Black voters in the South. "I will be ready to defend our democracy and stand there in honor of Congressman Lewis," she said, "and fight to protect the vote of everyone who turned out and cast a vote in this historic election cycle."

She heard there might be protests in Washington, so she arrived at the Capitol complex early, figuring the heavily guarded area was the safest place for her to be. Ossoff's race was yet to be called, but the numbers looked promising. Another new member of her class, Representative Sara Jacobs of California, was planning to bring champagne over to her office for a toast. They started looking for cups. Then they received a text alert that their building was on lockdown.

» » » » » »

At 11 a.m., John Eastman took the stage at the "Save America" rally at the Ellipse, a large oval park south of the White House. Standing next to Rudy Giuliani, he wore a floppy brown hat, camel overcoat, and red paisley scarf, "looking every bit the Batman villain," wrote the *Los Angeles Times*.

Giuliani said that Eastman, "the professor," was there to explain "how [the Democrats] cheated" in the Georgia runoff "and how it was exactly the same as what they did on November 3rd."

The conspiracy theories about the election had only escalated since

Eastman had testified before the Georgia legislature a month earlier. "The old way" of voter fraud, he told tens of thousands of Trump supporters who had gathered near the National Mall, "was to have a bunch of ballots sitting in a box under the floor and when you needed more you pulled them out in the dark of night." Now, he alleged, "they put those ballots in a secret folder in the machines, sitting there waiting until they know how many they need." Giuliani flashed a thumbs-up.

Eastman had spent January 4 meeting with Vice President Mike Pence in the Oval Office, urging him to reject the state-level certification of Electoral College votes for Biden when he presided over the Senate, which had never been done before in US history. He had drafted a six-page memo outlining how Pence could unilaterally reject the votes or send them back to GOP-controlled legislatures to reverse the outcome. Pence and his aides said he had no power to do this, citing the ceremonial role of the vice president when Congress counted the results. A federal judge would later call Eastman's actions "a coup in search of a legal theory."

"All we are demanding of Vice President Pence is this afternoon, at 1 o'clock, he let the legislatures of the states look into this so we can get to the bottom of it and the American people know whether we have control of our government or not," Eastman said to loud cheers. Giuliani clapped and nodded approval.

Eastman became more animated as he spoke. "We no longer live in a self-governing republic if we can't get the answer to this question," he said, banging his fists on the lectern. "Anybody that is not willing to do it does not deserve to be in office!" Giuliani pumped his fist. "God bless you," he said as Eastman exited the stage.

Trump took the podium next, urging his supporters to march to the US Capitol. "You'll never take back our country with weakness," he said.

» » » » » »

Williams was finalizing her speech for the House debate when her husband, Leslie, who had worked for eight years as an aide to John

Lewis, called. "What's going on?" he asked her. "I'm watching C-SPAN and they just removed Speaker Pelosi from the chamber."

Williams turned on the TV and saw a man with a Confederate flag marching through the Capitol.

It belonged to Kevin Seefried, fifty-one, from Laurel, Delaware, who wore a black sweatshirt and tan Carhartt vest. He had a teardrop tattoo under his eye, a popular image among prison inmates. He had driven to Washington at 3 a.m. with his wife, his son, and his son's girlfriend, to attend the "Save America" rally. They had planned to leave after, but they heeded Trump's call to march to the Capitol.

At 2:13 p.m., he climbed into the Senate building after his twenty-one-year-old son, Hunter, punched through a glass window, one of the first fifteen rioters to enter the Capitol. He soon ran into US Capitol Police officer Eugene Goodman, a Black man greatly outnumbered by the almost entirely white mob.

Seefried jabbed his flagpole at Goodman to keep him back. "Where are the members at?" he shouted. "Where are they counting the votes?" When Goodman told Seefried to leave the area outside the Senate chamber, he responded defiantly, "You can shoot me, but we're coming in."

Seefried, who worked in construction and avidly subscribed to Trump's stolen election claims, brought the flag from his home in rural Delaware, a slave state that had fought with the Union in the Civil War after explicitly rejecting secession. He regarded it as "a symbol of an idealized view of Southern life and Southern heritage." It was the first time the rebel flag had been flown inside the Capitol. "We're taking back our country," he told Goodman.

Seefried was photographed walking mid-stride through the second floor of the Capitol next to two paintings. On his left was a portrait of the Massachusetts senator Charles Sumner, a fervent abolitionist who was brutally attacked with a cane by the South Carolina representative Preston Brooks for denouncing slavery during a speech on the Senate floor in 1856. Behind Seefried was a portrait of the Great Nullifier,

John Calhoun, the South's foremost defender of slavery, who called it not a "necessary evil" but a "positive good."

There, in one image, lay the fundamental tension throughout US history between white supremacy and multiracial democracy, made ever starker by an angry white mob storming the Capitol a day after the election of the first Black senator in Georgia.

Williams was gripped by fear. "I knew exactly what that symbol was meant to say to me—that white supremacists had taken over our Capitol," she said. "That I was in a place that they didn't want me to be."

As a Black woman representing Georgia, she feared for her life. She was instructed to go to a safe location, but hadn't been told where it was. A senior member of Congress told her staff they were supposed to communicate over walkie-talkies, but Williams's office never received any. There was a loudspeaker system in the Capitol, but it wasn't working in her office. She was supposed to have a panic button in case of emergency, but it hadn't been installed.

"I just sat there terrified," she said. She told her staff to move away from the windows, turn off the lights, and close the blinds. Her chief of staff disabled location sharing on her phone so no one could find them. Stacey Abrams called to make sure she was okay. Williams could hear rioters going door to door looking for members of Congress. "Every noise I heard, I thought it was someone coming to breach where we were," she said.

At 4:16 p.m., in between dueling speeches where Biden denounced "an unprecedented assault" on American democracy and Trump told his supporters "we had an election that was stolen from us," the media called the race for Ossoff, giving Democrats control of the Senate. This seismic moment was treated as an afterthought. Williams and Jacobs never got to do their toast.

"We are still on lockdown," Williams tweeted an hour later. "I'm still safe. Armed domestic terrorists stormed the US Capitol to stop the peaceful transfer of power in our Country. In America."

That evening, after police had finally cleared the building, Williams sat in the center aisle of the House chamber. The door behind her was shattered, a symbol of the worst attack on the Capitol since British soldiers had shelled the building during the War of 1812.

Now the threat to democracy came from within. Despite the violence, the Georgia GOP Representative Jody Hice, who earlier in the day had tweeted "this is our 1776 moment," moved ahead with a challenge to Georgia's results, citing an "unprecedented amount of fraud and irregularities." The Georgia representatives Rick Allen, Buddy Carter, and Marjorie Taylor Greene stood next to him.

But the GOP senator Kelly Loeffler, whom Warnock had defeated, withdrew her support for the objection, which needed to be seconded by at least one senator to proceed. "The events that transpired have forced me to reconsider, and I cannot now, in good conscience, object to the certification of these electors," a visibly shaken Loeffler said on the Senate floor, looking like she had seen a ghost.

Still, challenges to the election in Arizona and Pennsylvania were debated, with 65 percent of House Republicans voting to overturn the results. At 3:45 a.m., Pence affirmed Biden's victory. "Joseph R. Biden Jr. of the state of Delaware has received for President of the United States, 306 votes," he announced. "Donald J. Trump of the state of Florida has received 232 votes."

Williams returned home around 4 a.m. Her five-year-old son was asleep, but her husband had waited up. She embraced him, then sat down and cried.

» » » » » »

That Sunday, Warnock delivered a sermon from the pulpit of Ebenezer Baptist Church in Atlanta, where Martin Luther King Jr. had been baptized and eulogized.

A banner from the congregation congratulated him on his "historic Senate win." He hadn't said much since January 6, saving his thoughts for his weekly address, which he titled "God's victory over violence." Speaking before an empty sanctuary because of COVID,

wearing a black suit and turquoise tie, he showed a video of him celebrating in his office as he took the lead in the Senate race, jumping up
and down and hugging members of his campaign.

"Georgia had elected its first Black Senator and its first Jewish senator," Warnock said. "Then, as we were basking in the glory of all that
represented, it seemed like we could only have a few hours to celebrate.
Just as we were trying to put on our celebration shoes, the ugly side of
our story, our great and grand American story, began to emerge."

He then showed a video of the mob storming the Capitol.

"We saw the crude and the angry and the disrespectful and the violent break their way into the people's house, some carrying Confederate
flags—signs and symbols of an old world order passing away," he said.

He portrayed the juxtaposition of the events of January 5 and January 6 as a battle between two clashing Americas, a new multiracial
majority that was ascendant in states like Georgia versus an angry
conservative white minority that was resorting to increasingly extreme tactics as its longtime hold on power slipped away.

"I asked myself, Lord, why could we not just have a few hours to
bask in the glory of what God is doing?" Warnock said, his voice rising. "Here it is: the old world order is surely passing away. Those on the
other side of history are rising to take their place as equal members in
the human family . . . Because the old order is slipping away, sometimes it responds violently and desperately."

Throughout US history, gains for those communities that had been
excluded from the promise of American democracy had all too often
been followed by equally intense efforts to roll back that progress. That
was especially clear on January 6. "If you cut the head off a snake, it
shakes and moves violently, not because it is living, but because it is dying," Warnock said. "So there is both victory in this moment and there
is violence in this moment. There is fantastic opportunity and there is
fierce opposition."

Though the insurrection had been inspired by months of lies
about the election, the plan hatched by Georgia Republicans in early
December—to pass new restrictions on voting in response to those

falsehoods—moved forward. The "fierce opposition" to multiracial democracy had not diminished since the assault on the Capitol, but it had begun to take on more sophisticated, less visible forms that would receive far less attention than the insurrection itself.

On January 7, the Republican speaker of the Georgia House, David Ralston, announced at the state capitol that he was creating a new special committee on election integrity to rewrite the state's voting laws. "People are concerned," he told reporters, "and I think we have to speak to those concerns."

9

THE INSURRECTION THROUGH OTHER MEANS

On September 3, 1868, Henry McNeal Turner rose to speak in the Georgia House of Representatives to fight for his political survival. He was one of thirty-three new Black state legislators elected that year in Georgia, a revolutionary change in the South after 250 years of slavery. Eight hundred thousand Black voters had been registered across the region following the end of the Civil War, and the share of Black male Southerners who were eligible to vote skyrocketed from 0.5 percent in 1866 to 80.5 percent two years later.

These Black legislators had helped to write a new state constitution guaranteeing voting rights for former slaves. Yet just two months after the Fourteenth Amendment granted full citizenship rights to Black Americans, Georgia's white-dominated legislature introduced a bill to expel the Black lawmakers, arguing that the state's constitution protected their right to vote but not to hold office. "You bring both Congress and the Republican Party into odium in this state," said Joseph E. Brown, who had served as governor during the Confederacy years, when "you confer upon the Negroes the right to hold office . . . in their present condition."

Turner was shocked. Born free in South Carolina, he'd been appointed by Lincoln as the first Black chaplain in the Union Army. After the war, he settled in Macon, Georgia's fifth-largest city, where he was elected to the legislature. As a gesture of goodwill, he'd pushed to restore voting rights to ex-Confederates. But now white members of the legislature—both Democrats and Republicans—were turning on their Black colleagues.

"There are persons in this legislature today who are ready to spit their poison in my face, while they themselves opposed, with all their power, the ratification of this Constitution," Turner said in the House chamber. "They question my right to a seat in this body, to represent the people whose legal votes elected me. This objection, sir, is an unheard of monopoly of power."

His passionate speech would become a rallying cry for the civil rights movement one hundred years later. "Am I a man?" he asked. "If I am such, I claim the rights of a man. Am I not a man because I happen to be of a darker hue than honorable gentlemen around me?"

But his pleas went unheeded. The legislature voted to expel the Black lawmakers, who weren't even allowed to participate in the vote. "The sacred rights of my race," said Turner, were "destroyed at one blow." White members sat as the Black legislators exited the chamber, with Turner brushing dust off his feet, "in imitation of Christ." Soon he was getting death threats from the Ku Klux Klan. "We should neither be seized with astonishment or regret" if he were to be lynched, editorialized the *Weekly Sun* of Columbus, Georgia. Two weeks later, one of the ousted Black legislators, Philip Joiner, led a twenty-five-mile march from Albany to the small town of Camilla in southwest Georgia, where white residents opened fire, killing a dozen or more of the mostly Black marchers.

And so Reconstruction—the country's first attempt at multiracial democracy—all but ended in Georgia almost as soon as it began. Outraged Republicans in Washington attempted to reinstate it, putting the state under military rule again, purging ex-Confederates from the legislature, and giving Black members their seats back. Georgia became the last Southern state to rejoin the Union and one of the last to ratify the Fifteenth Amendment, which granted Black men the right to vote and prohibited the denial of voting rights based on race or color.

But in the 1870 election, Georgia's white majority united to reclaim the state and vote out the Black members again, backed up by KKK violence that kept many Black people from the polls. "There is not language in the vocabulary of hell strong enough to portray the outrages that have been perpetrated," Turner wrote to Massachusetts's Senator Charles Sumner. Five years after the war ended, ex-Confederates, known as Redeemers, had retaken Georgia. "The Southern whites will never consent to the government of the Negro," said the Democratic US senator Benjamin Hill. "Never!" Georgia became a blueprint for how white supremacy would be restored throughout the South.

One hundred and fifty years later, another Georgia legislator representing Macon rose to defend the rights Turner had fought for. Like Turner, the Democratic state senator David Lucas was an African Methodist Episcopal minister. In 1974, at just twenty-four, he became the first Black member of the legislature to represent Macon since Reconstruction. He was a product of the Second Reconstruction of the 1960s, when the country passed civil rights laws, including the Voting Rights Act, to restore multiracial democracy. With his colorful suits and Honda 750 motorcycle, he stood out among the good ol' boys in the state capitol.

On February 23, 2021, Lucas, now seventy-one, took to the Senate podium to oppose a new voter ID requirement for mail-in ballots introduced by Georgia Republicans. It no longer allowed voters to request a mail ballot online but instead required them to print a signed application, a cumbersome process for voters without access to a printer. In 2005, Republicans had specifically exempted mail-in ballots from the state's voter ID law, believing that more rural and elderly voters would be the ones casting them. But now they were changing the rules after the Black share of mail-in voters increased by eight points in 2020 and the white share fell by thirteen points.

The measure was one of fifty restrictive voting bills introduced by Georgia Republicans after the state went blue and Trump tried to overturn the results. "Every last one of these elections bills are about the election didn't turn out the way you wanted and you want to perpetuate the lie that Trump told you," Lucas said on the Senate floor.

Though Republicans had crafted the state's voting laws, the flood of bills took aim at every method that facilitated broad voter participation: eliminating automatic voter registration, ending the ability of any voter to cast a mail-in ballot, curtailing mail ballot drop boxes, cutting Sunday voting, even preventing nonprofit groups from giving food and water to voters who waited in long lines. "At the end of the day, many of these bills are reactionary to a three-month disinformation campaign that could have been prevented," said Raffensperger. Most of the bills were cosponsored by Republicans who backed Texas's unsuccessful lawsuit to throw out Georgia's election results.

While Georgia Republicans argued the goal was to "restore the confidence of our public in our election system," some party leaders let the true aim slip. "If we don't do something about voting by mail," Lindsey Graham said after the election, "we're going to lose the ability to elect a Republican in this country."

Lucas, the in-house historian of Georgia's Legislative Black Caucus, said the voter ID bill before the legislature that day "reminds me of the election of 1876." He told the story of the disputed presidential contest, marred by white supremacist violence during America's centennial, that culminated in President Rutherford B. Hayes ordering the withdrawal of federal troops that were guarding the statehouses in Louisiana and South Carolina, marking the end of Reconstruction. (The troops did not leave the South entirely, as is commonly alleged, but returned to their home barracks and stopped protecting Black voting rights.) "When they pulled out the federal troops," said Lucas, "that's when we had Jim Crow and folks got lynched."

This history was personal for Lucas. When he was thirteen and playing four square with friends, the police picked him up and falsely accused him of throwing a rock through a white driver's windshield. They took him to a convenience store, where the driver got in the back of the police car, placed a gun to his head, "and told me he'd kill me," Lucas said. Later, as a student at Tuskegee University, he worked on the campaigns of the first Black legislators elected in Alabama since Reconstruction and helped a Black professor of political science register Black voters in the area. As he canvassed small-town dusty roads, white men in pickup trucks would drive by with shotguns and ask him, "Why are you registering folks to vote?"

After forty-five years in office, he told his colleagues, he couldn't believe he still had to defend his right to vote. What should have been the country's most fundamental democratic principle remained the most contested. "I will not go home and tell those folks who voted that I took away the right for you to vote," Lucas vowed on the Senate floor, wiping away tears with a white handkerchief.

Lucas invoked the history of Reconstruction for good reason: the overthrow of multiracial democracy in the South was a stark reminder of how quickly hard-won rights, even when enshrined in the Constitution, could be effectively nullified. The Second Reconstruction that began in the 1960s was marked by long, slow advancement that reached a peak in 2020, when Black voters in Georgia turned out in record numbers to elect the state's first Black and Jewish US senators. "After I finished crying, I was just so elated, that Georgia stands alone in the South," said the state representative Al Williams, who marched from Selma to Montgomery with John Lewis and was arrested seventeen times during the civil rights movement. "A Jewish guy and a Black Baptist preacher—who would have ever thought it?"

But the white backlash that followed those victories—an attempt to overturn the election, an insurrection at the US Capitol, a record number of bills to restrict voting rights—had all the makings of a concerted attempt to end the Second Reconstruction. The same pattern that existed during Reconstruction—the enfranchisement of Black voters, followed by the manipulation of election laws to throw out Black votes, culminating in laws passed to legally disenfranchise Black voters—was repeating itself.

Once again, the party of white grievance was rewriting the rules of American democracy to protect itself from the rising influence of new demographic groups. "Nobody's putting in a literacy test, nobody's putting in a poll tax," said Yale University historian David Blight, a leading scholar of Reconstruction. "But there are all kinds of ways for

how to just restrict voting this time. Rather than utter disfranchisement, they are obviously going for: Knock off 5 percent of the Black
vote, and you can once again win Georgia."

» » » » » »

On March 23, 2021, three days before the Georgia legislature would
pass a sweeping bill rolling back access to the ballot, Jessica Anderson,
the executive director of Heritage Action for America, met with Brian
Kemp and urged him to quickly sign the legislation when it reached
his desk. She was a thirty-five-year-old former Trump administration
official in the Office of Management and Budget with long blond hair
and an attack-dog personality.

"I had one message for him," Anderson, who led the sister organization to the Heritage Foundation, one of the country's most influential conservative think tanks, recounted to top donors during an
exclusive retreat in Tucson, Arizona, a month later. "Do not wait to
sign that bill. If you wait even an hour, you will look weak. This bill
needs to be signed immediately."

Kemp followed Anderson's advice, announcing the signing of the
"Election Integrity Act" an hour after its passage from his office in the
state capitol.

Though Kemp had resisted Trump's attempt to overturn the election by certifying the 2020 results, he eagerly embraced the effort to
rewrite Georgia's voting laws in the months that followed. "There's
no doubt there were many alarming issues with how the election was
handled," the governor said, echoing the disinformation spread by
Trump, "and those problems, understandably, led to the crisis of confidence in the ballot box here in Georgia."

Nearly six minutes in, he abruptly stopped his speech. "What's the
problem?" he asked an aide.

Park Cannon, a young Black Democratic state representative who
represented a historic section of downtown Atlanta that included

Ebenezer Baptist Church, had gathered with a group of voting rights activists outside Kemp's office.

"The governor is signing a bill that affects all Georgians," said Tamara Stevens, a former Republican who had joined daily protests against the bill at the capitol for nearly a month. "Why is he doing it in private and why is he trying to keep elected officials who are representing us out of the process?"

When Cannon knocked on the governor's door demanding to see the signing, two white Georgia state patrol troopers told her, "You're under arrest." They grabbed her arms, put her in handcuffs, and forcefully dragged her from the statehouse.

"Why am I under arrest?" she pleaded with the officers. "There is no reason for me to be arrested, I'm a legislator. Do not touch me."

She was taken to Fulton County jail and charged with two felonies, in a scene that recalled the brutal crackdowns against civil rights activists during the Jim Crow era.

Warnock, who was Cannon's pastor, visited the jail close to 11 p.m. as a crowd of supporters chanted, "Let her go!"

"What we have witnessed today," he told reporters, "is a desperate attempt to lock out and squeeze the people out of their own democracy."

As Cannon was detained, Kemp signed the bill alongside six white male Republican lawmakers, under a painting of a slave plantation. "If you don't like being called a racist or Jim Crow, then stop acting like one," Democratic state senator Nikki Merritt told her Republican colleagues. Abrams called the law "Jim Crow in a suit and tie."

Facing sustained protests at the capitol from voting rights groups and criticism of the bill from some of the state's largest companies, including Delta Airlines, Georgia Republicans backed away from a handful of the most extreme proposals, such as eliminating automatic voter registration, no-excuse absentee voting, and Sunday voting. But the final bill, known as SB 202, still included sixteen provisions that restricted ballot access, and at the eleventh hour new sections were added giving the legislature more control over how elections were run to entrench their power through more obscure means.

The legislature removed Raffensperger, the most vocal Republican to defend the 2020 election results, as chair and voting member of the state election board, which oversaw the certification of elections, and gave itself the power to appoint a majority of the board's members. The state election board, in turn, had new authority to take over county election boards it viewed as "underperforming," raising the possibility that election officials appointed by and beholden to the heavily gerry-mandered legislature could take over voting operations in Democratic strongholds. These changes could make it easier for GOP officials to decline to certify close elections, exactly what Trump had tried and failed to pull off in 2020.

What voting rights groups didn't realize at the time was how the most powerful groups in the conservative movement had orchestrated the passage of the bill behind the scenes, using it as a template to re-write voting laws nationwide. Anderson told donors that Heritage Action had crafted key parts of the Georgia law and was doing the same with similar bills for Republican state legislators across the country. "In some cases, we actually draft them for them," she said at a Ritz-Carlton perched in the hills of the Sonoran Desert, "or we have a sentinel on our behalf give them the model legislation so it has that grassroots, from-the-bottom-up type of vibe."

The Georgia law had "eight key provisions that Heritage recom-mended," Anderson said, including policies severely restricting mail ballot drop boxes, preventing election officials from sending absentee ballot request forms to voters, making it easier for partisan workers to monitor the polls, preventing the collection of mail ballots, and restricting the ability of counties to accept donations from nonprofit groups seeking to aid in election administration. All of these rec-ommendations came straight from Heritage's list of "best practices" drafted that February. With Heritage's help, Anderson said, Georgia became a "model for the rest of the country."

By the time Kemp had signed SB 202, more than 350 restrictive

voting laws had been introduced in forty-seven states, the most concentrated attempt to roll back ballot access since the Voting Rights Act
had passed in 1965, eclipsing the wave of antivoter bills that passed
after the 2010 election in depth and breadth. It was no coincidence
that so many GOP-controlled states—from Georgia to Florida to
Arizona—were rushing to pass similar pieces of legislation in such a
short period of time. In Wisconsin, Scott Walker said after the election that "state lawmakers have to take action to restore integrity to
the voting process" and called for mail ballots to be limited only to
people in nursing homes and members of the military, even though
he'd voted by mail in six of the previous eight elections. Wisconsin
Republicans responded by passing a series of bills that made it more
difficult to obtain and return mail ballots, tightened voter ID requirements, banned private grants to election offices, and gave the heavily gerrymandered legislature more power over how elections were
administered.

Republican legislators claimed they were simply tightening up
election procedures to address concerns about fraud in the 2020 election. But Anderson's comments revealed how a group of conservative
insiders who had been pushing for restrictions on voting for decades
had capitalized on Trump's baseless claims about the 2020 election to
finally get them passed. Assisting these efforts, Kobach had become
general counsel for a new conservative group, Alliance for Free Citizens, that drafted model legislation promoting proof-of-citizenship
laws for voter registration and reducing access to mail ballots. Some
of the leading figures who had tried to overturn the election quickly
pivoted to this new fight; the Claremont Institute president, Ryan Williams, said that John Eastman was "still very involved with a lot of the
state legislators and advising them on election integrity stuff."

To "create this echo chamber," as Anderson put it, Heritage was
spending $24 million over two years in eight battleground states—
Arizona, Michigan, Florida, Georgia, Iowa, Nevada, Texas, and Wisconsin—to pass and defend restrictive voting legislation. Every Tuesday
the group led a call with right-wing advocacy groups like the Susan B.

Anthony List, Tea Party Patriots, and Freedom Works to coordinate the efforts at the highest levels of the conservative movement. "We literally give marching orders for the week ahead," Anderson said. "All so we're singing from the same song sheet of the goals for that week and where the state bills are across the country."

Though the bills had been sold as advancing "election integrity," they were aimed more at helping GOP candidates take back power. "We are going to take the fierce fire that is in every single one of our bellies," Anderson told the donors, "to right the wrongs of November."

The forces behind the drive to rewrite the country's voting laws were leading the push to entrench minority rule on multiple fronts: not just restricting access to the ballot, but transforming the courts, undercutting the census, drawing new gerrymandered maps, reducing the size of the country's nonwhite population, and reshaping the election system. Trump's delegitimization of the electoral process gave Republicans a sweeping opening to redefine core democratic institutions and limit who could exercise basic democratic rights. After their success in Wisconsin, they made Georgia a new laboratory for oligarchy.

》 》 》 》 》 》

"There is a clear national need for a Republican conservative counterpart to [the] Brookings [Institution]," Pat Buchanan wrote in a memo to Nixon in 1970, "which can generate the ideas Republicans can use." Three years later, the Heritage Foundation was cofounded by Paul Weyrich, a pugnacious activist from Wisconsin and admirer of Barry Goldwater on a mission to create a conservative power structure that would rival the more liberal think tanks that dominated Washington at the time.

Weyrich, who was also Heritage's first president, went on to cofound the American Legislative Exchange Council (ALEC), which paired corporations with conservative state legislators to draft model legislation, and the Moral Majority with Jerry Falwell, which mobilized evangelical voters behind GOP causes and candidates. Heritage received major funding from leading right-wing donors such as Charles and David Koch, the Bradley Foundation, Richard Mellon Scaife, and Joseph Coors. Weyrich, a dogged behind-the-scenes organizer, became known as "the Lenin of social conservatism."

Speaking in 1980 at a meeting of fifteen thousand evangelical Christians supporting Reagan in Dallas, Weyrich bluntly articulated his radical views on voting rights. "I don't want everybody to vote," he said. "Elections are not won by a majority of the people. They never have been from the beginning of our country and they are not now. As a matter of fact, our leverage in the elections quite candidly goes up as the voting populace goes down." Those words became a mantra for conservative activists who sought to discourage broad participation in the political process.

In the years since, the Heritage Foundation became the driving force behind much of the Republican Party agenda, claiming that two-thirds of its policy recommendations were enacted under the presidencies of Reagan and Trump.

In 2010, as opposition on the right to the Obama administration reached a fever pitch, Heritage launched Heritage Action, a dark money group that did not have to disclose its donors but received at least $500,000 from the Koch brothers. The goal was to connect the Heritage Foundation to the growing Tea Party movement and to enable the group to undertake more aggressive political activities, such as leading opposition to the Affordable Care Act and promoting a government shutdown in 2013. This right-wing advocacy alienated some Republicans on Capitol Hill, with the former Oklahoma senator Tom Coburn accusing the group of "destroying the Republican Party."

The former Heritage Foundation president Jim DeMint described the relationship between the Heritage Foundation and Heritage Action as "the one-two punch." The foundation wrote the policy, and Heritage Action turned it into law.

At the Arizona event, Jessica Anderson introduced Heritage Foundation fellow Hans von Spakovsky as the mastermind behind the nationwide push to restrict voting rights. He had spent two decades aggressively promoting in GOP circles the myth of widespread voter fraud.

During the George W. Bush administration, von Spakovsky was a special counsel at the Justice Department's Civil Rights Division, where he played a key role in the department's approval of a 2005 voter ID law from Georgia—among the first of its kind—over objections from career department lawyers, who found it to be discriminatory. While advocating internally for the law, von Spakovsky published a law review article under the pseudonym "Publius" praising voter ID laws, in a move that experts said violated Justice Department ethics guidelines.

"It's like he goes to bed dreaming about this, and gets up in the morning wondering, 'What can I do today to make it *more* difficult for people to vote?'" John Lewis once said of von Spakovsky.

In 2017, von Spakovsky was one of the driving forces behind Trump's ill-fated Commission on Election Integrity. He argued the commission should exclude Democrats and "mainstream Republican officials and/or academics," and helped Kobach draft the controversial letter requesting sensitive voter data from all fifty states.

Though Anderson called von Spakovsky "the premier election law expert across this country," his work had not fared well in court. During a trial challenging Kansas's proof-of-citizenship law for voter registration, Kobach hired von Spakovsky to support his claim that votes by noncitizens had swung US elections. But under questioning, von Spakovsky admitted he couldn't name a single election where noncitizen voting had decided the outcome. A federal judge, in striking down the law, wrote that the court gave "little weight to Mr. von Spakovsky's opinion," citing "several misleading and unsupported examples of noncitizen voter registration."

Nonetheless, von Spakovsky's sensationalist claims about stolen elections and advocacy for policies that restricted voting had found an increasingly receptive audience among Republicans following Trump's attempt to overturn the 2020 election.

"The one good thing that came out of last year's elections," von

Spakovsky said at the Heritage Action event in April, "is I think finally a lot of members of the public, and particularly state legislators,
realized that these vulnerabilities exist, have existed for a long time
and have figured out in many states we really need to do something
to fix it."

» » » » » »

On July 30, 2020, as Trump tweeted that he might try to delay the presidential election because of "INACCURATE & FRAUDULENT" mail
voting, many of the country's leading preachers, activists, and politicians gathered at Ebenezer Baptist Church for the funeral of John
Lewis, who had passed away from pancreatic cancer at eighty years old.

The organist played "We Shall Overcome" as the dignitaries, including dozens of members of Congress wearing masks that said
"Good Trouble," filed in. Sitting in the pews were three former US
presidents: Clinton, Bush, and Obama. Warnock, dressed in a Kente
cloth–trimmed minister's robe, welcomed them to "America's freedom church."

Lewis's family, aides, and friends—including Speaker of the House
Nancy Pelosi and Bernice King, the youngest child of Martin Luther
King Jr.—recounted his incredible life story: how he grew up the son
of sharecroppers in the Black Belt of Alabama, heard King on the radio, and began preaching to his chickens. How he took part in nearly
every major event of the civil rights movement: the sit-ins that integrated lunch counters; the Freedom Rides that desegregated interstate bus travel; the March on Washington, where he was the youngest
speaker; the "Bloody Sunday" march in Selma that led to the passage
of the Voting Rights Act, which he led. How, in the five decades since,
he'd become the moral voice of the Congress, a winner of the Presidential Medal of Freedom, and the country's most ardent defender of
democracy.

"He loved America," Warnock said, "until America learned to love
him back."

The night before, Warnock had thought about what Lewis must have been feeling when he crossed the Edmund Pettus Bridge in Selma and saw a sea of Alabama state troopers waiting for him. "He had no reason, really, to think that he could win," Warnock said. "I think we look back on the victories of the civil rights movement as if they were inevitable, when they were actually quite improbable."

Three hours in, Warnock invited Obama to deliver the closing eulogy. But the first Black president, standing a few feet above the flag-draped casket, didn't just want to reminisce about Lewis's life or issue yet another statement praising him as a hero. He wanted the Congress to counter the attacks on voting rights and the gutting of the Voting Rights Act that Lewis had spent the last years of his life fighting against.

"You want to honor John?" he asked. "Let's honor him by revitalizing the law that he was willing to die for." The congregants stood and cheered.

"Naming it the John Lewis Voting Rights Act is a fine tribute," Obama said. "But John wouldn't want us to stop there." He called for policies like automatic voter registration, expanding early voting, banning partisan gerrymandering, and admitting Washington, DC, and Puerto Rico as new states to create a more representative government and participatory democracy. "And if all this takes eliminating the filibuster—another Jim Crow relic—in order to secure the God-given rights of every American, then that's what we should do," he said emphatically.

Obama gave Warnock an elbow bump as he stepped down from the lectern. Warnock put his hand on Lewis's casket, bowed his head, and said a final prayer. Lewis's body was taken to South-View Cemetery in Atlanta, founded by former slaves in 1866 so that Black Atlantans could have a burial ground of their own when whites would not accept them.

Many of the policies highlighted by Obama were included in two bills championed by Lewis—the For the People Act and another bill to restore the Voting Rights Act—that had passed the Democratic-controlled House a year earlier but were never taken up by the

GOP-controlled Senate. Even after Lewis's passing, when tributes to his life poured in across America, these ambitious reforms appeared doomed with Republicans in control of much of Washington.

Warnock was a preacher that day, not a candidate for Senate. But after Biden's victory and his party's improbable wins in Georgia a few months later, suddenly the unthinkable seemed possible, and Warnock dedicated the next year to making Lewis's unfinished work a reality.

» » » » » »

On March 17, 2021, a week before Georgia passed SB 202, Warnock gave his first major speech on the floor of the US Senate.

"We elected Georgia's first African American and Jewish senator, and, hours later, the Capitol was assaulted," Warnock told his colleagues. "We see in just a few precious hours the tension very much alive in the soul of America."

When he was born in 1969 in the projects of Savannah, Warnock said, Georgia still had two arch-segregationist senators, Richard B. Russell and Herman E. Talmadge, the son of the former governor Eugene Talmadge. After the Supreme Court's 1954 *Brown v. Board of Education* decision, Talmadge predicted that "blood will run in the streets of Atlanta" if schools were desegregated. He didn't vote for a single civil rights bill during his twenty-three years in the Senate.

Warnock noted that he now held the Senate seat "where Herman E. Talmadge sat." That was progress, but the immediate backlash to his election showed just how entrenched the reactionary forces in American politics had become. Once again, his home state was at the center of a heated national debate over voter suppression. "We are witnessing right now a massive and unabashed assault on voting rights unlike anything we have seen since the Jim Crow era," he said, pointing to the hundreds of restrictive bills championed by the likes of Heritage Action. "This is Jim Crow in new clothes."

When Lyndon Johnson signed the Voting Rights Act to outlaw Jim Crow–era voter suppression tactics, he compared it to the last battle over slavery, to redress not just the country's original sin, but the failed hope of Reconstruction. The defeat of the Confederacy was "an American victory but also a Negro victory," Johnson said. "Yet for almost a century, the promise of that day was not fulfilled."

Warnock said he thought often about what would have happened if the Voting Rights Act had not passed in 1965, if the country had not intervened to enforce the Fifteenth Amendment after it had been ignored for so many years. "If we had not acted in 1965, what would our country look like?" he asked his fellow senators. "Surely, I would not be sitting here. Only the eleventh Black senator in the history of our country. And the first Black senator in Georgia. And maybe that's the point."

That day, Democratic senators had reintroduced the For the People Act, known as HR 1, which contained many of the pro-voter reforms Obama had highlighted at Lewis's funeral: nationwide automatic and Election Day registration, two weeks of early voting in every state, guaranteed access to vote-by-mail, prohibitions on discriminatory voter purging and voter ID laws, and a ban on partisan gerrymandering for congressional elections. It would counter the restrictive voting laws passed in states like Georgia and represent the largest expansion of voting access since the Voting Rights Act. Though the debate over voting rights had become increasingly partisan, polls showed that nearly 70 percent of the public supported the bill. "Much of what HR 1 is trying to do is restore majority rule in America," said the Maryland congressman John Sarbanes, the chief sponsor of the bill in the House, which had passed it in early March.

Yet it faced formidable obstacles in the Senate. Republican senators unanimously opposed the bill, with Senator Ted Cruz of Texas calling it "the single most dangerous piece of legislation before Congress." Given this GOP intransigence, Warnock urged Democrats to approve the bill with a simple majority vote, rather than the sixty votes required to overcome the filibuster and pass most legislation, a bold proposal opposed by at least two Democratic moderates, Joe Manchin of West Virginia and Kyrsten Sinema of Arizona, along with President Biden, whom Warnock called after his speech.

"This issue—access to voting and preempting politicians' efforts to restrict voting—is so fundamental to our democracy that it is too important to be held hostage by a Senate rule," Warnock argued as he closed his remarks. "It is a contradiction to say we must protect minority rights in the Senate while refusing to protect minority rights in the society."

» » » » » »

On a Sunday in early July 2021, the Texas state representative Celia Israel, a Democrat from Austin, was attending a dress fitting with her longtime partner and preparing for their wedding on the floor of the Texas House in a few days when she received a text from State Representative Gina Hinojosa that they needed to speak urgently.

"Are you in jail?" Israel asked her.

"No," Hinojosa responded. "I hate to tell you this, but your wedding isn't going happen on Thursday."

A day later, Israel was on one of two charter flights with fifty of her Democratic colleagues. They were fleeing the state to prevent Texas Republicans from assembling the quorum necessary to pass a sweeping package of voting restrictions that went even further than Georgia's law.

Their destination: Washington, DC, where they hoped to persuade the Congress to pass the For the People Act and the John Lewis Voting Rights Act.

"We are going to use that time to plead with our friends and allies and leaders in the Congress that the time is now," Democratic caucus chair Chris Turner said when the planes arrived at Dulles International Airport that evening. "You must pass strong federal voter protection legislation."

Texas was already the most difficult state in the country to vote in. Only those who were over sixty-five years old, out of town during in-person voting, or had a medical condition that kept them from the polls (COVID-19 didn't count) could qualify for a mail ballot. Under the state's voter ID law, a handgun permit was an acceptable form of identification to cast a ballot but a student ID was not. There was no online registration, and grassroots voter registration drives were nearly impossible, which explained why Texas had three million unregistered voters, who were overwhelmingly younger people of color, far more than any other state.

Texas had become a majority-minority state in 2004 and its demographics suggested it should be as competitive as Georgia. But the state's strict limits on ballot access prevented the state's population changes from transforming the electorate and kept power firmly in the hands of conservative white Republicans.

Now, even though Trump had carried the state by six points, Texas Republicans were seeking to put in place even tougher restrictions on voting: "the Election Integrity Protection Act of 2021" repealed the methods used in Houston's Harris County, the state's largest area, to increase voter turnout in 2020, such as drive-thru voting and extended voting hours. It banned all mail ballot drop boxes, added new ID requirements for mail ballots, cut Sunday voting, granted "free movement" to partisan poll watchers when votes were being cast and counted, and made it a felony for election officials to send unsolicited mail ballot applications to voters. Heritage Action took credit for "19 provisions" in the bill.

Most notably, the act, which was sponsored by a Republican from exurban Houston who had traveled to Pennsylvania after the election to help Trump challenge the election results, made it easier to overturn future elections. The losing candidate would no longer have to prove before a court that individual fraudulent votes had swung an election but rather that the number of allegedly fraudulent votes could have exceeded the margin of victory, precisely what Trump had argued in 2020. The introduction to the bill said it was intended to preserve "the purity of the ballot box," the exact language used by Congress when it repealed the Reconstruction enforcement laws in 1893.

To Texas Democrats, this was not a coincidence.

Back in August 1890, the surviving ex-Confederate leaders in Mississippi had convened in the state capitol of Jackson to draft a new state constitution that would disenfranchise Black voters once and for all. Mississippi had a Black majority, but the state's conservative white leaders sought to ensure permanent control.

"We want to make a government of the correct political majority," said the Mississippi Democratic senator James Z. George, a Confederate brigadier general who held the former seat of Jefferson Davis. "Good government in Mississippi can only come from the predominance of influence and political power in the white race."

The constitutional convention established a dizzying array of devices to eliminate Black suffrage, including a poll tax and the disqualification of prospective voters who committed minor crimes like "obtaining goods under false pretenses," offenses for which Black people were disproportionately charged. The centerpiece of the plan was a requirement that any voter "be able to read any section of the Constitution of this State; or he shall be able to understand the same when read to him, or give a reasonable interpretation thereof." This "understanding clause" gave local white election officials enormous power to turn away Black voters, while permitting local whites who might fail such a test to vote regardless.

Republicans in Congress—at the time the party of civil rights— followed the Mississippi convention with outrage. That summer, the House of Representatives passed a bill sponsored by the Massachusetts representative Henry Cabot Lodge, a protégé of Charles Sumner, empowering federal supervisors to oversee registration, voting, and ballot counting in the South and giving federal judges the power to invalidate fraudulent election results. "The Government which made the Black man a citizen of the United States is bound to protect him in his rights as a citizen of the United States, and it is a cowardly Government if it does not do it!" Lodge said.

Senate Republicans vowed to approve the Lodge bill. Senator John Ingalls of Kansas, addressing Senator George directly, placed dozens of newspaper articles from Mississippi in the *Congressional Record* and read aloud from a *Jackson Clarion Ledger* story where delegates boasted of securing "to the white race a fixed and permanent majority."

Because Republicans controlled the Senate, Democrats staged a dramatic filibuster—the first of many Southern-led efforts to kill civil rights legislation—giving exhaustive speeches and using a variety of procedural delays to derail the bill. They eventually persuaded a group of western Republicans from sparsely populated mining states who feared the expansion of suffrage to Chinese immigrants and wanted to focus instead on economic benefits for their region to join them in killing the bill in early 1891.

Following the bill's defeat, Democrats suppressed the Black vote so efficiently that they gained unified control of the federal government in 1893 for the first time since before the Civil War. They promptly repealed the laws that had been used to enforce Reconstruction and protect Black suffrage, bidding goodbye to what the Mississippi congressman Hernando Money called "an offensive theory of majority rule."

"Let every trace of the reconstruction measures be wiped from the statute books; let the States of this great Union understand that the elections are in their own hands," House Democrats wrote in an 1893 report. "Responding to a universal sentiment throughout the country for greater purity in elections many of our States have enacted laws to protect the voter and to purify the ballot."

Following the adoption of the Mississippi plan and failure of the Lodge bill, by 1907 every Southern state had changed its constitution to disenfranchise Black voters. By the early 1900s, only 7 percent of Black residents were registered to vote in seven Southern states and Black turnout fell from 61 percent of the voting-age population in 1880 to just 2 percent in 1912.

When the Texas legislature first debated the new voting restrictions in May 2021, the Democratic state representative Rafael Anchia referenced the language from the end of Reconstruction. "Did you know that this purity of the ballot box justification was used during the Jim Crow era to prevent Black people from voting?" he asked his GOP colleagues.

That month, Democrats blocked the bill for the first time, staging a covert walkout of the House chamber ahead of a midnight deadline to pass it before the legislative session ended on Memorial Day weekend. After the Texas governor, Greg Abbott, called a new special legislative session to approve the bill, Democrats formulated the risky idea of fleeing to Washington, leaving their families on a day's notice and defying arrest warrants issued by state authorities back home.

A day after Texas Democrats arrived in Washington, Biden traveled to the National Constitution Center in Philadelphia to deliver his most extensive condemnation of the GOP-backed laws making it harder to vote.

"We're facing the most significant test of our democracy since the Civil War," the president said, surrounded by images of Benjamin Franklin and quotes from Daniel Webster and Theodore Roosevelt. He framed the choice facing the nation as "democracy or autocracy."

Though Biden called passage of the For the People Act "a national imperative," missing from his impassioned remarks, much to the chagrin of voting rights supporters, was any mention of the filibuster, which Republicans had used to prevent Democrats from bringing the bill to the Senate floor a few weeks earlier. Biden refrained from laying out a plan to pass the legislation, only saying, "we have to be clear-eyed about the obstruction we face."

An hour after Biden's remarks concluded, Texas Democrats met with Vice President Kamala Harris at the office of the American Federation for Teachers near Capitol Hill. She compared their actions to Frederick Douglass appealing to the Congress to pass the Fifteenth Amendment in 1867 and women marching down Pennsylvania Avenue in 1913 for the right to vote.

Yet in the weeks that followed, as Texas Democrats crisscrossed the offices of members of Congress, they failed to secure a meeting with the president.

"He won't meet with us on Zoom like this, and I'm trying to be tactful, but I don't know how else to say it, man," State Representative Richard Peña Raymond of Laredo told the US representative Lloyd Doggett of Austin in a moment of frustration. "I'm just pissed off at this point. He doesn't give us the respect the way you have."

A few weeks after his speech in Philadelphia, Biden attended a town hall hosted by CNN in Cincinnati, Ohio. Despite his address on voting rights, the president had spent the summer focused on passing the infrastructure and social spending bills (Build Back Better) that were the centerpiece of his domestic agenda. He said he agreed with Obama that the filibuster was a "relic of the Jim Crow era" and its abuse was "pretty overwhelming." But if the Senate scrapped it, Biden said, it would "throw the entire Congress into chaos and nothing will get done."

» » » » » »

As the White House prioritized preserving the filibuster over passing voting rights legislation, Republicans launched an all-out campaign to kill the For the People Act.

Heritage Action led the conservative coalition opposing the bill. "HR 1 is basically the dream bill of every left-wing advocacy group we've been fighting against for years on election issues," von Spakovsky said at the group's donor event in April.

At the beginning of the year Heritage put out "a short summary of the worst provisions" of the bill, he said. "Now, you all know congressional staffers don't like reading 900-page bills. That fact sheet we put out is being used by congressional staffers, members of Congress, to go up and fight HR 1." The group dubbed the bill the "Corrupt Politicians Act," a label that was soon being used by leading Republicans like Ted Cruz.

"We've made sure that every single member of Congress knows just how bad the bill is," Jessica Anderson added. "Then we've made sure there's an echo chamber of support around these senators driven by your Heritage Action activists and sentinels across the country where we've driven hundreds of thousands of calls, emails, placed letters to the editor, hosted events, and run television and digital ads."

The group focused particular attention on Manchin, organizing a rally in West Virginia in March urging him to "stand up for WV values," even as it bused in conservative activists from states hundreds of miles away. After having "a bit of fun with Manchin," Anderson told donors, the group ran ads urging vulnerable Democratic senators to preserve the filibuster to block the bill.

Anderson described the fight in existential terms. "It's an all-hands-on-deck moment," she said in April. "If we don't win this, we lose our republic, period."

That same month, Kobach announced his campaign for Kansas attorney general, citing his opposition to HR 1. "If the Biden Administration tries to nationalize our election laws and stops us from using photo ID in Kansas, they will have to get through me first," he said at a launch event outside the old Sedgwick County Courthouse in Wichita.

Manchin had cosponsored the For the People Act in the previous session of Congress. But in June 2021, he announced that he no longer supported it. He called the right to vote "fundamental to our American democracy" but wrote that "protecting that right . . . should never be done in a partisan manner."

Manchin's position ignored how landmark legislation securing voting rights, such as the Fourteenth and Fifteenth Amendments, had passed on party-line votes. His red line also created a fundamental asymmetry between the parties, with state-level Republicans using party-line majorities to undermine voting rights while Democrats in the Senate were unable to protect voting rights in the same manner.

Madison's fear of a Senate dominated by small states was personified by Manchin. He hailed from one of the smallest and whitest states in the country, one of only three to lose population over the previous decade, largely because of its reliance on a fading coal industry. Though Manchin represented just 0.5 percent of the country's population, as the last conservative Democrat in a deep red state, he was able to almost single-handedly dictate the priorities of a 50-50 Senate.

Manchin's support for the filibuster intensified the countermajoritarian bias of the Senate, allowing a small minority of senators to block bills supported by large bipartisan majorities. Ironically, Manchin had firsthand experience with this.

After the 2012 Sandy Hook Elementary School shooting, he sponsored bipartisan legislation with the Pennsylvania Republican Pat Toomey requiring background checks for gun sales. Eighty-six percent of Americans supported the bill, but it was blocked by senators who represented just 38 percent of the country. The fifty-four senators supporting Manchin-Toomey represented 76 million more Americans than the forty-six senators opposing it. After the vote, President Obama slammed "this continuing distortion of Senate rules," but Manchin didn't abandon his support for the filibuster.

In early August, shortly after the fifty-sixth anniversary of the Voting Rights Act, the Senate adjourned for the summer without passing any voting rights bills. After thirty-eight days in Washington, Texas Democrats reluctantly returned home with little to show for it.

Within two weeks, Texas Republicans muscled through their package of voting restrictions on a party-line vote, providing a stark contrast to the inaction in Washington. They removed the provisions that cut Sunday voting and made it easier to overturn elections after a public outcry, but otherwise kept intact the original bill that led to two Democratic walkouts. Republicans admitted during the closing debate that they didn't want to encourage increased political participation, despite the state's ranking forty-fifth in the country in voter turnout in 2020. "I'm not sure the goal of the state is to actively seek out voters," said the GOP state representative Andrew Murr, the bill's lead sponsor. "The state is not so proactive that it tries to grab all the voters."

After the Texas bill passed, voting rights activists ratcheted up the pressure on the White House. Ben Jealous, the president of People for the American Way and the former head of the NAACP, requested a meeting with the White House chief of staff Ron Klain and his deputy Bruce Reed. When he received no reply, he joined a group of religious and civil rights leaders protesting outside the White House gate. "Mr. President," he said through a bullhorn, "tell your party in the Senate to fix the rules so that we can get the voting rights bill through." Jealous was arrested on October 5 and spent the night in a jail cell with "the most aggressive roaches you've ever seen."

A month later—a year before the midterm elections—forty voting rights groups held a video call with Vice President Harris, whom Biden had put in charge of his voting rights strategy. That fall, Warnock and other Democratic senators had worked doggedly behind the scenes to persuade Manchin to support a new voting rights bill, the Freedom to Vote Act, which preserved much of the For the People Act. The groups hoped to receive marching orders from Harris on how to pass it. After showing up an hour late, she spoke for just six minutes, offered little more than platitudes, and left staff members to answer questions. "Nothing substantive came out of it," said Cliff Albright, cofounder of Black Voters Matter, who had been arrested with Jealous. "It was very frustrating."

The White House remained fixated on lobbying Manchin to support Biden's economic bills instead of passing the Freedom to Vote Act. If he waded into "the debate on the filibuster," Biden told CNN in October, "I lose at least three votes right now to get what I have to get done on the economic side of the equation." Voting rights activists were flabbergasted when the administration listed the passage of the infrastructure bill as the first item in a fact sheet touting the steps it had taken to "restore and strengthen American democracy" ahead of a global democracy summit in early December.

Warnock's frustration boiled over a week later. He had been told for nearly a year that it was impossible to change the Senate rules to pass voting rights legislation, but on December 14 Republicans allowed Democrats to pass a bill to raise the country's debt limit on a simple majority vote to avoid an economic crisis. It was "a point of moral dissonance for me," Warnock said on the Senate floor, "to change the Senate rules only for the benefit of the economy when the warning lights on our democracy are flashing at the same time." If Democrats could act alone to raise the debt ceiling, he argued, they could do the same for voting rights legislation. "How do we in good conscience justify doing one and not the other?" he asked his colleagues.

After watching Warnock's remarks, which he called "very moving," Manchin walked out of the Capitol trailed by TV cameras.

"Are you anywhere to the point where you could vote yes on proceeding [to voting rights legislation]?" a reporter asked him.

Warnock, wearing a black N95 mask, caught up to Manchin and patted him on the chest.

"I've got to check with my pastor," Manchin joked.

"You should check with the pastor," Warnock responded.

"I can't get into negotiations like this right now," Manchin said.

"Did you hear that?" Warnock said. "He's checking with the pastor. That means we're getting ready to pass voting rights!"

Everyone laughed as Manchin stepped into a black SUV, but the weary look in Warnock's eyes showed he was being pushed to the breaking point.

A few days later, Manchin announced he opposed Biden's Build Back Better bill, leaving the president's signature domestic priority in shambles. Months of lobbying from the White House, with the premise that pushing voting rights legislation would jeopardize Manchin's support for Biden's economic agenda, had backfired.

Biden had long maintained that passing popular pieces of legislation would "prove democracy works" and restore the legitimacy of the democratic process. But his administration's single-minded focus on economic policy—and its elusive pursuit of bipartisanship—had failed to blunt the growing radicalization of the GOP or stop the onslaught of bills undermining democracy at the state level. The time had come—some worried it had already passed—to confront these threats to democracy head on.

» » » » » »

On January 11, 2022, the president traveled to Georgia, "the belly of the beast," to deliver the speech on voting rights that activists had been begging him for a year to give.

The visit, on a crisp and clear Monday afternoon, was rich with symbolism. Biden rode on Air Force One with Warnock and Nikema Williams. He laid a wreath at the crypt of Martin Luther King and Coretta Scott King. He met with members of Georgia's congressional delegation at Ebenezer Baptist Church. From there, he made his way to the grounds of two historically Black colleges, Clark Atlanta University and Morehouse College, for his main remarks.

After months of resistance, Biden announced that he supported changing the Senate rules, "whichever way they need to be changed," to pass voting rights legislation. "When it comes to protecting majority rule in America," the president said, "the majority should rule in the United States Senate."

The endgame of the GOP, he said, was "to turn the will of the voters into a mere suggestion—something states can respect or ignore." He asked members of Congress, "How do you want to be remembered? . . . Do you want to be the on the side of Dr. King or George Wallace? Do you want to be on the side of John Lewis or Bull Connor? Do you want to be on the side of Abraham Lincoln or Jefferson Davis? This is the moment to decide."

Biden said he had been having conversations behind the scenes with senators for two months but was "tired of being quiet," slapping the lectern for emphasis. "May God protect the sacred right to vote," he said as he ended. "I mean it. Let's go get this done."

Yet to some activists who had been on the frontlines of battling voter suppression, Biden's speech was too little, too late. Stacey Abrams was a prominent no-show, tersely saying she had a scheduling conflict. A coalition of groups who led the fight against SB 202, including Black Voters Matter and the New Georgia Project, announced they were boycotting it. They called the president's visit "an empty gesture, without concrete action, without signs of real, tangible work."

This was the speech Biden should have delivered in Philadelphia the previous summer, the activists argued, when the eyes of the nation were captivated by Texas Democrats, coming on the heels of outcry over SB 202, and public and private pressure might have convinced Manchin and Sinema to change their minds. Instead, Biden's reluctance to use his bully pulpit and powers of persuasion as president left a void that conservative groups like Heritage Action were all too happy to fill. "All kinds of energy and momentum," said LaTosha Brown, "has been squandered."

Two days after visiting Georgia, Biden headed to Capitol Hill to speak to the Senate Democratic caucus. Minutes before their weekly lunch, Sinema launched a sneak attack, restating her opposition to changing the chamber's rules during a speech on the Senate floor.

Her home state of Arizona had been an epicenter of Trump's attempt to overturn the election. For much of 2021, Republicans had conducted a months-long audit that sought to reverse the results and had passed numerous changes to state law making it more difficult to vote. For the past two weeks, a group of college students from Arizona had been on a hunger strike outside the White House in a last-ditch attempt to convince Sinema to pass the Freedom to Vote Act.

But she was unmoved, bordering on uninterested, by these developments. She'd recently held a Zoom call with leading civil rights groups and hadn't even bothered to turn her camera on. "Efforts to fix these problems on bare majorities on a party-line basis only exacerbate the root causes that gave way to these state laws in the first place," Sinema said on the Senate floor. (She would formally leave the Democratic Party before the end of the year.)

Biden left his lunch with Senate Democrats sounding deflated. "I hope we can get this done," he told reporters. "The honest to God answer is: I don't know whether we can get this done."

A week later, shortly after Martin Luther King Day, Democrats combined the Freedom to Vote Act and John Lewis Voting Rights Act into one bill, and the Senate finally held the debate on voting rights legislation and the filibuster that was long overdue.

Mitch McConnell called it "the most important day in the history of the Senate as an institution" and accused Democrats of inciting a "fake panic over election laws" while ignoring the fake panic over voter fraud that had led to the passage of those laws in the first place. He said Democrats were trying to "break the Senate," even though he had changed the body's rules just a few years earlier to confirm three of Trump's Supreme Court justices with a simple majority vote, creating yet another asymmetry in the governing process.

On his 365th day in office, Warnock made one last appeal to his colleagues. As he had done in his maiden speech, he contrasted his election on January 5 with the insurrection on January 6. The aim of that violent attack was "now being pursued through partisan voter suppression laws in state legislatures," he said on the Senate floor. "Here's the question tonight: America, are we January 5th, or are we January 6th?"

As Warnock spoke, members of the Congressional Black Caucus, including Nikema Williams, sat at the back of the chamber. Sinema skipped his speech and Manchin watched it expressionless. He had already made up his mind.

Late that afternoon, Manchin stood on the Senate floor in front of a giant blue sign that read "the United States Senate has never been able to end debate with [a] simple majority."

The filibuster had been the "tradition of the Senate [for] 232 years," Manchin argued, playing "an important role in stabilizing our democracy from the transitory passions of the majority."

He cited Madison to make his point, but Manchin had misread the history behind the institutions that Madison helped create. Madison had intended the Senate to function as an elite body of distinguished wise men, chosen by state legislatures and given long terms, in order serve as a check on the popularly elected House. But he wanted the body to operate on the basis of majority rule.

The filibuster was not part of the Constitution and had emerged as an accident of history when the Senate failed to specify how to end debate on a bill in 1805. The founders called for a supermajority only in specific circumstances, such as approving constitutional amendments, foreign treaties, and removing impeached officials. If routine legislation were subject to such a requirement, "the fundamental principle of free government would be reversed," Madison wrote in Federalist

No. 58. "It would be no longer the majority that would rule: the power would be transferred to the minority."

Senator Angus King, an independent from Maine who had been negotiating with Manchin for months in a futile effort to persuade him to modify the Senate rules, said that "you can't have it both ways—it's either majority rule or it's minority rule."

In preserving the rights of the Senate minority over the rights of minority voters, the chamber was repeating the mistakes that had doomed Reconstruction, King said, pointing specifically to the failure of the Lodge bill.

"That filibuster echoed in this country for 75 years," King said. "I pray that we don't look back on this day and realize the level of mistake they made in 1891."

After twelve hours of debate, the proposal to change the Senate rules to pass the Freedom to Vote: John R. Lewis Act narrowly failed at 10:30 p.m. Sinema stood and loudly shouted "aye" to oppose it. The first person to congratulate her was the Louisiana senator John Kennedy, one of six Republicans who had objected to counting the Electoral College votes in her home state on January 6.

The vote underscored how unrepresentative of the country the Senate had become. The forty-eight Democrats who supported reforming the filibuster represented 34 million more Americans than the fifty-two senators who upheld it. Manchin and Sinema collectively represented 2.8 percent of the US population but had killed the Democrats' last, best chance to protect and expand voting rights for tens of millions of Americans.

"Our failure to pass voting rights in this moment, when the democracy itself is under assault, is not only a public policy failure, in my view, it's a moral failure," Warnock said. He was proud that he had convinced every Democrat to support the voting rights bill, but admitted, "we just could not get every single member to see that the urgency of the moment required us to not allow any Senate rule to usurp and supplant people's fundamental right to vote."

He argued that those who blocked voting rights legislation would find themselves on the wrong side of history. "I think when the history of this period is written, our children, our grandchildren, will ask, 'What were you doing when our house of democracy was on fire?'" he said. "'What were you doing when we witnessed the most violent assault on the United States Capitol that we've seen since the War of 1812? What were you doing when that cancer metastasized into voter suppression bills and laws all across the states, all across the country?' All of us need to stand up and be counted at this moment."

The juxtaposition between his victory in Georgia and the insurrection the next day would always be personal for Warnock. "We are caught somewhere between January 5th and January 6th," he said that evening. In this push and pull, the insurrectionists were winning.

10

DEMOCRACY ON THE BALLOT

In 2018, Democrats swept every statewide race in Wisconsin, ending nearly a decade of hard-edged Republican rule. "The voters spoke," Tony Evers, the state's superintendent of education, said at a raucous victory party in Madison after defeating Scott Walker for the governorship. "A change is coming, Wisconsin!"

But Robin Vos, the GOP leader in the assembly, and his senate counterpart, Scott Fitzgerald, had other ideas. Less than a month after the election, the GOP-controlled legislature convened an unprecedented lame-duck session to strip power from the incoming Democratic governor. They confirmed eighty-two Walker nominees before Evers took office without holding a hearing on many of them, and they blocked the new governor from making administrative changes to state laws and following through on key campaign promises, such as withdrawing the state from a Republican-backed lawsuit challenging Obamacare. The legislature also shortened the state's early voting period, which had contributed to record turnout in 2018, to suppress future Democratic turnout in urban areas. "How much more Third World country can you get?" asked the Wisconsin Democratic congressman Mark Pocan.

Protestors descended on the state capitol, denouncing the session as a legislative coup. Walker, whose tenure had been defined by aggressive efforts to entrench his party's power, was booed loudly in the capitol rotunda when he appeared at a ceremony lighting the state's forty-foot balsam fir Christmas tree, decorated with dairy-themed ornaments, and he was serenaded with chants of "Respect the Vote."

Russ Hahn, a fifty-three-year-old lawyer from Kenosha, held a sign that read "GOP Grinch Steals Democracy." "It's an attack on the entire citizenry of Wisconsin," he said.

Voters disapproved of the lame-duck session by a two-to-one margin. More than 1,400 Wisconsinites registered to testify against the GOP proposals—there was one hastily assembled hearing in a tiny legislative room—and not a single member of the public spoke in favor of them.

In the wee hours of the morning on December 5, when the legislature considered a final bill that no Democrat had seen in advance, the ninety-one-year-old state senator Fred Risser, the longest serving state legislator in America, rose to express his displeasure. He'd served with twelve different governors since joining the legislature in 1962, six Democrats and six Republicans. He'd been president of the senate five times. He'd never seen anything like this. "The Republicans haven't debated," he said. "They've come down with bills that we haven't had a chance to read and they don't even come up to defend them . . . That's not democracy. That's not the body that I joined."

The bill cleared the state senate at 6:04 a.m., one hour before the sun rose, giving literal meaning to democracy dying in darkness. After the vote, members of Indivisible Madison, a local progressive group, dressed in black and held a "funeral for democracy," singing Tom Petty's "I Won't Back Down."

In 2018, Republican candidates for the assembly had won 46 percent of the vote statewide but retained 64 percent of the seats in the legislature thanks to the brutally efficient gerrymander they drew at the beginning of the decade. Though Democrats had won more votes and had public opinion on their side, Republicans claimed that only they could legitimately govern. "If you took Madison and Milwaukee out of the state election formula," Vos said of the state's two largest and most Democratic cities, home to 850,000 people, "we would have a clear majority."

Evers was a mild-mannered, grandfatherly figure who could not be more old-school Wisconsin. He liked polka, the card game Euchre, and a daily Egg McMuffin. "He's got more of a Clark Kent vibe than a Superman vibe," Obama joked when he campaigned for him. After serving as the state's school superintendent for nearly a decade, he ran against Walker on meat-and-potato issues; his signature phrase on the campaign trail was "fix the damn roads." But after his election, he quickly found himself in an existential battle to preserve democracy in the state.

Evers called the lame-duck session "an attack on the will of the people, our democracy, and our system of government." He later viewed the soft coup in Wisconsin as a practice run for the full-on coup attempted by Trump in 2020. "It's the same deal, except they were successful in Wisconsin," Evers said. "They weren't successful in Washington, DC. There are things that have never happened before in the state of Wisconsin because of that lame duck session."

In the years that followed, the Republican-dominated legislature went on to refuse to confirm members of Evers's cabinet, blocked his appointments to key state agencies, and cut his popular budget priorities, including money for health care, schools, and roads.

The lame-duck session showed how much influence the legislature could wield without broad public support, the very type of power grab Republicans hoped to replicate in other states. As the crucial 2022 midterm elections approached, Republicans didn't just want to defeat Evers and reclaim one-party rule in Wisconsin. They wanted full control over how elections were run and certified in the state and across the country. After rewriting the country's voting laws, the next phase of their plan was to take over the election system itself.

» » » » » »

Two days after the 2020 election, Cleta Mitchell, a veteran GOP elections lawyer who called herself "the consigliere to the vast right-wing conspiracy," emailed her longtime friend John Eastman.

"A movement is stirring," she told Eastman. "But needs constitutional support."

She asked Eastman if he could write "a legal memo outlining the constitutional role of state legislators in designating electors?" As a former state legislator in Oklahoma from 1976 to 1984, Mitchell believed that "where state exec branch officials have rewritten or ignored state election law" the legislatures had the power to "reclaim that constitutional duty and designate the electors" regardless of the popular vote winner of the state, which Mitchell claimed was merely "advisory."

"Am I crazy?" she asked.

At least to Eastman, she was not. By November 28, he had produced a seven-page memo, "For POTUS," agreeing with Mitchell's assertion that state legislatures had the exclusive authority to determine the method for appointing presidential electors, giving them the power to override the choice of the voters. "Legislatures simply *must* investigate," he wrote, "and then, if convinced that the election was too fraught with risk of fraud to be properly certified, exercise their prerogative to legislatively designate a slate of electors."

In the weeks that followed, Mitchell helped lead the legal effort to overturn the election, and Eastman provided the constitutional theory behind it.

A day after the election, Mitchell was in Montana working for a Republican Senate candidate when she received a call from the White House chief of staff, Mark Meadows. He asked her to go to Atlanta to investigate the vote count. She was on the next flight out.

She quickly began assembling lawyers to challenge the results in Georgia, whom she called "team deplorables." On January 2, she participated in the call where Trump asked Raffensperger to "find 11,780 votes" to nullify Biden's win. She repeated several false claims about the election, alleging that eighteen thousand ballots were scanned at State Farm Arena after GOP poll monitors were ejected and that 4,500 people voted in Georgia who were registered out of state.

"Those numbers that we got that Ms. Mitchell was just saying, they're not accurate," Ryan Germany, counsel for the secretary of state, responded.

When Mitchell's participation in the call became public, she was forced to leave the white-shoe law firm in Washington, DC, where she had been a longtime partner, representing a who's who of GOP candidates, including Trump, and conservative organizations like the National Rifle Association. She landed as a senior fellow at the Conservative Partnership Institute, an "America first" think tank run by Meadows after he left the White House and the former Heritage Foundation president Jim DeMint. It had become a kind of Trump administration-in-exile, funded by Trump's PAC and other top right-wing donors and housing at least twenty key operatives who tried to overturn the election.

As head of the group's "Election Integrity Network" she worked closely with allies like Heritage Action to draft new restrictions on voting and raised money for the audit in Arizona that sought to reverse Biden's victory. After changing the country's voting laws to advantage Republicans, she moved on to taking over the machinery of the election system.

With her blond bob and affinity for pearls, the seventy-two-year-old Mitchell had long acted as the tart-tongued grandmother of the conservative election integrity movement. As the board secretary of the Bradley Foundation, she helped distribute millions of dollars to groups that spread unfounded claims of voter fraud and advocated for strict curbs on ballot access, such as the Heritage Foundation's Election Law Reform Initiative, run by her friend Hans von Spakovsky.

She used those connections in 2022 to partner with the RNC and outside groups like Heritage Action to recruit "a volunteer army of citizens" in key swing states that would be the eyes and ears of the Stop the Steal movement inside election offices and at the polls, determining who was counting the votes and which votes were counted. As Trump himself put it, "sometimes the vote counter is more important than the candidate."

Mitchell was "arming people to fight back against the radical left," she told Steve Bannon, one of the coarchitects of the strategy, "to keep them from stealing it ever again."

"Are these active workshops where they actually understand how to take over and grab hold of and control the local apparatus in their local elections and then to network throughout the country so that we have an apparatus that is unbreakable?" Bannon asked Mitchell before a summit in Virginia in April 2022.

"That's absolutely what we're doing," Mitchell said.

At a training session in New Mexico, Eastman explained how these new recruits could gather information that could be used to contest election outcomes. "Document what you've seen, raise the challenge. And [note] which of the judges on that election board decline to accept your challenge. Get it all written down," Eastman said at an Election Integrity Network meeting in Albuquerque. "That then becomes the basis for an affidavit in a court challenge after the fact."

At a summit for "election integrity" activists in Arizona in March 2022, cosponsored by Heritage Action and Tea Party Patriots, Mitchell explained the ideology that motivated this new movement.

The goal of the Democrats, first articulated by Jesse Jackson and more recently by politicians like Stacey Abrams, was to create a "new American majority" of "young people, people of color, unmarried women" that would "render conservatives obsolete," she said in her Oklahoma drawl at a hotel ballroom in south Phoenix. "That's one hundred and fifty million people constituting 64 percent of the people who can vote in America, and they are targeting those groups to change America. What do they do? They believe you can expand access to democracy by underrepresented populations . . . It's a place the left sees as a great target of opportunity, and we have to make sure that doesn't happen."

She ridiculed Democrats and nonprofit groups for trying to "register and turn out the vote of the most vulnerable people in our society" and wanting to "bring democracy to your doorstep. I want to pause right here: we don't live in a democracy." The hundreds of mostly older white activists in the room applauded. "For the left, everything is about democracy. The Democracy Fund, the democracy this, the democracy that. Biden gives speeches about, you know, the attacks on our democracy. We live in a constitutional republic."

This frequent conservative refrain was inspired by a 1961 speech in Chicago delivered by Robert Welch, a wealthy candy executive and founder of the far-right John Birch Society, in which he proclaimed, "This is a Republic, not a Democracy. Let's keep it that way!"

Welch drew heavily on the history of the founding era, citing the framers' distaste for direct democracy in places like ancient Greece, which Madison defined as "a society consisting of a small number of citizens, who assemble and administer the government in person." A republic, in contrast, was "a government in which the scheme of representation takes place."

To Welch, the chief danger in a democracy was majority rule. "In a democracy there is a centralization of governmental power in a simple majority," he said in September 1961. "And that, visibly, is the system of government which the enemies of our republic are seeking to impose on us today."

Welch believed the Constitution created by the founders was divinely inspired and should not be changed by a majority vote. "Those certain unalienable and divine rights cannot be abrogated by the vote of a majority any more than they can by the decree of a conqueror," he said. "The idea that the vote of a people, no matter how nearly unanimous, makes or creates or determines what is right or just becomes as absurd and unacceptable as the idea that right and justice are simply whatever a king says they are."

To Welch, early twentieth-century reforms like a progressive income tax and the direct election of US senators were evidence of democracy's dangerous leveling spirit. The expansion of democratic rights in the 1960s was even more frightening. The Birch Society sought to impeach Earl Warren, who they claimed had "taken the lead in the drive to convert this country into a democracy," and said the civil rights movement was trying to establish an "independent Negro-Soviet Republic."

In reality, the attempt to distinguish between a "democracy" and a "republic" was a false dichotomy premised on a misreading of history;

Madison strove to combine the two forms of government, creating a democratic republic where representatives would refine and filter the views of the public to achieve an enduring consensus, diminish the influence of any one faction, and protect minority rights. The Constitution could be amended to reflect changing times and circumstances if a sufficiently large majority demanded it.

The conservative invocation of a republic, on the other hand, was used throughout US history to protect oligarchies of privilege—such as Southern slaveholders or corporate robber barons—from the pressure of popular majorities. Under Mitchell's conception of a republic, states had a free hand to pass discriminatory voting laws and any government action to promote broader political participation violated states' rights and individual liberty. If democracy was the enemy, that justified nearly any attempt by the right to subvert core democratic institutions.

This antipathy to democracy was shared not just by the activists Mitchell was recruiting, but by a record number of candidates running for key election positions in the 2022 midterms.

» » » » » »

On a sticky Friday in early August, thousands of Trump supporters decked out in red and carrying flags that said "Trump won" streamed into the fairgrounds in Waukesha County—the longtime GOP stronghold twenty miles west of Milwaukee—to welcome the former president back to Wisconsin for the first time since he had begrudgingly left office.

The former Wisconsin Supreme Court justice Michael Gableman, whom the legislature had tapped to lead a sprawling thirteen-month investigation into the 2020 election, delivered the opening invocation. "Almighty and merciful god," Gableman said, "we thank you for the courage and wisdom of our 45th president."

He was followed by the state representative Janel Brandjten, one of fifteen legislative Republicans from Wisconsin who wrote to Pence a day before January 6 and urged him not to certify the state's electoral votes. Vos had named her chair of the assembly's election committee.

"We know what happened in 2020," Brandjten said.

"They stole the election," someone in the crowd yelled.

Storms in New York delayed Trump's arrival until the evening. But he said "global warming will not stop us from going" to Wisconsin.

"We won this state by a lot," Trump told his supporters, standing in front of a blue "Save America" banner. "The election was rigged and stolen and now our country is being systematically destroyed."

But it had been "an exceptional week for the America first movement," he bragged. GOP candidates for governor that he had endorsed in Arizona and Michigan, Kari Lake and Tudor Dixon, had won their primaries after refusing to accept the outcome of the 2020 election.

Now Trump was rallying support for the Wisconsin gubernatorial candidate Tim Michels, a wealthy construction executive who owned a $17 million mansion in Connecticut and a penthouse on Manhattan's Upper East Side. Michels had trekked to Mar-a-Lago to win Trump's endorsement in the primary, telling the media that he didn't think Trump "did anything wrong" on January 6 and "would be president right now if we had election integrity."

"My number one priority is election integrity," the fifty-nine-year-old Michels said to cheers when he bounded on stage in a dark suit and blue tie. "If we don't have fair and transparent elections, our entire constitutional system comes crumbling down. This is the United States of America. It's not some third world country. It's not some Banana Republic. We should not even be having this conversation twenty-one months after the election. Was it rigged? Was it fixed? I'm gonna stop it." He left the stage to chants of "USA! USA!"

Four days later, Michels upset Rebecca Kleefisch, who had been Walker's lieutenant governor and the preferred candidate of the GOP establishment. Both had run hard to the right, but Michels separated himself by saying he would consider signing a bill to decertify the 2020 election, embracing a radical effort to reinstall Trump in office by reversing the state's Electoral College votes long after Biden had become president, which Kleefisch said was "not constitutionally possible."

Trump claimed in Wisconsin his record in the primaries was 45-0, which was overstating things but not by much. Michels's victory capped a remarkably successful effort by Trump and his allies to reshape the Republican Party in the image of the Big Lie. A majority of Republican nominees, three hundred in total, for the House, Senate, and crucial statewide positions with authority over election administration—such as governor, secretary of state, and attorney general—had denied or questioned the outcome of the 2020 election. Election deniers were running on the ballot in every single state except for North Dakota and Rhode Island. "That's akin to giving a robber a key to the bank," said Colorado secretary of state Jena Griswold, chair of the Democratic Association of Secretaries of State.

In a year in which seemingly the entire GOP had radicalized against democracy, Republicans in Wisconsin were on the cutting edge of attacking free and fair elections. Trump had made the state a focal point of his obsession to overturn the election. Nearly three-quarters of Republicans in the legislature had taken steps to discredit the results, and GOP candidates who cast doubt on the outcome were nominated for governor, attorney general, and secretary of state.

Like he did with Brian Kemp, Trump directed much of his ire at Vos—the driving force behind GOP dominance in the state—calling him a "Democrat, actually," for saying that the legislature did not have the power to decertify the election. So Vos sought to placate Trump in other ways.

In June 2021, as he faced a resolution at the state GOP convention calling for his resignation because he was not sufficiently supportive of "a real election investigation and a forensic audit," Vos hired Michael Gableman to lead a taxpayer-funded review of the 2020 election.

Gableman, a divisive figure in state politics since his 2008 defeat of Louis Butler and lightning rod decisions upholding key parts of Walker's agenda, was hardly an unbiased observer. The former justice appeared at a pro-Trump rally days after the November election, telling a crowd in Milwaukee: "Our elected leaders—your elected leaders—have allowed unelected bureaucrats at the Wisconsin Elections Commission to steal our vote."

Gableman admitted after Vos hired him that "most people, myself included, do not have a comprehensive understanding or even any understanding of how elections work." Despite his limited knowledge of the election process, Gableman made a number of eye-opening moves, including threatening to jail the Democratic mayors of Green Bay and Madison for not responding to subpoenas.

In March 2021, Gableman appeared before Janel Brandtjen's committee with an interim report and said, "I believe the legislature ought to take a very hard look at the option of decertification," even though he left that conclusion out of the draft report he gave to Vos and later told the speaker that decertification was a "practical impossibility." He also told the legislature that in future elections "the thumb should be on the scale in favor of withholding certification of electors."

Two weeks later, Vos met with Eastman, who by that time had become a central figure in multiple state and federal investigations into Trump's attempt to overturn the election. Jefferson Davis, a conservative activist named after the former Confederate president, introduced Eastman as the man who "tried to save our country single-handedly on January 5th and 6th."

If few legal scholars had supported Trump's effort to reverse the 2020 results, even fewer argued that the former president could be reinstalled after Biden had assumed office. But Eastman doubled down on the fringiest of fringe theories. "The Wisconsin Legislature," he said in a packed meeting room on the third floor of the state capitol, "in my view, not just up until January 6 or inauguration, but today as well, has the ability to look at the assessment and say, you know, our election was illegally certified." There were loud cheers and chants of amen.

Although Vos had conceded after the election that Biden had won, he left the meeting with Eastman alleging there had been "widespread fraud" in the state. A recount requested by Trump and multiple independent investigations, including a legislative-ordered audit, had uncovered no such thing. An extensive report by a conservative group, the Wisconsin Institute for Law and Liberty, also found "no evidence of widespread voter fraud."

But the lies spread by Trump and his allies had made voting harder in Wisconsin in tangible ways. That July, the conservative majority on the Wisconsin Supreme Court outlawed most mail ballot drop boxes, arguing they were not authorized under state law. A few months later, another decision by a conservative judge in Waukesha County prevented election officials from correcting small errors on absentee ballot certificates, such as a missing zip code, leading to fears that more ballots would be thrown out in 2022.

The GOP-controlled legislature wanted to go further and had passed a series of bills, vetoed by Evers, that would make it more difficult to vote and give itself more authority over how elections were administered and certified. (The legislature had also passed new redistricting maps in 2021, over Evers's objections, that gave Republicans a near-supermajority, further entrenching their power for the next decade.)

After a campaign finance scandal in both parties, in 2007 the legislature had created a panel of retired judges—known as the Government Accountability Board—to oversee state campaign finance laws and elections. It was well-respected until Republicans disbanded the board in 2015 after it investigated Walker for allegedly illegally coordinating with conservative dark money groups. The legislature replaced it with the Wisconsin Elections Commission, modeled after the Federal Election Commission, with an equal number of Democratic and Republican appointees and a nonpartisan staff. Republicans praised the commission, which issued guidance to the state's 1,800 municipalities, until Trump blamed its attempts to make voting easier during the pandemic for his defeat.

In the fall of 2021, Christopher Schmaling, the Trump-backed sheriff of Racine County, accused the commission of breaking state law by unanimously recommending in March 2020 that election clerks mail absentee ballots to nursing home residents to limit the spread of COVID-19 instead of sending poll workers to assist in person. Schmaling argued that five of six commissioners should face criminal prosecution, and Vos called on its nonpartisan director, who had been unanimously confirmed by the state senate in 2019, to resign. Shortly thereafter, the US senator Ron Johnson—who had attempted to hand deliver a slate of pro-Trump electors from Michigan and Wisconsin to Pence on January 6—met with Vos and told him the legislature should "reclaim [its] authority over our election system."

In Wisconsin, presidential elections were certified by the governor while the commission chair certified nonpresidential elections. If elected, Michels had promised to dismantle the commission, which would give Republicans total control over how elections were certified, potentially opening the door to overturning future elections through more sophisticated and ostensibly legal means than Trump had used in 2020.

If Republicans retook control of the state in 2022, Evers warned, "I think they'll probably pass [certification] off to the legislature and that will give them essentially carte blanche to muck up an election. For example, a presidential election." As the midterms approached, this nightmare scenario was dangerously close to becoming a reality.

Ten days before the election, on an unseasonably warm Saturday afternoon, Obama visited Wisconsin for a rally at a high school gym in Milwaukee, surrounded by giant American and Wisconsin flags.

He wore a powder blue shirt with his sleeves rolled up. Evers sat behind him on stage, wearing black glasses and a fleece vest. A sign on the podium urged voters to cast their ballots early.

The prognosis for democracy appeared bleak to downright apocalyptic. Most pundits predicted a "red wave" that would give Republicans control of both houses of Congress and sweep many of the most extreme election deniers into power in crucial state races. Inflation was at a forty-year high and gas prices were close to $4 a gallon. A majority of voters disapproved of the job Biden was doing as president.

Obama had experienced his own "shellacking" in the midterms in 2010, seeing firsthand how GOP control of key swing states had led to a steady undermining of democratic norms and institutions over the past decade in places like Wisconsin. Now he wanted to persuade Democrats, independents, and perhaps even some moderate Republicans that this was no ordinary off-year election and that protecting democracy should be the overriding issue in the campaign.

"I get that right now, today, democracy might not seem like the top priority, especially because people have other things they're worried about," the former president said. "But we have seen throughout history what happens when we lose democracy."

He ridiculed Michels for flirting with decertifying the election. "To say the obvious, if someone's openly obsessed with changing the results of the last election, he probably shouldn't be in charge of overseeing this one coming up," Obama said.

In a playful tone, he gently ribbed Evers while highlighting the importance of the governor's race. "Don't let the glasses and necktie fool you, because Tony is tough . . . He might be democracy's best hope in Wisconsin."

With Biden's approval rating underwater, Obama crisscrossed the country in the final days of the campaign—starting in Georgia and ending in Pennsylvania, with Wisconsin, Michigan, Nevada, and Arizona in between—to emphasize that "democracy is at stake in this election."

The GOP threat to fair elections was brought into sharp relief two days later, on Halloween, when Michels, during a campaign stop in the small city of Watertown, promised that "Republicans will never lose another election in Wisconsin after I'm elected governor."

Evers immediately turned Michels's quote, which seemed to personify how Republicans wanted to make one-party rule voter-proof, into a TV ad. "Did you know Tim Michels pledged to rig future elections?" it said. "He'll try to overthrow the will of the people. Is that the kind of divisive radical you want as governor?"

The White House tried to amplify these warnings, with Biden

determined to use the bully pulpit to defeat election denialism with a vigor he did not show until it was too late when it came to passing voting rights legislation.

On September 1, the president visited Independence Hall in Philadelphia, where the Constitution had been drafted, for a prime-time speech. The movement to subvert the election system threatened America's experiment as a laboratory for democracy, Biden warned, and sought to delegitimize the very institutions created by the founders. He described the ideals of "equality and democracy" as the "the rock upon which this nation is built" but said they were now "under assault." At the root of this new effort to roll back democracy were long-contested ideas about freedom and who was entitled to exercise one of the country's most essential rights. "I will not stand by and watch the most fundamental freedom in this country—the freedom to vote and have your vote counted—be taken from you and the American people," Biden pledged.

Much of the media ignored Biden's speech, deeming it too "political." None of the major networks covered it live. ABC aired a game show called "Press Your Luck." CBS showed a rerun of "Young Sheldon," and NBC an old episode of "Law and Order."

Less than a week before the election, Biden delivered another prime-time address, from Union Station in Washington, to reiterate what was at stake in the midterms, the first major election since January 6. "I wish I could say the assault on our democracy ended that day, but I cannot," he said, blocks from where the Capitol had been ransacked. "As I stand here today, there are candidates running for every level of office in America—for governor, Congress, attorney general, secretary of state—who won't commit . . . to accepting the results of the elections that they're running in. This is the path to chaos in America. It's unprecedented. It's unlawful. And it's un-American."

Republicans mocked Biden for ignoring bread-and-butter issues.

"I don't remember hearing anything about inflation, about gas, about [the] border, about fentanyl, about crime," GOP House leader Kevin McCarthy told Fox News.

Even some top Democrats questioned whether it was the best use of the president's time. "Issues of democracy are hugely important at this moment and in next week's election. Totally appropriate for @POTUS to address them," tweeted David Axelrod, Obama's former chief strategist. "Still, as a matter of practical politics, I doubt many Ds in marginal races are eager for him to be on TV tonight."

But the state of democracy was not an abstract concern in Wisconsin and other key states. Forty-four percent of Americans said that the future of democracy was their primary consideration when they voted, according to an Associated Press poll, ranking higher than any other issue except inflation. The fear of irrevocably losing free and fair elections, combined with a backlash to the Supreme Court's decision that summer overturning *Roe v. Wade*, which criminalized abortions in states like Wisconsin, helped stave off the worst outcomes for democracy and showed how determined a majority of voters were to defend their fundamental rights.

"I think people understand here that Republicans are trying to suppress their votes and trying to rig the game in their favor," said the state representative Greta Neubauer, the Democratic leader in the Wisconsin Assembly. "It is something that I think was motivating to voters and to volunteers."

In the early hours of Wednesday morning, the Associated Press called the governor's race for Evers. He was re-elected by 3.5 points—triple his margin in 2018 and practically a landslide by Wisconsin standards—marking the first time since 1962 that the state had voted for a Democratic governor while a Democratic president was in office.

When he spoke at his victory party at the Orpheum Theater in Madison at 1 a.m., even the typically understated governor was in a jubilant mood. "Holy mackerel, folks, how about that?" he asked cheering supporters. "You showed up because you saw that democracy was on the brink of [extinction] and you decided to do a damn thing about it."

And Wisconsin voters were not alone. Voters in the six major battlegrounds where Trump tried to overturn the results—Arizona,

Georgia, Michigan, Nevada, Pennsylvania, and Wisconsin—rejected election-denying candidates who sought to control their states' election systems. The reactionary movement to institutionalize the insurrection had captured the headlines and taken over the Republican Party, but it had repelled a larger proportion of the electorate, who voted to preserve core democratic norms.

"There was a coordinated effort to make defending democracy a critical part of the election cycle," said the Michigan secretary of state, Jocelyn Benson, a Democrat who defeated a Republican candidate who had claimed that Trump won the election and that the January 6 attack was carried out by left-wing anarchists. "And it really took hold in the states where voters had witnessed firsthand the efforts and the tactics that were employed in 2020 to try to diminish their voice and their vote and dismantle democracy. Because of that, we were able to be successful in making it clear to voters on both sides of the aisle that democracy was at stake in this election, and with their vote, they could save it by rejecting the same people who tried to stop them from having their vote counted in 2020."

Of the forty-six election deniers who advanced to the general election in races for governor, attorney general, and secretary of state, only fifteen won, all in states that voted for Trump in 2016 and 2020. Though Mitchell had recruited thousands of conservative activists to watch the polls, there were few major problems at voting sites, largely because the fraud they had claimed was rampant never materialized and traditional election administrators held their ground.

Biden, while visiting Bali to meet with Chinese leader Xi Jinping, celebrated the outcome. "It was an emphatic statement," the president said, "that in America, the will of the people prevails."

11

NEW-SCHOOL ELECTION DENIAL MEETS OLD-SCHOOL VOTER SUPPRESSION

On a bright, crisp Saturday morning in late October 2022, Stacey Abrams's purple campaign bus arrived in Stone Mountain, Georgia. The city of 6,700 outside of Atlanta was best known for its nearby state park, where the Ku Klux Klan burned a cross on the hillside to signal the rebirth of the organization in 1915. The Klan and the United Daughters of the Confederacy commissioned a 1,700-foot-high granite relief sculpture of the Confederate leaders Robert E. Lee, Thomas "Stonewall" Jackson, and Jefferson Davis to honor the fallen heroes of the white South, which the legislature underwrote after the *Brown v. Board of Education* decision. It was finally completed in 1970, five years after the Voting Rights Act was passed.

Stone Mountain's connection to white supremacy had long been an affront to civil rights activists. "Let freedom ring from Stone Mountain of Georgia," Martin Luther King Jr. said in his "I Have a Dream" speech. Abrams called the monument "a blight on our state" after white supremacists marched through the streets of Charlottesville, Virginia, in 2017, but state law prohibited its removal. In 2000, however, the town installed a large Freedom Bell downtown, next to a gazebo and the railroad tracks. In the present day, the town of Stone Mountain is nearly three-quarters Black, and Biden won 83 percent of the vote in surrounding DeKalb County.

"I know where we are," Abrams said as she campaigned alongside the actress Kerry Washington and Democratic candidates for secretary of state and attorney general. "We're in Stone Mountain. And this ain't the Stone Mountain it used to be, is it?"

"No, no!" voices in the diverse crowd of roughly two hundred yelled back.

"We're standing next to that Freedom Bell. And on November 8, that bell's going to ring loud, ain't it?" Abrams asked to cheers.

Abrams, who for the second time was seeking to become the first Black woman governor in US history, was constantly reminded of the tension between the Old and New South. Her campaign bus had a sign inside depicting in emojis all the white men who had been governor of Georgia, followed by an image of her smiling face, with the tagline: "GA Governors Make History."

If the burdens of the past and a difficult midterm environment for Democrats weren't challenging enough, Abrams faced an additional problem in her rematch with Brian Kemp. Her opponent, whom she called "the chief architect of modern day voter suppression," was now being hailed in many quarters as a heroic defender of democracy.

"In 2018, Kemp was the Trumpy candidate accused of subverting democracy; now he's the candidate who defied Trump to defend it," *Time* magazine wrote. Because he certified Biden's victory in Georgia over Trump's objections and then easily defeated a Trump-endorsed primary challenger in May 2022, Kemp "wrote the GOP playbook for subduing Trump's election fury," said CNN.

Trump had vowed to end Kemp's political career and recruited the former GOP senator David Perdue, who tried to throw out his state's electoral votes, to challenge him. But instead the former president may have saved Kemp by allowing him to appear like a moderate without ever having to moderate any of his hard-line policy positions, such as supporting a six-week abortion ban, the right to carry a handgun practically anywhere without a permit, refusing to expand Medicaid while Georgia hospitals closed, and enthusiastically signing SB 202.

Kemp's certification of the last election—and the media's fawning coverage of it—allowed him to distance himself from the scores of GOP candidates who had questioned the election results. But Abrams argued that Kemp was a different kind of election denier. That he defended how votes were counted in 2020, she noted, overshadowed how he'd sought to limit access to the ballot over the course of his career.

"When you are willing to deny election access, you are just as guilty of undermining democracy," she said in the back of her wood-paneled campaign bus. "We've got to expand our language to understand that election denial begins with who can vote and ends with how the votes get counted."

That Kemp was now regarded as a voice of reason—and a champion of fair elections, no less—showed how far to the right the center of gravity had moved within the Republican Party, and, by extension, across American politics. "When our bar is so low," Abrams said, "anyone can step over it."

Abrams faced renewed scrutiny in 2022 for challenging how Kemp had conducted the 2018 election, when he was both secretary of state and a candidate for governor, which provided an early glimpse of how election officials could manipulate the rules to shape outcomes to their liking.

Abrams didn't challenge the certification of the election like Trump did, nor did she try to overturn the results. But Kemp and his allies highlighted her nonconcession speech to paint her as a proponent of "the original Big Lie." (Her lawsuit after the election to reform Georgia's voting laws led to key administrative changes that broadened voting access but was ultimately unsuccessful in federal court.)

Meanwhile, Kemp's role in institutionalizing Trump's election lies had mostly been forgotten, even though the governor admitted he signed SB 202 because of his unhappiness with the 2020 election. "I was as frustrated as anyone else with the results, especially at the federal level," he said during a GOP primary debate in May. "And we did something about it with Senate Bill 202."

The governor's race was the first major test of the new voting law. While new-school election denialism was largely defeated in 2022, old-school voter suppression still had an impact.

In the run-up to the election, conservative activists, taking advantage of a provision that allowed unlimited challenges to voter eligibility, questioned the qualifications of one hundred thousand voters, claiming they no longer lived at the correct address. Though close to 90 percent of the challenges were dismissed at the county level, they led to confusion and accusations of voter intimidation; in some cases, voters showed up at the polls and were told they could not vote because someone had contested their eligibility.

A few days before the election, Stephanie Friedman, a fifty-year-old mother of three from France who became a naturalized US citizen in 2016, went to cast her ballot at a library in the north Atlanta suburbs. There was no line, and she thought it would take two minutes to vote early. But when she checked in with poll workers, they informed her that her eligibility had been challenged. She didn't know who had done it or why.

A supervisor called the main Fulton County election office, and, after waiting twenty minutes, they confirmed that Friedman was eligible to vote and could cast a ballot that day. But the experience left her frightened and angry, and she worried that voters "who are more vulnerable" and were challenged on days when there were longer lines at the polls "are going to turn around and not vote."

The wide range of new restrictions on mail voting also worked to limit voting options. Democrats promoted mail voting in 2018 and on a much larger scale during the pandemic to increase turnout in Georgia, including among Black voters and other constituencies that were less likely to go to the polls. But they were forced to dramatically scale back those efforts in 2022, instead choosing to put their resources behind encouraging voters to cast ballots in person during the early voting period.

On the first Friday of early voting, Warnock led a golf cart parade to the polls in Peachtree City, a lakefront community thirty miles south of Atlanta.

"It's great to be in the land of the golf carts," he joked.

"Welcome to the South!" a woman in the crowd shouted back.

Republicans carried Fayette County, which included Peachtree

City, by forty-one points in 2000, but Trump won it by only seven points in 2020, a sign of how the state was changing.

"If you turn out, I know how it's going to turn out," said Warnock, who was locked in a close race for re-election.

He hopped in a golf cart with a Warnock sign in the front and led a procession through tall pine trees, around the lake, and to the polling site at the local library, where the line stretched out the door.

A few days later, Abrams spoke at a Black church in Lithonia, fifteen minutes from Stone Mountain, to encourage people to vote on Sunday, when Black churches held "Souls to the Polls" drives.

When the pastor asked how many people had already voted, roughly 80 percent of the hands went up.

As a result of these efforts, Georgia saw record turnout during the early voting period for a midterm, with more than two million ballots cast, well above 2018 levels. Yet that high turnout was spun by Republicans not as a sign of successful organizing against voter suppression efforts, but as evidence that barriers to the ballot box didn't exist, which furthered the GOP narrative that democracy was not under threat.

"How many turnout records do we have to break before Stacey Abrams and President Biden apologize to Georgia?" Gabriel Sterling, the chief operating officer for Raffensperger, told Fox News.

In the end, the effect of SB 202 was less noticeable than the rhetoric of the election deniers running for office, but still significant.

Mail voting fell by 81 percent in Georgia compared to 2020, far more than in other battleground states. Even with Warnock and Abrams at the top of the ticket, the Black share of the electorate dropped to its lowest level since 2006. White turnout was nearly nine points higher than nonwhite turnout, the largest racial gap in a decade. As voting rates decreased for core Democratic constituencies, the passage of SB 202 motivated 142,000 "disenfranchised conservatives," who voted in the 2020 presidential race but stayed home in the January Senate runoffs, to return to the polls in 2022, said the former GOP senator Kelly Loeffler.

Georgia's new voting law wasn't the only reason Abrams lost to Kemp by seven points, but it was almost certainly a contributing factor.

» » » » » »

The consequences of SB 202 became much clearer when Warnock faced another runoff election, this time against the scandal-plagued former Georgia Bulldogs star running back Herschel Walker. Walker was close to a deity in the football-crazed state but had been dogged for months by reports that he had multiple children he did not acknowledge, had paid for women to have abortions, and had a pattern of domestic abuse. He had also loudly claimed that the 2020 election had been stolen and said that Georgia officials who certified the results, which included Kemp and Raffensperger, should be jailed.

Though the runoff system was set up to advantage conservative candidates, Republicans radically changed it after Warnock and Ossoff were elected to the Senate.

SB 202 shortened the runoff period from nine weeks to four, cutting the number of mandatory early voting days from sixteen to five and leaving practically no time to vote by mail. This compressed time frame—which heightened fears of long lines and rejected ballots—was compounded by an unexpected announcement by Raffensperger days after the election that the lone Saturday of early voting would be canceled because of a state holiday following Thanksgiving that was originally created to honor Robert E. Lee.

Raffensperger had earned a lot of goodwill by standing up to Trump during the 2020 election and testifying publicly before the January 6 committee. He was featured on the cover of *Time* before the election as one of "the defenders" of democracy fighting "to save America's elections." But voting rights activists were aghast at his decision. "A Confederate holiday should not prevent the protection of democracy," said Gerald Griggs, president of the Georgia NAACP.

Warnock immediately sued to reinstate Saturday voting. A court quickly ruled in his favor. "I work during the week, and on the weekend you have more time," said Fulton County Superior Court judge Thomas Cox. "There are other Georgians who may only have limited time off, and that may be Saturday." Republicans appealed to the Georgia Supreme Court but were unsuccessful.

More than seventy thousand people voted that Saturday, with turnout especially high in diverse metro Atlanta counties. The next day, Warnock led a march to a polling site during "Souls to the Polls" with civil rights leader Andrew Young and Martin Luther King III. He waited an hour to cast his ballot at the Metropolitan Library in southwest Atlanta. "The only reason we were able to vote yesterday is because I sued them," he said.

Raffensperger's attempt to curtail early voting backfired on Republicans. More than 150,000 voters cast ballots that weekend—the second highest weekend turnout during the past four elections—and the Black share of the electorate was higher than in November 2020.

Warnock welcomed Obama back to Georgia before the last day of early voting, where they made a final plea for voters to go to the polls. "I'm inspired by this strong early vote turnout, but I don't want us to be lulled to sleep," Warnock said. "The other side is already playing games."

That Friday, there were long lines across metro Atlanta. Nearly every polling place in Fulton County saw lines over an hour, with the longest wait of three hours at the East Point library. "These wait times result from bad policy choices," tweeted the Democratic state representative Michelle Au. "This reflects not just voter enthusiasm, but also severely limited options to vote within a highly compressed timeframe resulting from SB 202."

As the state broke early voting records, Republicans once again claimed the high turnout proved that SB 202 did not restrict ballot access, without acknowledging that voters were determined to wait in the long lines created by the shortened early voting period.

"Claims of voter suppression in Georgia," said Raffensperger, "are conspiracy theories no more valid than Bigfoot."

On Election Night, December 6, the results seesawed back and forth. First Warnock was up, then Walker, then Warnock for good when large counties in Atlanta finished reporting their results. Warnock had improved on his margin from November in nearly every county, building what he called "a multi-racial, multi-religious coalition of conscience." The networks called the race at 11 p.m.

Warnock appeared on stage at the Marriott Marquis in downtown Atlanta to loud chants of "six more years."

"Y'all settle down," he told his supporters. He had something he wanted the entire country to hear.

"There are those who would look at the outcome of this race and say that there's no voter suppression in Georgia," Warnock said.

"No!" his supporters yelled.

"Let me be clear," he continued. "Just because people endured long lines that wrapped around buildings, some blocks long, just because they endured the rain and the cold, and all kinds of tricks in order to vote, doesn't mean that voter suppression does not exist. It simply means that you, the people, have decided that your voices will not be silenced."

After Warnock's victory, which gave Democrats a 51-49 advantage in the Senate, the chamber took up legislation to reform the Electoral Count Act of 1887. Trump and Eastman had tried to exploit ambiguities in the antiquated law to overturn the results. A bipartisan group of lawmakers sought to "Trump-proof" the act by raising the threshold for members of Congress to object to Electoral College votes, prohibiting state legislatures from changing the method of designating electors after the election, requiring governors to certify those electors, and specifying that Congress could only count a slate of electors validated by a court if a dispute over the result arose.

"The 117th Congress began under the shadow of a violent insurrection," said the Senate majority leader, Chuck Schumer, "so it is fitting that one of our final actions will be passing a bill safeguarding our elections from future dangers."

Warnock supported these changes, but said they were no substitute for the voting rights legislation the Senate had failed to pass at the beginning of the year.

"We cannot in good conscience abhor election subversion in our presidential elections while at the same time turning a blind eye when the voices of voters are suppressed and subverted on a local and state level," Warnock said on the Senate floor a few days before Christmas. "It is a contradiction that I cannot abide."

Republicans claimed that the defeat of high-profile election deniers and Democrats' relative success overall showed that democracy was not in grave danger.

"The midterms have busted the myth of conservative 'minority rule,'" wrote the conservative *Washington Post* columnist Jason Willick.

But that argument ignored the structural and practical threats to democracy that remained embedded in the system.

Despite the losses by election deniers in key battlegrounds, more than two hundred skeptics of the 2020 election were still elected to Congress and top state offices across the country. Few GOP members of Congress who objected to the results paid a price, but those who attempted to hold Trump accountable for the insurrection, such as the Wyoming representative Liz Cheney, lost their primaries or were forced into retirement.

Aggressive partisan gerrymandering by Republicans in states including Florida, Georgia, Texas, and Tennessee—combined with Supreme Court decisions refusing to strike down racially gerrymandered maps in Alabama and Louisiana before the election—helped Republicans narrowly retake the House.

After Warnock's victory, the Senate Democratic caucus represented 58 percent of the country and 56 million more Americans than Republicans but enjoyed only a two-seat majority, reflecting the continued unrepresentativeness of the body. Democrats came one seat short of having the votes necessary to reform the filibuster to pass voting rights legislation.

And the antidemocratic strains that had infected much of the GOP showed no signs of subsiding. Less than a month after the election,

Trump called for "the termination" of the Constitution. "UNPREC-
EDENTED FRAUD REQUIRES UNPRECEDENTED CURE!" he
wrote on Truth Social. Other conservative intellectuals dug in deeper
against democratic norms. "Elections—and therefore consent and
popular sovereignty—are no longer meaningful," wrote Glenn Ellmers,
a colleague of Eastman's at the Claremont Institute.

Before the year ended and Democrats lost unified control of Washington, Warnock made one last push to approve the Freedom to Vote:
John R. Lewis Act. He asked for unanimous consent to pass it during
the Electoral Count Act debate.

The Nebraska GOP senator Deb Fischer blocked it with an objection. "This is one of those election takeover bills," she said.

"What I would want to ask her is whether she thinks the 1965 Voting Rights law was a federal takeover of state elections and local elections," Warnock asked after Fischer had left the floor. "Without the
1965 Voting Rights law, I would not be standing here." He vowed, "I
will not rest until we live up to that moral obligation."

» » » » » »

There was at least one prominent election denier who won in 2022.

Kris Kobach had hoped to take a job in the second term of a Trump
administration, where he was being vetted for a position. But after
Biden won, he threw his hat in the ring for Kansas attorney general,
the state's top legal office. "I decided to run for attorney general the
day that President Biden was sworn into office," he said.

He'd tried to help Trump overturn the election. On January 6, he'd
participated in a small rally at the statehouse in Topeka, calling on
Congress not to certify the election results, echoing Eastman's claim
that state legislatures still had the power to appoint pro-Trump electors. "At this late stage in the process, ultimately the authority rests
with the state legislatures," he said.

Kobach was dismayed that only Texas had the "backbone" to file
the lawsuit before the Supreme Court that he had proposed challeng-

ing the "election shenanigans" he claimed took place in 2020. He was running for attorney general so that Kansas could stand "shoulder to shoulder" with Texas, whose controversial attorney general, Ken Paxton, had been indicted for securities fraud and impeached by the state House. "I'll think you'll see Kansas be recognized as the other state not to be messed with along with Texas," Kobach said in a debate.

He pledged to create a special litigation unit focused on suing the federal government, recruiting lawyers from across the country to work in it. Kobach's campaign signs said "Sue Joe Biden!"

"I'll wake up every morning having my breakfast, thinking about what our next lawsuit against Joe Biden is going to be," he vowed.

Politicians in both parties scoffed at Kobach's chances. The past few years had not gone well for him.

In June 2018, a federal court struck down his signature law requiring proof of citizenship for voter registration, which had blocked thirty-five thousand people from registering to vote. "The magnitude of potentially disenfranchised voters," wrote Judge Julie Robinson, "cannot be justified by the scant evidence of noncitizen voter fraud." The alleged cases of voter fraud Kobach had presented before the court, which he called "the tip of the iceberg," was "only an icicle," Robinson wrote.

The trial was a disaster for Kobach. He was held in contempt of court for withholding crucial evidence and ordered by Robinson to take legal education classes for errors he made while representing the state. Kansas had to pay nearly $2 million in court fees to the ACLU, even though Kobach had often described himself as the group's "worst nightmare."

His other priorities hadn't fared much better. As the only secretary of state with the power to prosecute voter fraud cases, he'd obtained only a dozen minor convictions, most against elderly voters—many of them Republicans—who'd voted twice because they owned property in two states and didn't realize they were ineligible. They received small fines. He hadn't convicted a single noncitizen of illegal voting, despite claiming that such fraud was "pervasive."

He tried to use the secretary of state position as a springboard to higher office, but he lost races for governor in 2018 and for the GOP primary for US Senate in 2020. After he left office, he served as counsel for We Build the Wall alongside board chair Steve Bannon, who had twice been indicted for misusing funds that were supposed to go toward building a private wall along the US-Mexico border. Kobach was fined $30,000 by the FEC for taking donations from the group during his senate bid and not reporting it.

But Kobach's campaign for attorney general came at a fortuitous time. He had embraced the cause of "election integrity" long before it was fashionable within the Republican Party and his claims of widespread voter fraud were now being embraced by a record number of Republicans, even though they had been thoroughly debunked in court. On the campaign trail, Kobach said he wanted to hunt for new cases of illegal voting and ban mail ballot drop boxes. "You have to have an attorney general who understands that fraud does exist," Kobach said in a debate. "Those on the left who say there's no election fraud are simply ignoring reality."

He won the GOP primary despite being opposed by most of the state's Republican establishment and powerful groups like the Kansas Chamber of Commerce. "This result shows that the swamp in Topeka cannot pick the candidates and decide who wins," he said.

In the general election, he faced Democratic candidate Chris Mann, a little-known former prosecutor and police officer. The understated Mann called Kobach a "comic book villain" but Kobach won by sixteen thousand votes even as Democratic governor Laura Kelly was reelected. Though Kansas was a comfortably red state, Kobach was one of just five nonincumbent election deniers to win a key statewide office with oversight of the election process in 2022.

"I don't care who you are or where you come from, you gotta love a comeback story," he said to cheers at a victory party at the Hotel Topeka. "Tomorrow we begin the process of taking America back and the Kansas attorney general's office is going to be very directly involved in that process."

The attorney general's office was a better fit for Kobach than secretary of state. His hard-line positions on immigration and voting could be instantly nationalized. And he now had a direct pipeline to the Supreme Court, whose conservative supermajority was increasingly sympathetic to his once-radical views.

12

THE GERRYMANDERING OF HISTORY

On January 11, 1870, twenty-two-year-old John Roy Lynch of Natchez walked to the front of the Mississippi House chamber and took the oath of office from Judge E. G. Peyton. Seven years earlier, Lynch had been an enslaved person in Louisiana, not even recognized by the Supreme Court as a citizen of the United States. Now he was vowing to support and defend a constitution whose protections finally applied to him. "You are beginning a new era in the history of Mississippi, and entering upon untried experiments," Greene C. Chandler, a prominent judge and lawyer, told the thirty-five Black legislators elected for the first time.

It was the first integrated legislative session in the history of the state. Less than a decade earlier, Mississippi had been the second state in the Confederacy to secede after South Carolina. Now ex-slaves were taking the places of their former owners, exemplifying the startling changes that were occurring throughout the South. Within days of taking office, Lynch and his colleagues ratified the Fourteenth and Fifteenth Amendments, making it possible for Mississippi to rejoin the Union five years after the end of the war.

Even more remarkable was what happened next: The legislature appointed Hiram Revels, a Black minister also from Natchez, to complete the unexpired US Senate term of Jefferson Davis. This astonished the few Southern Democrats who remained in Congress. They argued that Revels, because of the 1857 *Dred Scott* decision, had not been a US citizen long enough to qualify as a senator. But the radical Republicans who dominated the Senate voted 48-8 to admit him as a new member.

At 4:40 p.m. on February 25, 1870, the Senate gallery rose with a buzz as Revels entered the chamber, took the oath of office, and became the first Black senator in US history. Senator Simon Cameron of Pennsylvania said that he had prophesied the day, telling Davis when he left the chamber in 1861: "I believe, in the justice of God, that a Negro some day will come and occupy your seat."

America had finally begun to live up to the lofty rhetoric of the country's founding document, which proclaimed equality in theory but limited such rights in practice. "The Fifteenth Amendment was conceived in the womb of the Declaration of Independence," Mississippi's first Black secretary of state, James Lynch (no relation to John), said during a celebration at the state capitol in 1870. "The alarming voice in favor of nullification . . . the menaces of Calhoun . . . these are over."

John Roy Lynch, born to an enslaved Black mother and a white father from Ireland who managed a plantation in Louisiana, joined the legislature at a time of great opportunity in the state. Mississippi was a wasteland after the war—even the capitol dome was cracked and on the brink of collapse—and needed to be thoroughly rebuilt. The legislature authorized the construction of new roads and railroads. It repaired public buildings and created new hospitals. It set up the first system of public education, building three thousand schools attended by seventy thousand students, where Black children sang, "We are rising, We are rising, We are rising, as a people."

In its first six months of 1870, the legislature passed 325 new laws and resolutions. The judicial code was completely revamped, all public places integrated, and any law that "discriminate[d] between citizens or inhabitants of this state, founded on race, color, or previous condition of servitude" was repealed. This burst of activity was all the more impressive because most of the new Black legislators, including Lynch, had little formal education. After the war, Lynch had attended a school for Black children run by Northern teachers for four months before the Klan ran them out of town, then surreptitiously continued his studies by overhearing the lessons from a local white school in the alley across from his job at a photography shop.

Thanks to strong support from Black voters, Republicans won a sweeping victory in 1872 and Lynch, at twenty-four, was elected the first Black speaker of the Mississippi House, the first Black man to hold that position in any state. He had fair skin and good looks, slender with wavy hair and a Van Dyke beard, and spoke in a refined manner that impressed whites. "He is one of the most intelligent men of his race, is conservative in his views, and distinctly Caucasian in his habits," wrote the historian James W. Garner.

At the end of his term, the House considered a resolution thanking Lynch for "the able, efficient, and impartial manner in which he presided over the deliberations of this body." John Calhoun of Marshall County moved to strike the word "impartial," but the resolution was overwhelmingly adopted. Lynch was given a gold watch and chain inscribed with his name and title, which he kept for the rest of his life as a family heirloom.

A year later, Lynch made history again, running for Congress and becoming the first Black member of the US House from Mississippi. He was also the youngest member of Congress at twenty-six, representing the sixteen counties in the southern part of the state, from the Mississippi River to the Alabama border. He joined half a dozen other Black Congressmen in the body, entering as the House was debating a bill drafted by Charles Sumner to ban discrimination in hotels, trains, and all public accommodations. It was the last of the major civil rights bills taken up by Congress during Reconstruction.

Lynch drew on his own experience to make a persuasive case for the legislation. "Here am I, a member of your honorable body, representing one of the largest and wealthiest districts in the State of Mississippi," he told his colleagues. Yet when he traveled by train to Washington through the South, "I am treated, not as an American citizen, but as a brute. Forced to occupy a filthy smoking-car both night and day, with drunkards, gamblers, and criminals; and for what? Not that I am unable or unwilling to pay my way; not that I am obnoxious in my personal appearance or disrespectful in my conduct; but simply because I happen to be of a darker complexion."

The issue, Lynch said, was much bigger than whether he could ride in an integrated train car. It struck at the heart of a debate that defined Reconstruction: Were those who had previously been excluded from the Constitution's protections truly free after abolition and entitled to the full benefits of citizenship? On the House floor in February 1875, Lynch took aim at "the Calhoun school of impracticable state rights theorists" who "seem to forget that the Constitution as it is, is not in every respect the Constitution as it was."

The civil rights bill passed in March 1875. Despite this victory, when Lynch returned to Mississippi later that spring, the atmosphere had changed. "The political clouds were dark," he wrote. "Democrats were bold, outspoken, defiant, and determined."

It was the high-water mark of Black politics in the state. In addition to Lynch and the US senator Blanche K. Bruce, Blacks comprised more than 40 percent of the legislature and held the offices of lieutenant governor, secretary of state, and secretary of education. As Black influence grew, outnumbered whites resorted to increasingly extreme tactics to regain power. "The condition of public affairs in 1875," wrote Judge Frank Johnston, a prominent leader of white conservatives, "had grown intolerable to the white men who for years had submitted in silence to the humiliation of negro domination."

That year, segregationist whites took back the state by force, forming militia groups that attacked integrated political meetings and kept Black voters from the polls. President Ulysses S. Grant, worried about inflaming public sentiment ahead of the 1876 presidential election, refused to send federal troops to the state to protect the biracial government. "The legitimate state government, the one that represented the honestly expressed will of a majority of the voters of the state, was, in the fall of 1875, overthrown through the medium of a sanguinary revolution," wrote Lynch. He lost his seat in Congress a year later, when Democratic election officials invalidated nearly five thousand votes cast for him.

Lynch stuck around Mississippi after Reconstruction ended and became Republican Party chair, nominating a full statewide ticket in

1889 for the first time since 1875. That inspired Democrats to rewrite the state constitution in 1890 to enshrine a wide variety of Jim Crow tactics that virtually eliminated the Black vote.

Eight years later, Cornelius Jones, a Black lawyer from the Mississippi delta, challenged the Mississippi constitution on behalf of Henry Williams, a Black man convicted of murder by an all-white jury. Because Blacks were blocked from voting in Mississippi, they could no longer serve on juries based on the voter registration rolls and were denied equal protection, Jones argued.

But the Supreme Court, two years after it enshrined the doctrine of "separate but equal" in *Plessy v. Ferguson*, unanimously upheld the Mississippi constitution. Its provisions "do not, on their face, discriminate between the white and negro races, and do not amount to a denial of the equal protection of the law," Justice Joseph McKenna wrote in *Williams v. Mississippi*. "It has not been shown that their actual administration was evil, but only that evil was possible under them." The widespread suppression of Black votes was an evil the court ignored.

Lynch had passed the Mississippi bar in 1896, but after the *Williams* decision he left the state for Chicago, as part of a great migration of 1.5 million Black Southerners to the North.

» » » » » »

In 1913, Lynch published *The Facts of Reconstruction*, one of the first histories of the era written by a Black participant.

"Very much, of course, has been written and published about Reconstruction, but most of it is superficial and unreliable; and, besides, nearly all of it has been written in such a style and tone as to make the alleged facts related harmonize with what was believed to be demanded by public sentiment," Lynch wrote. His main purpose was "to present the other side."

The histories of Reconstruction written by Lynch's contemporaries described the period as a tragic farce, not because multiracial democracy had been overturned so violently and abruptly, but because it had been attempted at all. Blacks were portrayed as ignorant and corrupt, undeserving of the benefits of citizenship, duped by greedy Northern "carpetbaggers" and conniving Southern "scalawags."

In 1874, James Pike, a prominent reporter with the *New York Tribune*, published *The Prostrate State: South Carolina Under Negro Government*. He portrayed the state legislature as "a mass of black barbarism" and used repellent racial stereotypes. "Sambo," he wrote, "is already his own leader in the Legislature." Pike was revolted by the emergence of majority rule in the state, lamenting that "300,000 white people, more or less composing the intelligence and property-holders of the State, are put under the heel of 400,000 pauper blacks, fresh from a state of slavery and ignorance the most dense." Pike's dispatches for the *Tribune*, which were reprinted in pro-Republican newspapers across the country, and his subsequent book helped turn Northern sentiment against Reconstruction, influencing the federal government's decision not to intervene to protect Black voting rights.

This critique of Reconstruction was reinforced by the first serious histories of the era. In the late 1880s, James Ford Rhodes, an Ohio industrialist turned amateur historian, began publishing a highly popular seven-volume *History of the United States from the Compromise of 1850 to the Final Restoration of Home Rule at the South in 1877*. "No large policy in our country," he wrote, "has ever been so conspicuous a failure as that of forcing universal negro suffrage upon the South." He referred to Reconstruction as the "oppression of the South by the North."

Lynch critiqued Rhodes's work in a series of articles in the *Journal of Negro History* in 1917 and 1918. "I regret to say that, so far as the Reconstruction period is concerned, it is not only inaccurate and unreliable but it is the most biased, partisan, and prejudiced historical work I have ever read," he wrote.

The integrated state governments under Reconstruction "were the best governments those States ever had before or have ever had since," Lynch argued, because "they were the first and only governments in that section that were based upon the consent of the governed."

Lynch's defense of Reconstruction was overshadowed by the writings of white historians who were hostile to Black suffrage. This historiography was institutionalized by Columbia University historian William Archibald Dunning and his crop of influential PhD students, many of whom traveled from the South to study with him. They were the first generation of professional historians who produced seminal works on Reconstruction overall and detailed studies of each Southern state that defined how the era was understood for decades. The Dunning school provided "an intellectual foundation for Jim Crow," the Columbia University historian Eric Foner wrote.

Dunning, a New Jerseyan who served as president of the American Historical Association and the American Political Science Association, opposed the effort to grant new rights to former slaves. "To stand the social pyramid on its apex was not the surest way to restore the shattered equilibrium in the South," he wrote in *Essays on the Civil War and Reconstruction*, published in 1898. "The enfranchisement of the freedmen and their enthronement in political power was as reckless a species of statecraft as that which marked 'the blind hysterics of the Celt' in 1789–95."

Dunning's students went further. Walter L. Fleming, author of *Civil War and Reconstruction in Alabama*, defended the KKK and collaborated with the United Daughters of the Confederacy. Even the most fair-minded of these histories were ripe with bias. In *Reconstruction in Mississippi*, James W. Garner praised Lynch but wrote that the desire of Black legislators to become speaker of the house was "another illustration of their greed for political power." The integrated government in Mississippi had collapsed, Garner wrote, because "a superior race will not submit to the government of an inferior one."

The contributions of Black politicians were downplayed and ridiculed, if mentioned at all, by Dunning and his contemporaries. In *Freedom's Lawmakers: A Directory of Black Officeholders During Reconstruction*, Foner described how Alexander St. Clair Abrams, author of Georgia's legislative manual, deleted Black lawmakers from the volume's biographical sketches after ex-Confederates retook the state. It would be foolish to document "the lives of men who were but yesterday our slaves, and whose past careers, probably, embraced such menial occupations as boot-blacking, shaving, table waiting, and the like," he wrote. It was as if the likes of Lynch and Henry McNeal Turner had never existed.

This weaponization of history propelled the Lost Cause movement, led by Confederate veterans and their families, which promoted reconciliation efforts with the North by portraying the Civil War not as a fight to maintain slavery, but as a noble struggle to preserve an old-time Southern way of life. As Reconstruction laws were wiped off the books, monuments were erected to Confederate generals throughout the South, with a hundred thousand people turning out in Richmond, Virginia, on Memorial Day 1890 to see the unveiling of a giant statue of Robert E. Lee on horseback.

"The Southern victory over Reconstruction replaced Union victory in the war and Jim Crow laws replaced the Fourteenth Amendment in their places of honor in national memory," David Blight wrote in *Race and Reunion: The Civil War in American Memory*. If students attended a school named after Robert E. Lee, celebrated a holiday honoring him, passed his statue in the town square every day, and read about the horrors of the war and evils of Reconstruction in their textbooks, they would think that Jim Crow was as American as apple pie.

D. W. Griffith's 1915 film *The Birth of a Nation*, based on the novel *The Clansman* by Thomas Dixon Jr., brought this ideology to the mainstream. The son of a Confederate army colonel in Kentucky, Griffith promoted the most odious racial stereotypes in his three-hour silent epic, depicting Black members of the South Carolina legislature barefoot, eating fried chicken, and drinking whiskey while passing a law legalizing interracial marriage. A former slave attempts to rape a white woman before the KKK heroically appears on horseback to prevent Blacks from voting on Election Day, returning white rule to the South. It was the first film ever shown at the White House, and it revived the KKK, which had been dormant since the end of Reconstruction but used the film to recruit millions of new members in its second iteration. Ushers dressed in white robes for screenings.

Two years after the film's premiere, as racist propaganda once dismissed during Reconstruction was accepted by many in the North, Lynch voiced his hope that "a fair, just, and impartial historian will, someday, write a history covering the Reconstruction period, in which an accurate account based upon actual facts of what took place at the time will be given."

W.E.B. Du Bois, the Harvard-trained sociologist and cofounder of the NAACP, answered that call in 1935, publishing *Black Reconstruction: An Essay Toward a History of the Part Which Black Folk Played in the Attempt to Reconstruct Democracy in America, 1860–1880*. It was much more than an essay. At 729 pages, it represented the first major history of Reconstruction written by a Black author that put the struggles and achievements of Black Americans at the center of the narrative.

Reconstruction, Du Bois argued, was not a tragic error but a "splendid failure," one that enshrined equality in the Constitution, laid the foundation for multiracial democracy, and created the South's first public schools and other notable reforms. His last chapter, "The Propaganda of History," was a scorching indictment of how a generation of white historians had portrayed Reconstruction. He was "literally aghast at what American historians have done to this field," Du Bois wrote.

"In order to paint the South as a martyr to inescapable fate, to make the North the magnanimous emancipator, and to ridicule the Negro as the impossible joke in the whole development, we have in fifty years, by libel, innuendo and silence, so completely misstated and obliterated the history of the Negro in America and his relation to its work and government that today it is almost unknown," he concluded. "This may be fine romance, but it is not science. It may be inspiring, but it is certainly not the truth. And beyond this it is dangerous. It is not only part foundation of our present lawlessness and loss of democratic ideals; it has, more than that, led the world to embrace and worship the color bar as social salvation and it is helping to range mankind in ranks of mutual hatred and contempt, at the summons of a cheap and false myth."

Though reviewed favorably in *The New York Times*, Du Bois's monumental work was largely dismissed by white historians at the time. University of Chicago historian Avery Craven called it "a half-baked Marxian interpretation" and "badly distorted picture of the Negroes' part in Southern life." But four years after its publication, the South Carolina–born historian Francis Simkins, who had studied under Dunning, published a remarkably frank rebuke to his colleagues in the *Journal of Southern History*.

"A biased interpretation of Reconstruction caused one of the most important political developments in the recent history of the South, the disfranchisement of the blacks," Simkins wrote in 1939. "The fraud and violence by which this objective was first obtained was justified on a single ground: the memory of the alleged horrors of Reconstruction."

He condemned the "extremely partisan judgment" of his fellow white historians and called for "more moderate, saner, perhaps newer views of [t]his period," which he hoped would "aid in the solution of the South's great race problem."

That awakening wouldn't occur until the 1960s, when the civil rights movement sought to tear down the architecture of white supremacy in all facets of American life and create a Second Reconstruction.

On February 23, 1968, Martin Luther King Jr. appeared at Carnegie Hall, alongside James Baldwin and Pete Seeger, to celebrate Du Bois's one hundredth birthday, five years after his death.

It would be King's last major speech in New York City, delivered six weeks before his assassination in Memphis. Du Bois "before anyone else and more than anyone else, demolished the lies about Negroes in their most important and creative period of history," King said. "The truths he revealed are not yet the property of all Americans but they have been recorded and arm us for our contemporary battles."

» » » » »

A case from Mississippi concerning the fundamental meaning of the Reconstruction amendments would give the conservative movement its biggest victory in the culture wars in the past fifty years—and show the lengths they would go to to rewrite history to achieve that end.

On June 24, 2022, Justice Samuel Alito authored the majority opinion in *Dobbs v. Jackson Women's Health Organization* overturning *Roe v. Wade*, a once-unthinkable outcome that took away a constitutionally protected right for the first time in US history.

"We cannot turn the clock back to 1868," Earl Warren had written in *Brown v. Board of Education*, but that's precisely what Alito had done. He pointed to history 67 times to justify his decision, most notably the passage of the Fourteenth Amendment in 1868, which the Court in *Roe v. Wade* said protected the right to privacy. Since abortion was not mentioned in the Constitution, Alito wrote, it must be "deeply rooted in this nation's history and tradition." But until the *Roe* decision in 1973, the right to an abortion "was entirely unknown in American law," he wrote. "When the Fourteenth Amendment was adopted, three quarters of the States made abortion a crime at all stages of pregnancy." He was interpreting the rights of women based on a period fifty years before they had the right to vote.

The sources Alito cited in support of his historical narrative included a thirteenth-century English judge who advocated for human slavery and a seventeenth-century jurist who executed two women for "witchcraft," defended marital rape, and said fourteen-year-olds should be subject to capital punishment. But the problem wasn't just that Alito relied on sketchy and antiquated historical sources. It's that he got the facts about the past wrong too.

His opinion claimed that "an unbroken tradition of prohibiting abortion on pain of criminal punishment persisted from the earliest days of the common law until 1973." But from the founding of the country through the Civil War, abortion was legal in a majority of states prior to the first signs of fetal movement, known as "quickening," which usually occurred around sixteen to twenty weeks into a pregnancy.

Meanwhile, he downplayed the sexist and nativist motivations behind restrictions on abortion that passed prior to the Fourteenth

Amendment's ratification. In 1857, Massachusetts doctor Horatio Storer and his allies in the newly formed American Medical Association launched a campaign to ban abortions to preserve traditional gender roles and protect Anglo-Protestant dominance from a growing Catholic population. As the country expanded westward and the South was rebuilt, would the frontier "be filled by our own children or by those of aliens?" Storer asked. "This is a question that our own women must answer; upon their loins depends the future destiny of the nation."

But even after states like Ohio banned abortion in 1867 following Storer's lobbying, alleging that women were "living in a state of legalized prostitution" and permitting "our broad and fertile prairies to be settled only by the children of aliens," still only a minority of states outlawed the procedure pre-quickening before the Fourteenth Amendment's enactment. "The court adopted a flawed interpretation of abortion criminalization that has been pressed by anti-abortion advocates for more than 30 years," said a joint statement from the American Historical Association and the Organization of American Historians.

Originalism claimed to be grounded in an authentic reading of the framers' intentions, but Alito was redefining what counted as legitimate history, cherry-picking the past to suit his present-day interests. In so doing, he turned the Fourteenth Amendment, which was meant to guarantee equal citizenship to African Americans and protect rights that included bodily autonomy for formerly enslaved women after decades of rape and forced pregnancies, into a vehicle used to set the progress of women back 150 years.

"When the majority says that we must read our foundational charter as viewed at the time of ratification (except that we may also check it against the Dark Ages), it consigns women to second-class citizenship," Justices Stephen Breyer, Sonia Sotomayor, and Kagan wrote in dissent.

Conservatives were prevailing in these cultural battles because they had aggressively taken hold of the country's countermajoritarian institutions. A Supreme Court supermajority constructed through a series of antidemocratic maneuvers, which owed its existence to presidents who lost the popular vote and senators representing a minority of Americans, had issued a decision opposed by more than 60 percent of the public that rescinded a fundamental right for tens of millions of women. They had frozen the Constitution in the country's undemocratic past, when a majority of Americans were excluded from political participation, in order to issue radical rulings at odds with precedent and popular sentiment. They were using the conservative capture of the courts to take America back in time.

As a rejoinder, Alito said his decision simply returned "the issue of abortion" from unelected judges "to the people's elected representatives." In Wisconsin, Vos had made a similar argument when Republicans stripped Evers of power. The legislature was "the most representative branch of government and the closest to the people of Wisconsin," he claimed in 2018.

But Wisconsin showed how disconnected "the people's elected representatives" could be from the people themselves, largely because of court rulings legalizing gerrymandering, voter suppression, and dark money that gave the legislature a free hand to entrench its own power and ignore popular sentiment. Evers twice called special sessions of the legislature to repeal an 1849 law criminalizing all abortions in Wisconsin, even in cases of rape or incest, that immediately went into effect following the *Dobbs* decision. Both times GOP leaders gaveled in and out within seconds, despite polls showing that 63 percent of Wisconsinites opposed overturning *Roe v. Wade* and 83 percent believed abortion should be allowed in cases of rape or incest.

Evers had a favorite phrase that was inscribed on the ceiling of the ornate conference room where he signed bills and made announcements: "the will of the people is the law of the land." After Republicans refused to debate changing the abortion law, he said angrily, "when it comes to reproductive freedom, the will of the people isn't the law of the land."

Dobbs was not a one-off. A day before Alito selectively deployed history to take away abortion rights, Justice Thomas selectively deployed history to dramatically expand gun rights by striking down a New York law from 1913 requiring a "special need for self-protection" to obtain a concealed carry permit, a decision opposed by eight in ten New Yorkers.

For the past decade, the courts had judged gun restrictions based on the text of the Second Amendment and the government's modern-day interest in protecting public safety. Thomas deemed the latter "one step too many." Gun restrictions could only be constitutional, he wrote, if they matched the "historical tradition of firearm regulation" that existed when the Second Amendment was ratified in 1791 and the Fourteenth Amendment in 1868, which the Court said extended protections for gun rights to the states. He went so far as to cite *Dred Scott*, widely considered one of the worst decisions in Supreme Court history, to support his contention that "public carry was a component of the right to keep and bear arms."

Thomas's rigid history test ignored the forty-five thousand gun deaths in the United States per year, the mass shootings that killed twenty-one people in Uvalde and ten in Buffalo just weeks earlier, the record support for gun regulation following those atrocities, and the fact that modern weapons of war like AR-15s, which can fire nine hundred rounds per minute, were in no way comparable to an eighteenth-century musket. The court was creating "a one-way ratchet that will disqualify virtually any 'representative historical analogue' and make it nearly impossible to sustain common-sense regulations necessary to our nation's safety and security," Breyer dissented. "A standard that relies solely on history is unjustifiable and unworkable."

Much like defenders of the South had reshaped the memory of Reconstruction to support the establishment of Jim Crow, powerful forces in the Republican Party and the conservative movement were distorting history to impose a reactionary ideology on a changing society that would preserve the power structure of the past. They were gerrymandering history to justify the gerrymandering of politics and culture.

» » » » » »

On September 9, 1912, Sleety Mae Crow, an eighteen-year-old girl in Georgia's Forsyth County, was found beaten and unconscious on the banks of the Chattahoochee River, thirty miles north of Atlanta in the foothills of the Appalachian Mountains.

The next day, the county sheriff arrested three Black men who were allegedly seen in the area, despite no physical evidence or motive linking them to the crime. When twenty-four-year-old Rob Edwards, known as Big Rob, was taken to the jail in the county seat of Cumming, a mob of two thousand whites overwhelmed the single deputy guarding him. They beat Edwards with a crowbar, shot him repeatedly, then dragged him through the streets before hanging his mutilated body from a telephone pole in the town square.

Two Black teenagers, Ernest Knox and Oscar Daniel, were tried and convicted in a single day. Five thousand people—half the population of Forsyth County—watched their hangings.

After Crow was buried, armed white men on horseback with guns, dynamite, and kerosene went door to door at night in the Black community, burning down houses and telling residents to leave within twenty-four hours or be killed. Within a few weeks, nearly all of the 1,098 Black residents had fled. Only thirty Black people remained by 1920, and soon they would leave too. It was the largest expulsion of Black people from a single county in American history.

Seventy-five years later, in January 1987, the civil rights activist Hosea Williams, who marched next to John Lewis on Bloody Sunday, led a small group of fifty Black and white demonstrators through Forsyth County, which at the time contained only one Black resident out of a population of thirty thousand, to commemorate the racial expulsion and celebrate the newly created Martin Luther King Jr. holiday. A much larger crowd of angry whites—including members of the

Klan—threw bottles and rocks at Williams as he sang "We Shall Over-come." They carried Confederate flags, shouted "Nigger, go home!" and held signs that said, "Racial Purity is Forsyth's Security." It was Bloody Sunday in color. "We've got a South Africa in the back yard of Atlanta," Williams said.

It wasn't until the winter of 2021—109 years after the expulsion—that the Community Remembrance Project of Forsyth County un-veiled a blue historical marker in the town square of Cumming to mark where Edwards was lynched and detail the "mob violence" that forced Black residents to flee. It was a small symbol of how the country was finally grappling with its racist past.

The previous summer, after the murder of George Floyd and other unarmed Black men and women at the hands of police, between 15 million to 26 million people marched in support of the Black Lives Matter movement, the largest mass demonstrations in American history. Three-quarters of Americans said racism and racial discrimi-nation were a "big problem" in society, up twenty-six points from 2015. Books about antiracism shot to the top of the bestseller list. The US military said it would change the names of nine bases commemorat-ing Confederate generals. Statues honoring the likes of Calhoun and Lee were removed from cities such as Charleston and Richmond. Fair-fax, Virginia, renamed Robert E. Lee High School after John Lewis.

But as was often the case throughout American history, this "ra-cial reckoning," as Biden called it, led to an equally potent "counter-reckoning" among aggrieved conservative whites. Trump fanned the flames of white grievance, calling Black Lives Matter activists "domes-tic terrorists" and denouncing the effort to remove the symbols of the Confederacy.

"Our nation is witnessing a merciless campaign to wipe out our history, defame our heroes, erase our values and indoctrinate our children," Trump said during a speech at Mount Rushmore on July 3, 2020.

That fall, he authorized the creation of the 1776 Commission to restore "patriotic education." It was dominated by members of conservative think tanks like the Heritage Foundation and Claremont Institute but included no historians of the United States.

The commission issued its report two days before Trump left office. It likened "progressivism" to fascism and slavery as "challenges to America's principles" and compared the prolife movement to "great reforms" such as abolition. Though released on Martin Luther King Day, it claimed that the civil rights movement "almost immediately turned to programs that ran counter to the lofty ideals of the founders . . . not unlike those advanced by Calhoun and his followers."

Historians quickly dismissed the report as right-wing agitprop. "They're using something they call history to stoke culture wars," said James Grossman, the executive director of the American Historical Association.

But some scholars warned that historians ignored it at their own peril. "The 1776 Report will undoubtedly shape deliberations about history and social studies education at the local and state levels, especially in places where right-wing activists have taken over educational policymaking," predicted New York University historian Tom Sugrue.

》 》 》 》 》 》

In April 2022, Brian Kemp made a trip to Forsyth County, not to visit the lynching memorial but to sign a bill banning the teaching of "divisive concepts" in K–12 schools. The concepts prohibited under the Protect Students First Act included the idea that "the United States of America is fundamentally racist" and that a student "bears individual responsibility for actions committed in the past by other individuals of the same race" or should feel "anguish, guilt, or any other form of psychological distress" from instances of racism. (It ignored the distress of actually being subjected to racism.)

"We put students and parents first by keeping woke politics out of the classroom," the governor said at a local education center just a few miles from where Edwards had been lynched, before a nearly all-white group of state legislators, parents, and students. Months earlier, the Forsyth County school district, after protests from white parents, had banned eight books for allegedly explicit material, including Toni Morrison's debut novel, *The Bluest Eye.*

Kemp didn't mention the irony of signing a law preventing teachers from addressing America's racist past in a county that had forcibly expelled all of its Black residents a century earlier.

"What supports white supremacy more than making rules to say you can't talk about racism or white supremacy?" asked Jaha Howard, a Democratic candidate for state superintendent of education.

The Georgia bill followed a flurry of similar laws passed by GOP-controlled legislatures.

Texas prohibited teaching that "slavery and racism are anything other than deviations from, betrayals of, or failures to live up to the authentic founding principles of the United States, which include liberty and equality."

Kentucky stated that "the institution of slavery and post-Civil War laws enforcing racial segregation and discrimination were contrary to the fundamental American promise of life, liberty, and the pursuit of happiness, as expressed in the Declaration of Independence, but that defining racial disparities solely on the legacy of this institution is destructive to the unification of our nation."

Florida banned an AP African American studies course and relented only after the work of prominent Black writers was removed. The revised curriculum approved by the state board of education claimed that enslaved people "developed skills" that "could be applied for their personal benefit," and instructed teachers that when students learned about racial massacres against Black people, such as the lynching in Forsyth County, they should note "acts of violence perpetrated against and by African Americans." The state's Stop W.O.K.E. Act also prohibited schools and businesses from using any training programs that suggested that an individual was "inherently racist, sexist, or oppressive, whether consciously or unconsciously."

In the first two years following Trump's presidency, nineteen states passed laws restricting how history and current events could be taught, the same number of states that had passed laws making it harder to vote during the same period. There was remarkable overlap between the attacks on education and voting rights, and the conservative groups behind them.

The Republican sponsor of Georgia's Protect Students First Act said he used language from model legislation drafted by the Heritage Foundation, which claimed that "slavery, legal racial discrimination, and racism are so inconsistent with the founding principles of the United States" and that "America and its institutions are not systemically racist." The foundation's president, a Black woman named Kay James, had been ousted early in 2021 after being criticized by Tucker Carlson for condemning the "ugly racism that stains our nation's history and afflicts us like a cancer of the soul" following the murder of George Floyd. She was replaced by a conservative leader from Texas who said the group's priorities would be "education, education, and education."

This was a new front in an old war. Conservatives had long focused on taking over local school boards and reshaping education. In the 1970s, the Heritage Foundation sent organizers to a West Virginia county where parents complained the textbooks were "anti-Christian" and "anti-white," helping to foster a new "parental rights" movement. Paul Weyrich told the platform committee of the Republican National Convention in 1976 that public school textbooks were "being used to denigrate their parental authority, to deride the values upon which this country has been built, to mock, sneer, vituperate."

Though educators said critical race theory (CRT)—a forty-year-old academic framework arguing that racism was not just the product of individual prejudice but systemically embedded in American society—was not taught in Georgia public schools, Heritage Action said the concept had "infiltrated Georgia schools with the goal to re-shape K–12 education, teaching children that everything must be viewed through the lens of race." The group had made the crusade against CRT its top priority along with passing state-level voting restrictions, turning an obscure academic concept into the centerpiece of a new culture war that opposed any effort to redress racial discrimination. Conservative groups and politicians sought to censor and rewrite history to preserve the dominant status of a shrinking white minority. "It could turn out to be one of the most important conservative grassroots fights since the Tea Party movement," Jessica Anderson said.

In the summer of 2021, Heritage Action launched a website—saveourschools.com—and released a "Reject Critical Race Theory" e-book so that conservative activists could "understand what CRT is, identify it in their community's schools, and issue FOIA requests to expose how school administrators are promoting CRT." That December, the Heritage Foundation and Heritage Action organized a letter from conservative groups calling on state legislatures "to reject the racial prejudice inherent in Critical Race Theory." Shortly thereafter, bills restricting how race and history could be taught began moving quickly through the Georgia legislature and their prevalence increased by 250 percent nationwide.

Voter suppression and history suppression went hand-in-hand. One tactic was aimed at reshaping the composition of the electorate and preventing historically disenfranchised communities from exercising true political power, while the other tactic sought to prevent the next generation from understanding why those groups faced discrimination in the first place and how that legacy impacted present-day disparities in voting, housing, jobs, policing, and many other facets of life. As the Supreme Court clung to a distorted version of the past to roll back fundamental rights, conservatives were whitewashing the teaching of history to prevent honest conversations about contemporary inequities. "They are trying to manipulate power and exert their influence at both ends of the spectrum by limiting those who can cast ballots now, and by indoctrinating those who can cast ballots later," said Janai Nelson, president of the NAACP Legal Defense Fund.

For Warnock, who was steeped in history as pastor of King's church while also on the frontlines of fighting attacks on voting rights, the connection between the two tactics was impossible to ignore. "It's hard to miss the fact that in this moment, when we're seeing a kind of unabashed and unembarrassed emergence of bigotry unlike anything I've seen in my lifetime, as a post–civil rights generation baby, there is at the same time an effort afoot to rob our young people of the tools that give them the vocabulary and tools of analysis for understanding what's happening," he said. "It's a dangerous combination. And people of goodwill, regardless of their politics, have to stand up and reject this idea that our children are somehow so weak and so unable to handle the truth of history that we must hide it from them."

In the fall of 2021, as educational gag orders proliferated in GOP-controlled states, the Library of America released a new version of *Black Reconstruction*, edited by Eric Foner and Henry Louis Gates Jr.

"We have too often a deliberate attempt so to change the facts of history that the story will make pleasant reading for Americans," Du Bois wrote in the last chapter. He was "astonished" by "the recurrence of the idea that evil must be forgotten, distorted, skimmed over . . . We must forget that George Washington was a slave owner, or that Thomas Jefferson had mulatto children." The problem with this philosophy, he wrote, "is that history loses its value as an incentive and example; it paints perfect men and noble nations, but it does not tell the truth."

» » » » » »

The defeat of Reconstruction and the attempt to overthrow the Second Reconstruction—in politics and culture—were both driven by the fear that new demographic groups were on the verge of forming enduring multiracial coalitions.

That majority-minority future had already arrived among the country's youth. The 2020 census revealed that for the first time in US history a majority of the population younger than eighteen were people of color. They comprised 55 percent of public school students in grades

K–12. The graduating high school class of 2022–2023 would be the last in which white students were a majority.

The panic over the "browning of America" motivated the most extreme elements of the GOP. On the one-year anniversary of the January 6 insurrection, the University of Chicago's Project on Security and Threats released a detailed study of the more than seven hundred people arrested for breaching the Capitol.

They were 93 percent white and 85 percent male. But some of the findings were surprising. Unlike many Republicans, the insurrectionists didn't come from the country's reddest or most rural counties. Instead, they were more likely to reside in counties that had experienced the most significant declines in the white population, such as Harris County, Texas, and Putnam County, New York. The study painted a portrait of a political movement "driven by racial cleavages and white discontent with diversifying communities."

In a larger national poll, the Chicago Project found that 8 percent of the public believed that Biden's presidency was "illegitimate" and that force was "justified" to return Trump to power. Of these 21 million Americans, three-quarters agreed that "the Democratic Party is trying to replace the current electorate . . . with new people, more obedient voters from the Third World." Fears of a "Great Replacement" were the "most important driver of [the] insurrectionist movement," the survey concluded.

In the 1990s, when Buchanan first raised the issue of white displacement, he was ahead of his time in understanding that so many political fights were really about culture.

"Today in too many of our schools, children are being robbed of their innocence," Buchanan said when he launched his 1996 presidential campaign in Manchester, New Hampshire, nearly three decades before the conservative outcry over CRT. "Their minds are being poisoned against their Judeo-Christian heritage, against America's heroes and American history, against the values of faith, family and country." It was a battle, he said, that "we can't walk away from."

As Buchanan spoke, four Jewish college students from New York rushed the stage, chanting "Buchanan is a racist" and holding signs that said, "Buchanan Equals David Duke Without the Sheet."

After they were tackled by security, Buchanan raised his arms triumphantly and held two thumbs up in a Nixon-like gesture. He seemed to relish the confrontation. "Now you know what we're fighting against in this country," he said to cheers.

EPILOGUE: A NEW LABORATORY FOR DEMOCRACY

On November 6, 2018, Katie Fahey stepped to the podium at a ballroom in Detroit's Atheneum Suite Hotel carrying a flute of champagne in each hand.

"Hey Michigan," she told a crowd of jubilant supporters. "We just amended the state Constitution!"

Her group, Voters Not Politicians (VNP), had passed a landmark ballot initiative to end gerrymandering in one of the country's most gerrymandered states. That result—and the events that led to it—were altogether improbable.

Two years earlier, Fahey was a twenty-seven-year-old political novice from the Grand Rapids area who worked as a program manager for a recycling nonprofit. Two days after the 2016 election, dismayed by Trump's ten-thousand-vote upset victory in Michigan and the GOP's stranglehold over state politics, she'd posted on Facebook before leaving for work: "I'd like to take on gerrymandering in Michigan. If you're interested in doing this as well, please let me know." She added a smiley face emoji for a millennial touch.

When she got to the office, she saw that her post was going viral with likes and positive replies. But she knew little about the topic at hand. She googled "how do you end gerrymandering?" and visited the website Ballotpedia. She learned that Michigan was one of two dozen states that allowed citizens to put ballot initiatives directly before the voters. But doing so required gathering 315,000 signatures in 180 days, a prospect that seemed insurmountable. The only thing Fahey had ever organized was the Grand Rapids Improv Festival.

Nancy Wang, an environmental law professor at the University of Michigan, was one of the people who responded to Fahey's Facebook post, becoming head of the group's policy committee. "We were very excited to learn that there was something we could do, even though to take advantage of direct democracy was very daunting," she said. "The path was basically impossible but there was a path."

But to the surprise of everyone, themselves included, Fahey and four thousand volunteers recruited through social media collected 428,000 signatures in 110 days with no paid staff—which had never been done before in Michigan history—to put an initiative on the ballot. It called for an independent citizens commission, instead of the state legislature, to draw new political districts. "Redistricting and gerrymandering seemed like that fundamental issue where we could really start changing the system and trust it again," Fahey said.

But getting an initiative on the ballot was one thing; upending the state's political system was quite another. Since 2011, Republicans in Michigan had enshrined minority rule on a scale that rivaled neighboring Wisconsin.

With the help of the national GOP, Michigan Republicans drew legislative maps in 2011 that allowed them to "cram ALL the Dem garbage," in the words of one GOP staffer, into as few seats as possible to maximize Republican power. The following year, Republican state legislative candidates received only 46 percent of statewide votes but controlled 54 percent of seats. That outcome—where Republicans got a minority of votes but a majority of seats—repeated itself in every major state legislative election for the next decade. The GOP's national redistricting group, which was advised by Tom Hofeller, wrote that "the effectiveness" of their strategy was "perhaps most clear in the state of Michigan." In 2019, a federal court called Michigan's legislative maps "a gerrymander of historical proportions."

Republicans had transformed the state from a blue-collar Rust Belt Democratic stronghold to a Wisconsin-like laboratory for oligarchy. The state's Republican governor, Rick Snyder, a wealthy business executive elected in 2010 who called himself "one tough nerd," was a close ally of Scott Walker who implemented similar policies, such as cutting taxes for corporations and curtailing labor rights. Michigan had its own version of the Bradley Foundation in the DeVos family, owners of the multilevel marketing company Amway, which had spent more than $100 million backing conservative candidates and causes in the state to promote the values of "God, America, Free Enterprise." (Betsy DeVos served as Trump's education secretary.) A state that had once embodied the American dream, making the cars that symbolized the country's prosperity, had become known as a place where "good ideas go to die," said Michael Li of the Brennan Center for Justice.

The GOP's grip on power allowed them to ignore the will of the voters. Shortly after taking office in 2011, Michigan Republicans passed a law dramatically expanding the governor's ability to appoint emergency managers to run financially troubled cities. In practice, this allowed unelected bureaucrats appointed by white Republicans to govern majority-Black cities like Detroit and Flint. Fifty-two percent of Black residents in Michigan—compared with only 2 percent of whites—lived in places under emergency management. This was another form of nullification, denying a majority of the state's Black population the right to be represented by officials they elected.

Michigan voters viewed the emergency manager law as an attack on representative democracy and repealed it through a ballot referendum in 2012. It passed in seventy-six of the state's eighty-three counties. But a month later, despite Snyder's claim that "we clearly heard, recognized and respected the will of the voters," he signed a new bill that reinstated the emergency manager law and included a provision that it could not be repealed again at the ballot box. Shortly thereafter, the emergency manager Snyder appointed in Flint made the decision to change the city's water supply from a treated water plant in Detroit to the polluted Flint River, causing one of the worst public health disasters in recent American history.

"It felt like until we got politicians actually having to be responsive to the will of the people, nothing would change," Fahey said. "If something as big as the Flint water crisis didn't change behavior in Lansing, what would?"

Flint became exhibit A for why Fahey and her fellow volunteers wanted to restore legitimacy to the state's broken political institutions. In her office she kept a quilted map of the state's districts created by volunteers that proclaimed, "All political power is inherent in the people," quoting the opening words of the state constitution. That became the guiding light for Fahey and her fellow organizers.

"Maybe I was a naïve twentysomething, but I just wanted to believe in the concept of democracy again," she said. "When you go back and look at the Declaration of Independence, it says government should come from the consent of the governed."

That basic idea, which was so fundamental to the country's founding but challenged throughout American history, propelled Voters Not Politicians to a shocking victory in 2018, with 61 percent of voters approving their ballot initiative. The group survived a challenge from the Michigan Chamber of Commerce that tried to disqualify the initiative before the state Supreme Court and a barrage of negative ads from the DeVos-funded Michigan Freedom Fund that sought to defeat it at the ballot box. "VNP really was revolutionary," Wang said. "We showed that even in this day of huge moneyed interests fighting against people, people actually have a way of winning."

That same year, a coalition of groups led by state chapters of the ACLU, League of Women Voters, and NAACP spearheaded another ballot initiative, passed by 66 percent of voters, that dramatically expanded voter access in the state through policies like automatic and Election Day registration and no-excuse absentee voting. In addition to its gerrymandered maps, Michigan had some of the country's most restrictive voting laws: it was one of only two states, alongside Mississippi, that had done nothing to increase ballot access in previous decades. This led to persistent gaps in voter participation: 76 percent of whites were registered to vote compared to 68 percent of Asian Americans, 67 percent of African Americans, and 49 percent of Hispanics. "When you have a system that is so arcane, you have a democratic system that is excluding large numbers of individuals," said Sharon Dolente, an attorney for the Michigan ACLU who became a senior adviser to the new Promote the Vote coalition.

Collectively, the two ballot initiatives represented the largest expansion of democracy in the state in decades. And the fact that they were spearheaded by citizens, not lawmakers, and approved directly by the voters across party lines, resurrected the idea that states could become laboratories of democracy again. "It's a great success story for democracy," said Jocelyn Benson, a former voting rights lawyer who was elected secretary of state in 2018. "And it shows how when states are laboratories for democracy, in a voter-centric way, they can demonstrate ways to make democracy healthier across the country."

» » » » » »

Still, despite these major advances for democracy, Michigan was far from a postpartisan utopia.

On April 30, 2020, days after Trump tweeted "Liberate Michigan!," armed protesters wearing camouflage fatigues and bulletproof vests and carrying semiautomatic rifles slung over their shoulders, occupied the state capitol in Lansing to protest Democratic governor Gretchen Whitmer's stay-at-home order during the pandemic. One lawmaker later called it a "dress rehearsal" for the insurrection. At least two of the protesters would subsequently be among the fourteen people charged in a failed plot to kidnap Whitmer and bomb the state capitol.

Trump focused on Michigan early in his attempt to overturn the 2020 results. Two days after the election, his supporters tried to stop votes from being counted at the TCI Center in Detroit, raucously banging on the doors to be let in. The GOP leaders of the Michigan legislature flew to the White House when Trump lobbied them to appoint their own electors to reverse Biden's 154,000-vote margin of victory in the state. The state board of canvassers came perilously close to refusing to certify the election result, which would've plunged the country into a constitutional crisis. Sixteen Republicans were charged with felonies by the state's attorney general for fraudulently posing as pro-Trump electors and attempting to overthrow the will of the state's voters.

Two years later, Republican candidates who denied the outcome of the election were nominated to run for governor, attorney general, and secretary of state. Cleta Mitchell trained conservative activists in the state to be poll watchers, urging them to engage in "hand-to-hand combat with the Left."

To counteract these threats, the groups behind the two 2018 ballot initiatives—Voters Not Politicians and Promote the Vote—teamed up to oppose the election deniers and pass a third ballot initiative protecting voting rights. Once again, the prodemocracy efforts succeeded. All the election deniers running for statewide office were defeated in the midterms. And 60 percent of voters approved a new ballot initiative to expand voting access through policies like nine days of early voting and funding for ballot drop boxes while combating election subversion by requiring that election results be certified strictly based on county vote totals, with no interference from partisan actors. Voters also passed another ballot initiative, with 57 percent support, enshrining the right to "reproductive freedom" in the Michigan constitution.

A year earlier, new political districts for the state legislature and US House had been drawn by a citizens' commission composed of four Democrats, four Republicans and five independents, chosen at random from a group of ten thousand applicants to represent the demographics of the state. The commission included not just the usual lawyers, but a pastor, a real estate agent, a bank manager, a tech specialist, and others who didn't work in politics full-time.

Rather than reflecting brazen political calculations, the maps they drew were intended to promote "partisan fairness" and preserve "communities of interest." An increase in the number of competitive districts and lines that more accurately reflected the state's demographics allowed Democrats to narrowly flip both houses of the legislature in 2022, giving them control of state politics for the first time in forty years.

In 2018, Whitmer had won the governor's race by just over 400,000 votes, but Republicans maintained control of the legislature, 19-17 in the Senate and 58-52 in the House.

Four years later, Whitmer won re-election by 400,000 votes again, but this time Democrats took control of the Senate 20-18 and the House 56-54 after winning 51 percent of the statewide vote.

"This is what happens when you get rid of gerrymandering," Anthony Eid, an independent member of the redistricting commission, tweeted after the election. "The people who get the most votes win."

To voting rights activists, the real cause for celebration was not the Democratic victories, but that the makeup of the legislature followed the statewide vote for the first time in more than a decade. "It led to election results that are fair and that followed the will of the people," Fahey said. The state set a record for voter turnout in a midterm.

Lawmakers then passed policies that responded to the will of the majority of voters. After the constitution was amended to protect reproductive rights, the legislature repealed the state's abortion ban from 1931, which had been reinstated after the *Dobbs* decision. "Who would like to watch me slay a zombie?" Whitmer said as she signed the bill in April 2023, surrounded by doctors and prochoice advocates.

These developments stood in stark contrast to Wisconsin, where voters had little power to change the composition of the heavily gerrymandered legislature or repeal unpopular policies, like its 1849 abortion ban. In September 2022, Governor Evers asked legislators to authorize a constitutional amendment that would give voters the chance to rescind the abortion ban through a ballot referendum. But GOP leaders gaveled in and out of the special legislative session within fifteen seconds, taking no action. That November, Evers was re-elected with 51 percent of the vote and Democrats won four out of five statewide races, but Republicans retained 67 percent of state Senate seats and 65 percent of Assembly seats, coming just two seats short of the supermajority needed to override Evers's vetoes and regain total control of the state.

The disconnect between the legislative agenda under minority rule and public sentiment in Wisconsin recalled the conditions that led reformers to lobby for ballot initiatives at the turn of the twentieth century. With Jim Crow firmly entrenched in the South and corporate robber barons and corrupt party bosses in control of much of the industrial North, there were growing complaints that democratic institutions were no longer responsive to popular demands.

The outrage led to a new movement for direct democracy. In 1898, South Dakota became the first to adopt the initiative and referendum process. Over the next two decades, nearly twenty more states followed suit, including Michigan in 1908. Voters organized and passed a series of initiatives to boost representative democracy, through reforms like the direct election of senators, women's suffrage, abolition of the poll tax, and the power to recall public officials. William S. U'Ren, a reform activist in Oregon who led the People's Power League, called the ballot initiative "the best means available for overthrowing government by plutocracy in the American states." These state-based efforts laid the groundwork for the constitutional amendments that were enshrined during the Progressive Era.

The prodemocracy activists in Michigan believed they were following in the footsteps of this progressive tradition. The passage of three ballot initiatives in four years to broaden and protect representative democracy showed how faith in the legitimacy of government institutions could be restored and how freedom and core democratic rights could be expanded even in a heavily polarized and divided battleground state. "There might not be very much alignment on social issues or identity issues, but there's a lot on democracy issues," said Wang, who became executive director of Voters Not Politicians after the 2018 election. "And more and more people are realizing that that is at the core of a functional government."

With Washington gripped by paralysis and the barriers to deep structural change seemingly insurmountable on a federal level, activists like Wang saw Michigan as a national model. "That's where the opportunity lies right now," Wang said. "There's a lot of opportunity in states like Michigan. That's why you see a lot of really exciting grassroots energy, because federal . . ." Her voice trailed off. "That is very daunting."

» » » » » »

While the Michigan constitution could be amended by voters through a simple majority vote, the US Constitution is far more difficult to change, with any amendment requiring the approval of two-thirds of both houses of Congress and three-quarters of states. This double supermajority requirement—combined with increased partisan polarization—explains why every major effort to amend the Constitution in the past fifty years has failed.

In 1965, after the Supreme Court's "one person, one vote" decisions and the passage of the Voting Rights Act, Lyndon Johnson tapped Senator Birch Bayh, a young Democrat from Indiana, to lead an effort to pass a constitutional amendment abolishing the Electoral College and electing the president through a national popular vote. Johnson called it "the next logical outgrowth of the persistent and inevitable movement toward the democratic ideal" of every vote counting equally.

Democrats and Republicans had both idealistic and pragmatic reasons to oppose the Electoral College. Johnson worried that Democratic electors unhappy with his policies on civil rights and Vietnam might vote against him. And in 1968, George Wallace came within fifty-three thousand votes in three states of denying Richard Nixon a majority of Electoral College votes, which would've thrown the election to the House of Representatives for the first time since 1824. Because each state delegation received one vote in such a scenario regardless of population, twenty-six states representing just 20 percent of the country's population could decide the presidency. In 1823, Thomas Jefferson had called that provision "the most dangerous blot in our constitution." Nixon, too, came out in favor of abolishing the Electoral College after his election.

A remarkably broad coalition, ranging from the Chamber of Commerce to the American Bar Association to the AFL-CIO, supported a national popular vote. So did 80 percent of the public, which meant it had a good chance of being ratified by three-quarters of states. "The rule of the majority," testified AFL-CIO president George Meany, "is the very essence of democracy."

On September 18, 1969, the House of Representatives approved the Bayh amendment by a landslide vote of 338-70, with huge majorities of both parties voting for it.

But in the Senate, the coalition of Southern states and small states that had conspired in 1787 to give each state the same number of senators regardless of population and to prevent the direct election of the president once again joined forces to defend the Electoral College. Like John Calhoun before the Civil War, the Southern senators wanted specific protections for Southern whites to be maintained in the Constitution, even as they were outnumbered nationally. They had benefited from the three-fifths clause during slavery and the increase in Southern electoral votes after the war when Black residents were counted as full citizens, even as they were disenfranchised during Jim Crow. "The Electoral College is one of the South's few remaining political safeguards," wrote the Alabama senator James Allen in October 1969. "Let's keep it."

Southern senators opposed to the civil rights movement, like Dixiecrat Strom Thurmond of South Carolina, staged a lengthy filibuster, knowing that a popular vote election would give Black voters the same power as white voters. On September 29, 1970, the Bayh amendment finally came up for a vote, with fifty-three senators supporting it and thirty-four opposing (thirteen senators missed the vote). Sixty percent of senators voting that day supported eliminating the Electoral College, but it fell short of the two-thirds supermajority needed to break a filibuster and send the amendment to the states for ratification. That killed the best chance for the Congress to bring presidential elections in line with other core democratic principles.

The Senate was facing "a bigger question right now than the success or failure of direct election," Bayh said on the floor. The fundamental issue, he believed, was "whether our system will work." As had occurred so often throughout American history, the system allowed a small minority to thwart the agenda of a much larger majority. The thirty-four senators who stopped the amendment came from states with only 27 percent of the nation's population.

Even when huge majorities of Congress did support an amendment, a small minority of states could still block it. That occurred twice in the 1970s, when Congress passed the Equal Rights Amendment, which enshrined legal protections regardless of gender, and the District of Columbia Voting Rights Amendment, which would have given the nation's capital full representation in the Electoral College and Congress, counteracting the conservative white bias of both institutions by granting voting rights to a city with a large Black population. Yet both times they failed to win ratification in three-quarters of states.

"It is clear," President Franklin Roosevelt said in 1937, "that any determined minority group in the nation could, without great difficulty, block ratification by one means or another in at least thirteen states for a long period of time." That was even more true in the present day, as the gap between large and small states widened and organized interest groups had more power than ever to sway minority forces.

In Congress, thirty-four senators from the seventeen smallest states—representing as little as 7 percent of the nation's population— could defeat a Constitutional amendment, while the smallest thirteen states—representing just 4 percent of the US population—could do the same.

The founders attempted to strike a balance between allowing the Constitution to change with the times and preserving the stability of democratic government. Requiring supermajorities in both Congress and the states would guard against "that extreme facility which would render the Constitution too mutable," Madison wrote in Federalist No. 43, while avoiding "that extreme difficulty, which might perpetuate its discovered faults."

But compared to other countries and state constitutions, the founders made the federal Constitution much harder to amend. After the passage of the Bill of Rights in 1791, the Constitution has been altered only seventeen times in 230-plus years, mostly during periods of great upheaval, such as the 1860s, the Progressive Era, and the 1960s. Far from preserving key democratic institutions, this incapacity to change has destabilized them, trapping the founding document in an antiquated past and leading to a growing divide between elected leaders and the shifting demographics of the country. Public opinion polls show that huge majorities believe that abortion rights should be codified, gun regulation should be tightened, campaign spending limited, and the right to vote enshrined as a fundamental protection. But it is impossible to imagine any of these efforts, however popular, resulting in a successful Constitutional amendment any time soon.

The Michigan constitution, on the other hand, had been rewritten four times through state constitutional conventions since its drafting in 1835, most recently in 1963. That constitution reflected the values of the civil rights movement, including protections against racial discrimination and safeguarding citizens' civil and political rights. It could be modified through direct citizen involvement and had been amended more than thirty times since then to reflect new popular movements.

That's why activists like Fahey and Wang decided to focus on state politics. Direct democracy was hardly a panacea; only half the states offer ballot initiatives and even in those that do, lawmakers frequently tried to undermine them or make the process more difficult. After voters in half a dozen states passed ballot initiatives protecting reproductive rights in 2022, the next year GOP-controlled legislatures in states including Arkansas, North Dakota, and Ohio sought to make it harder to get such initiatives on the ballot and tried to increase the number of votes needed to approve them, from simple majorities to supermajorities. These legislative power grabs followed the playbook pioneered by Republicans in Wisconsin, who showed how quickly a reactionary minority could take control of democratic mechanisms and warp them to entrench their power. But, despite these persistent barriers to majority rule, many states still offered a pathway toward expanding democracy that was currently foreclosed on the federal level, barring a massive national movement for systemic reform.

State constitutions empower popular majorities in ways that the federal constitution does not. They were specifically designed to be a majoritarian counterweight to the countermajoritarian features of America's political institutions. State constitutions in places like Michigan were built around a "democracy principle" that embraced the "values of popular sovereignty, majority rule, and political equality," wrote Miriam Seifter, a law professor at the University of Wisconsin. "From provisions declaring that all political power resides in the people, to the express protection of the right to vote, to the relative ease of amendment, to the direct election of numerous state officials with no equivalent of the Senate or electoral college, state constitutions are filled with provisions espousing democracy."

Those were the values that prodemocracy activists in Wisconsin, after watching a conservative white minority subvert democratic institutions for more than a decade, were hoping to recapture in the spring of 2023.

» » » » » »

Before the 2022 election, Wisconsin Democratic Party chair Ben Wikler devised a three-part strategy to restore democracy in the state. First, Democrats had to re-elect Evers and preserve his veto power. After narrowly accomplishing those two goals in the midterms, the third and most important part of the plan revolved around winning an open seat on the Wisconsin Supreme Court in April 2023, which would flip its balance of power for the first time in fifteen years. The court could then roll back the undemocratic and unpopular policies passed by Wisconsin Republicans through cases reinstating fair redistricting maps, voting rights, labor rights, and abortion rights. "The possibility now exists to be able to actually turn Wisconsin into a state that Bob La Follette wouldn't be horrified by," Wikler said.

Wikler, a tall and loquacious forty-one-year-old with boundless energy, was born in Madison and deeply invested in Wisconsin's progressive tradition. He stuffed envelopes for the congressional campaign

of his godmother at eleven and led his first protest at fourteen, object-
ing to an exclusive marketing agreement between Coca-Cola and the
Madison public schools. He left the state for college and became Washington director of the liberal group MoveOn.org, dealing with big national issues like climate change and health care. But after leading the
coalition that prevented congressional Republicans from repealing the
Affordable Care Act in 2017, he thought more seriously about moving
back home. "The real fight going forward was at the state level and nowhere was that more true than in Wisconsin," he said.

After volunteering for Evers in 2018, he came home for good just as
the legislature convened the lame-duck session stripping the new governor of power. "It was a microcosm of the whole Republican strategy
since 2011, which has been to rig our system to ensure that the GOP
would have control even when voters wanted the opposite," Wikler
said. Though his background was in progressive organizing, not partisan politics, the next year he was elected to lead the state Democratic
Party. "The alternative," he said, "was a GOP that was trying to permanently put our democracy in chains." He believed passionately in
using grassroots organizing to combat entrenched power; one poster
in his office said, "Brats, Cheese, and Beer Can Save Democracy."

Ever since Michael Gableman defeated Louis Butler in 2008 and
Republicans took over the governor's mansion and legislature in 2011,
the Wisconsin Supreme Court had been a key driver of GOP efforts to
make their majorities voter-proof and turn the state into what Wikler
called "a democracy-free zone." It upheld the legislature's gerrymandered maps, strict voter ID law, and lame-duck measures while approving Walker's repeal of collective bargaining rights for unions (Act
10) and ending the John Doe investigation into his fundraising practices. The symbiosis between the legislature and the court created an
almost impenetrable antidemocracy feedback loop in the state. "Right
now, the state Supreme Court is an extension of the Republican legislature," Wikler said after the 2022 election.

The two judicial candidates running to replace the retiring conservative chief justice in April 2023 had vastly different views on the direction of the state and the role of the courts in the democratic process.

The liberal judge backed by Democrats, sixty-year-old Janet Protasiewicz, who served for more than twenty-five years as an assistant district attorney in the Milwaukee area before being elected as a county judge in 2014, got her start in politics by protesting Scott Walker's agenda. She grew up in a Polish family with parents who were teachers on Milwaukee's blue-collar south side. She worked her way through college and law school before taking a job with the state. As a member of the public employee union for state prosecutors, she joined thousands of protesters at the state capitol in 2011 to oppose Act 10. "I signed the governor's recall petition, and I came to this beautiful city and I marched at the Capitol in protest of Act 10," she said in Madison before the election. Now, in a full circle moment, she had the power to roll back Walker's agenda. "This is their chance to undo everything that we've done over the past dozen years," Walker said.

Her campaign was premised on restoring majority rule in Wisconsin. Her supporters saw the state court as a potential counterweight to the conservative takeover of the US Supreme Court. Unlike many prospective judges, Protasiewicz wasn't afraid to talk about her beliefs. She called the legislature's maps "positively rigged" and asserted that "women have the right to choose." At a candidate forum early in the campaign, she said she decided to run because "I could not sit back and watch extreme right-wing partisans hijack our supreme court."

On the other hand, her opponent Daniel Kelly, a former conservative justice from 2016 to 2020 who was appointed by Walker to fill a vacancy on the court, had played a key role in the conservative takeover of the state. He was a former president of the Milwaukee chapter of the Federalist Society, worked for the Bradley Foundation, and served on the board of the Bradley-funded Wisconsin Institute for Law and Liberty, which brought lawsuits that led the court to uphold gerrymandered maps and invalidate mail ballot drop boxes. Kelly defended the legislature's first round of redistricting maps before a federal court as a lawyer in private practice in 2012 and praised the next round of maps passed in 2021.

In 2020, when the Wisconsin Supreme Court came one vote short of ruling in favor of Trump's lawsuit to overturn the election in the state, Kelly worked on another strategy to nullify Biden's victory, consulting with Wisconsin Republicans on a plan to appoint their own electors in violation of the popular vote. After that, he joined the state GOP on an "Election Integrity Roundtable" tour before the 2022 midterms that one Democratic lawmaker called a "conspiracy theory roadshow."

His campaign received millions of dollars in backing from dark money groups. Kelly's top outside funder was Wisconsin Manufacturers and Commerce, one of Walker's closest allies during the John Doe investigation. His second-largest supporter was right-wing megadonor Richard Uihlein, an Illinois-based shipping magnate who bankrolled the Save America rally that preceded the insurrection, and multiple groups—such as the Tea Party Patriots and Cleta Mitchell's Conservative Partnership Institute—that promoted election denial. Protasiewicz called Kelly "a true threat to our democracy."

The race had huge state and national implications and would determine whether the GOP's efforts to undermine democracy in Wisconsin would finally be reversed or be irrevocably cemented. "It is the single most important election in 2023 in the opening salvo to 2024," said Steve Bannon.

On April 4, 2023, the same day as Trump appeared in court in Manhattan to face thirty-four felony charges in a hush money scheme, Wisconsin voters chose democracy over oligarchy in a landslide, electing Protasiewicz by eleven points. The state saw record turnout for a state supreme court election, even as negative ads flooded the airwaves. "This election was a release valve for twelve years of Democratic rage in Wisconsin about Republicans rigging our state and smashing our democracy—and then using that power to rip away our rights," Wikler tweeted.

At her victory party at the Saint Kate Hotel in downtown Milwaukee, Protasiewicz entered the room with the court's three liberal justices, all women, behind her, to Lizzo's "About Damn Time." The new majority clasped hands on stage and raised their arms triumphantly, as someone called them "the fab four."

Protasiewicz's supporters held blue signs that said "Freedom," which was a dominant theme for the night and in the larger struggle for control of Wisconsin. "Ultimately, you can trace all these fights back to that basic question, whether freedom is the birthright of every American and every new American or whether freedom should be a privilege that is accorded to those who already have all the wealth and all the power anyway," Wikler said. "That question has been the struggle at the heart of American politics since our founding and before. And Wisconsin, at its best, has always been a leader in the fight for that freedom."

After a decade of seeing their rights taken away, Wisconsinites were ready to restore them. "Too many have tried to overturn the will of the people," Protasiewicz said. "Today's result shows that Wisconsinites believe in democracy and the democratic process."

Following her success in Michigan, Fahey had helped prodemocracy activists in Wisconsin build a movement against gerrymandering by passing local resolutions calling for fair maps and creating a model independent redistricting commission. Wisconsinites looked wistfully at the expansion of democracy in Michigan in 2018 and 2022, but now there was hope that after years of being a laboratory for oligarchy, the state was on the verge of becoming a representative democracy again.

"My goal—and the goal for millions of people who have been involved in voting and marching and organizing and knocking on doors—was for Wisconsin to become a democracy and to become a laboratory for democracy, in line with its best traditions," Wikler said after the election. "The question of how to build a thriving multiracial democracy is still a central question for the whole United States. And Wisconsin should be at the forefront of figuring that out."

Protasiewicz's win wasn't the only good news for democracy that spring. Voters in Wisconsin and Illinois also rejected scores of right-wing school board candidates who sought to censor the teaching of education and gerrymander history. The 1776 Project, a conservative political action committee funded by Richard Uihlein, said only a third of the sixty-three candidates it had backed in the two states won their races. "The extremists got trounced," said J. B. Pritzker, the Democratic governor of Illinois.

But the proponents of minority rule, at the state and national level, wouldn't give up control easily. Following Protasiewicz's victory, Cleta Mitchell told top donors at an RNC meeting that Republicans needed to limit polling places on college campuses after high youth turnout in Wisconsin, cut early voting, and repeal same-day voter registration and the automatic mailing of ballots to registered voters. "Our constitutional republic's survival is at stake," she said. Republicans in the Wisconsin legislature also threatened to impeach Protasiewicz before she had even heard a case if she didn't recuse herself from cases challenging the state's gerrymandered maps, an extraordinary move that would effectively nullify her landslide election.

And two days after the Wisconsin Supreme Court election, the Tennessee House of Representatives, where Republicans had a two-thirds supermajority partly due to gerrymandering, voted to expel two Black Democratic lawmakers who held a protest on the House floor calling for gun control legislation after a shooter killed six people, including three nine-year-olds, with an AR-15 at a Nashville elementary school. But instead of banning assault weapons, Republican legislators assaulted democracy, in a chilling scene that recalled the expulsion of Black lawmakers like Henry McNeal Turner in Georgia in 1868. "We're at war for our republic," said the Republican state representative Scott Cepicky.

"We are losing our democracy to White supremacy, we are losing our democracy to patriarchy, we are losing our democracy to people who want to keep a status quo that is damning to the rest of us and damning to our children and unborn people," responded the state representative Justin Pearson, a twenty-eight-year-old from Memphis who was one of the two expelled lawmakers.

The contrast between the events in Wisconsin and Tennessee showed how contested the ideas of freedom, legitimacy, and American citizenship remained and how the forces behind the status quo would go to nearly any length to preserve their hold on power.

NOTES

EPIGRAPH

xii *"The supreme issue"*: Quoted in Dan Kaufman, *The Fall of Wisconsin* (New York: W. W. Norton & Company, 2018), 282.

PROLOGUE: FEAR OF A WHITE MINORITY

3 *"If present trends hold"*: Quoted in John Aloysius Farrell, "OPEN DOORS / CLOSING MINDS," *Boston Globe*, February 23, 1992.

3 *"we have an illegal"*: Quoted in Carol Goar, "U.S. Hopeful Snipes at Multiculturalism," *Toronto Star*, May 10, 1995.

3 *"Buchanan Fence"*: Quoted in John Toole, "Buchanan: Take Back Streets from Homeless," *Union Leader* (Manchester, N.H.), December 24, 1991.

3 *"Make America First Again"*: Quoted in John King, "Political Notebook: Candidates Sign in," Associated Press, December 23, 1991.

3 *"Let's Make America Great"*: Quoted in Bud Kennedy, "How Reagan's 'Make America Great Again' Became a Trump Takeaway," *Fort Worth Star-Telegram*, July 19, 2016.

4 *"Time to Rethink Immigration?"*: Peter Brimelow, *National Review*, June 22, 1992.

4 *"America will become a"*: Peter Brimelow, "Immigration: Dissolving the People," *Baltimore Sun*, June 4, 1995.

4 *"New projections show that"*: Scripps Howard, "Minority Population Projected Up By 2050," *Plain Dealer* (Cleveland, Ohio), December 4, 1992.

4 *"new restrictionism"*: Quoted in Tom Gjelten, *A Nation of Nations* (New York: Simon & Schuster, 2015), 245.

4 *"The question we Americans"*: Quoted in Arthur Brice, "Immigration: One Candidate Grabs Issue," *The Atlanta Journal and Constitution*, March 6, 1992.

4 *"a sleepy and segregated"*: Quoted in Tim Alberta, "'The Ideas Made It, But I Didn't,'" *Politico Magazine*, May/June 2017.

5 *"The Negroes of Washington"*: Quoted in Timothy Stanley, *The Crusader* (New York: Thomas Dunne Books, 2012), 17.

5 *"stand with the great"*: Quoted in Sam Tanenhaus, "When Pat Buchanan Tried to Make America Great Again," *Esquire*, April 5, 2017.

5 *"silent majority"*: Ibid.

6 *"be discriminated against in"*: Public Law 89-236, GovInfo, October 3, 1965, https://www.govinfo.gov/content/pkg/STATUTE-79/pdf/STATUTE-79-Pg911.pdf.

6 *"Initially, the visit would"*: Quoted in Harry F. Rosenthal, "President Advised to Keep Distance From King Widow," Associated Press, December 1, 1986.

6 *"liberal issues"*: Quoted in Stanley, *The Crusader*, 56.

6 *"the second era of Reconstruction"*: Quoted in Stephen Chapman, "Buchanan Courts Segregationist Vote," *St. Louis Post-Dispatch*, March 10, 1992.

7 *"a beautiful monument"*: "Buchanan Campaign Rally," Atlanta, Ga., C-Span, February 29, 1992, https://www.c-span.org/video/?24755-1/buchanan-campaign-rally.

7 *"an act of regional"*: Quoted in Ben Smith III, "Challenger Lambastes Rights Act," *The Atlanta Journal and Constitution*, March 1, 1992.

7 *"They both tried to"*: Quoted in Stanley, *The Crusader*, 177.

7 *"The way to deal"*: Quoted in Derrick Z. Jackson, "Buchanan Leads GOP Down the Road of White Supremacy," *Boston Globe*, February 21, 1996.

7 *"I think Pat Buchanan"*: Quoted in Chapman, "Buchanan Courts Segregationist Vote."

7 *"Who speaks for the"*: Quoted in Jon Margolis, "Democrats May Lose Among New Immigrants," *Chicago Tribune*, March 3, 1994.

7 *"The Buchanan Brigade"*: Quoted in Lloyd Grove, "Campaign Notebook," *The Washington Post*, February 19, 1992.

8 *"a cultural war"*: "Pat Buchanan 1992 Republican Convention Address," Houston, Tex., C-Span, August 17, 1992, https://www.c-span.org/video/?31255-1/pat-buchanan-1992-republican-convention-address.

8 *"probably sounded better in"*: Quoted in John Warner, "If Only Molly Ivins Could Say Something Now," *Chicago Tribune*, April 25, 2018.

8 *"equip the Border Patrol"*: Quoted in "Buchanan Supporters Claim Victory on Illegal Immigration Plank," Associated Press, August 12, 1992.

8 *"They don't build lighthouses"*: Ibid.

8 *"the true sons and daughters"*: "Buchanan Campaign Speech," Manchester, N.H., C-Span, February 20, 1996, https://www.c-span.org/video/?70046-1/buchanan-campaign-speech.

8 *"intoxication with 'democracy'"*: Patrick J. Buchanan, "Worship of Democracy Already Brings Third World Disillusionment," *The Oregonian*, January 10, 1991.

8 *"equal justice for the"*: Patrick J. Buchanan, *Suicide of a Superpower* (New York: Thomas Dunne Books, 2011), 349.

8 *"The Founding Fathers did"*: Ibid., 191.

9 *"We're not a democracy"*: Mike Lee, Twitter post, October 7, 2020, 9:34 p.m., https://twitter.com/SenMikeLee/status/1314016169993670656.

9 *"rule by majority"*: Mike Lee, "Of Course We're Not a Democracy," October 20, 2020, https://www.lee.senate.gov/2020/10/of-course-we-re-not-a -democracy.

10 *"the superior force of"*: James Madison, "The Federalist Papers: No. 10," November 23, 1787, https://avalon.law.yale.edu/18th_century/fed10.asp.

12 *"government of the people"*: Remarks by Abraham Lincoln, Gettysburg, Pa., November 19, 1863, https://presidentlincoln.illinois.gov/visit/whats -inside/exhibits/online-exhibits/gettysburg-address-everett-copy/.

1. LABORATORY FOR OLIGARCHY

13 *"map room"*: Quoted in Emily Bazelon, "The New Front in the Gerrymandering Wars: Democracy vs. Math," *The New York Times Magazine*, August 29, 2017.

13 *"Public comments on this"*: Quoted in Patrick Marley, Daniel Bice, and Jason Stein, "Lawmakers Were Made to Pledge Secrecy over Redistricting," *Milwaukee Journal Sentinel*, February 6, 2012.

13 *"Aggressive"*: Quoted in *Whitford v. Gill*, 15-cv-421-bbc (W.D. Wis. 2016), 11.

13 *"The maps we pass"*: Ibid., 15.

14 *"This looks fair to"*: Quoted in Patrick Marley, "Parties Joust over Wisconsin Redistricting Plan," *Milwaukee Journal Sentinel*, July 13, 2011.

14 *"We Back the Badge"*: Quoted in Ari Berman, "How the GOP Rigs Elections," *Rolling Stone*, January 24, 2018.

14 *"It's a prime example"*: Ibid.

15 *"I voted for every"*: Quoted in Shawn Johnson, "Van Wanggaard Fights to Reclaim His Old State Senate Seat in 21st District," Wisconsin Public Radio, August 5, 2014.

15 *"Keeping Christ in Christmas"*: Quoted in Berman, "How the GOP Rigs Elections."

15 *"nobody knew who I"*: Ibid.

15 *"I tried to serve"*: Ibid.

15 *"It was unwinnable for"*: Ibid.

16 *"Even when Republicans are"*: *Whitford v. Gill*, 78.

16 *"The basic principle of"*: Quoted in Kaufman, *The Fall of Wisconsin*, 23.

16 *"a laboratory for wise experimental"*: Ibid., 5.

16 *"do it anywhere in"*: Scott Walker with Marc Thiessen, *Unintimidated* (New York: Sentinel, 2013), 8.

17 *"the last remaining moderate"*: Steven Elbow, "Outgoing Republican State Sen. Dale Schultz Vents His Spleen at the GOP," *The Capital Times*, December 19, 2014.

17 *"In the 1980s and"*: Quoted in Ari Berman, "The GOP's War on Voting Is Working," *The Nation*, June 29, 2016.

17 *"used procedures that would"*: Quoted in James B. Nelson, "Wisconsin Rep. Robin Vos Says Voter Fraud Accounted for a Portion of Lehman's Victory Margin over Wanggaard in Senate Recall," PolitiFact, July 6, 2012.

17 *"Anyone who argues"*: Ibid.

18 *"We've got to think"*: Quoted in Jessie Opoien, "Former Republican Staffer Names Wisconsin Senators Who Were 'Giddy' About Voting Law Changes," *The Capital Times*, May 16, 2016.

18 *"What I'm concerned about"*: Ibid.

18 *"giddy"*: Ibid.

18 *"It made me physically"*: Quoted in Berman, "The GOP's War on Voting Is Working."

18 *"nip . . . in the bud"*: Ibid.

18 *"too much access"*: Ibid.

19 *"We should be pitching"*: Quoted in Jack Craver, "Schultz: 'I Am Not Willing to Defend Them Anymore,'" *The Capital Times*, March 26, 2014.

19 *"The Wisconsin experience"*: Quoted in Ari Berman, "Rigged: How Voter Suppression Threw Wisconsin to Trump," *Mother Jones*, November/December 2017.

19 *"international communist conspiracy"*: Quoted in John Savage, "The John Birch Society Is Back," *Politico Magazine*, July 16, 2017.

20 *"the war of ideas"*: Mary Bottari, "Weaponized Philanthropy: Document Trove Details Bradley Foundation's Efforts to Build Right-Wing 'Infrastructure' Nationwide," Exposed by CMD, May 5, 2017.

20 *"go big and go"*: Quoted in Patrick Healy and Monica Davey, "Behind Scott Walker, a Longstanding Conservative Alliance Against Unions," *The New York Times*, June 8, 2015.

20 *"We supplied the ideas"*: Ibid.

20 *"If Act 10 is enacted"*: Quoted in Ari Berman, "How Wisconsin Became the GOP's Laboratory for Dismantling Democracy," *Mother Jones*, October 25, 2022.

21 *"We ❤ UW"*: Deborah Ziff, "On Campus: UW-Madison students to Walker: 'Don't Break My ❤,'" *Wisconsin State Journal*, February 28, 2011.

21 *"independent political spending"*: Citizens United v. Federal Election Commission, 558 US 310 (2010).

22 *"We've spent a lot"*: Quoted in Stacey Singer, "Altruist's Other Role: Antagonist; David Koch Boosts Cancer Research, Far-Right Causes," *Palm Beach Post*, February 19, 2012.

22 *"Today, every other governor"*: Quoted in Andy Kroll, "VIDEO: Scott Walker's Divide-and-Conquer Strategy Is 'The New Model for the Country,'" *Mother Jones*, June 2, 2012.

22 *"Corporations. Go heavy after"*: Quoted In Ed Pilkington and the Guard-

ian US interactive team, "Leaked Court Documents from 'John Doe Investigation' in Wisconsin Lay Bare Pervasive Influence of Corporate Cash on Modern US Elections," *The Guardian*, September 14, 2016.

22 *"The Governor is encouraging"*: Ibid.

22 *"third Koch brother"*: Quoted in Bruce Murphy, "Dark Money's Front Man," *The Progressive*, January 22, 2016.

23 *"my Karl Rove"*: Quoted in Bottari, "Weaponized Philanthropy."

23 *"run thru one group"*: Quoted in Pilkington, "Leaked Court Documents from 'John Doe Investigation.'"

23 *"recall isn't the Wisconsin"*: Quoted in Kaufman, *The Fall of Wisconsin*, 158.

24 *"soup to nuts campaign"*: Quoted in Pilkington, "Leaked Court Documents from 'John Doe Investigation.'"

24 *"That's inside baseball"*: Quoted in Marc Fisher, "Wisconsin Gov. Scott Walker's Recall Vote: Big Money Fuels Small-Government Fight," *The Washington Post*, March 25, 2012.

24 *"tremendous influence"*: Remarks by Robert M. La Follette, "The Danger Threatening Representative Government," Mineral Point, Wis., July 4, 1897, https://www.wisconsinhistory.org/pdfs/lessons/EDU-SpeechTranscript -SpeechesLaFollette-DangerThreatening.pdf.

24 *"We are facing a"*: Quoted in Ari Berman, "How the Money Primary Is Undermining Voting Rights," *The Nation*, June 8, 2015.

25 *"independent expenditures, including those"*: *Citizens United v. FEC*.

25 *"red flag"*: Quoted in Pilkington, "Leaked Court Documents from 'John Doe Investigation.'"

25 *"We should discuss this"*: Ibid.

25 *"lead-bearing paint"*: Quoted in "Walker's Worst 100: A Chronicle of the Assault on Democracy in Wisconsin," Wisconsin Democracy Campaign, April 26, 2016.

25 *"Not since the days"*: Ibid.

26 *"the government in Washington"*: Quoted in Benjamin I. Page, Larry M. Bartels, and Jason Seawright, "Democracy and the Policy Preferences of Wealthy Americans," *Perspectives on Politics* 11, no. 1 (March 2013).

26 *"economic elites and organized groups"*: Martin Gilens and Benjamin I. Page, "Testing Theories of American Politics: Elites, Interest Groups, and Average Citizens," *Cambridge University Press*, September 18, 2014.

26 *"the majority does not"*: Ibid.

26 *"criminal scheme"*: Quoted in James Hohmann, "Walker Allegedly in 'Criminal Scheme,'" *Politico*, June 19, 2014.

27 *"Louis Butler worked to"*: "Racist, Misleading Wisconsin Supreme Court Election Ad: 'Prosecutor,'" YouTube, March 4, 2010, https://www.youtube .com/watch?v=1haqLYB1cw0.

27 *"law and order judge"*: Quoted in Dee J. Hall, "High Court Race Could Be Replay of Last Year's Election," *Wisconsin State Journal*, January 3, 2008.

27 *"the most racist ad"*: Quoted in John Nichols, "Michael Gableman Ran the Most Racist Ad in the History of Wisconsin Politics," *The Capital Times*, October 12, 2021.

27 *"reckless disregard for the truth"*: Quoted in "Gableman's Ad Drags State Politics to New Low," *The Capital Times*, March 22, 2018.

28 *"Loophole Louie"*: Quoted in Stacy Forster and Patrick Marley, "Rebuttals Shed Light on Accusations Before Supreme Court Vote," *Milwaukee Journal Sentinel*, March 30, 2008.

28 *"This system is broken"*: Quoted in Viveca Novak, "Winning Ugly in Wisconsin," FactCheck.org, April 4, 2008.

28 *"the conservative judicial majority"*: Quoted in Dave Zweifel, "Prosser Takes Low Road on Conflicts," *The Capital Times*, March 23, 2011.

28 *"If Justice Prosser loses"*: Quoted in Patrick Marley, "Walker Agenda Could Be Stopped If Prosser Is Defeated, Governor's Attorney Says," *Milwaukee Journal Sentinel*, April 5, 2011.

28 *"leading the coalition to"*: Quoted in Pilkington, "Leaked Court Documents from 'John Doe Investigation.'"

28 *"weak on criminals"*: Quoted in "Smear Groups, Candidates Spent $5.4 Million on Supreme Court Race," Wisconsin Democracy Campaign, April 19, 2011.

29 *"absolutely indispensable"*: Quoted in Brendan Fischer, "Prosecutor in Scott Walker Probe Asks Justices to Recuse," *The Center for Media and Democracy's PR Watch*, February 13, 2015.

29 *"Club for Growth–Wisconsin was"*: Quoted in Pilkington, "Leaked Court Documents from 'John Doe Investigation.'"

29 *"total bitch"*: Quoted in Lincoln Caplan, "The Destruction of the Wisconsin Supreme Court," *The New Yorker*, May 5, 2015.

29 *"highly unusual"*: Quoted in Lynn Adelman, "How Big Money Ruined Public Life in Wisconsin," *Cleveland State Law Review*, June 16, 2017, https://papers.ssrn.com/sol3/papers.cfm?abstract_id=3086693.

29 *"brave individuals"*: Quoted in Pilkington, "Leaked Court Documents from 'John Doe Investigation.'"

30 *"My career in the"*: Quoted in Brendan Fischer, "In 'Extraordinary' Move, WI Supreme Court Fires Scott Walker Prosecutor to Stave-Off SCOTUS Review," *The Center for Media and Democracy's PR Watch*, December 3, 2015.

30 *"They went way, way"*: Matthew Rothschild, interview conducted by the author, March 11, 2022.

31 *"like 1939 Germany"*: Quoted in Dave Zweifel, "Plain Talk: Scott Walker and Friends Want It Both Ways on John Doe Leakers," *The Capital Times*, September 28, 2016.

31 *"It was just a"*: Quoted in Berman, "How the GOP Rigs Elections."

31 *"a laboratory for plutocracy"*: Rothschild, interview.

2. THE FURY OF DEMOCRACY

32 *"open the main business"*: Max Farrand, ed., *Records of the Federal Convention of 1787* (New Haven, Conn.: Yale University Press, 1937), 1:18.

32 *"would decide forever the"*: Quoted in Woody Holton, *Unruly Americans and the Origins of the Constitution* (New York: Hill and Wang, 2018), 108.

32 *"Our chief danger arises"*: Farrand, *Records*, 1:26.

33 *"corrected and enlarged"*: Quoted in Richard Beeman, *Plain Honest Men* (New York: Random House, 2009), 88.

33 *"restrain, if possible"*: Farrand, *Records*, 1:58.

33 *"all men are created"*: "Declaration of Independence: A Transcription," National Archives, https://www.archives.gov/founding-docs/declaration -transcript.

34 *"mother principle"*: Quoted in Michael Klarman, *The Framers' Coup* (New York: Oxford University Press, 2016), 606.

34 *"For if liberty and"*: Quoted in Robert Dahl, *A Preface to Democratic Theory* (Chicago: University of Chicago Press, 1956), 34.

34 *"a government by its"*: Quoted in Donald Lutz, *Popular Consent and Popular Control* (Baton Rouge: Louisiana State University Press, 1980), 40.

34 *"where annual elections end"*: Quoted in Holton, *Unruly Americans*, 196.

34 *"VOX POPULI VOX DEI"*: Ibid., 164.

35 *"Government is, or ought"*: Quoted in Terry Bouton, *Taming Democracy* (New York: Oxford University Press, 2007), 53.

35 *"The general disease which"*: Quoted in Klarman, *Framers' Coup*, 86.

36 *"whenever any form of"*: Declaration of Independence, National Archives.

36 *"the malcontents"*: Quoted in Klarman, *Framers' Coup*, 93.

36 *"mankind left to themselves"*: Quoted in Holton, *Unruly Americans*, 219.

36 *"I was once as strong"*: Ibid., 21.

36 *"endeavoring to give the"*: Quoted in Robert A. Goldwin and William A. Schambra, eds., *How Democratic Is the Constitution?* (Washington, DC: AEI Studies, 1980), 128.

37 *"not a little tainted"*: Quoted in John MacGregor Burns, *The Deadlock of Democracy* (Englewood Cliffs, N.J.: Prentice-Hall, 1963), 12.

37 *"A little rebellion now"*: Quoted in Jack N. Rakove, *Original Meanings* (New York: Knopf, 1996), 34.

37 *"had more perhaps than"*: Quoted in Holton, *Unruly Americans*, 6.

37 *"What has been the"*: Farrand, *Records*, 1:132.

38 *"into question the fundamental"*: Quoted in Rakove, *Original Meanings*, 48.

38 *"It is much more"*: Quoted in Gordon Wood, *The Creation of the American Republic 1776-1787* (Chapel Hill: University of North Carolina Press, 1998), 413.

38 *"all its powers directly"*: Quoted in Myron Magnet, "James Madison and the Dilemmas of Democracy," *City Journal*, Winter 2011.

38 *"To secure the public"*: Madison, "Federalist No. 10."

39 *"Who does not see"*: Quoted in Lance Banning, *The Sacred Fire of Liberty* (Ithaca, N.Y.: Cornell University Press, 1995), 93.

39 *"the most trifling minority"*: Quoted in Greg Weiner, *Madison's Metronome* (Lawrence: University of Kansas Press, 2012), 10.

39 *"No other rule exists"*: Ibid., 6.

39 *"Had every Athenian citizen"*: Quoted in Rakove, *Original Meanings*, 236.

40 *"Wherever the real power"*: Quoted in Wood, *Creation*, 410.

40 *"If a majority were"*: Quoted in Henry Steele Commager, *Majority Rule and Minority Rights* (New York: Oxford University Press, 1943), 10.

40 *"the great majority of"*: Quoted in Banning, *Sacred Fire*, 183.

41 *"to enlarge the sphere"*: Farrand, *Records*, 1:134.

41 *"to frame a republican"*: Ibid., 136.

41 *"the total exclusion of"*: James Madison, "The Federalist Papers: No. 63," February 26, 1788, https://guides.loc.gov/federalist-papers/text-61-70#s-lg-box-wrapper-25493450.

41 *"the only defense against"*: Quoted in Banning, *Sacred Fire*, 129.

41 *"great anchor of the"*: Quoted in Magnet, "James Madison and the Dilemmas of Democracy."

41 *"the rights of property"*: Ibid.

41 *"the aristocratic part of"*: Quoted in Klarman, *Framers' Coup*, 208.

41 *"The Senate ought to"*: Quoted in Banning, *Sacred Fire*, 181.

42 *"distinguished for their rank"*: Quoted in Klarman, *Framers' Coup*, 210.

42 *"nothing but a permanent"*: Farrand, *Records*, 1:299.

42 *"James the Caledonian"*: Max Farrand, *The Framing of the Constitution of the United States* (New Haven, Conn.: Yale University Press, 1962), 21.

42 *"If we are to"*: Farrand, *Records*, 1:151.

42 *"the commercial and monied"*: Ibid., 154.

43 *"As all authority was"*: Ibid., 179.

43 *"N. Jersey will never"*: Ibid.

43 *"The number of Representatives"*: Quoted in Beeman, *Plain, Honest Men*, 151.

43 *"equally in the power"*: Ibid.

44 *"the present claims of"*: Farrand, *Records*, 1:495.

44 *"I do not, gentlemen"*: Ibid., 500.

44 *"vehemence unprecedented"*: Quoted in Klarman, *Framers' Coup*, 194.

44 *"A government founded in"*: Quoted in Banning, *Sacred Fire*, 153.

45 *"depart from justice in"*: Quoted in Klarman, *Framers' Coup*, 199.

45 *"a more objectionable minority"*: Ibid., 185.

45 *"The Great Concession is"*: Daniel Wirls and Stephen Wirls, *The Invention of the United State Senate* (Baltimore, Md.: Johns Hopkins University Press, 2004), 96.

45 *"Every idea of proportion"*: Alexander Hamilton, "Federalist No. 22," De-

cember 14, 1787, https://guides.loc.gov/federalist-papers/text-21-30#s-lg
-box-wrapper-25493335.

46 *"the number of free inhabitants"*: Quoted in Beeman, *Plain, Honest Men*, 88.
46 *"free inhabitants"*: Ibid., 107.
46 *"This was nothing more"*: Quoted in Sean Wilentz, *No Property in Man* (Cambridge, Mass.: Harvard University Press, 2018), 64.
46 *"express security ought to"*: Ibid.
46 *"Upon what principle is"*: Farrand, *Records*, vol. II, 222.
47 *"did not well see"*: Ibid., vol. I, 587.
47 *"would never confederate on"*: Ibid., 593.
48 *"In this one instance"*: Holton, *Unruly Americans*, 189.
48 *"The security the"*: Quoted in David Waldstreicher, *Slavery's Constitution* (New York: Hill and Wang, 2010), 86.
48 *"lie over for the"*: Quoted in Beeman, *Plain, Honest Men*, 201.
48 *"The blessings in which"*: Remarks by Frederick Douglass, "What to the Slave Is the Fourth of July?" Rochester, N.Y., July 5, 1852, https://www.blackpast.org/african-american-history/speeches-african-american-history/1852-frederick-douglass-what-slave-fourth-july.
49 *"a covenant with death"*: William Lloyd Garrison, "A Covenant with Death and an Agreement with Hell," Farmington, Mass., Massachusetts Historical Society, https://www.masshist.org/object-of-the-month/objects/a-covenant-with-death-and-an-agreement-with-hell-2005-07-01.
49 *"in favor of an"*: Farrand, *Records*, 1:69.
49 *"no government could long"*: Ibid., 49.
49 *"Wilson was a minority"*: Holton, *Unruly Americans*, 129.
49 *"should be the guardian"*: Farrand, *Records*, vol. II, 52.
50 *"The people are uninformed"*: Ibid., 57.
50 *"The extent of the"*: Ibid., 31.
50 *"people at large will"*: Ibid., 29.
50 *"The people will be"*: Quoted in Jesse Wegman, *Let the People Pick the President* (New York: St. Martin's Press, 2020), 69.
51 *"It would be as"*: Farrand, *Records*, vol. II, 57.
52 *"the Slave Power"*: Wegman, *Let the People Pick the President*, 105.
53 *"a necessary defense against"*: Farrand, *Records*, vol. II, 202.
53 *"the freeholders"*: Ibid., 203–4.
53 *"should not depress the"*: Quoted in Klarman, *Framers' Coup*, 179.
54 *"The people will not"*: Farrand, *Records*, vol. II, 201.
54 *"This valuable privilege of"*: Quoted in Historical Society of Pennsylvania, *Pennsylvania and the Federal Constitution, 1787-1788* (Lancaster, Pa.: Inquirer Printing and Publishing, 1888), 598.
54 *"Universal male suffrage was"*: Rosemarie Zagarri, *Revolutionary Backlash* (Philadelphia: University of Pennsylvania Press, 2008), 180.
55 *"the genius of our"*: "Constitution Celebration," Philadelphia, Pa., C-Span,

September 17, 1987, https://www.c-span.org/video/?151155-1/constitution
-celebration.

55 *"flagwaving fervor"*: Thurgood Marshall, "The Constitution's Bicentennial: Commemorating the Wrong Document?" *Vanderbilt Law Review,*
vol. 40: 1337.

56 *"The change now proposed"*: Herbert J. Storing, ed., *The Complete Anti-
Federalist* (Chicago: University of Chicago Press, 1981), vol. 4, article 5,
document 5.

56 *"swallow up all us"*: Quoted in Pauline Maier, *Ratification* (New York: Simon & Schuster, 2011), 555.

57 *"The original Constitution"*: Richard B. Morris, "The People of the Constitution," in *A Grand Experiment: The Constitution at 200,* ed. John Allphin
Moore and John E. Murphy (Lanham, Md.: Rowman & Littlefield, 1997).

3. THE NEW NULLIFICATION

58 *"The Union is in"*: Remarks by John C. Calhoun, Washington, DC, March
4, 1850, http://nationalhumanitiescenter.org/ows/seminarsflvs/Calhoun
.pdf.

59 *"a permanent and hopeless"*: Quoted in Jamelle Bouie, "America Holds
Onto an Undemocratic Assumption from Its Founding: That Some People
Deserve More Power Than Others," *The New York Times Magazine,* Au-
gust 14, 2019.

59 *"radical error"*: John C. Calhoun, *A Disquisition on Government* (Charleston, S.C.: Steam Power-Press of Walker and James, 1851), 30.

59 *"Tariff of Abominations"*: Quoted in James H. Read, *Majority Rule versus
Consensus* (Lawrence: University of Kansas Press, 2009), 3.

60 *"It is this negative"*: Calhoun, *Disquisition,* 35.

60 *"to give to each division"*: Ibid., 25.

60 *"concurrent majority"*: Ibid., 35.

60 *"the smallest fraction"*: James Madison to Edward Everett, National
Archives, August 28, 1830, https://founders.archives.gov/documents
/Madison/99-02-02-2138.

61 *"the Great Nullifier"*: Quoted in Sam Tanenhaus, "Original Sin," *The New
Republic,* February 10, 2013.

61 *"the most solid and"*: Remarks by John C. Calhoun, Washington, DC,
February 6, 1837, https://constitutingamerica.org/speech-on-reception-of
-abolition-petitions-by-john-c-calhoun-1782-1850-reprinted-from-the-u
-s-constitution-a-reader-published-by-hillsdale-college.

61 *"utterly unqualified to possess"*: Quoted in Read, *Majority Rule,* 127.

61 *"The whites are a"*: Ibid., 132.

61 *"The two great divisions"*: Ibid., 145.

61 *"The South, the poor"*: Quoted in David Morris Potter, *The South and the
Concurrent Majority* (Baton Rouge: Louisiana State University Press,
1972), 4.

61 *"A majority, held in"*: Remarks by Abraham Lincoln, Washington, DC, March 4, 1861, https://avalon.law.yale.edu/19th_century/lincoln1.asp.

61 *"to a political and"*: Quoted in Richard Hofstadter, *The American Political Tradition and the Men Who Made It* (New York: Vintage, 1989), 103.

62 *"the sentiment of the"*: Calhoun, *Disquisition*, 332.

62 *"Second American Revolution"*: Quoted in C. Vann Woodward, *Reunion and Reaction* (New York: Little Brown, 1951), 4.

62 *"the principal philosopher of"*: Quoted in Tanenhaus, "Original Sin."

63 *"If there is anyone"*: "Barack Obama Victory Speech," Chicago, Ill., C-Span, November 4, 2008, https://www.c-span.org/video/?282164-2/barack-obama-victory-speech.

64 *"coalition of the ascendant"*: Ronald Brownstein, "Obama's Gamble," *National Journal*, June 28, 2012.

64 *"Democrats are getting the"*: Quoted in Conor Dougherty, "Minority Turnout Was Critical to Obama's Election, Data Show," *The Wall Street Journal*, July 21, 2009.

64 *"No other country has"*: Quoted in Sam Roberts, "Minorities in U.S. Set to Become Majority by 2042," *The New York Times*, August 14, 2008.

64 *"What are the seemingly"*: Patrick J. Buchanan, "A.D. 2041-End of White America?" *CNS News*, October 18, 2011.

65 *"go Pat go"*: "Buchanan Campaign Speech," February 20, 1996.

65 *"extreme"*: Quoted in Katharine Q. Seelye, "Dole Says Buchanan Is Extreme in Outlook," *The New York Times*, February 24, 1996.

65 *"Pitchfork Pat"*: George F. Will, "Pitchfork Pat," *The Washington Post*, February 29, 1996.

65 *"Look, he's a Hitler"*: Quoted in Francis X. Clines, "Trump Quits Grand Old Party for New," *The New York Times*, October 25, 1999.

66 *"The people who put"*: Patrick J. Buchanan, *State of Emergency* (New York: Thomas Dunne Books, 2006), 52.

66 *"Obama's election represents multiculturalism"*: Quoted in Christopher S. Parker and Matt A. Barreto, *Change They Can't Believe In* (Princeton, N.J.: Princeton University Press, 2014), 157.

66 *"Because we don't have"*: Quoted in Faith Davis Johnson, "Savvy About Civics," *Dallas Morning News*, April 4, 2010.

66 *"pass on our culture"*: Quoted in Ed Pilkington, "Prejudice and Principle Brew at Tea Party Meet," *The Guardian*, February 6, 2010.

67 *"Taxed Enough Already"*: Ibid., 2.

67 *"The evidence is pretty"*: Devin Burghart, interview conducted by the author, February 9, 2022.

67 *"Obama is destroying the"*: Parker and Barreto, *Change*, 50.

67 *"is as big a"*: Quoted in Stephanie Mencimer, "Tea Partiers: The Most Oppressed Minority?" *Mother Jones*, November 17, 2010.

68 *"take our country back"*: Quoted in Frank Rich, "The Rage Is Not About Health Care," *The New York Times*, March 27, 2010.

68 *"The White Anglo-Saxon"*: Quoted in Devin Burghart, "Tea Party Nation Warns of White Anglo-Saxon Protestant 'Extinction,'" Institute for Research and Education on Human Rights, March 29, 2011.

68 *"For the first time"*: Patrick J. Buchanan, "Losing White America," July 23, 2010, https://buchanan.org/blog/losing-white-america-4248?doing_wp _cron=1612885397.0971629619598388671875.

68 *"popular pressure"*: Quoted in Lawrence Rosenthal and Christine Trost, *Steep: The Precipitous Rise of the Tea Party* (Berkeley: University of California Press, 2010), 35.

68 *"a fit of populist"*: Ibid.

69 *"The Founding Fathers originally"*: Quoted in Devin Burghart, "Tea Party Leaders Attack Constitution," IREHR, November 30, 2010.

69 *"We've got a great"*: Quoted in W. Gardner Selby, "Gov. Rick Perry Recaps His Comment on Texas Seceding from the United States; Does He Repeat Accurately?" *PolitiFact*, April 22, 2010.

69 *"No, it is not"*: Patrick J. Buchanan, "Secession in the Air," February 12, 2010, https://buchanan.org/blog/secession-in-the-air-3584.

70 *"Illegal Means Illegal"*: "07 13 2010 Kris Kobach Part 1," Overland Park, Kan., YouTube, July 19, 2010, https://www.youtube.com/watch?v=bEUFyT _aeFE&t=354s.

70 *"Elect Kris Kobach"*: Ibid.

70 *"the man behind Arizona's"*: Ibid.

70 *"we built the law"*: Ibid.

70 *"explicitly racist behavior"*: Quoted in Addy Barr, "Tea Party to NAACP: 'Grow Up,'" *Politico*, July 13, 2010.

71 *"What do Obama and"*: Quoted in "An Obama Birther for Kansas Secretary of State?" *Washington Independent*, July 13, 2009.

71 *"We're not motivated by"*: Kris Kobach Part 1, YouTube.

71 *"very suspicious"*: "07 13 2010 Kris Kobach Part 2" YouTube, July 19, 2010, https://www.youtube.com/watch?v=rL5ilS8lciw&t=2s.

71 *"Joe, Joe, Joe"*: "Sheriff Joe Arpaio Part 1," YouTube, July 20, 2010, https:// www.youtube.com/watch?v=ITGkRQddrEA.

72 *"I took away their"*: "Sheriff Joe Arpaio Part 2," YouTube, July 20, 2010, https://www.youtube.com/watch?v=vrLCxesJObc.

72 *"He should be running"*: "Sheriff Joe Arpaio Part 3," YouTube, July 20, 2010, https://www.youtube.com/watch?v=fX7c4J88Yxk.

72 *"I want Kansas to"*: "04-14-11 Kris Kobach at Hutch PFA," Hutchinson, Kan., Vimeo, https://vimeo.com/22465601.

72 *"I can sum up"*: Quoted in Julie Clements, "Malkin Makes Visit to Butler County with Kobach," *El Dorado Times*, November 9, 2009.

72 *"on the verge of"*: Quoted in Deborah Hastings, "Fact Check: GOP Vitriol Rages over Community Group," Associated Press, October 16, 2008.

73 *"new Southern strategy"*: Lorraine C. Minnite, *The Myth of Voter Fraud* (Ithaca, N.Y.: Cornell University Press, 2010), 90.

73 *"In Kansas, the illegal"*: Quoted in Rachel Slajda, "Voter Fraud Candidate Kris Kobach Wins in Kansas," *Talking Points Memo*, November 3, 2010.

73 *"incidents"*: Expert Report of Lorraine C. Minnite, *Fish v. Kobach*, No. 2:16-cv-02105.

73 *"the Cadillac of voter"*: Quoted in John Hanna, "Kan. Gov. Signs Bill Requiring Photo ID at Polls," Associated Press, April 18, 2011.

73 *"If a state enacted"*: Kris Kobach, interview conducted by the author, March 3, 2017.

74 *"Of the 11 states"*: Wendy Weiser and Erik Opsal, "The State of Voting In 2014," Brennan Center for Justice, www.brennancenter.org/analysis/state-voting-2014.

74 *"fraudulent ballots"*: Quoted in Angie Haflich, "Kobach Addresses State Issues, Criticism," *The Garden City Telegram*, May 31, 2013.

75 *"It was almost like"*: Charles Stricker III, interview conducted by the author, February 23, 2017.

75 *"in suspense"*: "Kobach Issues 90-Day Limit for Incomplete Registrations," Associated Press, September 18, 2015.

77 *"clash of civilizations"*: Samuel P. Huntington, *The Clash of Civilizations and the Remaking of World Order* (New York: Simon & Schuster, 1996).

77 *"It seems likely that"*: Quoted in Gay Seidman, "Mr. Huntington Goes to Pretoria," *Harvard Crimson*, November 5, 1987.

77 *"touched on a lot"*: Kobach, interview.

78 *"Some of the problems"*: Michael J. Crozier, Samuel P. Huntington, and Joji Watanuki, *The Crisis of Democracy* (New York: New York University Press, 1975), 113.

78 *"potentially desirable limits to"*: Ibid.

78 *"In itself, this marginality"*: Ibid., 114.

78 *"Why the South Must"*: *National Review*, August 25, 1957.

79 *"Over most of this"*: James Jackson Kilpatrick, "Must We Repeal the Constitution to Give the Negro the Vote?" *National Review*, April 20, 1965.

79 *"What is wrong in"*: Quoted in Kevin M. Schultz, "William F. Buckley and National Review's Vile Race Stance," Salon.com, June 7, 2015.

79 *"While Muslims pose the"*: Quoted in David Montejano, "Who Is Samuel P. Huntington?" *Texas Observer*, August 13, 2004.

80 *"do not appear to"*: Samuel P. Huntington, "The Hispanic Challenge," *Foreign Policy*, October 28, 2009.

80 *"the large and continuing"*: Samuel P. Huntington, *Who Are We?* (New York: Simon & Schuster, 2004), 317.

80 *"Buchanan with footnotes"*: Alan Wolfe, "Review: Who Are We? The Challenges to America's National Identity by Samuel P. Huntington," *Foreign Affairs*, May/June 2004.

80 *"What the vote for"*: Samuel T. Francis, *Revolution from the Middle* (Raleigh, N.C.: Middle American Press, 1997), 214.

81 *"It was not popular"*: Quoted in Ari Berman, "The Man Behind Trump's Voter-Fraud Obsession," *The New York Times Magazine*, June 13, 2017.

81 *"While the other"*: Ibid.

81 *"When Buchanan was pushing"*: Quoted in Rachel L. Swarns, "Outcry on Right Over Bush Plan on Immigration," *The New York Times*, February 21, 2004.

82 *"mandated ethnic profiling"*: Berman, "The Man Behind Trump's Voter-Fraud Obsession."

82 *"great success"*: Ibid.

82 *"We plan to make"*: Quoted in Matt Schudel, "John Tanton, Architect of Anti-Immigration and English-Only Efforts, Dies at 85," *The Washington Post*, July 21, 2019.

82 *"I've come to the"*: Quoted in Carly Goodman, "John Tanton Has Died. He Made America Less Open to Immigrants—and More Open to Trump," *The Washington Post*, July 18, 2019.

83 *"As Whites see their"*: Quoted in Gustavo Arellano, "John Tanton, Quiet Architect of America's Modern-Day Anti-Immigrant Movement, Dies at 85," *Los Angeles Times*, July 18, 2019.

83 *"diabolical Jewish control"*: Quoted in "John Tanton Is The Mastermind Behind the Organized Anti-Immigration Movement," Southern Poverty Law Center, June 18, 2022.

83 *"the end of the white"*: Quoted in Berman, "The Man Behind Trump's Voter-Fraud Obsession."

83 *"the proliferation of other"*: Quoted in Mark Potok, "The Dark Legacy of John Tanton, the Anti-Immigration White Nationalist Who Set the Stage for Trump," *The Daily Beast*, July 23, 2019.

83 *"demographic and other trends"*: "Memo: John Tanton to Otis Graham," March 3, 1993, via SPLC https://www.splcenter.org/sites/default/files/blog/wp-content/uploads/2010/06/tanton_graham_030393.pdf.

83 *"reduction of the European-American"*: Ibid.

84 *"People and groups tied"*: "Dennis Moore Kris Kobach TV Debate Kansas House District 3," YouTube, October 22, 2004, https://www.youtube.com/watch?v=ai5puBPbcs8.

84 *"amnesty"*: Ibid.

84 *"I want to just"*: Quoted in Berman, "The Man Behind Trump's Voter-Fraud Obsession."

84 *"a field study"*: Ibid.

84 *"If you have a"*: Kobach, interview.

85 *"the ACLU's worst nightmare"*: The Kris Kobach Show, KCMO, January 22, 2017, https://audioboom.com/posts/5534478-january-22-2017-hour-1.

85 *"strategy of replacing American"*: Quoted in Ahiza Garcia, "Kobach: Obama's Lawlessness Could Lead To 'Ethnic Cleansing' In America," *Talking Points Memo*, November 20, 2014.

85 *"when one culture or"*: Ibid.
85 *"For the first time"*: Burghart, interview.

4. THE DEATH OF THE AUTOPSY AND THE BIRTH OF THE BIG LIE

86 *"the most public and"*: "RNC Chair Reince Priebus Speaks at March 18, 2013 National Press Club Breakfast," Washington, DC, YouTube, March 18, 2013 https://www.youtube.com/watch?v=DCL40bHHVuw.
87 *"The demographics are changing"*: Quoted in Mackenzie Weinger, "Bill O'Reilly: 'The White Establishment Is Now the Minority,'" *Politico*, November 6, 2012.
87 *"I went to bed"*: Quoted in Abena Agyeman-Fisher, "Limbaugh On Obama Win: 'I Went To Bed Last Night Thinking We've Lost The Country,'" NewsOne, November 7, 2012.
87 *"The demographic winter of"*: Patrick J. Buchanan, "The Bell Tolls for the 'New Majority,'" June 14, 2013, https://buchanan.org/blog/the-bell-tolls-for-the-new-majority-5616.
87 *"The nation's demographic changes"*: Republican National Committee, "Growth & Opportunity Project," https://www.wsj.com/public/resources/documents/RNCreport03182013.pdf.
88 *"attrition through enforcement"*: Berman, "The Man Behind Trump's Voter-Fraud Obsession."
88 *"I'm for self-deportation"*: Quoted in Lucy Madison, "Romney on Immigration: I'm for 'Self-Deportation,'" CBS News, January 24, 2012.
88 *"If Hispanic Americans perceive"*: RNC, "Growth & Opportunity Project."
88 *"not generating enough angry"*: Quoted in Rosalind S. Helderman and Jon Cohen, "As Republican Convention Emphasizes Diversity, Racial Incidents Intrude," *The Washington Post*, August 29, 2012.
88 *"The reince revolution is"*: Newt Gingrich, Twitter post, March 18, 2013, https://mobile.twitter.com/newtgingrich/status/313673503599624192?lang=bn.
88 *"controversial and bold"*: Jennifer Rubin, "GOP Autopsy Report Goes Bold," *The Washington Post*, March 18, 2013.
88 *"scathing self-analysis"*: Neil King, "GOP Issues Scathing Self-Analysis," *The Wall Street Journal*, March 18, 2013.
88 *"It's really hard to"*: Quoted in Benjy Sarlin, "How the GOP Stopped Worrying About Latinos and Learned to Love the Base," *MSNBC.com*, July 1, 2013.
89 *"'missing' white voters"*: Sean Trende, "The Case of the Missing White Voters," *RealClearPolitics*, November 8, 2012.
89 *"improving their vote share"*: Sean Trende, "Does GOP Have to Pass Immigration Reform?" *RealClearPolitics*, June 25, 2013.
89 *"Democrats liked to mock"*: Ibid.
89 *"downscale, blue-collar whites"*: Sean Trende, "The Case of the Missing White Voters, Revisited," *RealClearPolitics*, June 21, 2013.

89 "*'racial polarization' scenario*": Trende, "Does GOP Have to Pass Immigration Reform?"

90 "*a strategy from which*": Buchanan, *Suicide of a Superpower*, 349.

90 "*Is the way to*": Patrick J. Buchanan, "Requiem for a Grand Old Party," World Net Daily, May 9, 2013, https://www.wnd.com/2013/05/requiem -for-a-grand-old-party/.

90 "*will create millions of*": Patrick J. Buchanan, "Will the GOP Embrace Amnesty," April 19, 2013, https://buchanan.org/blog/will-the-gop-embrace -amnesty-5541.

90 "*The people the Republicans*": Quoted in Thomas B. Edsall, "Should Republicans Just Focus on White Voters?" *The New York Times*, July 3, 2013.

91 "*hardline position on immigration*": Quoted in Sarlin, "How the GOP Stopped Worrying About Latinos and Learned to Love the Base."

91 "*baloney*": Ibid.

91 "*we've got to look*": Quoted in Rachel Weiner, "Sean Hannity: I've 'Evolved' on Immigration," *The Washington Post*, November 8, 2012.

91 "*Not only do I*": Quoted in Sarlin, "How the GOP Stopped Worrying About Latinos and Learned to Love the Base."

91 "*Kill the Bill*": William Kristol and Rich Lowry, "Kill the Bill," *National Review*, July 9, 2013.

91 "*It's the defining struggle*": Quoted in Molly Ball, "The Immigration Fight Is the Battle for the Soul of the GOP," *The Atlantic*, July 17, 2013.

91 "*Any politician who thinks*": Quoted in John Eligon, "Kansas Official Holds Line Against Moderation in Debate on Immigration," *The New York Times*, July 14, 2013.

92 "*American civilization and culture*": Quoted in Ball, "The Immigration Fight Is the Battle for the Soul of the GOP."

92 "*Judeo-Christian values*": Quoted in Matt Vasilogambros and National Journal, "A Rant on Western Civilization by Rep. Steve King," *The Atlantic*, July 25, 2013.

92 "*the Great Replacement*": Quoted in Trip Gabriel, "Before Trump, Steve King Set the Agenda for the Wall and Anti-Immigrant Politics," *The New York Times*, January 10, 2019.

92 "*Culture and demographics are*": Quoted in German Lopez, "Rep. Steve King's Latest Racist Remarks Are Far from His First," *Vox*, March 13, 2017.

92 "*I'd like to see*": Ibid.

93 "*amnesty for illegal immigrants*": Quoted in Lindsey Boerman, "Meet David Brat, the Man Who Ousted Eric Cantor," CBS News, June 11, 2014.

93 "*enforcement of current*": Quoted in Molly Ball, "Kellyanne's Alternative Universe," *The Atlantic*, April 2017.

93 "*the intellectual infrastructure*": Ibid.

93 "*rapists*": Quoted in Olivia Nuzzi, "Donald Trump's Sorry He Offended You, Not Sorry for What He Did," *The Daily Beast*, October 7, 2020.

94 *"the Flight 93 election"*: Publius Decius Mus, "The Flight 93 Election," *Claremont Review of Books*, September 5, 2016.

94 *"The more multiracial, multiethnic"*: Quoted in Aaron Rupar, "Trump Promotes Pat Buchanan Column That Makes White Nationalist Case for His Border Wall," *Vox*, January 14, 2019.

95 *"Voting is important to"*: Quoted in Berman, "Rigged: How Voter Suppression Threw Wisconsin to Trump."

95 *"many dishonest people undermined"*: Quoted in Anita Weier, "Assembly Nods to Voter ID; Senate Likely to Oppose It," *The Capital Times*, November 7, 2001.

95 *"This particular election was"*: Quoted in Berman, "Rigged."

96 *"It was their first"*: Ibid.

97 *"customer-initiated cancellation"*: Ibid.

97 *"disenfranchised a number of"*: Ibid.

97 *"primary focus"*: Quoted in Jessie Opoien, "As Madison Expands Early Voting, Scott Walker Says Keeping Voter ID in Place Is Priority," *The Capital Times*, August 18, 2016.

98 *"I think Hillary Clinton"*: Quoted in Berman, "Rigged."

98 *"Perhaps the biggest drags"*: Sabrina Tavernise, "Many in Milwaukee Neighborhood Didn't Vote—and Don't Regret It," *The New York Times*, November 20, 2016.

98 *"a load of crap"*: Quoted in Matthew DeFour, "Donald Trump's Victory Completes Eight-Year Political Reversal in Wisconsin," *Wisconsin State Journal*, November 14, 2016.

98 *"aided and abetted by"*: Quoted in Rebecca Traister, "Inside Hillary Clinton's Surreal Post-Election Life," *New York Magazine*, May 26, 2017.

98 *"Hillary Clinton Blames Voter"*: Becket Adams, "Hillary Clinton Blames Voter Suppression for Losing a State She Didn't Visit Once During the Election," *Washington Examiner*, May 31, 2017.

99 *"main reason"*: Quoted in Ari Berman, "A New Study Shows Just How Many Americans Were Blocked From Voting in Wisconsin Last Year," *Mother Jones*, September 25, 2017.

99 *"We have hard evidence"*: Ibid.

99 *"Selma of the North"*: Patrick D. Jones, *The Selma of the North* (Cambridge, Mass.: Harvard University Press, 2009).

99 *"I'd want to live"*: Quoted in Whet Moser, "Why Is Milwaukee So Politically Polarized?" *Chicago Magazine*, May 7, 2014.

99 *"We don't want Wisconsin"*: Quoted in Alec MacGillis, "The Unelectable Whiteness of Scott Walker," *The New Republic*, June 15, 2014.

99 *"I looked 12 until"*: Quoted in Berman, "Rigged."

100 *"We're moving into a"*: Ibid.

100 *"Whoever comes next, this"*: Quoted in Traister, "Inside Hillary Clinton's Surreal Post-Election Life."

101 *"Kobach Strategic Plan for"*: Quoted in Berman, "The Man Behind Trump's Voter-Fraud Obsession."

101 *"extreme vetting"*: Ibid.

101 *"Stop Aliens From Voting"*: Quoted in Ari Berman, "Trump Election Commission Leader Sought a Radical Change to a Key Voting Law," *Mother Jones*, October 6, 2017.

101 *"the problem of noncitizens"*: Quoted in Ari Berman, "Kris Kobach Wants to Make It Harder to Vote Nationwide—But He's Already Failing Back Home in Kansas," *Mother Jones*, November 28, 2017.

101 *"I won the popular"*: Ibid.

101 *"I think the president-elect"*: Quoted in Berman, "The Man Behind Trump's Voter-Fraud Obsession."

102 *"Study: Voting by Non-Citizens"*: Joel B. Pollak, "Study: Voting by Non-Citizens Tips Balance for Democrats," *Breitbart News*, October 26, 2014.

102 *"Jaw-Dropping Study Claims"*: Jim Geraghty, "Jaw-Dropping Study Claims Large Numbers of Non-Citizens Vote in U.S.," *National Review*, October 24, 2014.

102 *"If we apply that"*: Quoted in Bryan Lowry, "Trump Adviser Backs Claim of Millions Voting Illegally," *The Wichita Eagle*, December 1, 2016.

102 *"Thus the best estimate"*: Quoted in Berman, "The Man Behind Trump's Voter-Fraud Obsession."

103 *"the claim Trump is"*: Quoted in John Hanna, "Kobach Supports Trump's Voting Fraud Claims," Associated Press, December 1, 2016.

103 *"It's the most inappropriate"*: Quoted in "TRANSCRIPT: ABC News Anchor David Muir Interviews President Trump," ABC News, January 25, 2017.

103 *"I have seen no"*: Ibid.

103 *"We may never know"*: Quoted in Ari Berman, "The Trump Administration Is Trying Again to Get Data on Every American Voter," *Mother Jones*, July 27, 2017.

103 *"improper voter registrations and"*: Quoted in Berman, "The Man Behind Trump's Voter-Fraud Obsession."

104 *"This is a first"*: "Kobach: This Is a First of Its Kind Effort vs Voter Fraud," Tucker Carlson Tonight, Fox News, September 12, 2017.

104 *"VOTER FRAUD PANEL"*: Donald J. Trump, Twitter post, July 1, 2017, https://twitter.com/realdonaldtrump/status/881137079958241280?lang=en.

104 *"voter inconsistencies and irregularities"*: Remarks by President Trump and Vice President Pence at the Presidential Advisory Commission on Election Integrity Meeting, Washington, DC, Trump White House Archives, July 19, 2017.

104 *"this commission has no"*: Ibid.

104 *"the full first and"*: Quoted in Ari Berman, "The Trump Administration Is Planning an Unprecedented Attack on Voting Rights," *The Nation*, June 30, 2017.

104 *"very helpful in the"*: Quoted in "PACEI Dunlap Documents July 18 Release," American Oversight, 358, July 18, 2018, https://embed .documentcloud.org/documents/4635501-PROD001-0005992.

104 *"a waste of taxpayer"*: Quoted in Berman, "The Trump Administration Is Planning an Unprecedented Attack on Voting Rights."

104 *"a pretext to validate"*: Ibid.

105 *"go jump in the"*: Quoted in Ari Berman, "The Trump Administration's Voter-Suppression Plans Are Backfiring Badly," *The Nation*, July 5, 2017.

105 *"the President's Commission has"*: Ibid.

105 *"this hastily organized experiment"*: Ibid.

105 *"I've been studying America's"*: Ibid.

105 *"both without precedent and"*: Quoted in Ari Berman, "Meet the Vote Suppressors and Conspiracy Theorists on Trump's 'Election Integrity' Commission," *The Nation*, July 11, 2017.

106 *"We do need an"*: Quoted in Berman, "The Man Behind Trump's Voter-Fraud Obsession."

106 *"alarming evidence of voter fraud"*: Ibid.

106 *"the first concrete evidence"*: Ibid.

106 *"200 legitimate voters may"*: Ibid.

106 *"The Commission may compare"*: Quoted in Vann R. Newkirk II, "Inside Trump's Voter-Fraud Crusade," *The Atlantic*, August 8, 2018.

107 *"He already has policy"*: Quoted in John Hanna, "Kobach Says He Won't Pre-judge Voter Fraud Panel's Findings," Associated Press, May 18, 2017.

107 *"thousands . . . brought in on"*: Quoted in Eli Stokols, "Trump Brings Up Vote Fraud Again, This Time in Meeting with Senators," *Politico*, February 10, 2017.

107 *"To put the 5,526"*: "Email from Kossack to Kobach—September 7, 2017—'This is not public,'" PACEI Dunlap Documents, American Oversight, 61, https://embed.documentcloud.org/documents/4635501 -PROD001-0005992#document/p61/a444775.

107 *"exclusive"*: Kris W. Kobach, "Exclusive—Kobach: It Appears That Out-of-State Voters Changed the Outcome of the New Hampshire U.S. Senate Race," *Breitbart News*, September 7, 2017.

108 *"flooding across borders"*: Quoted in Ari Berman, "Kris Kobach Won't Stop Spreading Voter Fraud Falsehoods," *Mother Jones*, September 12, 2017.

108 *"The result, as we"*: Ibid.

108 *"Politically and philosophically he"*: Matthew Dunlap, interview conducted by the author, April 1, 2022.

109 *"You have a right"*: Quoted in Berman, "Kris Kobach Won't Stop Spreading Voter Fraud Falsehoods."

109 *"What are we working"*: Dunlap, interview.

110 *"to participate meaningfully in"*: Quoted in Ari Berman, "Trump's Voter Fraud Commission Is Being Sued by One of Its Commissioners," *Mother Jones*, November 9, 2017.

110 *"WTF?"*: Quoted in Newkirk, "Inside Trump's Voter-Fraud Crusade."

110 *"indefensible"*: Quoted in David Daley, "Kobach and Trump's Spectacular Voter-Fraud Failure," *Rolling Stone*, April 27, 2020.

110 *"rather than engage in"*: "Statement by the Press Secretary on the Presidential Advisory Commission on Election Integrity," Trump White House Archives, January 3, 2018.

110 *"a tactical shift where"*: Quoted in Josh Binder, "Exclusive–Kris Kobach: Voter Fraud Commission 'Being Handed Off' to DHS, Will No Longer Be 'Stonewalled' by Dems," *Breitbart News*, January 3, 2018.

110 *"no Commission records or"*: Quoted in Melanie Schmitz, "Oops! White House Admits It Has Zero Evidence of Voter Fraud in 2016 Election," Think Progress, January 17, 2018.

110 *"Mr. Kobach is not"*: Ibid.

110 *"Staff Report"*: Quoted in Jessica Huseman, "Election Commission Documents Cast Doubt on Trump's Claims of Voter Fraud," *ProPublica*, August 3, 2018.

110 *"They wanted to have"*: Dunlap, interview.

111 *"the sections on evidence"*: "Matthew Dunlap, letter to Vice President Pence and Secretary Kobach," August 3, 2018, http://paceidocs.sosonline .org/PDF/Dunlap%20PACEI%20Docs%20Findings%20letter%20-%20FI NAL.080318.pdf.

111 *"I thought this was"*: Dunlap, interview.

111 *"Many people are voting"*: Quoted in Ari Berman, "Donald Trump Shut Down His Election Fraud Commission, But He Hasn't Given up on Voter Suppression," *Mother Jones*, January 4, 2018.

111 *"The narrative"*: Dunlap, interview.

5. THE MOST DANGEROUS BRANCH

112 *"this partisan impeachment sham"*: Quoted in Rebecca Klar, "GOP Lawmaker Holds Moment of Silence on House Floor for People Who Voted for Trump," *The Hill*, December 18, 2019.

112 *"I would like you"*: Quoted in Justin Wise, "Trump Claims He Asked Ukraine to Do US a 'Favor,' Not Him," *The Hill*, December 5, 2019.

112 *"The framers predicted that"*: "Senator McConnell on Impeachment Trial Vote," Washington, DC, C-Span, February 5, 2020, https://www.c-span .org/video/?468922-14/senator-mcconnell-impeachment-trial-vote&event =468922&playEvent.

113 *"Corrupting an election to"*: Quoted in "Read the Full Text: Mitt Romney's Remarks on Impeachment Vote," *Politico*, February 5, 2020.

113 *"the Senate can now"*: "McConnell: 'The Senate Can Now Get Back to the Business of the American People,'" February 11, 2020, https://www .republicanleader.senate.gov/newsroom/remarks/mcconnell-the-senate-can -now-get-back-to-the-business-of-the-american-people.

113 *"My motto for the"*: "McConnell on Hugh Hewitt," February 11, 2020,

https://www.republicanleader.senate.gov/newsroom/press-releases/mccon
nell-on-hugh-hewitt.

114 *"The Voting Rights Act is"*: Quoted in Ari Berman, "Why Are Conservatives Trying to Destroy the Voting Rights Act?" *The Nation*, February 6,
2015.

114 *"Things in the South have"*: "Brief of State of Alabama As Amicus Cu-
riae Supporting Petitioner," *Shelby County v. Holder*, No. 12-96, January 2,
2013.

115 *"Nearly 50 years later"*: *Shelby County v. Holder*, 570 US 529 (2013).

115 *"unconstitutional poll tax"*: Quoted in Ari Berman, "The Country's Worst
Voter-ID Law Was Just Struck Down," *The Nation*, July 20, 2016.

115 *"with almost surgical precision"*: Quoted in Adam Liptak and Michael
Wines, "Strict North Carolina Voter ID Law Thwarted After Supreme
Court Rejects Case," *The New York Times*, May 15, 2017.

116 *"Can you give an"*: "Nomination Hearing," Washington, DC, U.S. Senate
Committee on the Judiciary, December 4, 2019, https://www.judiciary
.senate.gov/committee-activity/hearings/12/04/2019/nominations.

116 *"needed to be updated"*: Ibid.

116 *"He's someone with a"*: Ibid.

117 *"It sounds like it"*: Ibid.

117 *"the institutional equivalent of"*: Jack Bass, *Taming the Storm* (New York:
Doubleday, 1992), 132.

117 *"What do you see as"*: "Nomination Hearing," Senate Judiciary Committee.

118 *"the worst voting rights"*: "Civil Rights Organizations Call for Defeat of
Andrew Brasher's Nomination to Eleventh Circuit," NAACP, January 13,
2020.

118 *"Arizona on steroids"*: Quoted in Raymond A. Mohl, "The Politics of Expulsion: A Short History of Alabama's Anti-Immigrant Law, HB 56,"
Journal of American Ethnic History 35, no. 3 (Spring 2016).

118 *"A bad day for turkeys"*: Quoted in George Talbot, "Kris Kobach, the Kansas Lawyer Behind Alabama's Immigration Law," *AL.com*, October 16,
2011.

119 *"Alabama is now the"*: Quoted in Julia Preston, "In Alabama, a Harsh Bill
for Residents Here Illegally," *The New York Times*, June 3, 2011.

119 *"We are convinced that"*: Quoted in Campbell Robertson and Julia Preston, "Appeals Court Draws Boundaries on Alabama's Immigration Law,"
The New York Times, August 21, 2012.

119 *"the worst abomination in"*: Quoted in Molly Runkle, "Judge William
Pryor—A Southern Conservative Who Speaks His Mind," *SCOTUSblog*,
January 30, 2017.

120 *"The ACLU and Planned Parenthood"*: Quoted in Leadership Conference on Civil and Human Rights, "Oppose the Confirmation of Andrew
Brasher to the U.S. Court of Appeals for the Eleventh Circuit," December
3, 2019.

120 *"Sexual relationships between men"*: Ibid.

120 *"little effect on gun"*: Quoted in "Nomination of Andrew Lynn Brasher to the U.S. Court of Appeals for the Eleventh Circuit, Questions for the Record," Senate Judiciary Committee, December 11, 2019, https://www .judiciary.senate.gov/imo/media/doc/Brasher%20Responses%20to%20 QFRs.pdf.

120 *"He's not just unqualified"*: "Senate Session," Washington, DC, C-Span, February 10, 2020, https://www.c-span.org/video/?469127-1/senate-session.

121 *"He is known as"*: Carrie Campbell Severino, "Congratulations to Andrew Brasher for Appointment as Solicitor General of Alabama," *National Review*, February 21, 2014.

121 *"couldn't be more thrilled"*: Carrie Severino, Twitter post, November 6, 2019, https://twitter.com/jcnseverino/status/1192140610528043009.

121 *"guard the Constitution and"*: Alexander Hamilton, "Federalist No. 78," https://guides.loc.gov/federalist-papers/text-71-80#s-lg-box-wrapper -25493470.

121 *"a protector of the"*: Quoted in Clarence Page, "The Legacy of Thurgood Marshall," *Chicago Tribune*, June 29, 1991.

122 *"discrete and insular minorities"*: *United States v. Carolene Products Company*, 304 US 144 (1938).

122 *"havens of refuge for"*: Quoted in David Kaplan, *The Most Dangerous Branch* (New York: Crown, 2018), 17.

122 *"minority rights revolution"*: Quoted in Steven M. Teles, *The Rise of the Conservative Legal Movement* (Princeton, N.J.: Princeton University Press, 2010), 24.

122 *"Impeach Earl Warren"*: Quoted in John Wicklein, "Birch Society Will Offer $2,300 For Impeach-Warren Essays," *The New York Times*, August 5, 1961.

122 *"strict constructionists"*: "Draft (Buchanan): The New Court," October 23, 1968, President Richard Nixon—Pat Buchanan Papers, https://www .paperlessarchives.com/FreeTitles/Nixon-BuchananPapers.pdf.

122 *"American economic system is"*: Quoted in "Captured Courts," Senate Democratic Policy & Communications Committee, May 2020.

123 *"the virtues of individual"*: Ibid.

123 *"racial entitlement"*: Quoted in Amy Davidson Sorkin, "In Voting Rights, Scalia Sees a 'Racial Entitlement,'" *The New Yorker*, February 28, 2013.

123 *"Equal Gratification"*: Quoted in Daniel S. Lucks, "Originalism Threatens to Turn the Clock Back on Race," *The Washington Post*, October 13, 2020.

123 *"In approaching this problem"*: *Brown v. Board of Education of Topeka*, 347 US 483 (1954).

124 *"The original Constitution does"*: "Southern Manifesto on Integration," March 12, 1956, https://www.thirteen.org/wnet/supremecourt/rights /sources_document2.html.

124 *"constitutional cases clocks must"*: Quoted in Calvin Terbeek, "Clocks

Must Always Be Turned Back," *Cambridge University Press*, March 16, 2021.

124 *"They needed a way"*: Nan Aron, interview conducted by the author, May 31, 2022.

124 *"not acting as an"*: Quoted in "Captured Courts."

125 *"We're going to have"*: Ibid.

125 *"We have seen our"*: "2017 National Lawyers Convention, White House Counsel McGahn," Washington, DC, C-Span, November 17, 2017, https://www.c-span.org/video/?437462-8/2017-national-lawyers-convention-white-house-counsel-mcgahn.

125 *"I never would have"*: Quoted in Charles Homans, "Mitch McConnell Got Everything He Wanted. But at What Cost?" *The New York Times Magazine*, January 22, 2019.

125 *"If we stop this"*: Quoted in Alec MacGillis, *The Cynic* (New York: Simon & Schuster, 2014), 65.

126 *"Low voter turnout is"*: Mitch McConnell, "Should US Simplify Voter Registration?" *The Christian Science Monitor*, October 1, 1991.

126 *"the corrosive and distorting"*: *McConnell v. Federal Election Commission*, 540 US 93 (2003).

126 *"worst Supreme Court decision since"*: Quoted in MacGillis, *The Cynic*, 71.

127 *"Judge Kallon has a"*: Quoted in Mary Troyan, "Obama Appoints Judge Abdul Kallon to 11th Circuit," *Montgomery Advertiser*, February 11, 2016.

127 *"too late now"*: Ibid.

127 *"a Republican President will"*: Quoted in Al Franken, "How Ending the Blue Slip Damaged the Federal Courts Forever," *Democracy Docket*, August 25, 2021.

127 *"Granting any more lifetime"*: Heritage Action, "MEMO: Fight Obama's Overreach by Refusing to Confirm Nominees," January 15, 2016.

127 *"the decision not to"*: Quoted in Homans, "Mitch McConnell Got Everything He Wanted."

127 *"The Supreme Court ended"*: Quoted in Carl Hulse, *Confirmation Bias* (New York: Harper, 2019), 152.

128 *"do-nothing Congress"*: Quoted in "'Turnip Day' Session," U.S. Senate, July 26, 1948, https://www.senate.gov/artandhistory/history/minute/Turnip_Day_Session.htm.

128 *"to move judges like"*: Quoted in Homans, "Mitch McConnell Got Everything He Wanted."

128 *"super-minoritarian"*: Joshua P. Zoffer and David Singh Grewal, "The Counter-Majoritarian Difficulty of a Minoritarian Judiciary," *California Law Review*, October 2020.

6. THE NEW AMERICAN MAJORITY

130 *"call out in a"*: Quoted in Aaron Gould Sheinin, "Voting-Rights Project Launched," *The Atlanta Journal-Constitution*, August 15, 2013.

130 *"We were short on"*: Quoted in Greg Bluestein, *Flipped* (New York: Viking, 2022), 148.

130 *"genteel poor"*: Quoted in Darren Sands, "Stacey Abrams Wants to Be the First Black Woman Governor. But First She Has to Win the Nomination," *Buzzfeed News*, August 17, 2017.

131 *"We ask you to"*: "Stacey Abrams Made This Famous Speech 26 Years Before the State of the Union Response," NowThis/YouTube, February 5, 2019, https://www.youtube.com/watch?v=u9Fz6GqjMC8.

131 *"the present initiatives around"*: Gabriel Salguero and Rev. Delman Coates, "Why We Can't Wait: The Future of the US Democracy," *The Huffington Post*, July 19, 2013.

131 *"The last few weeks"*: Quoted in Adam Nagourney, "Zimmerman Acquittal Sparks New Debate in Martin Killing," *The New York Times*, July 15, 2013.

132 *"The first and most"*: Ben Jealous, "True South: Unleashing Democracy in the Black Belt 50 Years After Freedom Summer," Center for American Progress, June 16, 2014.

132 *"If you change Georgia"*: "Voting Rights and Southern Demographics," Washington, DC, C-Span, June 16, 2014, https://www.c-span.org/video/?319980-1/voting-rights-south.

133 *"civically engage the rising"*: Quoted in Carol Anderson, "Brian Kemp's Lead in Georgia Needs an Asterisk," *The Atlantic*, November 7, 2018.

133 *"Democrats are working hard"*: Quoted in Carol Anderson, "Brian Kemp, Enemy of Democracy," *The New York Times*, August 11, 2018.

133 *"significant illegal activities"*: Quoted in Kristina Torres, "Voter Drive Faces Fraud Allegations," *The Atlanta Journal-Constitution*, September 11, 2014.

133 *"fishing expedition"*: Quoted in Jamelle Bouie, "Georgia's Democrats Have Registered More Than 85,000 Minority Voters (and Counting). Republicans Never Saw It Coming," *Slate*, September 12, 2014.

133 *"You don't have to"*: Quoted in Kristina Torres, "State Backs Down on Scope of Voter Fraud," *The Atlanta Journal-Constitution*, September 18, 2014.

134 *"politically incorrect conservative"*: Quoted in Jelani Cobb, "Stacey Abrams's Fight for a Fair Vote," *The New Yorker*, August 12, 2019.

134 *"I got a big truck"*: Quoted in William Cummings, "Georgia Gubernatorial Candidate Brian Kemp Suggests Truck Is for Rounding Up 'Illegals,'" *USA Today*, May 10, 2018.

134 *"The approach of trying"*: Quoted in Jonathan Martin and Richard Fausset, "Black, Female and Running for Governor: Can She Win in the South?" *The New York Times*, May 19, 2018.

134 *"New American majority"*: Ibid.

135 *"counter to the most"*: "Full text of Carter's letter to Georgia secretary of state," Associated Press, October 29, 2018.

135 *"tilt the playing field"*: Quoted in Ari Berman, "Brian Kemp's Win In Georgia Is Tainted by Voter Suppression," *Mother Jones*, November 16, 2018.

135 *"As a naturalized United States"*: Declaration of Amos Amoadu Boadai, *Georgia State Conference of The NAACP v. Brian Kemp*, Case 2:16-cv-00219-WCO, September 14, 2016.

135 *"no match, no vote"*: Quoted in "Why the Voting Rights Act Matters," *The New York Times*, June 12, 2009.

136 *"flawed system"*: Quoted in Brentin Mock, "How Dismantling the Voting Rights Act Helped Georgia Discriminate Again," CityLab, October 15, 2018.

136 *"I've become very"*: "Georgia House, Day 23 Morning," Atlanta, Ga., GPB Lawmakers/YouTube, February 23, 2017, https://www.youtube.com/watch?v=6iXkQbtuIgs#action=share.

136 *"We'll see what"*: Ibid.

137 *"may represent the largest"*: Alan Judd, "Georgia's Strict Laws Lead to Large Purge of Voters," *The Atlanta Journal-Constitution*, October 27, 2018.

137 *"This was definitely foreseeable"*: Quoted in "Georgia Voters Express Frustrations After Being Turned Away from Polls!" *Ebony*, Facebook, November 6, 2018, https://www.facebook.com/ebonymag/videos/georgia-voters-express-frustrations-after-being-turned-away-from-polls-this-was-/1964119023702589/?paipv=0&eav=AfZFqoNCsy3NLwTiw1UXs_WRIy0ylYjU5Fa2JFuvEKy4NH65DQRfnuRn_gk36U98ooU&_rdr.

138 *"Maybe the South hasn't"*: Quoted in Mark Niesse and Nick Thieme, "Precinct Closures Harm Voter Turnout in Georgia, AJC Analysis Finds," *The Atlanta Journal-Constitution*, December 13, 2019.

138 *"possible cyber crimes"*: Quoted in Allan Smith, "Kemp Charges Georgia Democrats with Attempted Voter Hack," NBC News, November 4, 2018.

138 *"subvert the Constitution"*: Quoted in Eric Geller, "Elections Security: Federal Help or Power Grab?" *Politico*, August 28, 2016.

138 *"perhaps the most outrageous"*: Richard L. Hasen, "Brian Kemp Just Engaged in a Last-Minute Act of Banana-Republic Level Voter Manipulation in Georgia," *Slate*, November 4, 2018.

139 *"illegals to vote"*: Quoted in Naomi Lim, "Republican Gubernatorial Candidate in Georgia: Stacey Abrams 'Wants Illegals to Vote,'" *Washington Examiner*, October 15, 2018.

139 *"so excited to vote"*: Phoebe Einzig-Roth, interview conducted by the author, November 15, 2018.

139 *"The thing that infuriates"*: Quoted in Ari Berman, "The United States Is Becoming a Two-Tiered Country with Separate and Unequal Voting Laws," *Mother Jones*, November 19, 2018.

140 *"We are seeing unfold"*: Quoted in Jenny Jarvie, "Georgia's Bitter Contest Not Over Yet," *Los Angeles Times*, November 8, 2018.

140 *"To watch an elected"*: "Full Speech: Stacey Abrams Ends Candidacy for

Georgia Governor," Atlanta, Ga., NBC News/YouTube, November 16, 2018, https://www.youtube.com/watch?v=G1YXTP7u8Ds.

7. THE INSTITUTIONAL COUP

142 *"talk to someone about"*: "April-5-2017-Email-From-Brooke-Alexander. pdf," April 5, 2017, via US House Oversight and Reform Committee, https://s3.documentcloud.org/documents/4616790/April-5-2017-Email -From-Brooke-Alexander.pdf.

142 *"at the direction of"*: Quoted in "Commerce Department's Administrative Record for Census Citizenship Question Lawsuits," via Hansi Lo Wang/ NPR, June 8, 2018, 775–776, https://apps.npr.org/documents/document .html?id=4500011-1-18-Cv-02921-Administrative-Record#document/p775 /a428456.

142 *"a just and perfect"*: Quoted in "Hidden Figures: How Donald Trump Is Rigging the Census," *Mother Jones*, May/June 2018.

143 *"Immigrants and their families"*: Ibid.

144 *"I am mystified why"*: Quoted in Hansi Lo Wang, "How the 2020 Census Citizenship Question Ended Up in Court," NPR, November 4, 2018.

144 *"We need to work"*: Ibid.

145 *"Where is the DoJ"*: Ibid.

145 *"Since this issue will"*: Ibid.

145 *"Justice staff did not"*: Ibid.

145 *"The AG is eager"*: Ibid.

145 *"is very costly"*: Ibid.

145 *"more effective enforcement"*: Quoted in Ari Berman, "We Now Know Why Steve Bannon and Kris Kobach Lobbied for a Citizenship Question on the Census," *Mother Jones*, June 11, 2018.

145 *"solely"*: Quoted in Hansi Lo Wang, "How the 2020 Census Citizenship Question Ended Up In Court."

146 *"Sec Ross has reviewed"*: Quoted in Hansi Lo Wang, "Documents Detail the Secret Strategy Behind Trump's Census Citizenship Question Push," NPR, July 20, 2022.

146 *"Voting rights enforcement has"*: Quoted in Ari Berman, "Trump Administration Creates Census Crisis With Move to Suppress Immigrant Responses," *Mother Jones*, March 27, 2018.

146 *"leads to the problem"*: Quoted in Berman, "We Now Know Why Steve Bannon and Kris Kobach Lobbied for a Citizenship Question on the Census."

146 *"A person [whose] very"*: Kris W. Kobach: "Exclusive-Kobach: Bring the Citizenship Question Back to the Census," *Breitbart News*, January 30, 2018.

147 *"No taxation without representation"*: Quoted in Ari Berman, "Trump's Stealth Plan to Preserve White Electoral Power," *Mother Jones*, January/ February 2020.

147 *"rotten boroughs"*: Ibid.

147 *"There can be no"*: Ibid.

147 *"legal voters"*: Ibid.

147 *"No one will deny"*: Ibid.

147 *"Representatives shall be apportioned"*: Ibid.

148 *"We have admitted the"*: Quoted in Wayne Dawkins, *Emanuel Celler: Immigration and Civil Rights Champion* (Oxford: University Press of Mississippi, 2020), 36.

148 *"It is hoped to"*: Quoted in Jia Lynn Yang, *One Mighty and Irresistible Tide* (New York: W. W. Norton & Company, 2020), 42.

148 *"America must be kept"*: Ibid., 54.

148 *"AMERICA OF THE MELTING"*: David A. Reed, "AMERICA OF THE MELTING POT COMES TO END," *The New York Times*, April 27, 1924.

149 *"The racial composition of"*: Ibid.

149 *"one state in which"*: Quoted in Daniel Okrent, *The Guarded Gate* (New York: Simon & Schuster, 2019), 376.

149 *"It was America"*: Quoted in Adam Serwer, "White Nationalism's Deep American Roots," *The Atlantic*, April 2019.

149 *"It is not best"*: Quoted in Berman, "Hidden Figures: How Donald Trump Is Rigging the Census."

149 *"more distinctly American population"*: Quoted in Berman, "Trump's Stealth Plan to Preserve White Electoral Power."

150 *"The exclusion of aliens"*: Ibid.

150 *"be composed of contiguous"*: Quoted in Margo Anderson, *The American Census* (New Haven, Conn.: Yale University Press, 1988), 153.

150 *"in the typical state"*: Stephen Ansolabehere and James M. Snyder Jr., *The End of Inequality* (New York: W. W. Norton, 2008), 31.

151 *"one person, one vote"*: *Reynolds v. Sims*, 377 US 533.

151 *"apportioned on a population"*: Ibid.

151 *"The fundamental principle of"*: Ibid.

151 *"the greatest peace-time"*: Ansolabehere and Snyder, *The End of Inequality*, 240.

151 *"advantageous to Republicans and"*: Quoted in Michael Wines, Deceased G.O.P. Strategist's Hard Drives Reveal New Details on the Census Citizenship Question," *The New York Times*, May 30, 2019.

152 *"eligible voters their fundamental"*: Quoted in Berman, "Trump's Stealth Plan to Preserve White Electoral Power."

152 *"This would amount to"*: Ibid.

152 *"inform our principal's decision"*: "May 30, 2019 Exhibits," via Hansi Lo Wang/NPR, May 30, 2019, 52, https://www.documentcloud.org/documents/6077735-May-30-2019-Exhibit.html#document/p63/a504019.

152 *"radical departure from"*: Ibid., 62.

153 *"Democratic districts could geographically"*: Ibid.

153 *"As the Framers of"*: *Evenwel v. Abbott*, 578 US ___ (2016).

153 *"Without a question on"*: Hofeller, "May 30, 2019 Exhibits."

154 *"Please make certain that"*: Quoted in Hansi Lo Wang, "Emails Show Trump Officials Consulted With GOP Strategist on Citizenship Question," NPR, November 12, 2019.

154 *"It is fine as"*: Ibid.

154 *"block level citizen voting"*: Quoted in "Exhibit A," Case 1:18-cv-02921-JMF, May 30, 2019, 54, https://s3.documentcloud.org/documents/6077735/May-30-2019-Exhibit.pdf.

155 *"the kid with the"*: Quoted in Robert Draper, "The League of Dangerous Mapmakers," *The Atlantic*, October 2012.

155 *"Gerrymander of the Year"*: Quoted in Wallace Turner, "California G.O.P. Seeks to Void Redistricting," *The New York Times*, September 22, 1981.

155 *"It's a paradox, but"*: Quoted in Tom Baxter, "Minorities Could Gain Vote Clout; Redistricting Puts House Seats on Line," *The Atlanta Journal and Constitution*, April 7, 1991.

155 *"Project Ratfuck"*: Quoted in Michael Kelly, "Segregation Anxiety," *The New Yorker*, November 20, 1995.

156 *"The gerrymander overcometh all"*: Quoted in Peter Skerry, "Sampling Error," *The New Republic*, May 31, 1999.

156 *"the only legalized form"*: Quoted in Judy Holland, "Control of Numbers Today Means Winning Tomorrow," *The Times Union* (Albany, N.Y.), December 12, 1999.

156 *"Now that we had"*: Republican National Committee, "Redistricting Essentials," November 12, 2010, https://s3.us-east-2.amazonaws.com/files.bridgemi.mike/Ex587.pdf.

156 *"to minimize the number"*: Quoted in Ari Berman, "Three Big Supreme Court Cases Hinge on the GOP's Controversial Gerrymandering Guru," *Mother Jones*, June 7, 2019.

157 *"to change as few"*: Ibid.

157 *"I propose that we"*: Ibid.

157 *"I acknowledge freely that"*: Quoted in Ari Berman, "The Supreme Court Could Green-Light Extreme Partisan Gerrymandering," *Mother Jones*, March 25, 2019.

157 *"The process Dr. Hofeller"*: Quoted in Berman, "Three Big Supreme Court Cases Hinge on the GOP's Controversial Gerrymandering Guru."

157 *"seems to have been"*: *Department of Commerce v. New York*, 588 US __ (2019).

158 *"political questions beyond the"*: *Rucho v. Common Cause*, 588 US __ (2019).

159 *"new rationale"*: Quoted in Ari Berman, "Trump Backs Down on the Census Citizenship Question," *Mother Jones*, July 11, 2019.

159 *"I'm here to say"*: Quoted in Berman, "Trump's Stealth Plan to Preserve White Electoral Power."

159 *"Some states may want"*: Ibid.

159 *"could encourage states to"*: Quoted in Jeremy Stahl, "Trump's Effort to Rig the Census Failed, but the Fight Is Far From Over," *Slate*, July 11, 2019.

159 *"All of you need"*: Quoted in Berman, "Trump's Stealth Plan to Preserve White Electoral Power."

160 *"States that welcome illegal"*: Kris W. Kobach, "Kobach: President Trump Was Absolutely Correct to Exclude Illegal Aliens from Apportionment," *Breitbart News*, July 22, 2020.

160 *"using covid to steal"*: Quoted in Ari Berman, "Trump Is Trashing the Constitution to Stay in Power," *Mother Jones*, November/December 2020.

161 *"the central nervous system"*: Ibid.

161 *"whole number of persons"*: Ibid.

161 *"a better understanding of"*: Ibid.

161 *"I am very concerned"*: "Hearing on the Census and Undocumented Immigrants," Washington, DC, C-Span, July 29, 2020, https://www.c-span.org/video/?474154-1/hearing-census-undocumented-immigrants.

162 *"I actually think President"*: Ibid.

162 *"over two hundred years of"*: Quoted in Lo Wang, "Documents detail the secret strategy behind Trump's census citizenship question push."

162 *"extremism in defense of"*: Quoted in Robert D. McFadden, "Henry V. Jaffa, Conservative Scholar and Goldwater Muse, Dies at 96," *The New York Times*, January 12, 2015.

162 *"twin relics of barbarism"*: Quoted in Dan Morain, "Anti-Gay Candidate Tests GOP Appeal," *Sacramento Bee*, April 7, 2010.

163 *"show trial"*: Quoted in "The Constitutionality of The Mueller Report," Fox News, May 12, 2019.

163 *"asserted obligation to"*: "Hearing on the Census and Undocumented Immigrants," C-Span.

163 *"brilliant . . . she doesn't meet"*: Quoted in Maeve Reston, "Trump's Birther Lie About Kamala Harris Magnifies Racist Themes of His Campaign," CNN, August 14, 2020.

164 *"a major delay"*: Quoted in Hansi Lo Wang, "How Trump Officials Cut the 2020 Census Short Amid the Pandemic," NPR, September 18, 2020.

164 *"will result in a"*: Quoted in Hansi Lo Wang, "Census Could Look 'Manipulated' If Cut Short By Trump Officials, Bureau Warned," NPR, September 20, 2020.

164 *"Any thinking person who"*: Quoted in Lo Wang, "How Trump Officials Cut the 2020 Census Short Amid the Pandemic."

165 *"Since the first time"*: "Presidential Advisory Commission on Election Integrity (PACEI) Documents 2606," via Hansi Lo Wang/NPR, 193, https://www.documentcloud.org/documents/7039978-Presidential-Advisory-Commission-on-Election.html#document/p193/a577027.

165 *"When I was at"*: Quoted in Hansi Lo Wang, "Amid Partisan Concerns, Another Trump Appointee Joins Census Bureau's Top Ranks," NPR, August 17, 2020.

165 *"I really would like"*: Ibid.

165 *"We have come up"*: Quoted in "Documents Show Far-Right Influence at Trump Commerce Department," *American Oversight*, March 30, 2021.

166 *"The [Commerce] department is"*: Quoted in Mike Schneider, "Biden White House Moves to Protect Data from Politics After Trump Census Pressure," Associated Press, January 18, 2022.

166 *"consistently pessimistic"*: Quoted in Michael Wines, "Census Memo Cites 'Unprecedented' Meddling by Trump Administration," *The New York Times*, January 15, 2022.

166 *"who were slow or"*: Ibid.

166 *"processing anomalies"*: Quoted in Hansi Lo Wang, "Supreme Court Looks for Ways to Wait Out Trump on Key Census Question," NPR, November 30, 2020.

166 *"number one priority"*: Quoted in Hansi Lo Wang, "Leaked Files Show Trump's Ability to Alter Census May Come Down to the Wire," NPR, December 2, 2020.

167 *"significant pressure"*: "MEMORANDUM FOR: Dr. Steven Dillingham, Director U.S. Census Bureau, From Peggy Gustafson, Inspector General," United States Department of Commerce, January 12, 2021.

167 *"the driving forces behind"*: Ibid.

167 *"In my opinion"*: Quoted in Tierney Sneed, "How Trump's Four-Year Crusade to Rig the Census Fell Apart," *Talking Points Memo*, February 1, 2021.

167 *"inconsistent with our nation's"*: Quoted in Hansi Lo Wang, "Biden Ends Trump Census Policy, Ensuring All Persons Living in U.S. Are Counted," NPR, January 20, 2021.

167 *"Our analysis of the"*: Quoted in Janie Boschma, Daniel Wolfe, Priya Krishnakumar, Christopher Hickey, Meghna Maharishi, Renée Rigdon, John Keefe and David Wright, "Census Release Shows America Is More Diverse and More Multiracial Than Ever," CNN, August 12, 2021.

168 *"diversity explosion"*: William H. Frey, "New 2020 Census Results Show Increased Diversity Countering Decade-Long Declines in America's White and Youth Populations," Brookings Institution, August 13, 2021.

168 *"population suppression"*: Quoted in Hansi Lo Wang, "The 2020 Census Had Big Undercounts of Black People, Latinos and Native Americans," NPR, March 11, 2022.

168 *"Today we learned that"*: Quoted in Tara Bahrampour, "2020 Census Undercounted Latinos, Blacks and Native Americans, Bureau Estimates Show," *The Washington Post*, March 10, 2022.

8. THE ELECTORAL COUP

169 *"flooded with reports from"*: "Second Georgia Senate Election Hearing," Atlanta, Ga., 11Alive/YouTube, December 3, 2020, https://www.youtube.com/watch?v=hRCXUNOwOjw. This hearing includes quotes from Ligon, Giuliani, Pick, and Eastman.

171 *"Wow! Blockbuster testimony"*: Quoted in David Wickert and Greg Bluestein, "Inside the Campaign to Undermine Georgia's Election," *The Atlanta Journal-Constitution*, December 31, 2021.

171 *"The President's team is"*: Gabriel Sterling, Twitter post, December 4, 2020, https://twitter.com/GabrielSterling/status/1334950232526884873.

171 *"Someone's going to:"* Quoted in Wickert and Bluestein, "Inside the Campaign to Undermine Georgia's Election."

172 *"With all due respect"*: "Second Georgia Senate Election Hearing," 11Alive.

172 *"criminal enterprise"*: *The State of Georgia v. Donald Trump, et al.*, Fulton County Superior Court, Clerk No. 23SC188947, August 14, 2023, https://www.scribd.com/document/665036274/Trump-Indictment-Georgia-081423#.

172 *"the big one"*: Quoted in Aaron Rupar, "Trump Says Texas's Challenge to His Election Loss Is 'the Big One,'" *Vox*, December 9, 2020.

172 *"I have been watching"*: Quoted in Tierney Sneed, "READ: The Template SCOTUS Election-Reversal Lawsuit That Trump Allies Pushed on LA's AG," Talking Points Memo, June 18, 2021.

172 *"Jeff is reviewing all"*: Ibid.

172 *"revised and streamlined"*: Ibid.

173 *"Trump's lawyers have a"*: Scott Walker, Twitter post, December 1, 2020, https://twitter.com/ScottWalker/status/1333950558445531137.

173 *"Using the COVID-19"*: Quoted in Sneed, "The Template SCOTUS Election-Reversal Lawsuit That Trump Allies Pushed on LA's AG."

173 *"If one player in"*: Quoted in Jim Rutenberg, Jo Becker, Eric Lipton, Maggie Haberman, Jonathan Martin, Matthew Rosenberg, and Michael S. Schmidt, "77 Days: Trump's Campaign to Subvert the Election," *The New York Times*, January 31, 2021.

173 *"Have you been in"*: Quoted in Sneed, "The Template SCOTUS Election-Reversal Lawsuit That Trump Allies Pushed on LA's AG."

174 *"Someone else in our group"*: Ibid.

174 *"suitcases full of ballots"*: *Texas v. Pennsylvania, et al.*, "Motion for Preliminary Injunction and Temporary Restraining Order," December 7, 2020.

174 *"far more important than"*: Kris W. Kobach, "Kobach: Texas Case Challenges Election Directly at Supreme Court," *Breitbart News*, December 7, 2020.

174 *"a large percentage of"*: *Texas v. Pennsylvania*, "Motion to intervene filed by Donald J. Trump, President of the United States," December 9, 2020.

174 *"the manner in which"*: *Texas v. Pennsylvania*, "Order in Pending Case," No. 22O155, December 11, 2020.

174 *"We have heard the"*: Georgia Senate Republican Caucus, "Majority Statement on Elections," December 8, 2020.

175 *"Georgia could be the"*: Quoted in Claire Simms, "President Obama Headlines Biden-Harris Rally in Atlanta," Fox5 Atlanta, November 2, 2020.

175 *"I don't know if"*: Ibid.

176 *"conscience of the Congress"*: Quoted in Katharine Q. Seelye, "John Lewis, Towering Figure of Civil Rights Era, Dies at 80," *The New York Times*, July 17, 2020.

176 *"Protesting is the diagnosis"*: Quoted in Simms, "President Obama Headlines Biden-Harris Rally in Atlanta."

176 *"the Abrams playbook"*: Stacey Abrams and Lauren Groh-Wargo, "The Abrams Playbook," September 9, 2019, https://drive.google.com/file/d/1A DcfRsKjPArby9cAzI2hblWVEOJPEYaj/view.

177 *"the line was already"*: Lucille Anderson v. Brad Raffensperger, "Complaint for Injunctive and Declaratory Relief," Case 1:20-mi-99999-UNA, August 6, 2020.

177 *"2018 was the cake"*: Quoted in Ari Berman, "Runoff Elections in Georgia Are Disasters for Democrats. Here's Why This Time Is Different," *Mother Jones*, December 7, 2020.

177 *"I tried to vote"*: Kevin Riley, Twitter post, June 9, 2020, https://twitter .com/ajceditor/status/1270504296124203008.

177 *"Complete Meltdown"*: AJC, Twitter post, June 10, 2020, https://twitter .com/ajc/status/1270655897912606727.

178 *"VOTE EARLY"*: Quoted in Maya King, "Georgia's Legacy of Voter Suppression Is Driving Historic Black Turnout," *Politico*, October 26, 2020.

178 *"When I would go"*: Quoted in Berman, "Runoff Elections in Georgia Are Disasters for Democrats."

179 *"STOP THE COUNT"*: Quoted in Aaron Rupar, "Trump's Desperate 'STOP THE COUNT!' Tweet, Briefly Explained," *Vox*, November 5, 2020.

179 *"the bunker"*: Quoted in Laura Thompson, "Meet the One-Woman Newsroom That Live-Tweeted Georgia's Biggest Election Story," *Mother Jones*, November 12, 2020.

179 *"crime-infested"*: Quoted in Greg Bluestein, "Heart of John Lewis' District Deals Blow to Trump," *The Atlanta Journal-Constitution*, November 6, 2020.

179 *"Could this be John"*: Quoted in Paulina Villegas, "John Lewis's Former District May Have Flipped Georgia Blue. It's Seen by Some as Divine Revenge," *The Washington Post*, November 6, 2020.

179 *"count every vote"*: "Georgia Reacts to Biden Win," Atlanta, Ga., GPB/ YouTube, November 7, 2020, https://www.youtube.com/watch?v=B9Uhe 3oMShk.

179 *"Yesterday we were helping"*: Ibid.

180 *"This moment"*: "Georgia Electoral College Vote," Atlanta, Ga., C-Span, December 14, 2020, https://www.c-span.org/video/?507287-1/georgia -electoral-college-vote.

181 *"long-term harm to"*: Quoted in Nicholas Fandos, "Representative Paul Mitchell Leaves Republican Party Over Its Refusal to Accept Trump's Loss," *The New York Times*, December 14, 2020.

181 *"In this battle for"*: "Joe Biden Speech After Electoral College Vote," Wilmington, Del., Rev.com, December 14, 2020, https://www.rev.com

/blog/transcripts/joe-biden-speech-after-electoral-college-vote-transcript
-december-14.

181 *"You voted like your"*: "President-elect Biden Remarks in Georgia," Atlanta, Ga., C-Span, December 15, 2020, https://www.c-span.org/video/?507318-1 /president-elect-biden-campaigns-democratic-senate-candidates-georgia.

181 *"With these two Senate"*: Ibid.

181 *"the new Georgia"*: Ibid.

182 *"this is a white man's"*: Quoted in Hank Klibanoff, "Pistols," Buried Truth Podcast/WABE, March 25, 2018.

182 *"Pistols"*: Ibid.

182 *"all we have to"*: Quoted in Berman, "Runoff Elections in Georgia Are Disasters for Democrats."

183 *"as a means"*: Ibid.

183 *"Blackest Bus in America"*: Quoted in Ari Berman, "Georgia's Runoffs Were a Tool of White Supremacy. But Black Voters Turned Out in Record Numbers," *Mother Jones*, January 6, 2021.

183 *"Having the entire country"*: Quoted in Berman, "Runoff Elections in Georgia Are Disasters for Democrats."

184 *"The governor's done nothing"*: Quoted in Aaron Blake, "Trump's Feud with Brian Kemp Says It All About the President's Voter Fraud Claims," *The Washington Post*, November 30, 2020.

184 *"the hapless Governor of"*: Ibid.

184 *"They have not earned"*: Quoted in Berman, "Runoff Elections in Georgia Are Disasters for Democrats."

185 *"Because this is America"*: "Rev. Raphael Warnock Speaks from Atlanta After Taking the Lead in Georgia's Senate Race," Atlanta, Ga., 11Alive/YouTube, January 6, 2021, https://www.youtube.com/watch?v=h6WRsupapAI &t=1s.

185 *"find 11,780 votes"*: Quoted in Amy Gardner, "'I Just Want to Find 11,780 Votes': In Extraordinary Hour-Long Call, Trump Pressures Georgia Secretary of State to Recalculate the Vote in His Favor," *The Washington Post*, January 3, 2021.

186 *"I will be ready"*: Quoted in "Election Night Live Continued," CNN, January 6, 2021.

186 *"Save America"*: Quoted in Laura K. Field, "What the Hell Happened to the Claremont Institute?" *The Bulwark*, July 13, 2021.

186 *"looking every bit the"*: Quoted in Gustavo Arellano, "John Eastman's Journey from Respectable O.C. Republican to Batman Villain," *Los Angeles Times*, June 20, 2022.

186 *"the professor"*: "User Clip: John Eastman at January 6 Rally," Washington, DC, C-Span, March 24, 2021, https://www.c-span.org/video/?c4953961 /user-clip-john-eastman-january-6-rally.

186 *"The old way"*: Ibid.

187 *"a coup in search"*: Quoted in Zoe Tillman, "A Judge Called Donald

Trump's Postelection Efforts 'A Coup in Search of a Legal Theory,'" *Buzzfeed News*, March 28, 2022.

187 *"All we are demanding"*: "John Eastman at January 6 Rally," C-Span.

187 *"You'll never take back"*: Quoted in Astead W. Herndon, "America in 2021: Racial Progress in the South, a White Mob in the Capitol," *The New York Times*, January 8, 2021.

187 *"What's going on?"*: Quoted in Jennifer Gerson, "Rep. Nikema Williams on the Capitol Insurrection & What Comes Next," *Bustle*, January 21, 2021.

188 *"Where are the members"*: Quoted in Ellie Kaufman, "Capitol Police Officer Goodman Says Mob on January 6 Looked Like 'Something Out of Medieval Times' at Trial of Man Who Carried Confederate Flag," CNN, June 13, 2022.

188 *"You can shoot me"*: Quoted in Michael Kunzelman, "Man Who Carried Confederate Flag into Capitol Heads to Trial," Associated Press, June 12, 2022.

188 *"a symbol of an"*: Quoted in Marisa Sarnoff, "Rioter Who Carried Confederate Flag While Chasing Black Police Officer Inside U.S. Capitol on Jan. 6 Gets Years in Prison," *Law & Crime*, February 9, 2023.

188 *"We're taking back our"*: Quoted in Spencer Hsu, Twitter post, June 13, 2022, https://twitter.com/hsu_spencer/status/1536384230426562562.

188 *"positive good"*: Remarks by John C. Calhoun, February 6, 1837.

189 *"I knew exactly what"*: Quoted in Gerson, "Rep. Nikema Williams on the Capitol Insurrection."

189 *"I just sat there"*: Ibid.

189 *"Every noise I heard"*: Ibid.

189 *"unprecedented assault"*: Quoted in Domenico Montanaro, "Timeline: How One of the Darkest Days in American History Unfolded," NPR, January 7, 2021.

189 *"we had an election"*: Quoted in Anne Gearan and Josh Dawsey, "Trump Issued a Call to Arms. Then He Urged His Followers 'to Remember This Day Forever!'" *The Washington Post*, January 6, 2021.

189 *"We are still on"*: Nikema Williams, Twitter post, January 6, 2021, https://twitter.com/NikemaWilliams/status/1346949732275548161.

190 *"this is our 1776"*: Quoted in Tia Mitchell, "Georgia Lawmakers Condemn U.S. Capitol Violence; Democrats Seek Trump's Removal," *The Atlanta Journal-Constitution*, January 7, 2021.

190 *"unprecedented amount of fraud"*: Quoted in David Wickert and Greg Bluestein, "Part 2: The Road to Jan. 6," *The Atlanta Journal-Constitution*, December 31, 2021.

190 *"The events that transpired"*: Ibid.

190 *"Joseph R. Biden Jr."*: Quoted in Montanaro, "Timeline: How One of the Darkest Days in American History Unfolded."

190 *"historic Senate win"*: *"11 AM Service"*: Atlanta, Ga., Ebenezer Baptist Church, January 10, 2021, https://livestream.com/historicebenezerbaptistchurch/events/9479172/videos/215839073.

190 *"God's victory over violence"*: Ibid.

192 *"People are concerned"*: Quoted in David Wickert, "Ralston Wants Review of Perceived Georgia Election Issues," *The Atlanta Journal-Constitution*, January 7, 2021.

9. THE INSURRECTION THROUGH OTHER MEANS

193 *"You bring both Congress"*: Quoted in Ari Berman, "Jim Crow Killed Voting Rights for Generations. Now the GOP Is Repeating History," *Mother Jones*, June 2, 2021.

194 *"There are persons in"*: Rev. Henry McNeal Turner, "I Claim The Rights Of a Man," September 3, 1868, https://www.blackpast.org/african-american -history/1868-reverend-henry-mcneal-turner-i-claim-rights-man/.

194 *"The sacred rights of"*: Quoted in Berman, "Jim Crow Killed Voting Rights for Generations."

194 *"imitation of Christ"*: Quoted in Stephen Ward Angell, *Bishop Henry McNeal Turner and African-American Religion in the South* (Knoxville, Tenn.: University of Tennessee Press, 1992), 88.

194 *"We should neither be"*: Quoted in Berman, "Jim Crow Killed Voting Rights for Generations."

195 *"There is not language"*: Ibid.

195 *"The Southern whites will"*: Ibid.

195 *"Every last one of"*: "'Free at Last'–Sen. David Lucas on SB 67," Atlanta, Ga., Fair Fight Action/YouTube, February 23, 2021, https://www.youtube .com/watch?v=ZXYIyRbmCOs.

196 *"At the end of"*: Quoted in Patricia Murphy, Greg Bluestein, and Tia Mitchell, "The Jolt: Why Georgia Elections May Never Be the Same," *The Atlanta Journal-Constitution*, February 24, 2001.

196 *"restore the confidence of"*: Quoted in Amy Gardner, "State GOP Lawmakers Propose Flurry of Voting Restrictions to Placate Trump Supporters, Spurring Fears of a Backlash," *The Washington Post*, February 19, 2021.

196 *"If we don't do"*: Quoted in Ari Berman, "Republicans Are Laying the Groundwork to Make It Harder to Vote," *Mother Jones*, November 10, 2020.

196 *"reminds me of the"*: Lucas on SB 67.

196 *"and told me he'd"*: Quoted in Berman, "Jim Crow Killed Voting Rights for Generations."

197 *"I will not go home"*: Lucas on SB 67.

197 *"After I finished crying"*: Quoted in Berman, "Jim Crow Killed Voting Rights for Generations."

197 *"Nobody's putting in a"*: Ibid.

198 *"I had one message"*: Quoted in Ari Berman and Nick Surgey, "Leaked Video: Dark Money Group Brags About Writing GOP Voter Suppression Bills Across the Country," *Mother Jones*, May 13, 2021.

198 *"There's no doubt there"*: "Governor Kemp on Georgia Voting and Elec-

tions Law," Atlanta, Ga., C-Span, March 25, 2021, https://www.c-span.org/video/?510309-1/governor-kemp-georgia-voting-elections-law.

199 *"The governor is signing"*: Quoted in Greg Bluestein, Twitter post, March 25, 2021, https://twitter.com/bluestein/status/1375224814147895298.

199 *"You're under arrest"*: Ibid.

199 *"Why am I under"*: Quoted in Gerald A. Griggs, Twitter post, March 25, 2021, https://twitter.com/AttorneyGriggs/status/1375219999057530883.

199 *"let her go!"*: Atlanta News First, Twitter post, March 25, 2021, https://twitter.com/ATLNewsFirst/status/1375280278290137092.

199 *"What we have witnessed"*: Ibid.

199 *"If you don't like"*: Quoted in Berman, "Jim Crow Killed Voting Rights for Generations."

199 *"Jim Crow in a"*: Ibid.

200 *"underperforming"*: Ibid.

200 *"In some cases"*: Quoted in Berman and Surgey, "Dark Money Group Brags About Writing GOP Voter Suppression Bills Across the Country."

200 *"eight key provisions"*: Ibid.

200 *"model for the rest"*: Ibid.

201 *"state lawmakers have to"*: Scott Walker, Twitter post, December 1, 2020, https://twitter.com/scottwalker/status/1333950917591252993.

201 *"still very involved with"*: Quoted in Lauren Windsor, Twitter post, October 27, 2021, https://twitter.com/lawindsor/status/1453477418245574656.

201 *"create this echo chamber"*: Quoted in Berman and Surgey, "Dark Money Group Brags About Writing GOP Voter Suppression Bills Across the Country."

202 *"We literally give marching"*: Ibid.

202 *"We are going to"*: Ibid.

202 *"There is a clear national"*: Quoted in Steven Rattner, "A Think Tank for Conservatives," *The New York Times*, March 23, 1975.

203 *"the Lenin of social"*: Quoted in David Grann, "Robespierre of the Right," *The New Republic*, October 26, 1997.

203 *"I don't want everybody"*: Quoted in Berman and Surgey, "Dark Money Group Brags About Writing GOP Voter Suppression Bills Across the Country."

203 *"destroying the Republican Party"*: Ibid.

203 *"the one-two punch"*: Ibid.

204 *"It's like he goes"*: Jane Mayer, "The Voter-Fraud Myth," *The New Yorker*, October 22, 2012.

204 *"mainstream Republican officials and"*: Quoted in Ari Berman, "Trump Election Commissioner Sought to Exclude Democrats and 'Mainstream Republicans,'" *Mother Jones*, September 13, 2017.

204 *"the premier election law expert"*: Quoted in Berman and Surgey, "Dark Money Group Brags About Writing GOP Voter Suppression Bills Across the Country."

204 *"little weight to Mr."*: Ibid.

204 *"The one good thing"*: Ibid.

205 *"INACCURATE & FRAUDULENT"*: Quoted in Ari Berman, "John Lewis Says the Right to Vote Is in Danger. Then Trump Threatens to Take It Away," *Mother Jones*, July 30, 2020.

205 *"We Shall Overcome"*: "Representative John Lewis Funeral Service in Atlanta, Georgia," Atlanta, Ga., C-Span, July 30, 2020, https://www.c-span.org/video/?474223-1/representative-john-lewis-funeral-service-atlanta-georgia.

205 *"He loved America"*: Ibid.

206 *"He had no reason"*: Raphael Warnock, interview conducted by the author, July 28, 2023.

206 *"You want to honor"*: "Representative John Lewis Funeral Service in Atlanta."

207 *"We elected Georgia's first"*: Senator Reverend Raphael Warnock, "Senator Warnock Delivers Maiden Speech on Voting Rights," Washington, DC, Twitter post, March 17, 2021, https://twitter.com/i/broadcasts/1vAxRwMePmNKl.

208 *"an American victory but"*: Remarks by Lyndon Johnson, Signing of the Voting Rights Act, August 6, 1965, Washington, DC, http://millercenter.org/president/speeches/speech-4034.

208 *"If we had not"*: "Senator Warnock Testifies at Senate Judiciary Committee Hearing on Voting Rights," Washington, DC, Senator Warnock/YouTube, April 20, 2021, https://www.youtube.com/watch?v=Z_qpy5IABrc.

208 *"Much of what HR 1"*: Quoted in Ari Berman, "The House Passes a Major Voting Rights Bill—and Creates a Helluva Battle in the Senate," *Mother Jones*, March 3, 2021.

208 *"the single most dangerous"*: Quoted in Berman, "Jim Crow Killed Voting Rights for Generations."

209 *"This issue—access to"*: Warnock, "Senator Warnock Delivers Maiden Speech on Voting Rights."

209 *"Are you in jail?"*: Quoted in Zach Montellaro, "Postponed Weddings, Stockpiled Insulin and Covid: The Bizarre Life of Texas Democrats in Exile," *Politico*, July 18, 2021.

209 *"We are going to"*: Quoted in CBS News, Twitter post, July 12, 2021, https://twitter.com/CBSNews/status/1414759048222842881.

210 *"the Election Integrity Protection"*: Quoted in Daniel Friend, "Breakdown of the Final Texas 'Election Integrity Protection Act of 2021,'" *The Texan*, May 29, 2021.

210 *"19 provisions"*: Quoted in Berman and Surgey, "Dark Money Group Brags About Writing GOP Voter Suppression Bills Across the Country."

210 *"the purity of the"*: Quoted in Alexa Ura, "Texas GOP's Voting Restrictions Bill Could Be Rewritten Behind Closed Doors After Final House Passage," *Texas Tribune*, May 7, 2021.

211 *"We want to make"*: Quoted in Dorothy Overstreet Pratt, *Sowing the Wind* (Oxford: University Press of Mississippi, 2017), 94.

211 *"obtaining goods under false"*: Quoted in Michael Perman, *Struggle for Mastery* (Chapel Hill: University of North Carolina Press, 2001), 83.

211 *"be able to read"*: Quoted in Vernon Lane Wharton, *The Negro in Mississippi, 1865-1890* (Chapel Hill: University of North Carolina Press, 1947), 214.

211 *"understanding clause"*: Quoted in Pratt, *Sowing the Wind*, 144.

211 *"The Government which made"*: Quoted in Charles W. Calhoun, *Conceiving a New Republic* (Lawrence: University Press of Kansas, 2006), 241.

212 *"to the white race"*: Quoted in *Congressional Record*: "Proceedings and Debates of the Fifty-First Congress," volume 22, part 1, 731, December 20, 1890.

212 *"an offensive theory of"*: Quoted in Perman, *Struggle for Mastery*, 23.

212 *"Let every trace of"*: Quoted in Berman, "Jim Crow Killed Voting Rights for Generations."

212 *"Did you know that"*: Quoted in Ura, "Texas GOP's Voting Restrictions Bill Could Be Rewritten Behind Closed Doors After Final House Passage."

213 *"We're facing the"*: Remarks by President Biden on Protecting the Sacred, Constitutional Right to Vote, Philadelphia, Pa., July 13, 2021, https://www.whitehouse.gov/briefing-room/speeches-remarks/2021/07/13/remarks-by-president-biden-on-protecting-the-sacred-constitutional-right-to-vote/.

213 *"He won't meet with"*: Quoted in Brandon Mulder and Madlin Mekelburg, "'I'm Just Pissed Off at This Point': Frustration Mounts as Texas Democrats Fail to Secure Biden Meeting," *Austin American-Statesman*, July 23, 2021.

214 *"relic of the Jim Crow"*: Remarks by President Biden in a CNN Town Hall with Don Lemon, Cincinnati, Ohio, July 22, 2021, https://www.whitehouse.gov/briefing-room/speeches-remarks/2021/07/22/remarks-by-president-biden-in-a-cnn-town-hall-with-don-lemon/.

214 *"HR 1 is basically"*: Quoted in Berman and Surgey, "Dark Money Group Brags About Writing GOP Voter Suppression Bills Across the Country."

215 *"a bit of fun with"*: Quoted in Ari Berman, "Manchin Says Voting Rights Are 'Fundamental' as He Torpedoes the Plan to Protect Them," *Mother Jones*, June 8, 2021.

215 *"It's an all-hands"*: Quoted in Berman and Surgey, "Dark Money Group Brags About Writing GOP Voter Suppression Bills Across the Country."

215 *"If the Biden Administration tries"*: Quoted in Andrew Bahl and Alice Mannette, "Kris Kobach Files for Kansas Attorney General Run as He Launches Another Bid for Statewide Office," *Topeka Capital-Journal*, April 29, 2021.

215 *"fundamental to our American"*: Joe Manchin, "Why I'm Voting Against the For the People Act," *Charleston Gazette-Mail*, June 6, 2021.

216 *"this continuing distortion of"*: Quoted in Reid J. Epstein, "Obama Laments 'Shameful Day,'" *Politico*, April 17, 2013.

216 *"I'm not sure the"*: Quoted in Ari Berman, "Texas Republicans Pass Voting Restrictions to Solidify Anti-Democratic Hold on Power," *Mother Jones*, August 31, 2021.

216 *"Mr. President"*: "No More Excuses: Voting Rights Now!" Washington, DC, PFAW/YouTube, October 5, 2021, https://www.youtube.com/watch?v=US_fwapIYcc.

217 *"the most aggressive roaches"*: Quoted in Peter Nicholas, "Is Biden Doing Enough to Protect Democracy?" *The Atlantic*, October 17, 2021.

217 *"Nothing substantive came out"*: Quoted in Sam Levine, "'Time Is Running Out': Can Congress Pass a Voting Rights Bill After Months of Failure?" *The Guardian*, December 6, 2021.

217 *"the debate on the"*: Remarks by President Biden in a CNN Town Hall with Anderson Cooper, Baltimore, Md., October 21, 2021, https://www.whitehouse.gov/briefing-room/speeches-remarks/2021/10/22/remarks-by-president-biden-in-a-cnn-town-hall-with-anderson-cooper-2/.

217 *"restore and strengthen American"*: Quoted in James Slattery, Twitter post, December 8, 2021, https://twitter.com/jcslattery/status/1468660827041456134.

217 *"a point of moral"*: Senator Warnock Takes to the Floor of the US Senate Calling for Immediate Action on Voting Rights, Washington, DC, Senate Warnock/YouTube, December 14, 2021, https://www.youtube.com/watch?v=VqfChZLe9qA.

218 *"very moving"*: Quoted in Tia Mitchell, "Warnock Says Senate Should Delay Holiday Recess to Focus on Passing Voting Bills," *The Atlanta Journal-Constitution*, December 14, 2021.

218 *"Are you anywhere to"*: Quoted in Manu Raju, Twitter post, December 14, 2021, https://mobile.twitter.com/mkraju/status/1470873958195109891?s=10.

218 *"prove democracy works"*: Quoted in David E. Sanger, "Biden Defines His Underlying Challenge With China: 'Prove Democracy Works,'" *The New York Times*, March 26, 2021.

218 *"the belly of the"*: Quoted in Laura Barron-Lopez and Christopher Cadelago, "'We Are Going Right to the Belly of the Beast': Biden Takes on Georgia," *Politico*, January 9, 2022.

219 *"whichever way they need"*: Remarks by President Biden on Protecting the Right to Vote, Atlanta, Ga., January 11, 2022, https://www.whitehouse.gov/briefing-room/speeches-remarks/2022/01/11/remarks-by-president-biden-on-protecting-the-right-to-vote/.

219 *"an empty gesture"*: Quoted in Jewel Wicker, "Georgia Activists Warn Biden Against a 'Photo Op' Visit That Lacks Voting Rights Plan," *The Guardian*, January 11, 2022.

220 *"All kinds of energy"*: Quoted in Laura Barron-Lopez and Maya King,

"Biden Confronts a Skeptical Base as He Pushes Voting Rights in Georgia," *Politico*, January 11, 2022.

220 *"Efforts to fix these"*: Quoted in Ari Berman, "GOP States Are Shredding Voting Rights and Joe Manchin and Kyrsten Sinema Are Now Complicit," *Mother Jones*, January 20, 2022.

220 *"I hope we can"*: Remarks by President Biden After Meeting with the Senate Democratic Caucus, Washington, DC, January 13, 2022, https://www .whitehouse.gov/briefing-room/speeches-remarks/2022/01/13/remarks-by -president-biden-after-meeting-with-the-senate-democratic-caucus/.

220 *"the most important day in"*: "Senate Session," Washington, DC, C-Span, January 19, 2022, https://www.c-span.org/video/?517308-1/senate-blocks -voting-rights-bill-fails-change-filibuster&live=.

220 *"fake panic over election"*: Mitch McConnell, "Just the Kind of Short-sighted Power Grab this Body Was Built to Stop," January 19, 2022, https:// www.republicanleader.senate.gov/newsroom/remarks/just-the-kind-of -shortsighted-power-grab-this-body-was-built-to-stop.

221 *"Here's the question tonight"*: Senator Warnock Fights for the Sacred Right to Vote on the Floor of the US Senate, Washington, DC, Senator Warnock/YouTube, January 19, 2022, https://www.youtube.com/watch?v =mCfoCoB-AGI.

221 *"the United States Senate has"*: Senate Session, C-Span, January 19, 2022.

221 *"tradition of the Senate"*: Quoted in Jonathan Chait, "Joe Manchin Falsely Says Senate Has Always Had the Filibuster," *New York Magazine*, January 10, 2022.

221 *"an important role in stabilizing"*: Senate Session, C-Span, January 19, 2022.

221 *"the fundamental principle of"*: James Madison, "Federalist No. 58," https:// guides.loc.gov/federalist-papers/text-51-60#s-lg-box-wrapper-25493434.

222 *"you can't have it"*: Senate Session, C-Span, January 19, 2022.

222 *"aye"*: Ibid.

222 *"Our failure to pass"*: Warnock, interview.

223 *"We are caught somewhere"*: Senate Session, January 19, 2022.

10. DEMOCRACY ON THE BALLOT

224 *"The voters spoke"*: Quoted in Ari Berman, "The Insurrection Was Put Down. The GOP Plan for Minority Rule Marches On," *Mother Jones*, March/April 2021.

224 *"How much more Third"*: Quoted in Patrick Marley, "Clerks Sour on Moving 2020 Presidential Primary," *Milwaukee Journal Sentinel*, November 21, 2018.

224 *"Respect the Vote"*: Quoted in Jessie Opoien and Katelyn Ferral, "Wisconsin Republicans Set to Pass Lame-Duck Bills Late Tuesday," *The Capital Times*, December 4, 2018.

225 *"GOP Grinch Steals Democracy"*: Ibid.

225 *"It's an attack on"*: Quoted in Mitch Smith and Monica Davey, "Lawmakers Clash and Protesters Chant Amid Fight Over Wisconsin Governor's Power," *The New York Times*, December 4, 2018.

225 *"The Republicans haven't"*: "Senate Floor Session," Madison, Wis., WisconsinEye, December 4, 2018, https://wiseye.org/2018/12/04/senate-floor -session-62/.

225 *"funeral for democracy"*: Hunter Saenz, Twitter post, December 5, 2018, https://twitter.com/Hunt_Saenz/status/1070442427432034306.

225 *"If you took Madison"*: Quoted in Molly Beck, "Did GOP Gerrymandering Limit Dems' Inroads in the Legislature?" *Milwaukee Journal Sentinel*, November 9, 2018.

226 *"He's got more of"*: "Former President Barack Obama Speaks in Milwaukee," Milwaukee, Wis., Channel 3000/YouTube, October 29, 2022, https:// www.youtube.com/watch?v=C6BMPXPbXIw.

226 *"fix the damn roads"*: Quoted in Mark Sommerhauser, "Evers and GOP in Standoff," *Wisconsin State Journal*, May 20, 2019.

226 *"an attack on the"*: Quoted in Scott Bauer, "Democrats Look to Other Lawsuits to Block GOP Lame-Duck Laws," Associated Press, June 21, 2019.

226 *"It's the same deal"*: Quoted in Ari Berman, "How Wisconsin Became the GOP's Laboratory for Dismantling Democracy," *Mother Jones*, October 25, 2022.

226 *"the consigliere to the"*: Quoted in David Freedlander, "Cleta Mitchell Is Training Thousands of Trump Loyalists to Monitor the Polls on Election Day," *New York Magazine*, October 20, 2022.

226 *"A movement is stirring"*: Quoted in Kyle Cheney, Twitter post, June 21, 2022, https://mobile.twitter.com/kyledcheney/status/1539204618252701696.

227 *"advisory"*: Quoted in Rick Hasen, "Cleta Mitchell, in Jan. 6 Committee Deposition, Expresses View that (Old) Electoral Count Act Is Unconstitutional and Legislatures Have Absolute Power over Electors; The People's Vote for President is Just 'Advisory,'" Election Law Blog, December 30, 2022.

227 *"Am I crazy?"*: Quoted in Cheney, Twitter post.

227 *"For POTUS"*: Quoted in Rosalind S. Helderman, "Trump Campaign Documents Show Advisers Knew Fake-Elector Plan Was Baseless," *The Washington Post*, June 20, 2022.

227 *"Legislatures simply* must *investigate"*: John C. Eastman, "The Constitutional Authority of State Legislatures to Choose Electors," *The American Mind*, December 1, 2020.

227 *"team deplorables"*: Quoted in Freedlander, "Cleta Mitchell Is Training Thousands of Trump Loyalists to Monitor the Polls on Election Day."

227 *"Those numbers that we"*: Quoted in "Read the Full Transcript and Listen to Trump's Audio Call with Georgia Secretary of State," CNN, January 3, 2021.

228 *"America first"*: "Conservative Partnership Institute: The Trump-aligned

$45M Institution Creating 'America First' Political Infrastructure," *Documented*, July 10, 2022.

228   *"Election Integrity Network"*: Quoted in Heidi Przybyla, "RNC Links Up with 'Stop the Steal' Advocates to Train Poll Workers," *Politico*, August 2, 2022.

228   *"a volunteer army of"*: Quoted in Alexandra Berzon, "Lawyer Who Plotted to Overturn Trump Loss Recruits Election Deniers to Watch Over the Vote," *The New York Times*, May 30, 2022.

228   *"sometimes the vote counter"*: "Trump: 'The Vote Counter Is More Important Than the Candidate,'" *Politico*, November 7, 2022.

228   *"arming people to fight"*: Quoted in Will Steakin, "Inside the Trump-Backed Effort to Take 'Control' of Elections Ahead of 2022 and 2024," ABC News, June 13, 2022.

229   *"apparatus that is unbreakable"*: Quoted in Sam Levine, "Republican Push to Recruit Election Deniers as Poll Workers Causes Alarm," *The Guardian*, June 30, 2022.

229   *"Document what you've seen"*: Quoted in Heidi Przybyła, "'Raise the Challenge': Eastman Exhorts Poll Watchers to Build a Record," *Politico*, October 28, 2022.

229   *"new American majority"*: Quoted in "Leaked Audio: Cleta Mitchell's Election Integrity Network Bringing Conspiracy Theorists Into Election System," *Documented*, August 2, 2022.

230   *"This is a Republic"*: Robert Welch, "Republics and Democracies," Chicago, Ill., September 17, 1961, https://thenewamerican.com/republics-and-democracies/.

230   *"a society consisting of"*: Quoted in Jamelle Bouie, "Alexandria Ocasio-Cortez Understands Democracy Better Than Republicans Do," *The New York Times*, August 27, 2019.

230   *"In a democracy there"*: Welch, "Republics and Democracies."

230   *"taken the lead in"*: Quoted in Max P. Peterson, "The Ideology of the John Birch Society" (MS thesis, Utah State University, 1966).

230   *"independent Negro-Soviet Republic"*: Quoted in John Savage, "The John Birch Society Is Back," *Politico*, July 16, 2017.

231   *"Trump won"*: "Jordan Klepper Fingers the Pulse—Wisconsin Trump Rally," *The Daily Show with Trevor Noah*, August 10, 2022, https://www.cc.com/video/czilsj/the-daily-show-with-trevor-noah-jordan-klepper-fingers-the-pulse-wisconsin-trump-rally.

231   *"Almighty and merciful"*: "Former President Trump Holds Rally in Wisconsin," Waukesha, Wis., C-Span, August 5, 2022, https://www.c-span.org/video/?522114-1/president-trump-holds-rally-wisconsin.

232   *"did anything wrong"*: "Michels Jan 6 WISN," Milwaukee, Wis., Democratic Party of Wisconsin/YouTube, August 2, 2022, https://www.youtube.com/watch?v=RO-EuRf_nq8.

232   *"would be president right"*: Quoted in Patrick Marley, "Candidate for

Governor Tim Michels Says 'Maybe' the 2020 Election Was Stolen Even Though Biden's Win Has Been Repeatedly Confirmed," *Milwaukee Journal Sentinel*, May 9, 2022.

232 *"My number one priority"*: "Former President Trump Holds Rally in Wisconsin," C-Span.

233 *"not constitutionally possible"*: Quoted in Scott Bauer, "Pence, Walker Tout Kleefisch in Wisconsin's 2022 Republican Primary for Governor," Associated Press, August 3, 2022.

233 *"That's akin to"*: Quoted in Ari Berman, "The Coming Coup: How Republicans Are Laying the Groundwork to Steal Future Elections," *Mother Jones*, January 13, 2022.

233 *"Democrat, actually"*: Quoted in Issac Yu, "Five Takeaways from Friday's Trump-Michels Rally in Waukesha," *Milwaukee Journal Sentinel*, August 6, 2022.

233 *"a real election investigation"*: Quoted in Berman, "How Wisconsin Became the GOP's Laboratory for Dismantling Democracy."

234 *"Our elected leaders"*: Ibid.

234 *"most people, myself included"*: Quoted in Patrick Marley and Natalie Eilbert, "Gableman Lacks Full Grasp of Elections," *Milwaukee Journal Sentinel*, October 7, 2021.

234 *"I believe the legislature"*: Quoted in Berman, "How Wisconsin Became the GOP's Laboratory for Dismantling Democracy."

234 *"practical impossibility"*: Ibid.

234 *"the thumb should be"*: Ibid.

234 *"tried to save our country"*: Quoted in Lauren Windsor, Twitter post, April 12, 2022, https://twitter.com/lawindsor/status/1513929147088789512.

234 *"The Wisconsin Legislature"*: Ibid.

235 *"widespread fraud"*: Quoted in Alexander Shur, "Vos: 2020 Election Can't Be Overturned," *Wisconsin State Journal*, March 17, 2022.

235 *"no evidence of widespread"*: Quoted in Patrick Marley, "Conservative Group Finds No Signs of Widespread Voter Fraud in Wisconsin but Urges Changes to Election Processes," *Milwaukee Journal Sentinel*, December 7, 2021.

236 *"reclaim [its] authority over"*: Quoted in Patrick Marley and Bill Glauber, "Ron Johnson Calls for Having Republican Lawmakers Take Over Federal Elections in Wisconsin," *Milwaukee Journal Sentinel*, November 10, 2021.

236 *"I think they'll probably"*: Quoted in Berman, "How Wisconsin Became the GOP's Laboratory for Dismantling Democracy."

236 *"red wave"*: Quoted in Dana Milbank, "Opinion: Biggest Loser of the Midterm Elections? The Media." *The Washington Post*, November 9, 2022.

237 *"shellacking"*: Quoted in Liz Halloran, "Obama Humbled By Election 'Shellacking,'" NPR, November 3, 2010.

237 *"I get that right"*: "Former President Barack Obama Speaks in Milwaukee," October 29, 2022.

237   *"Republicans will never lose"*: Quoted in Ari Berman, "How Democracy Nearly Died in Wisconsin," *Mother Jones*, January/February 2023.

237   *"Did you know Tim Michels"*: "Rigged," Tony Evers/YouTube, November 4, 2022, https://www.youtube.com/watch?v=6ZT-fP0U6js.

238   *"equality and democracy"*: Remarks by President Biden on the Continued Battle for the Soul of the Nation, Philadelphia, Pa., September 1, 2022, https://www.whitehouse.gov/briefing-room/speeches-remarks/2022/09/01/remarks-by-president-bidenon-the-continued-battle-for-the-soul-of-the-nation/.

238   *"political"*: Quoted in Paul Farhi, "As Biden Warned About Democracy's Collapse, TV Networks Aired Reruns," *The Washington Post*, September 2, 2022.

238   *"I wish I could"*: Remarks by President Biden on Standing up for Democracy, Washington, DC, November 2, 2022, https://www.whitehouse.gov/briefing-room/speeches-remarks/2022/11/03/remarks-by-president-biden-on-standing-up-for-democracy.

238   *"I don't remember hearing"*: Quoted in Berman, "How Democracy Nearly Died in Wisconsin."

239   *"Issues of democracy are"*: David Axelrod, Twitter post, November 2, 2022, https://twitter.com/davidaxelrod/status/1587894537032065024.

239   *"I think people understand"*: Ibid.

239   *"Holy mackerel, folks"*: Ibid.

240   *"There was a coordinated"*: Jocelyn Benson, interview conducted by the author, November 23, 2022.

240   *"It was an emphatic"*: Remarks by President Biden in a Press Conference, Bali, Indonesia, November 14, 2022, https://www.whitehouse.gov/briefing-room/speeches-remarks/2022/11/14/remarks-by-president-biden-in-a-press-conference-bali-indonesia.

11. NEW-SCHOOL ELECTION DENIAL MEETS OLD-SCHOOL VOTER SUPPRESSION

241   *"Let freedom ring from"*: "Read Martin Luther King Jr.'s 'I Have a Dream' speech in its entirety," NPR, January 16, 2023.

241   *"a blight on our"*: Quoted in Greg Bluestein, "Abrams Calls for Removal of Confederate Faces off Stone Mountain," *The Atlanta Journal-Constitution*, August 15, 2017.

241   *"I know where we"*: Quoted in Ari Berman, "Brian Kemp Is a Different Kind of Threat to Democracy," *Mother Jones*, November 3, 2022.

242   *"the chief architect of"*: Stacey Abrams, Twitter post, October 17, 2022, https://twitter.com/staceyabrams/status/1582146468106080257.

242   *"In 2018, Kemp was"*: Molly Ball, "Brian Kemp's Revenge," *Time*, October 7, 2022.

242   *"wrote the GOP playbook"*: Michael Warren, "How Brian Kemp Wrote the GOP Playbook for Subduing Trump's Election Fury," CNN, May 25, 2022.

243 *"When you are willing"*: Stacey Abrams, interview conducted by the author, October 22, 2022.

243 *"the original Big Lie"*: Quoted in Maya King, "Republicans Are Trying to Pin the 'Big Lie' on Stacey Abrams," *Politico*, December 23, 2021.

243 *"I was as frustrated"*: Quoted in Steve Benen, "Georgia's Kemp Accidentally Tells the Truth About Anti-Voting Law," *MSNBC/MaddowBlog*, May 3, 2022.

244 *"who are more vulnerable"*: Quoted in Berman, "Brian Kemp Is a Different Kind of Threat to Democracy."

244 *"It's great to be"*: Ibid.

245 *"How many turnout records"*: Quoted in Andrew Mark Miller, "Georgia Election Official Asks Biden, Abrams How Many Records They Need to Break to Get Apology," Fox News, October 23, 2022.

245 *"disenfranchised conservatives"*: Quoted in Patricia Murphy and Greg Bluestein, "The Jolt: Loeffler Report Says Ground Game, Voting Law Key to GOP Wins," *The Atlanta Journal-Constitution*, January 17, 2013.

246 *"the defenders"*: Charlotte Alter, "Conspiracy Theorists Want to Run America's Elections. These Are the Candidates Standing in Their Way," *Time*, September 20, 2022.

246 *"A Confederate holiday should"*: Quoted in Mark Niesse, "Saturday Voting Barred in US Senate Runoff After Ga. Holidays," *The Atlanta Journal-Constitution*, November 13, 2022.

247 *"I work during the"*: Quoted in Mark Niesse, "Judge Allows Saturday Voting Before U.S. Senate Runoff in Georgia," *The Atlanta Journal-Constitution*, November 18, 2022.

247 *"The only reason we"*: Quoted in Patricia Murphy, Greg Bluestein, Tia Mitchell, "The Jolt: Warnock Rallies Weekend Voters, but Walker Is Out of Sight," *The Atlanta Journal-Constitution*, November 28, 2022.

247 *"I'm inspired by this"*: "WATCH: Senator Raphael Warnock and Barack Obama Speak in Atlanta," Atlanta, Ga., WBRL, December 1, 2022, https://www.wrbl.com/news/politics/your-local-election-hq/watch-live-senator-raphael-warnock-and-barack-obama-speak-in-atlanta/.

247 *"These wait times result"*: Dr. Michelle Au, Twitter post, November 29, 2022, https://twitter.com/AuforGA/status/1597689598586810368.

247 *"Claims of voter suppression"*: "Raffensperger: Largest Early Voting Day in History Disproves Voter Suppression Claims," Georgia Secretary of State Office, November 29, 2022.

248 *"Y'all settle down"*: "Senator Warnock Election Runoff Victory Speech," Atlanta, Ga., C-Span, December 6, 2022, https://www.c-span.org/video/?524638-1/senator-raphael-warnock-declared-winner-georgia-senate-runoff.

248 *"Trump-proof"*: Greg Sargent, "The GOP Is Quietly 'Trump-Proofing' Our System Behind His Back," *The Washington Post*, December 20, 2022.

248 *"The 117th Congress began"*: "Senator Schumer Says Now Is Not the Time for U.S. to Waiver in Support of Ukraine," Washington, DC, C-Span, December 21, 2022, https://www.c-span.org/video/?c5047717/senator-schumer-time-us-waiver-support-ukraine.

249 *"We cannot in good conscience"*: "Sen. Warnock Urges Senate to Pass Voting Rights Legislation," Washington, DC, Senate Warnock/YouTube, December 21, 2022, https://www.youtube.com/watch?v=0INevHtt9IM.

249 *"The midterms have busted"*: Quoted in Jason Willick, "The Midterms Have Busted the Myth of Conservative 'Minority Rule,'" *The Washington Post*, December 1, 2022.

250 *"the termination"*: Quoted in Aaron Blake, "The Trump GOP's Desertion of 'Law and Order' Crosses a New Threshold," *The Washington Post*, December 5, 2022.

250 *"Elections—and therefore consent"*: Glenn Ellmers, "Hard Truths and Radical Possibilities," *American Greatness*, November 23, 2022.

250 *"This is one of"*: "Senate Session, Part 1," Washington, DC, C-Span, December 21, 2022, https://www.c-span.org/video/?524986-1/senate-confirms-lynne-tracy-us-ambassador-russia-93-2&event=524986&playEvent.

250 *"What I would want"*: "Sen. Warnock Urges Senate to Pass Voting Rights Legislation," December 21, 2022.

250 *"I decided to run"*: Quoted in John Hanna, "Kris Kobach Looks for Comeback in Kansas After Losing 2 Big Races," Associated Press, July 5, 2022.

250 *"At this late stage"*: Quoted in "Former Secretary of State Kris Kobach Attends Protest at Kansas State Capitol," KSNT Topeka, January 6, 2021.

250 *"backbone"*: Quoted in Tim Carpenter, "Attorney General Candidates Kobach, Mattivi and Warren Hunt for Votes, Work to Disarm Rivals," *Kansas Reflector*, March 13, 2022.

251 *"shoulder to shoulder"*: "Kansas Attorney General Debate," Wichita, Kan., 12 News Wichita, July 21, 2022, https://www.kwch.com/video/2022/07/22/kansas-attorney-general-debate/.

251 *"I'll think you'll see"*: Quoted in Jonathan Shorman, "How Far Will Kansas Go to Fight Biden? If Elected AG, Kobach Promises Dedicated Unit," *The Kansas City Star*, May 27, 2022.

251 *"Sue Joe Biden!"*: Quoted in Tim Carpenter, "Kobach Prevails in GOP Attorney General Race; Treasurer Campaign Very, Very Close," *Kansas Reflector*, August 3, 2022.

251 *"I'll wake up every"*: Quoted in Shorman, "How Far Will Kansas Go to Fight Biden? If Elected AG, Kobach Promises Dedicated Unit."

251 *"The magnitude of potentially"*: Quoted in Pema Levy, "Kris Kobach's Voter Suppression Law Was Just Struck Down in Kansas," *Mother Jones*, June 18, 2018.

251 *"the tip of the"*: Quoted in Jessica Huseman, "How the Case for Voter Fraud Was Tested—and Utterly Failed," *ProPublica*, June 19, 2018.

251 *"pervasive"*: Quoted in Ari Berman, "Kris Kobach Just Got Humiliated in Federal Court," *Mother Jones*, March 20, 2018.

252 *"You have to have"*: Quoted in Andrew Bahl, "Kris Kobach Says Opponents 'Ignoring Reality' on Voter Fraud, Wants to Ban Ballot Drop Boxes," *Topeka Capital-Journal*, October 18, 2022.

252 *"This result shows that"*: Quoted in Jonathan Shorman and Luke Nozicka, "Kris Kobach Narrowly Wins Kansas GOP Primary for Attorney General in Political Comeback," *The Kansas City Star*, August 3, 2022.

252 *"comic book villain"*: Quoted in Bahl, "Kris Kobach Says Opponents 'Ignoring Reality' on Voter Fraud, Wants to Ban Ballot Drop Boxes."

252 *"I don't care who"*: Quoted in Jonathan Shorman and Katie Moore, "Republican Kris Kobach Completes Comeback with Win in Kansas AG Race, Vowing to Fight Biden," *The Kansas City Star*, November 9, 2022.

12. THE GERRYMANDERING OF HISTORY

254 *"You are beginning a"*: Quoted in *The Daily Clarion*, January 13, 1870.

255 *"I believe, in the"*: Quoted in Lerone Bennett Jr., *Black Power, U.S.A.* (Chicago: Johnson Pub Co Inc, 1967), 236.

255 *"The Fifteenth Amendment was"*: Quoted in *Jackson Weekly Pilot*, April 9, 1870.

255 *"We are rising"*: Bennett Jr., *Black Power, U.S.A.*, 258.

255 *"discriminate[d] between citizens or"*: Quoted in Milton Meltzer, *Freedom Comes to Mississippi* (Westchester, Ill.: Follett, 1970), 107.

256 *"He is one of"*: James W. Garner, *Reconstruction in Mississippi* (New York: MacMillan Co., 1901), 295.

256 *"the able, efficient, and"*: John Roy Lynch, *Reminiscences of an Active Life* (Chicago: University of Chicago Press, 1970), xiii. Introduction by John Hope Franklin.

256 *"Here am I"*: John R. Lynch, "Speech on the Civil Rights Bill," Washington, DC, February 3, 1875, https://www.blackpast.org/african-american-history/1875-john-r-lynch-speech-civil-rights-bill/.

257 *"the Calhoun school of"*: Ibid.

257 *"The political clouds were dark"*: Lynch, *Reminiscences of an Active Life*, 163.

257 *"The condition of public"*: Frank Johnston, "Suffrage and Reconstruction in Mississippi," *Publications of the Mississippi Historical Society*, vol. VI, Oxford, Miss., 1902.

258 *"The legitimate state government"*: Lynch, *Reminiscences of an Active Life*, 135.

258 *"separate but equal"*: *Plessy v. Ferguson*, 163 US 537 (1896).

258 *"do not, on their"*: *Williams v. Mississippi*, 170 US 213 (1898).

258 *"Very much, of course"*: John R. Lynch, *The Facts of Reconstruction* (New York, Neale Publishing, 1913), 9.

258 *"to present the other"*: Ibid, 10.

259 *"carpetbaggers" and conniving Southern "scalawags"*: William A. Dunning, "The Undoing of Reconstruction," *The Atlantic*, October 1901.

259 *"a mass of black"*: James S. Pike, *The Prostrate State* (New York: D. Appleton, 1874), 67.

259 *"Sambo"*: Ibid., 38.

259 *"300,000 white people"*: Ibid., xv.

259 *"No large policy in"*: Quoted in David W. Blight, *Race and Reunion* (Cambridge, Mass.: Harvard University Press, 2001), 358.

259 *"oppression of the South"*: Ibid.

259 *"I regret to say"*: John R. Lynch, "Some Historical Errors of James Ford Rhodes," *The Journal of Negro History*, October 1917.

259 *"were the best governments"*: John R. Lynch, "More About the Historical Errors of James Ford Rhodes," *The Journal of Negro History*, April 1918.

260 *"an intellectual foundation for"*: Eric Foner, *The Second Founding* (New York: W. W. Norton & Company, 2019), 20.

260 *"To stand the social"*: William Archibald Dunning, *Essays on the Civil War & Reconstruction* (New York: Macmillan, 1898), 250.

260 *"another illustration of their"*: Garner, *Reconstruction in Mississippi*, 295.

260 *"a superior race will"*: Ibid., 408.

260 *"the lives of men"*: Eric Foner, *Freedom's Lawmakers* (Baton Rouge: Louisiana State University Press, 1996), xi.

261 *"The Southern victory over"*: Blight, *Race and Reunion*, 361.

262 *"a fair, just, and"*: Lynch, "Some Historical Errors of James Ford Rhodes."

262 *"splendid failure"*: W. E. B. Du Bois, *Black Reconstruction* (New York: Harcourt, Brace, and Company, 1935), 708.

262 *"literally aghast at what"*: Ibid., 725.

262 *"In order to paint"*: Ibid., 723.

263 *"a half-baked Marxian"*: Avery Craven, "Book Review: Black Reconstruction," *American Journal of Sociology*, January 1936.

263 *"A biased interpretation of"*: Francis B. Simkins, "New Viewpoints of Southern Reconstruction," *The Journal of Southern History*, February 1939.

263 *"The truths he revealed"*: "Honoring Dr. Du Bois, A Speech By Dr. Martin Luther King Jr., New York, February 23, 1968, https://credo.library.umass.edu/view/pageturn/mums312-b287-i008/#page/2/mode/1up.

264 *"We cannot turn the"*: Brown v. Board of Education of Topeka.

264 *"deeply rooted in this"*: Dobbs v. Jackson Women's Health Organization, 597 US __ (2022).

264 *"witchcraft"*: Quoted in Laura Bassett, "In Leaked Abortion Decision, Justice Alito Relies on Jurist Who Supported Marital Rape, Executed 'Witches,'" *Jezebel*, May 3, 2022.

264 *"an unbroken tradition of"*: Dobbs v. Jackson Women's Health Organization.

264 *"quickening"*: Quoted in Jennifer Schuessler, "The Fight Over Abortion History," *The New York Times*, May 4, 2022.

265 *"be filled by our own"*: Ibid.

265 *"living in a state"*: Quoted in Reva Siegel, "Memory Games: Dobbs's Originalism as Anti-Democratic Living Constitutionalism—and Some Pathways for Resistance," *Texas Law Review*, August 9, 2022, https://papers.ssrn.com/sol3/papers.cfm?abstract_id=4179622.

265 *"The court adopted a"*: American Historical Association, "History, the Supreme Court, and Dobbs v. Jackson: Joint Statement from the AHA and the OAH," July 2022.

265 *"When the majority says"*: *Dobbs v. Jackson Women's Health Organization*.

266 *"to the people's elected"*: Ibid.

266 *"the most representative branch of"*: Quoted in Ricardo Torres, "Racine Area Officials Respond to Special Session," *Racine Journal Times*, December 5, 2018.

266 *"the will of the"*: "News Conference: Gov. Evers on Reproductive Freedom," Madison, Wis., *Wisconsin Eye*, September 21, 2022, https://wiseye.org/2022/09/21/news-conference-gov-evers-on-reproductive-freedom/.

267 *"special need for self-protection"*: *New York State Rifle & Pistol Association Inc. v. Bruen*, 597 US __ (2022).

267 *"one step too many"*: Ibid.

267 *"a one-way ratchet"*: Ibid.

269 *"We Shall Overcome"*: Quoted in Casey Cep, "'Do You Think You're Not Involved?' The Racial Reckoning of 'Blood at the Root,'" *The New Yorker*, July 11, 2020.

269 *"Nigger, go home!"*: Quoted in Dudley Clendinen, "Thousands in Civil Rights March Jeered by Crowd in Georgia Town," *The New York Times*, January 25, 1987.

269 *"Racial Purity is Forsyth's"*: Quoted in Cep, "'Do You Think You're Not Involved?' The Racial Reckoning of 'Blood at the Root.'"

269 *"We've got a South"*: Ibid.

269 *"mob violence"*: Quoted in Ashlyn Yule, "Historical Marker Documenting 1912 Lynching Unveiled in Downtown Cumming," *Forsyth County News*, January 25, 2021.

269 *"big problem"*: Quoted in Nate Cohn and Kevin Quealy, "How Public Opinion Has Moved on Black Lives Matter," *The New York Times*, June 10, 2020.

269 *"racial reckoning"*: Quoted in Hakeem Jefferson and Victor Ray, "White Backlash Is a Type of Racial Reckoning, Too," *FiveThirtyEight*, January 6, 2022.

269 *"counter-reckoning"*: Ibid.

269 *"domestic terrorists"*: Quoted in Giovanni Russonello, "Why Most Americans Support the Protests," *The New York Times*, June 5, 2020.

269 *"Our nation is witnessing"*: Quoted in Annie Karni, "Trump Uses Mount Rushmore Speech to Deliver Divisive Culture War Message," *The New York Times*, July 3, 2020.

269 *"patriotic education"*: Quoted in Michael Crowley and Jennifer Schuessler, "Trump's 1776 Commission Critiques Liberalism in Report Derided by Historians," *The New York Times*, January 18, 2021.

270 *"progressivism"*: "The 1776 Report," The President's Advisory 1776 Commission, January 2021.

270 *"They're using something they"*: Quoted in Crowley and Schuessler, "Trump's 1776 Commission Critiques Liberalism in Report Derided by Historians."

270 *"The 1776 Report will"*: Quoted in Rebecca Onion, "Trump's '1776 Report' Would Be Funny If It Weren't So Dangerous," *Slate*, January 19, 2021.

270 *"divisive concepts"*: "House Bill 1084," Georgia General Assembly, April 28, 2022, https://www.legis.ga.gov/legislation/61477.

270 *"We put students and"*: Governor Brian Kemp, "April 28, 2022: Education Bill Signing Ceremony," Cumming, Ga., Facebook post, https://www.facebook.com/watch/live/?ref=watch_permalink&v=411042064186386.

271 *"What supports white supremacy"*: Quoted in James Oliphant and Gabriella Borter, "Partisan War over Teaching History and Racism Stokes Tensions in U.S. Schools," *Reuters*, June 23, 2021.

271 *"slavery and racism are"*: Quoted in Jamelle Bouie, "The Backlash Against C.R.T. Shows That Republicans Are Losing Ground," *The New York Times*, February 4, 2022.

271 *"the institution of slavery"*: Quoted in Jeremy C. Young and Jonathan Friedman, "America's Censored Classrooms," *Pen America*, August 17, 2022.

271 *"developed skills"*: Quoted in Lori Rozsa, "Florida Approves Black History Standards Decried as 'Step Backward,'" *The Washington Post*, July 19, 2023.

271 *"inherently racist, sexist, or"*: Quoted in Katie Reilly, "Florida's Governor Just Signed the 'Stop Woke Act.' Here's What It Means for Schools and Businesses," *Time*, April 22, 2022.

272 *"slavery, legal racial discrimination"*: The Heritage Foundation, "Protecting K–12 Students from Discrimination," https://www.heritage.org/protecting-k-12-students-discrimination.

272 *"ugly racism that stains"*: Quoted in Jeff Stein and Yeganeh Torbati, "Heritage Foundation, Former Powerhouse of GOP Policy, Adjusts in Face of New Competition from Trump Allies," *The Washington Post*, February 7, 2022.

272 *"education, education, and education"*: Ibid.

272 *"anti-Christian"*: Sarah Posner, Twitter post, June 23, 2021, https://twitter.com/sarahposner/status/1407778999451930628.

272 *"parental rights"*: "Religious Right's Agenda in Congress Has Some Advances," *New Hampshire Union Leader*, February 18, 1996.

272 *"being used to denigrate"*: Sarah Posner, *Unholy* (New York: Random House, 2020), 135.

272 *"infiltrated Georgia schools with"*: Heritage Action for America, "Georgia

House Votes to Protect Students from State-Sanctioned Racial Discrimination, Passes HB 1084," March 4, 2022.

273 *"It could turn out"*: Quoted in Theodoric Meyer, Maggie Severns, and Meredith McGraw, "'The Tea Party to the 10th Power': Trumpworld Bets Big on Critical Race Theory," *Politico*, June 23, 2021.

273 *"Reject Critical Race Theory"*: Heritage Action for America, "Reject Critical Race Theory," June 21, 2021.

273 *"understand what CRT is"*: Jessica Anderson, "Reading, Writing, and Racism: The NEA's Campaign to Gaslight Parents," *National Review*, July 10, 2021.

273 *"They are trying to"*: Quoted in Ronald Brownstein, "Republicans Are Trying to Suppress More Than Votes," *The Atlantic*, January 28, 2022.

274 *"It's hard to miss"*: Warnock, interview.

274 *"We have too often"*: Du Bois, *Black Reconstruction*, 713.

275 *"browning of America"*: Ezra Klein, "White Threat in a Browning America," *Vox*, July 30, 2018.

275 *"driven by racial cleavages"*: Chicago Project on Security & Threats, "American Face of Insurrection," January 5, 2022.

275 *"illegitimate"*: Chicago Project on Security & Threats, "Findings from the Fall 2021 CPOST (NORC) American Political Violence Survey," January 2, 2022.

275 *"Today in too many"*: "Buchanan Announcement," Manchester, N.H., C-Span, March 20, 1995, https://www.c-span.org/video/?64066-1/buchanan-announcement.

EPILOGUE: A NEW LABORATORY FOR DEMOCRACY

277 *"Hey Michigan"*: Quoted in Lauren Gibbons, "Michigan Redistricting Was Fraught. But It's a 'Poster Child of What Is Possible' in a Midwest Battleground," *MLive*, March 24, 2022.

277 *"I'd like to take"*: Quoted in David Daley, *Unrigged* (New York: Liveright, 2020), 73.

277 *"how do you end"*: Katie Fahey, interview conducted by the author, March 23, 2023.

278 *"We were very excited"*: Nancy Wang, interview conducted by the author, March 24, 2023.

278 *"Redistricting and gerrymandering seemed"*: Quoted in David Eggert, "Anti-Gerrymandering Group Defies Odds with 2018 Ballot Drive," Associated Press, November 19, 2017.

278 *"cram ALL the Dem"*: Quoted in Daley, *Unrigged*, 80.

278 *"perhaps most clear in"*: The Redistricting Majority Project, "2012 REDMAP Summary Report," January 4, 2013.

278 *"a gerrymander of historical"*: Quoted in Clara Hendrickson, "Redistricting Experts Weigh In on Results of First General Election Under New Maps," *Detroit Free Press*, December 1, 2022.

278   *"one tough nerd"*: Quoted in Molly Ball, "From 'One Tough Nerd' to Embattled Governor," *The Atlantic*, October 17, 2014.

279   *"God, America, Free Enterprise"*: Quoted in Zack Stanton, "How Betsy DeVos Used God and Amway to Take Over Michigan Politics," *Politico*, January 15, 2017.

279   *"good ideas go to"*: Quoted in Riley Beggin, "One Woman's Facebook Post Leads to Michigan Vote Against Gerrymandering," *Bridge Michigan*, November 7, 2018.

279   *"we clearly heard"*: Quoted in Jonathan Oosting, "Snyder Signs Replacement Emergency Manager Law: We 'Heard, Recognized and Respected' Will of Voters," *MLive*, December 27, 2012.

279   *"It felt like until"*: Fahey, interview.

280   *"All political power is"*: Quoted in Daley, *Unrigged*, 78.

280   *"Maybe I was a"*: Fahey, interview.

280   *"VNP really was revolutionary"*: Wang, interview.

280   *"When you have a"*: Sharon Dolente, interview conducted by the author, March 22, 2023.

281   *"It's a great success"*: Benson, interview.

281   *"Liberate Michigan"*: Quoted in Kathleen Gray, "In Michigan, a Dress Rehearsal for the Chaos at the Capitol on Wednesday," *The New York Times*, January 9, 2021.

281   *"dress rehearsal"*: Ibid.

282   *"hand-to-hand combat"*: Quoted in Olivia Rubin, "'Hand-to-Hand Combat with the Left': Recordings Show Trump-Funded Lawyer Cleta Mitchell Readying for Midterm Elections," ABC News, November 3, 2022.

282   *"reproductive freedom"*: Quoted in Quinn Yeargain, "Measures to Protect Abortion Rights Triumph on Tuesday," *Bolts*, November 9, 2022.

282   *"partisan fairness"*: Quoted in Mike Wilkingson, "Michigan Legislature: Redistricting Paves Way for Democrats to Seize Control," *Bridge Michigan*, November 9, 2022.

283   *"This is what happens"*: Ibid.

283   *"It led to election"*: Fahey, interview.

283   *"Who would like to"*: Quoted in Barbara Rodriguez, "Michigan Gov. Gretchen Whitmer Repeals 1931 Abortion Ban," *The 19th*, April 5, 2023.

284   *"the best means available"*: Quoted in Daniel A. Smith and Caroline J. Tolbert, *Educated by Initiative* (Ann Arbor: University of Michigan Press, 2004), 5.

284   *"There might not be"*: Wang, interview.

284   *"That's where the opportunity"*: Ibid.

285   *"the next logical outgrowth"*: Quoted in John F. Kowal and Wilfred U. Codrington III, *The People's Constitution* (New York: The New Press, 2021), 217.

285   *"the most dangerous blot"*: Quoted in Alexander Keyssar, *Why Do We Still*

Have the Electoral College? (Cambridge, Mass.: Harvard University Press, 2020), 3.

286 *"The rule of the"*: Ibid., 220.

286 *"The Electoral College is"*: Ibid., 259.

286 *"a bigger question right"*: Quoted in Warren Weaver Jr., "Senate Puts Off Direct Vote Plan," *The New York Times*, September 30, 1970.

287 *"It is clear"*: Quoted in Kowal and Codrington, *The People's Constitution*, 4.

287 *"that extreme facility which"*: Ibid., 5.

289 *"democracy principle"*: Miriam Seifter, "Saving Democracy, State by State?" *Univ. of Wisconsin Legal Studies Research Paper No. 1764*, January 23, 2023.

289 *"The possibility now exists"*: Ben Wikler, interview conducted by the author, November 10, 2022.

290 *"The real fight going"*: Ben Wikler, interview conducted by the author, April 6, 2023.

290 *"It was a microcosm"*: Wikler, interview, April 6, 2023.

290 *"The alternative"*: Ibid.

290 *"Brats, Cheese, and Beer"*: Ben Wikler, interview conducted by the author, September 14, 2022.

290 *"a democracy-free zone"*: Quoted in Berman, "The Insurrection Was Put Down. The GOP Plan for Minority Rule Marches On."

290 *"Right now, the state"*: Quoted in Ari Berman, "This Race Could Decide the Fate of Democracy in Wisconsin—and the 2024 Election," *Mother Jones*, April 3, 2023.

291 *"I signed the governor's"*: Quoted in Shawn Johnson, "Janet Protasiewicz Has Campaigned on Democratic Issues. If She Wins, the Wisconsin Supreme Court Could Weigh In on Them," Wisconsin Public Radio, April 2, 2023.

291 *"This is their chance"*: Quoted in John McCormack, "Scott Walker Sounds the Alarm About Wisconsin's Supreme Court Election," *National Review*, February 23, 2023.

291 *"positively rigged"*: Quoted in Berman, "This Race Could Decide the Fate of Democracy in Wisconsin—and the 2024 Election."

291 *"women have the right"*: Quoted in Ari Berman, "Progressives Win a Majority on the Wisconsin Supreme Court," *Mother Jones*, April 4, 2023.

292 *"Election Integrity Roundtable"*: Quoted in Berman, "This Race Could Decide the Fate of Democracy in Wisconsin."

292 *"a true threat to"*: Ibid.

292 *"it is the single most"*: Quoted in Johnson, "Janet Protasiewicz Has Campaigned on Democratic Issues. If She Wins, the Wisconsin Supreme Court Could Weigh In on Them."

292 *"This election was a"*: Ben Wikler, Twitter post, April 4, 2023, https://twitter.com/benwikler/status/1643423451288403968.

293 *"About Damn Time"*: Quoted in Patrick Marley, "Liberals Win Control

of Wisconsin Supreme Court Ahead of Abortion Case," *The Washington Post*, April 4, 2023.

293 *"the fab four"*: "Janet Protasiewicz Gives Victory Speech," Milwaukee, Wis., WISN 12 News/YouTube, April 4, 2023, https://www.youtube.com /watch?v=BRHRff1uzPo.

293 *"Freedom"*: Ibid.

293 *"Ultimately, you can trace"*: Wikler, interview, April 6, 2023.

293 *"Too many have tried"*: "Janet Protasiewicz Gives Victory Speech," April 4, 2023.

293 *"My goal"*: Wikler, interview, April 6, 2023.

294 *"The extremists got trounced"*: Quoted in Adam Gabbatt, "Rightwing Extremists Defeated by Democrats in US School Board Elections," *The Guardian*, April 21, 2023.

294 *"Our constitutional republic's survival"*: Quoted in Josh Dawsey and Amy Gardner, "Top GOP Lawyer Decries Ease of Campus Voting in Private Pitch to RNC," *The Washington Post*, April 20, 2023.

294 *"We're at war for"*: The Tennessee Holler, Twitter post, April 13, 2013, https://twitter.com/TheTNHoller/status/1646548124272324608.

294 *"We are losing our"*: Quoted in Dakin Andone, Ryan Young, Amy Simonson, and Steve Almasy, "Tennessee's Republican-Led House Expels 2 Democratic Lawmakers over Gun Reform Protest, Fails in Bid to Oust a Third," CNN, April 7, 2023.

ACKNOWLEDGMENTS

When I started working on this book in 2019, I had no idea how tumultuous the next five years would be. So many people supported me during this journey and helped bring this project to fruition. I would like to thank:

Eric Chinski, Tara Sharma, Lottchen Shivers, and the entire team at Farrar, Straus and Giroux. I'm so lucky to have published all three of my books with them.

Elyse Cheney and the Cheney Agency for believing in me and this book.

Taya McCormick-Grobow, Kristine Bruch, and the staff of Type Media Center for supporting my career in journalism for two decades.

Clara Jeffery, Monika Bauerlein, Dan Schulman, and all my wonderful colleagues at *Mother Jones* for their support, encouragement, and commitment to the best traditions of independent journalism.

The Park Foundation, the Schumann Media Center, and Emerson Collective for supporting this book and my reporting on voting rights. Special thanks to Adelaide Gomer, Michael Connor, Karen Kimball, Bill Moyers, Amy Low, Patrick D'Arcy, and Marcy Stech.

Annette Luba Lucas for supporting my speaking career.

Eyal Press for his friendship and mentorship.

Most of all I'm grateful to my family: my dad, Warren; my sister, Ali; my brother-in-law, Kahreen; my cousins Lisa, Lauren, Amy, and Randy; and my godparents, Janet and Steve. I'm especially thankful for my wife, Meredith, who put up with me even when we couldn't leave the house, and my kids, Nora and Tessa, who came of age quite literally during this project. I hope their generation creates a better democracy than the one we have now.

This book is dedicated to my mom, Harriet Berman, who passed away in July 2023, just as I was finishing the final manuscript. She was always my biggest supporter and a steadfast believer in peace and justice. I wish she could have read this book, but I hope it makes her proud.

INDEX

A NOTE ABOUT THE AUTHOR

Ari Berman is the national voting rights correspondent for *Mother Jones* and a reporting fellow at Type Media Center. He is the author of *Give Us the Ballot: The Modern Struggle for Voting Rights in America* (a finalist for the National Book Critics Circle Award for nonfiction) and *Herding Donkeys: The Fight to Rebuild the Democratic Party and Reshape American Politics*. His writing has also appeared in *The New York Times*, *The Washington Post*, and *Rolling Stone*, and he is a frequent commentator on MSNBC and NPR. He has won the Sidney Hillman Foundation Prize for Magazine Journalism and an Izzy Award for outstanding achievement in independent media. He lives in New Paltz, New York.

.